THE BOSTON OPERA COMPANY

Books by QUAINTANCE EATON

OPERA CARAVAN

OPERA PRODUCTION; A HANDBOOK

MUSIC AND RECORDINGS (*with Fred Grunfeld*)

THE BOSTON OPERA COMPANY

MUSICAL U.S.A. (*editor*)

THE WORLD OF MUSIC, an encyclopedia (*editor*)

THE BOSTON OPERA COMPANY

by QUAINTANCE EATON

APPLETON-CENTURY   New York

APPLETON-CENTURY
AFFILIATE OF
MEREDITH PRESS

Library of Congress Catalogue Card Number: 65-12607

MANUFACTURED IN THE UNITED STATES OF AMERICA FOR MEREDITH PRESS

VAN REES PRESS   •   NEW YORK

To D. J. C. and L. G.,

who made it all possible

ACKNOWLEDGMENTS

To try to thank the individuals who have assisted in a research project that extended over several years is manifestly a tricky affair, so I hope to be forgiven if a few chinks appear in my roll call. The more so because a little book in which I kept names, addresses, phone numbers and appointments simply disappeared one day, leaving me to patch up by memory.

The trail started in the New York apartment of Mrs. E. Gerry Chadwick, daughter of Eben D. Jordan, with Lauder Greenway, chairman of the board of the Metropolitan Opera and an opera buff second to none, and Alexander Steinert, composer. Mrs. Chadwick shared her memories of those days which to her were sheer enchantment. Mr. Greenway sent me to Jeska Swartz, the petite mezzo-soprano whose recollections provided a solid underpinning as well as many decorative details, and Mr. Steinert recommended me to his stepmother, who had been a faithful Boston Opera subscriber. Both ladies passed me on to numerous additional sources, for which I shall never be able to thank them enough.

Several newspaper men endured barrages of questions, chiefly Warren Storey Smith, formerly of the *Post*, and Arthur Wilson, early critic of the *Globe*. Both men's memories and opinions appear in the text. Current critics, Cyrus Durgin of the *Globe* and Rudolph Elie of the *Herald* (both of whom have since departed from this world), drew on their files, as did Alexander Williams, now with Little, Brown and Company. Mrs. Olin Downes in New York allowed me to browse through her late husband's scrapbooks.

To discover the indispensable writings of Philip Hale and H. T. Parker, I spent long hours in the Boston Public Library, assisted in the beautiful Brown Memorial room by music librarians Daniel Koury and Robert P. Giddings and assistants Alberta Kneeland, Mary Lou Little, and Maurice Carbonnel among others. I am grateful for the patience of Frank Bruno and Edward Monroe in the old newspaper archives. Dennis A. Dooley in the State House Library also got out old bound volumes, and Mary Reardon in the Harvard Theatre Library found many photographs and microfilmed a set of opera programs. David McKibbin in the art section of the Athenaeum gave generously of his knowledge both of old Boston society and of Sargent's paintings. The files of the New England Conservatory and the Harvard Music Association were made available. Alexander P. Clark of the Princeton University Library opened the Otto Kahn-Henry Russell correspondence at the kind intervention of Mr. Kahn's daughter, Mrs. John Barry Ryan, and Mrs. Mary Ellis Peltz allowed me to investigate Boston correspondence with the Metropolitan, now in the latter's archives. Joseph Urban's widow made her husband's files accessible at Columbia University Library. Philip L. Miller, head of the music division of the New York Public Library and his wife, Catharine, in charge of the Music Library, assisted with appropriate books and clippings. Mr. Miller wrote the copy to accompany the commemorative record album being issued by Columbia simultaneously with this history. Charles Jahant of Maryland, whose opera knowledge is inexhaustible, shared it in the matter of casts and singers. Kenton Coe did research in Paris. Arthur Knight and Dominic Rocha, opera aficionados of Providence, Rhode Island, told me many anecdotes and regaled me with their collection of memorabilia. John K. Colby of Phillips Academy passed along some memories, as did Dale Warren of Houghton Mifflin Company. Alexander Smallens remembered his Boston days as if they were yesterday.

Many old-timers recalled opera experiences, among them Arthur S. Tooker, who sent letters after reading some of mine which the *Herald* kindly printed, and many who have since passed away: Mrs. Alvan T. Fuller, who sang as Viola Davenport; Sidney C. Woodward, who lent some fragile old programs; Mrs. Wallace Goodrich, widow of the conductor, whose scrapbooks were crammed with information; Clara Endicott Sears, who generously presented me with her book about the Vendome Hotel; Mary Wheelwright and Mark A. De Wolfe Howe. New light was shed on the controversial Mrs. John L. Gardner by Morris

Carter, formerly curator of her museum and author of her biography. Socialites Mrs. Stanley McCormick, Mrs. Robert Herrick, Mrs. Albert C. Titcomb, Mrs. Philip French and Mrs. Frederick C. Dumaine, Sr., contributed anecdotes.

Mrs. Al Lothian uncovered a mine of information about early days; the manager, Demeter Zachareff, was helpful; the late Howard Potter sent a treasurable prospectus of the Rabinoff seasons; John McCormack's widow lent a book of memoirs; William E. Benswanger and Wilmar M. Jacoby of Pittsburgh recalled the opera tour; William Moran supplied some Chicago casts. Harriet O'Brien introduced me to several knowledgeable individuals and gave information about the opera house, as did Charles Hamilton, formerly lawyer for the Shuberts. Northeastern University officials provided a list of the contents of the cornerstone after the tragic demolition. George Harvey's daughter, Mrs. Esther Switzler, and his former assistant, Miss Gilkie (whose first name was plainly in that little book), supplied details of the contractor's difficulties during construction and the bombing incident.

Books consulted were so numerous that I shall not attempt to list them except to say that Cleveland Amory, whose *Proper Bostonians* still raises the hackles of elderly ladies, personally added to my store of tall and short tales. Mrs. Harriet Houghton Barry graciously shared information from her manuscript biography of Philip Hale.

Irreplaceable material was freely given by Russell's second wife, Donna, who in several visits in San Francisco and extensive correspondence revealed a portion of her life which undoubtedly brought painful memories. Similarly, Russell's elder son, Henry Tosti, talked candidly about his father and family, giving insights that otherwise could never have been discovered. Tosti's daughter, Dorothy, a writer and dancer in New York City, was also helpful.

Many friends helped lighten the days—and nights—that might easily have grown wearisome with work, among them the Ralph Tedfords, the John Cushmans, the Albert Titcombs, the Richard Ehrlichs, the Perry Rathbones, the Stephen Fassetts, and the Talcott Bankses.

My gratitude to my editor, Theodore Purdy, who belongs to that rare band of opera lovers who know and remember everything. And to Hayes Sturges, of similar accomplishments, who read the manuscript and made valuable suggestions and corrections.

Gerald Fitzgerald of *Opera News* brought his vast experience to reading and correcting galleys and compiling the index. Ira Glackens, author of *Yankee Prima Donna*, supplied priceless photographs; others came from Donna Russell, Mrs. Chadwick, *Opera News* and the Metropolitan Opera Archives.

Lastly, I shall always be thankful for Elizabeth Ames's invitation to the sanctuary of Yaddo, the artists' colony near Saratoga Springs, where more than half of this book was written. Over a couple of summers at Theodore Erickson's Point View in Jamestown, R.I., the long task was finally completed.

CONTENTS

ACT III

ACT IV

ACT V

ILLUSTRATIONS

following page 50

Prologue

1

BACKSTAGE

Never before or since in the history of the United States has grand opera occupied so much time as in the six months between November, 1909, and May, 1910. Three opera houses were going full steam in New York City—the Metropolitan, on Thirty-Ninth Street and Broadway; its light-opera sister, the New Theatre, at Sixty-Second and Central Park West; and Oscar Hammerstein's Manhattan Opera House, on West Thirty-Fourth Street—accounting for more than three hundred performances. Several companies industriously plied the road, titillating a number of cities with spectacle and song; and the new Boston Opera Company regaled the Hub with eighty-eight presentations, as well as adding forty-seven in a mid-season tour of eight cities.

These were the days of the ambitious scheme conceived by Otto H. Kahn, financier-patron of the Metropolitan; its object was to spread grand opera throughout the country, with the Metropolitan as fountainhead and benevolent partner in a top-level syndicate. With interlocking boards, the Metropolitan and Boston companies, later adding Chicago and Philadelphia, endeavored to establish an exchange of artists and occasionally repertoire in a grandiose network. This ideal proved unrealistic and overblown; the structure collapsed after a few brief seasons, but its effects are still felt. The same scheme periodically boils to the top of the operatic kettle in the effort to syndicalize an "industry" that stubbornly insists on maintaining the individuality and autonomy of its various parts.

The unusual expansion undertaken in the season of 1909–10 by the

3

Metropolitan had but one purpose: to fight the bumptious Oscar Hammerstein. Three years previously, this tough-grained impresario had astonished the world by building his rival Manhattan Opera House, and filling it with productions and singers that at first spelled unqualified success. Taking advantage of Heinrich Conried's indifference to the French repertoire at the Metropolitan, Hammerstein brought Mary Garden, Maurice Renaud, Charles Dalmorès, and Hector Dufranne to sing in such operas as Debussy's *Pelléas et Mélisande,* Charpentier's *Louise,* Massenet's *Thaïs,* and Offenbach's *Tales of Hoffmann;* engaged Luisa Tetrazzini, Nellie Melba, Alessandro Bonci, Giovanni Zenatello, and John McCormack for his Italian repertoire; and prospered mightily.

By 1909 Hammerstein had not only breached the citadel in New York but had spread his attack to seven outlying bastions of the Metropolitan. In Philadelphia he erected an opera house and, before the plaster had dried, cheekily opened a season on the same night as the Metropolitan's. In Chicago he treated the audience to Mary Garden's flamboyant personality; in Brooklyn, Baltimore, Pittsburgh, and Washington, he followed or preceded the Metropolitan so closely that his presence haunted the older company unmercifully. In Boston, Giulio Gatti-Casazza, who had taken over the Met in 1908, could not even get a foot in the door one season; Hammerstein secured a spring lease on the only temple of opera, the fifty-five-year-old Boston Theatre.

Going against Gatti-Casazza's conservative opinion, the Metropolitan extended its lines of communication farther and farther. The Italian manager was forced for two seasons to work in tandem with a former tenor, Andreas Dippel, who commanded a large share of the company's affection and enough power with the directorate to place him on equal footing with the man from La Scala. It was Dippel's policy to fight Hammerstein's fire with Metropolitan fire. The season of 1909–10 brought the climax; in addition to a full schedule at home, the Met played twenty-one evenings in Brooklyn, twenty in Baltimore, twenty-five in Philadelphia, and ten in Boston (at the new Opera House) during the season. Then a divided company visited twelve cities in the spring, giving thirty-two performances in Chicago, while other cities were receiving thirty-six. Not content with this unprecedented marathon, the company packed up and sailed for Europe in May, delighting the citizens of Paris (or most of them) with nineteen performances of Italian works, among them Puccini's *Manon Lescaut,* which the French capital had never before witnessed. Although Otto Kahn's patronage ensured that there would be no loss from this overseas junket, the total expansion put a heavy strain on the Metropolitan's coffers.

Hammerstein felt the competition even more keenly. At the beginning of the fateful season of 1909–10, cracks began to appear in his jerry-built empire. Kahn announced in April that the feckless entrepreneur had been vanquished—to the tune of a million and a quarter indemnity. Although he made sporadic attempts at comebacks, violating the provisions of his agreement with the Met, this marked the recession from his neap tide; his strength ebbed fast from here on. Chicago inherited most of his properties and singers; a few went to the Metropolitan.

In this atmosphere of tournament and troubadouring, the Boston Opera company began existence.

No resident grand opera company had ever before occupied a Boston stage. The Boston Theatre, built in 1854 on Washington Street to replace a previous structure on Federal Street that had burned in 1852, played host to virtually every important touring group; the performances ranged from drama, opera, comic opera, and oratorio to ballet and negro minstrel shows; clergymen and athletes also appeared on its stage. Embodying many architectural and acoustical principles "in advance of its time," according to a history by a later manager, Eugene Tompkins, the 3,140-seat auditorium opened with a stock company, then welcomed its first opera, performed by an English company headed by Louise Pyne. The bill included Auber's *Crown Diamonds*, the Boston première of *Maritana*, *The Bohemian Girl*, *Fra Diavolo*, *The Beggar's Opera*, and the inevitable *La Sonnambula*, which always seemed the first choice of impresarios in new quarters.

Grisi and Mario, with Arditi conducting, presented the first Italian opera in the shining new house, their troupe singing *Puritani*, *Lucrezia Borgia*, *Favorita*, *The Barber of Seville*, *Don Pasquale*, *Don Giovanni*, *Semiramide*, and *Norma*. This last brought in the highest receipts for the season —$4,225.

The procession was fairly begun: in rapid succession came Brignoli and Bertucca-Maretzek to give Boston its first *Guillaume Tell;* Adelaide Phillips, known before as a dancer and now singing Romeo to Mrs. John Woods' Juliet (she would later join the Boston Ideals); Maretzek's, Strakosch's, and Mapleson's celebrated troupes; various German companies, Clara Louise Kellogg, Anna Bishop with Gilmore's Band, and all the other musical caravans that played stands ranging from one night to several weeks. The Boston Ideals gained name and fame by bringing together an ideal cast for the popular new Gilbert and Sullivan attraction, *H. M. S. Pinafore,* which was performed at the theater in 1879. They went on to nationwide triumphs and were reconstructed as The Bostonians in 1887, with Henry Clay Barnabee as their uniquely beloved comedian.

For a short period, beginning in 1860, the theater changed its name to Academy of Music, to be in line with comparable theaters in New York, Brooklyn, Philadelphia, and Baltimore, all built as opera houses. A brilliant new chandelier was installed, which was replaced by small electric clusters in 1890.

Henry E. Abbey brought the new Metropolitan Opera here for its first out-of-town appearances in 1883; later he would operate in massive Mechanics Hall, but his successor returned to the Boston Theatre, and the interim German company liked these premises. Even after the new opera house rose on Huntington Avenue, the old theater kept its doors open for a decade or so.

Two men shared the responsibility for the daring Boston venture in the early part of the century. Henry Russell, a bold impresario from London, who had piloted a troupe named after the Naples San Carlo company through the United States for several seasons, enlisted the hearty support of Boston's department-store prince, Eben D. Jordan of Jordan-Marsh, who guaranteed a roof for Russell's coterie. As early as December, 1908, Jordan was invited to the board of the Metropolitan Opera, while Otto Kahn joined the newly formed Boston board. Similar exchanges between New York and Chicago and New York and Philadelphia existed as earnest of the halcyon days to come. Even Europe was drawn into the budding cartel. As Henry E. Krehbiel, perceptive critic for the New York *Tribune,* wrote: "Shall we not between St. Denis and St. George compound an opera company, half American, half Italian, that shall go to Constantinople and take the Turk by the beard?"

No boundaries existed for the dreams of these ambitious men. Opera should sweep the capitals of the New World, from whence the benison should descend even unto the Old. As late as the summer of 1913, Henry Russell wrote to Otto Kahn: "I cannot help feeling that, if the operatic situation in North America is properly handled and concentrated, the day will come when we can control the operatic destinies of the world. This, however, is purely Utopian, but I mention it because it coincides with your own views."

Even after the Metropolitan drew in its horns in an almost immediate retrenchment, Russell kept the dream alive. Just before the First World War, he conveyed the Boston company to Paris, with English co-operation; this tour proved to be the company's swan song. The beginning was, however, brave and beautiful.

Boston, insulated by Family Trusts and other sound Yankee precautions, hardly trembled in the copper panic of 1907, when, as Eben D. Jordan put it, New York trust companies were crashing into failure, national banks were tottering on the verge of ruin, and clearing house certificates were the order of the day. Boston was so little affected that the smooth routine of winter vacations suffered no interruption. Florida hotel registers showed their usual sprinkling of Boston names, while Jordan and his family spent an accustomed quiet month in Hot Springs, taking the waters, golfing, and enjoying Virginia's peaceful Indian summer.

There a visitor called one day on an urgent mission. Henry Russell found himself that black October day in New York with twenty-six artists and a chorus of fifty of his traveling company to be paid, but no payroll. Men who had promised to support his tour were haggardly contemplating the ruins of their hopes and their fortunes. In his predicament, Russell thought of Jordan's enthusiasm for the San Carlo performances in Boston the previous spring. In his memoirs, *The Passing Show*, Russell describes the emergency:

I put in a long distance call to Jordan's house, but to my bitter disappointment, the telephone was answered by the butler, who said Jordan was in Hot Springs. I made up my mind, however, that he was my only hope, and, collecting the few remaining dollars I possessed, took the train that night to Hot Springs. . . .

Jordan was a distinguished-looking man, a little blunt in manner, but his eyes had the kindest expression I have ever seen. His voice was deep and gruff, and by the way he spoke I gathered that my visit considerably surprised him.

"What the devil have you followed me to Hot Springs for?" was his greeting. This made me so nervous that I was rendered speechless . . . but within a half hour of the time I had entered the room, Jordan had handed me a certified cheque for twenty thousand dollars.

Jordan recalled afterward that he had been glad to be of service to a man "in a rather vexatious position," a man he was already beginning to admire. He sent Russell to the New England Conservatory, where the business manager, Ralph Flanders, arranged for the troupe to rehearse on the premises a week before their engagement at the Majestic Theatre.

Russell's earlier Boston visit had occurred the previous May, when his company had performed in the Park Theatre. Alice Nielsen, Florencio Constantino, and Fely Dereyne were the chief singers; the repertoire included *La Bohème, Don Pasquale,* and a bill of assorted acts from various operas, at a $2.50 top. Olin Downes, the new critic on the *Post,* found the company worthy of the highest praise, "an aggregation of artists thoroughly at home and in sympathy with each other, and understanding the dramatic requirements of opera. *Mirabile dictu,*" he concluded, "the chorus is alive and the orchestra respectable." Russell was encouraged to postpone his sailing date and give four extra performances.

Heinrich Conried and the Metropolitan had preceded the San Carlo company, moving into the Boston Theatre on April 1, with a debut by a favorite Massachusetts daughter as his chief attraction. Geraldine Farrar sang in *Faust* and *Madama Butterfly,* to the enchantment of her home town.

During Russell's spring season, the leaven of permanent opera had already begun to work in Boston. Immediately after the San Carlo's departure, a reporter for the *Post* plucked a scoop out of thin air, proclaiming that Boston's own opera company was as good as formed. His story on May 17 mentioned Mrs. John L. Gardner alone as a backer, then quoted Russell's extremely cagey remarks, which admitted no more than that the vigorous arbiter of Boston's cultural life was indeed prominently identified with music in this, the most musical city in the country. Boston equaled any city in the world, Russell added quickly, taking the play away from Mrs. Gardner and focusing on the city itself. The story concluded with these clairvoyant words: "No theater has been decided, but no doubt that if successful the company will have its own in a few years." This alert prophet's name, concealed from his readers, was John Royal, a cub reporter, later an executive at the National Broadcasting Company and a granddaddy of the entertainment world.

The winter season of the San Carlo, made possible by Jordan's generosity, opened on December 9, 1907, to an unusual amount of fanfare. Two thousand Bostonians were in their seats when the curtain rose, and more poured in, so that standees could be counted in the hundreds. "All of Back Bay turned out," crowed Russell, always deeply conscious of the importance of "important" people, and consequently inclined to be even more gratified by the composition of the audience than by its size.

The impresario chose *La Gioconda*, his good-luck opera, to open this 1907 winter season. He would have liked to engage his old friend Lillian Nordica for the title role, as he was to do in 1909, but the prima donna had other commitments. Her husband, George Young, who in other years had assisted Russell in meeting the inevitable deficits of an opera company, this time pronounced himself flat broke, one of the victims of the October panic. Failing Nordica, Russell signed a handsome soprano who had been singing at the Paris Opéra, Jane Noria, the former Josie Ludwig of St. Louis. Noria, whose assumed name and figure bore more resemblance to Nordica's than her voice and talents, was the wife of Gatti-Casazza's secretary, known as "Count Centanini," and thus might be considered close to the throne.

The entire cast of this 1907 "Gioconda" would be met in Boston again: the mezzo-sopranos Maria Claessens and Rosa Olitzka, the tenor Constantino, the baritones Blanchart and Pulcini, and the monocled Spanish bass, Andrés de Segurola. The conductor was Arnaldo Conti, the dependable *routinier*, who would wear himself out in Russell's service. The former light-opera favorite, Alice Nielsen, and the matinee idol of other days, Victor Maurel, were the only other names of distinction on the roster. But when the three weeks of performances had ended, opera *aficionados* agreed with the *Post* that "Grand Opera Delights All." Few of the Metropolitan's annual spring visits had been as brilliant, Jordan believed.

First-night gowns, magnificent by all accounts, foreshadowed the elegance of the Boston Opera Company's opening which was to astonish even those who participated in it. The Jordans entertained American opera's highest dignitary, Otto H. Kahn, tireless benefactor of the Metropolitan, and the New York company's secretary, Rawlins Cottenet. Another inescapable cynosure, Mrs. Jack Gardner, occupied a box.

Now Russell expressed himself as being supremely optimistic about a permanent company. Jordan's name and that of Frederick S. Converse, one of Boston's most distinguished men of music, appeared firmly attached to the mast. Jordan recalled that at a portentous meeting in the New England Conservatory (which had been founded by his father and continued to enjoy his own support), he had offered to build an opera house if Russell would undertake its artistic direction. Converse was to assume responsibility for subscriptions to the forty-six boxes, and Flanders would be the business manager.

The die was cast. News and pinpricks of rumor leaked out, but the official announcement waited a few months. In March 1908, Russell indulged in a bit of wishful thinking, as reported in a newspaper in Indianapolis, where the San Carlo troupe was playing:

I wish to have American people learn to like opera as it is liked in the old country, and not to consider it as a special function, as it is in this country at the moment. I wish to have street boys know opera so well that they will sing and whistle it instead of the wretched stuff that catches the ear for a moment in what is known as musical comedy. This rests largely with the women. They are the ones who cultivate the arts. To them opera looks for the spread of taste. They are the artistic backbone of the country.

Fortunately for the moment, Russell detected no sour notes in his rhapsody. For the first time in many years he basked in an artistic climate that seemed to him both healthy and congenial, as well as comfortably cushioned with the necessary wealth and buttressed by an impeccable society.

With the architect Parkman B. Haven, of the firm of Wheelwright and Haven, Jordan set off for an extensive inspection of the opera houses in Europe, determined to take advantage of the best and avoid mistakes if possible. Only a half-dozen great houses existed in America: the Philadelphia Academy of Music, dating from 1857 and still standing; the New Orleans French Opera House, built in 1859, to be razed by fire in 1919 and never restored; the Metropolitan Opera, built in 1883 and, though encrusted with glamour and boasting excellent acoustics, long since found to be inadequate backstage; the Chicago Auditorium, inaugurated in 1889 and considered the finest in the country by many (always excepting Philadelphians), and Oscar Hammerstein's two houses, the Manhattan in New York, and the new one in Philadelphia.

The founder of the Boston Opera House had set one condition to his unprecedented generosity: that the Opera Company be incorporated with a capital of at least $150,000, and that the forty-six boxes be guaranteed for three years at $2,000 per year. Jordan proposed to lease the house to the company for a similar period, expecting a 5 per cent yield on his investment, which was estimated at $700,000 (it rose to more than $1,000,000 before the building was completed). He also guaranteed the deficit for three years.

Subscriptions to the boxes offered no problem. With Converse's salesmanship, the forty-six went surprisingly fast. From the resulting $98,000, about $40,000 to $50,000 would be available annually to the company for operating purposes after rent and expenses had been paid. Now it remained to secure subscriptions to the stock. A company was formed, capitalized at $200,000, and shares were offered at $100 each; each buyer had the privilege of selecting one ticket before the public sale. Boston responded as never before to a semi-public cultural appeal. In less than six months the full sum had been realized, and orders were still pouring in. Somewhat dazed, the executive committee, which in addition to Converse and Flanders included two young businessmen, George R. Fearing, Jr., and Charles Hayden, decided to cable their principal. Jordan, still in Europe, received the heartening news that the demand for boxes exceeded the supply; furthermore, public interest showed so strongly that the committee advocated enlarging the house. Jordan and Haven cabled their consent, the latter making some quick adjustments in absentia. The seating capacity, initially planned at 2,200, was raised to 2,700. Eight added boxes brought the total to fifty-four. When the tallies all came in, the stock had been oversubscribed by $30,000. All $3 seats (the top price in the first season) were snapped up even before the repertoire and artists had been announced. It seemed that Boston was ready for a genuine welcome to its first resident opera company in a house of its own.

Gauging its approach shrewdly, the management stressed the educational values of grand opera. Native talent would be fostered through an opera school. In this concept, Russell merely followed a European tradition. The only such school in America had been established in 1903 by Conried at the Metropolitan Opera; it had not failed entirely, but had been allowed to fade out of the scene after 1907–08, Conried's final season. The Boston School already had steam up in its New England Conservatory headquarters, working in advance of the opening of the house. An American chorus, recruited in the fall of 1908, earnestly pursued its duties under Delfino Menotti, who would be *régisseur*-in-chief for the company. The faithful Conti would join them later to train the singers and take over the orchestra from Wallace Goodrich, the young conductor preparing it. Six scholarships were arranged, the donors including Mrs. Jordan; David Bispham, the noted Metropolitan baritone; Mrs. Jessie Baskerville; Nathan L. Amster, a board member of the opera company; Charles Hayden; and Geraldine Farrar. This was the first and almost the last contact that the Metropolitan's glamour girl had with the Boston company.

Russell promised other novel experiments, which the *Globe* prophesied would be watched carefully, particularly by the western cities, probably because of their democratic potential. First was a series of Saturday-night debut performances for young singers. This admirable experiment lasted barely half of one season. But more importantly, Russell eschewed the "star system." With one of those grandiloquent phrases so typical of him, he proclaimed that "every stockholder who signed the parchment buried in the Opera House cornerstone may also be said to have signed the death warrant of the star system in America." Thus Russell joined the procession of opera chieftains who, before and after his time, vowed to abolish the very stuff of which grand opera is made. In their attempts to reverse natural laws and hitch the stars to their wagons, only a few have even partially succeeded.

Russell, explaining his refusal to use the star system, began by complimenting the American audience for its independence of thought, claiming to anticipate its desire for artists instead of "names." How this delusion shattered under experience, he recounted in his memoirs, where he accuses England and New York of fostering the star system, with the Metropolitan the chief offender. "The petty quarrels, the jealousies, and the intrigues were unlimited," he wrote. "Singers like Eames, Sembrich, Calvé, Nordica, Melba, and Geraldine Farrar were allowed to dominate any opera in which they appeared. Scenery was modified to suit their taste, lights arranged to suit their complexions, tenors chosen to suit their affections and conductors thrown out to gratify their tempers." Russell here betrays his animosity for La Geraldine, never even partially explained. Rather maliciously, he writes that the Boston soprano believed she should have been chosen for the opening night of the Boston Opera. "It was my task to convince her that Nordica had two claims to her one— the first that she was a greater artist than Farrar, secondly that she had been a loyal friend in the days of my misfortune, and now the time had come to repay her." Whatever the reason for the rift, Farrar never sang with Russell, thereby practically depriving Boston of the rightful operatic services of one of its brightest native talents.

Although Russell never succeeded completely in eradicating the natural human desire to "see stars," it is to his credit that he subdued so many temperaments to his purpose and kept to a standard of production that lent to the five Boston years their peculiar artistic ambiance, never forgotten and never surpassed in the memories of those who experienced them.

The solemn moment of ground-breaking for the opera house passed in mid-July, but the August date to lay the cornerstone proved premature. Excavation at the St. Stephens Street end, where the stage would stand, had found water, the first note of bad luck in the prevailing harmony. All filled Back Bay area offered similar problems. For a building as heavy as this, extra precautions became necessary. A thirteen-foot-thick slab of concrete was sunk as a cradle at the danger point. Building resumed, but time and the budget had been stretched. Beginning of actual construction had to be delayed until August 20.

After three months, all lay in readiness for the definitive ceremony. On November 30, 1908, at 3 P.M., a shivering crowd of two hundred ("lovers of music, song-birds of the stage, and patrons of the art," according to the *Post*) gathered on a scaffolding near Huntington Avenue to watch and to sing the national anthem as the huge Deer Island granite slab, weighing more than a ton, was lowered into place. Then Eben D. Jordan ceremoniously wielded a silver trowel, smoothing the mortar. The symbolic deed was accomplished. Governor Curtis Guild tossed off classical allusions; and telegrams of congratulations arrived in flocks: from Otto H. Kahn and the entire Metropolitan Opera board, from the American singers Emma Eames, Geraldine Farrar, and David Bispham, from Andreas Dippel and from Alice Nielsen, who by rights should have been present, but who was filling a singing engagement elsewhere.

Prominent among the guests was Mrs. Gardner, who sat just behind Russell, as an all-too-candid photograph on the front page of the *Post* reveals. Also in the vicinity were Mrs. Hall McAllister, who arranged a series of sought-after musicales each season in the homes of First Family ladies, and Mrs. Stanley McCormick, braving the raw winds in a sealskin hat with a bright pink feather. She preceded her generous Chicago sister-in-law, Edith Rockefeller McCormick, into the operatic cheering section by only a few months. Musical figures of note included George W. Chadwick, admired composer; Max Fiedler, conductor of the Boston Symphony; and Wallace Goodrich, destined to play a solid role with the opera orchestra.

The stone block enclosed a bronze casket in which were preserved for future generations samples of the musical life of the day. Programs and yearbooks and prospectuses of Boston musical institutions, compositions by Mrs. H. H. A. Beach, George W. Chadwick, Frederick S. Converse, Walter Damrosch, Henry Hadley, Charles M. Loeffler, Edward Mac-Dowell, John Knowles Paine, and Horatio Parker found place. Perhaps more interesting to a later audience was a selection of phonograph records by great singers of the day: Farrar, Caruso, Homer, Nordica, Eames, and Nielsen. In the list given to the newspapers, Nordica appeared as the singer of "Dio possente" from Gounod's *Faust*, as well as "Fucidio." Warren Storey Smith, former critic, who examined the contents when the box was unearthed by Northeastern University (which now possesses its contents), easily spotted the latter as "Suicidio," from *La Gioconda,* but had to gain access to the disc itself to prove that the dramatic soprano had not left a rarity in the form of a baritone aria. David Bispham's name showed plainly on the label.

On that cold, windy day in November 1908, no premonition of the ultimate fate of the lyric temple-to-be shook the spirits of the animated gathering. A month later, the executive staff, employees, and attachés of the Boston Opera House presented a gold plaque, engraved with all their names, to Eben D. Jordan. It and the autograph book inscribed with the signatures of the company's great, near-great, and would-be-great are the only tangible souvenirs of the Boston Opera still preserved by Jordan's daughter.

2

FATHER AND SON
(Eben Jordan, Senior and Junior)

When Eben Jordan, Jr., decided to build an opera house for Boston, he reflected the spirit of his father, who liked to say: "There is a time for looking backward and a time for looking forward." Eben Junior had shown himself an experimenter from youth, "always willing to grab his hat and hurry out the door in quest of a new idea," according to a booklet published on the hundredth anniversary of Jordan Marsh Company, Boston's most famous department store. He clearly inherited a flair for large gestures as well as a love of beauty and music from his father, who counted the New England Conservatory among his beneficiaries, bought paintings, and generously bolstered many a talented young person's career under the cover of anonymity valued so highly by Boston's big donors. A man of tact, he always sensed the right moment to lend a hand, another quality he passed on to his son.

Eben Senior's professed fondness for "theatricals," as well as for music, expressed itself materially when he backed up Patrick Sarsefield Gilmore with dollars as well as moral support in the gigantic Peace Jubilees of 1869 and 1872, and earned from Gilmore the tribute: "If not the founder, he is surely the funder." The older man seemed to enjoy a gamble. His career probably inspired one of Horatio Alger's tales. Alger, himself a Massachusetts boy, lived concurrently with Jordan and must have admired his life and works. Eben was a prototype of the country boy who braves the big city with a dollar in his pocket and proceeds to make better than good.

15

Born October 13, 1822, the eighth generation descended from Robert Jordan, a "fearless, tireless" pioneer of Episcopalianism in Maine, the boy early learned to be self-reliant. With a quarter more than the traditional fortune-founding dollar, the lad landed in Boston harbor, armed with "good principles, sound health, habits of industry and economy, and the desire to achieve results by honest toil"—far better than money, Tristram Frost Jordan sagaciously pointed out in a "Jordan Memorial" published in 1882.

At sixteen, after working on a farm for the grand salary of four dollars a month, the future tycoon (a word unheard of in those days) entered the store of William T. Tenney and Company at Prince and Salem Streets. He was a chore-boy, only gradually allowed the responsibility of waiting on customers. Within two years he moved to Pratt's on Hanover Street, where he commanded a yearly salary of $275, out of which he saved part, "thus early adopting the rule of living within his income." At nineteen, a leading drygoods merchant, Joshua Stetson, offered to set him up in business. His rent for the store was $200 for the first year, his sales $8,000. Sentimentally, Tristram Frost records that Eben's first customer, an old lady, bought one-half yard of calico for seven cents—the only sale that day. At the end of four years, Eben was earning $100,000 yearly. Now he was a man of twenty-five, ready to swim in deeper waters. In two years he was ripe for the partnership that now suggested itself in the person of Benjamin L. Marsh, whose brother Charles joined them a year later. To build up the complex that is the Jordan Marsh Company, with its six acres of salesrooms and two thousand or more employees, was steady hard work, calling for self-education, thrift, and persistence, as well as daring.

Like Napoleon, said his admiring relative, Tristram Frost Jordan, Eben Jordan possessed the instinct to judge men, to draw them out and train them. Jordan Marsh contributed to the beatitude of its employees in many ways. The boon of a ladies' "waiting" room originated with this store, surely one of the enlightened inspirations of the nineteenth century. JM's sanctuary for female employees utilized the entire upper floor of the great corner tower for the girls' "diversion and pleasure." He treated the entire company to outings, sending many of his buyers to Europe, and even accompanying a group of twenty-seven there in 1882, introducing the flattered and flustered girls to such notables as the Lord Mayor of London, Victor Hugo, and President Grévy of France. At a reception in Paris, Lillian Nordica (born Norton, in Farmington, Maine), sang "divinely" for representatives of the store where her mother had worked as a dressmaker.

Even more startlingly did the firm conspire to make the customer happy. "Satisfaction or your money back" was first proclaimed in this Boston emporium. They were the first to sell on credit and guarantee refunds, ideas that jolted their competitors all over the world, who were forced to follow the leader. "The customer is always right" originated with Jordan. Others profiting from the Jordan progressive spirit were the daily papers, which very soon had to add pages to accommodate the mass advertising that distinguished the company from early days, never matched in bulk by rivals.

The appearance of the store meant a great deal to the Jordans. Not only were the fixtures periodically brought up to date, but the personnel came in for grooming. Promptly on the first day of May, all the girls appeared in white blouses. As the hour of autumn struck, on Labor Day, the blouses were changed to black.

Mittons succeeded Marshes at the turn of the century, when the name was amended to Jordan Marsh Company, and under the aegis of Allied Stores Mittons remain today as the guiding forces of the firm, minus both Marshes and Jordans. Mittons carry on the tradition of "looking forward," with a health department, library, reading room, men's game room, cafeteria, and other modern comforts for all JM employes.

Eben Jordan came along just too late to found a "First Family." Cleveland Amory estimates that this charmed circle of almost mythical sanctity and power reached its Golden Age just as Jordan was emerging as a personage in the retail world. Because of the comparative brevity of its existence, the Jordan dynasty had no opportunity to employ an important First Family gambit: marriage. The Jordans' money was accumulated through qualities a Proper Bostonian respects—hard and honest toil, salted by rectitude and peppered by a dash of the shrewd trading dear to the Yankee. But while Eben Senior probably never spent a foolish penny, he abhorred miserliness. What distinguished the Jordans almost above all other rich men was their love for spending their money, and spending it openly—not that they ever squandered wealth or displayed vulgar ostentation. Their taste and training were too sound.

The Jordans' secret benefactions, too, were carried on with an amplitude that matched any of their neighbors'. But it was the public expenditures, most often in the cause of musical culture and culminating in the opera house gesture, that set them apart. Later, to be sure, a few rich Bostonians ventured out from behind the wall of reticence, refuting by their yachts, stables, and travels James Russell Lowell's dictum that Boston society looked upon leisure as "the larceny of time that belongs to other people." But only Major Henry L. Higginson, the Symphony's angel, spent money on culture right out where everybody could see—and in such quantity.

The death of Eben Senior in 1895 brought tributes from admirers near and far. "None missed the funeral," the *Standard* noted, estimating the throng at four thousand. The Reverend E. Winchester Donald delivered the eulogy in Trinity Church. "It was refreshing," remarked the *Journal,* "to see the respect paid by the great department stores," showing that "business competition never produced bitterness in Boston." Pallbearers constituted a nice blend of business, First Family (the two not mutually exclusive), and close friends, including John P. Marquand, father of the novelist; S. P. Mandell, owner of *The Evening Transcript;* Otis E. Weld, the wine merchant; E. J. Mitton; Isadore Braggiotti; and Charles H. Taylor. Braggiotti, himself the founder of a family that cut a considerable swath in the artistic and political world, was Jordan's privileged private secretary. Of Jordan it was said that "he never forgot an error or a tardiness and never remembered a name," so that Braggiotti more often than not labored as "Mr. What's-his-name."

The King had passed; a new reign had begun.

Eben Junior in his youth aspired to a life of greasepaint. With that same Isadore Braggiotti, "Mr. What's-his-name," Eben and a third young man, Herbert Dumaresq, traveled around the world in their salad days, calling themselves the Rali-Rali Brothers. Eben's voice was a fine baritone; Braggiotti's a high tenor; Dumaresq's role is uncertain. Braggiotti's expansive personality, evidence of his Italian-Smyrnian parentage, made a deep impression on his companion. Only five-foot-ten, Isadore later put on weight to the amount of 200 pounds, yet never lost his buoyancy and gusto. "If you don't say charming things, you don't think charming things," is the way he explained his effusive manner, as described by his daughter Gloria in her book, *Born in a Crowd.* In his bachelor days, he had bought dozens of pairs of gloves, socks, shoes, and extra canes, heaps of checked waistcoats, piles of suits, most of which he never wore. Yet they all traveled with him wherever he and his ever increasing family

flitted. He was not handsome, but his extraordinary vitality drew people
of all sorts into his orbit. His mother had been a Boston Chadwick, aunt
of the Elbridge Gerry Chadwick whom Jordan's daughter Dorothy later
married. Isadore therefore was accepted among Boston's First Families,
as well as in any society throughout the world that he chose to honor.
His influence on young Jordan never waned; possibly the merchant's continuing absorption in music was due to him.

Jordan needed to draw on his own reservoir of confidence many times
during the five years of his responsibility as "angel" for the opera company. If he had decided instead to endow an art museum, stock a library,
or, in another cultural bloodline open to private patronage, pay the deficits
of a first-class symphony orchestra, he would not have experienced the
headaches peculiar to opera patronage. Though his name may be glorified
in the annals of monumental philanthropy, a man in such a position becomes fair game for sharpshooters from all compass points. If he stays
behind the scenes, his silent partnership may be branded as veiled dictator-
ship. Fortunately, Jordan never incurred this reputation; Henry Russell
vouched for his patron's rigid adherence to a hands-off policy in artistic
matters. Jordan's problem became that of the open benefactor, with no
place to hide except in the security of his own good conscience. After
the initial novelty wears thin, the ignorant public, regarding the artistic
venture as a "rich man's toy," does not even yet in America acknowledge
the vital day-to-day importance of the lyric theatre to a well-rounded life.
If its own responsibility is not immediately enlisted, this public can turn
indifference into a cruel weapon.

Furthermore the operatic "angel" hovers perilously over a world which
has its own way of blowing up everything it touches to its own larger-
than-life proportions. An opera company breeds its own culture in the
warm agar of temperament, talent, and display. And in the America of
the first decade of the twentieth century, more particularly in a Boston
just emerging from Victorianism, traces of the stigma attached to the
theatrical "green room" still lingered—the green room where gay blades
and scabbards from both sides of the footlights met to arrange assigna-
tions.

Jordan risked these dangers for love of an art. He possessed the ability
to accept the inevitable, once it had been determined. Although never
betraying to the public or even to any but his closest friends a sign of
disillusionment, many black moments awaited him, through which his

stalwart character and profound integrity carried him. Although no gambler, except for a private game of poker (he owned real estate, but never stocks and bonds), he followed an impulse without hesitation and without quibbling when it appealed completely to his vision. His operatic plunge may have seemed such an impulse, yet it was undertaken only after considerable thought. This combination of a stable mind with a winged imagination provided the true key to Jordan's personality and accomplishments. At his untimely death in 1916 (to which the hidden sorrows of the operatic adventure may have indirectly contributed), eulogies were rendered which, though more appropriate to his generation and to his somewhat reserved nature, did not show less feeling than those tendered to his more extroverted father. Among other tributes, Richard Henry Dana, in a memorial concert at the New England Conservatory, spoke of Jordan as "friendly and even affectionate to those who knew him well. Because of the absorption of his busy life," Dana continued, "his quick perceptions, and the need of using almost every moment to accomplish what he undertook, he did not give all acquaintances a chance to know him fully and appreciate his many finer qualities."

Henry Russell could have found no more agreeable and trustworthy backer than this man, so positive in character, and with the one trait invaluable in the circumstance: he believed in experts, and once chosen, he left them on their own authority to deliver the goods.

3

LITTLE MAN, BIG BOSS
(Henry Russell)

Henry Russell was one of those individuals who, forever at the center of a boiling pot, himself remains impervious to heat. With a charm described variously as mesmeric or reptilian, he inspired either fanatical love or hate. In a society that did not condone, but appeared not to notice publicly, he moved unscathed through scandals that would have ruined a less invulnerable spirit. Each of his first two wives passed him sympathetically along to the next; neither showed any jealousy. His elder son, whom he alternately ignored and disciplined, still shows a wistful loyalty and ungrudging respect, over a residue of bitterness both natural and inevitable. Russell cared little for children. Pretentious, snobbish, vain, of slighter stature than even the many tiny tenors he engaged, he fitted exactly the average man's idea of an impresario—a term, incidentally which he loathed, preferring to call himself an "artistic director." Lacking the business genius and capacity for self-effacement of a Gatti-Casazza, he possessed Maurice Grau's ability to handle stars, yet only a degree of that bygone impresario's tact. Lavish as Henry E. Abbey, cocksure as Heinrich Conried, Russell revealed innate taste akin to Oscar Hammerstein's but missed that great entrepreneur's flair for the real *beau geste*. Many of his qualities can be described only as uniquely Russell.

This wily yet winning man arrived in Boston with relatively little experience as absolute boss of an opera company. He had fallen into the job, as many another before and after him, there being no formal training that can produce the complete impresario. A short fall season at Covent

Garden in London in 1904 and a few weeks of opera alternating with drama at London's Waldorf Theatre in the spring of 1905 constituted his first ventures. Both proved dismal failures. Even the presence of Enrico Caruso, fresh from his first season at the Metropolitan and already a Covent Garden favorite, and the visit of Puccini to witness his *Manon Lescaut* did not save the fall season; nor did the Divine Duse rouse the indifferent London public during the theatrical spring season. Next Russell turned to America as a happy hunting ground for his operatic ambitions. Within two seasons his success mounted in cities scattered throughout the east and midwest. When his touring San Carlo company paused in Toledo to present *Aïda* and *Faust* in March, 1908, the *Blade* devoted an editorial column to this phenomenon: "When a comparative unknown can... impress the musical world of his greatness to such an extent that wealthy men of one of our largest cities lend themselves to support... a permanent opera house, there must be something extraordinary in the unlimited possibilities of this man and the class of grand opera he is capable of producing."

An American musical magazine of the time credited him with mastery of half-a-dozen languages, composition, conducting, and a thorough knowledge of the physiological conditions surrounding voice production. Many an entrepreneur has dared the deep waters of opera production with far less useful equipment.

Russell's lifelong preoccupation with music and the theater was, they would have said in his childhood, foreordained. He could not have escaped the lyric theater because he could not have denied heredity. As Jordan's father bequeathed an empire of commerce to his son, so Russell Senior left a heritage of the stage. Henry's father had barely been weaned when he found himself behind the footlights. The "vehicle" of this debut was a sketch called *Panzarro*, put on in the English shires. The three-year-old baby was carried on; although hardly a role of substance, it was a portent of what was to come. At five he learned piano; at eight he sang contralto in the choir. With a traveling children's company, he was entertained by Edmund Kean, the unrivaled tragedian, and deliciously frightened by the actor's pet lion. Kean gave young Henry Senior some advice he never forgot: "Learn to speak every word distinctly, boy. Slovenliness is the curse of our profession."

At a still tender age, Russell journeyed to Milan, where he met Rossini, Donizetti, and Bellini, reigning monarchs of Italian opera. He found a place as piccolo in the opera house leased by the banker Sarasi, who induced Bellini to give the youth lessons in composition. Michael (*Bohemian Girl*) Balfe became a bosom companion, and the two toured through Italy, hiring out their musical talents. In Paris, Russell encountered the composer Meyerbeer. Back in London, he made friends with Maria Malibran, who had sung her debut there as Rosina in *The Barber of Seville* in 1825, and with the violinist Charles de Bériot, later her husband. He also knew the demonic Paganini. About 1833 he set off on a long tour of the North American continent, sojourning in Rochester for eight years as organist at the First Presbyterian Church, earning three hundred dollars a year. He returned to England in 1841.

One day he heard the oracular Henry Clay, and determined on a new career. Kean's injunction had never been forgotten; now he put it to practical use. He became a monologuist, traveling the wide circuit that welcomed itinerant preachers, lecturers, and musicians. His decision to compose his own songs for his act brought him his chief claim to fame. Of the more than eight hundred ditties he tossed off, several still strike a nostalgic note; notably "Woodman, Spare That Tree!" and "A Life on the Ocean Wave," which was used by the marines as a regimental march. The prolific composer lived too soon for his financial good, selling his songs outright at an average of about $2.50 per song. The famous plea for conservation brought only $2. "Cheer, Boys, Cheer!" earned the highest price—$15.

Whether his son Henry took pride in these achievements is not known. Today's psychiatrists would find ample reason for Henry's preference for his mother in the fact that his famous father could not marry her until the boy had reached the age of twelve. Already married, Russell left his wife and their five children for two loves: travel and a tiny Portuguese beauty, the daughter of Lirolon de Lara, a painter of some renown. The sixty-year-old Henry Senior had successfully concealed his liaison, although he ran a dangerous risk by registering their son's birth under the name of Russell at Somerset House, where all English vital statistics are kept. A second son, Landon, was surnamed Ronald, the name his Portuguese mother had assumed. He became an accomplished pianist and conductor and appeared one day in the King's Honors list as Sir Landon.

Young Henry's first success, typically fortuitous, was attended by the trumpets of notoriety rather than by the quieter instruments of slow recognition. He won a libel suit brought by a disgruntled singing teacher, though the verdict publicly branded his hopes of becoming a singer as unjustified. His faulty eyesight had already turned him from the earlier study of medicine and science; now another profession seemed closed to him.

Although Henry opens his memoirs with an account of the trial, he does not mention the notoriety simultaneously heaped on his parents. The five earlier sons of Henry Senior, one of them a bishop, another Count Clarke Russell, author of sea tales, exposed their father's irregular union. Henry Junior brazened it out, though it undoubtedly left a deep wound, which he forever tried to salve by seeking the company of wealthy and ennobled folk—his memoirs show him more title-dropper than historian. "It has been my strange destiny," he wrote complacently, "to spend at least half my life with very rich people, opera being one of those expensive luxuries that demand the support of a millionaire." Prince Obolensky, a Tsarist refugee who sang in Melba's opera company, which Henry piloted through Australia later in his life, twitted Henry on his snobbery and his fondness for *"tutoying"* (using the familiar second person singular) the great lords and ladies whose paths he crossed so often. His second wife laughingly accused him of sounding like a head waiter. He retaliated that he didn't consider himself a snob; he merely didn't want to be bored.

Another heritage that Henry could not escape, and which his second wife believes contributed to his insecurity, was his Jewishness. Russell in itself was an adopted name: his father's family came from France and was known as Roussel. Henry could not claim an English ancestry. It should not have mattered to any member of this gifted tribe, almost all of whom have flourished happily in the limelight. Among Russell's grandchildren are a composer-actress-singer, a dancer-writer, a photographer, and an industrial psychologist. Had Henry settled down to earnest effort, he might have topped his brother Landon's achievements as pianist and conductor. But he preferred the path of Balzac's character who was "an artist to the aristocrats and an aristocrat to the artists." His society friends listened in rapture to his piano playing, his second wife recalls, but he would never play if a musician were present.

The libel trial twisted itself about to Henry's ultimate advantage. The wide publicity that had been given his claim of being a singing teacher himself, moreover a teacher in a "pathological sense," brought him eager pupils. "It is often from disillusionment that life takes its permanent color," he remarked philosophically.

Russell's teaching "method," based on a study of the art of breathing and the physiology of the throat, became the object of considerable jest in the press, and, indeed, later suffered ribald interpretation behind proper Bostonian hands as "horizontal breathing." However, it sufficed to draw to his studio in Curzon Street Lillian Nordica and several noted English singers, and it cured Eleonora Duse of a taut and fatigued throat that had impeded her vocal production. The incandescent actress remained his staunch friend for two decades, naming him the "Mano Secura" (Secure Hand), and often thanking him publicly for his timely help. What the treatment consisted of, in addition to manipulation of the tense throat muscles, was never made clear, but Alice Nielsen later vouched for the Duse's gratitude: "She would give him every dollar if he would go to London. He went—of course not for money, for he is an artist." As a friend of both D'Annunzio and Duse, Russell witnessed the storms and raptures of this famous liaison, enjoying the delightful companionship of the poet and playing by the hour piano reductions of the Wagnerian scores D'Annunzio adored. He was able to make the piano thunder like an orchestra. Often, Russell said, when the poet's inspiration outran his physical strength, "Duse would stand behind his chair while he wrote, and wind cloths dipped in ice-water around his forehead."

In Duse's service, Russell spent the autumn of 1903 in London as her guest at the Savoy Hotel, remaining another year when "she would not hear of my leaving her." Her staging of her lover's plays, which she championed fiercely, almost as a religious cause, showed her "an inspired prophet," intent on the perfection of every detail. Russell eagerly absorbed the ways of the theater, learning further technique from D'Annunzio himself while assisting with the production of several new plays. He began to dread returning to the "comparatively dull life of a singing master." When De Sanna, director of the San Carlo Opera in Naples, sought an opera company with which to surround a current flame (a second-rate singer, the only kind, as Russell's friend Don Prospero Cellini, the critic, assured him, ever to get exploited exactly in this manner), and decided that the company should be in London (as far from Naples as possible), he offered the job to Russell. To this company, in addition to Caruso, the fledgling intendant mustered Caruso's sister-in-law, Rina Giachetti, from

whom his wife Ada had become estranged. Russell made very sure Caruso
did not know of her presence in the troupe until he landed in London.
Another principal soprano was to play a greater role in Russell's life than
the entire company combined. Her name: Alice Nielsen. Eleanora De
Cisneros, an American née Eleanora Broadfoot, joined the contralto ranks.
Russell's tenors included Francesco Vignas, who had spent the season of
1893–94 at the Metropolitan. The three chief baritones provided a strong
contingent: the experienced Mario Ancona, well known throughout the
musical world; the virile Mario Sammarco, who would sing with Hammerstein, Campanini, and Russell in America; and the young Pasquale Amato,
who had not yet made his debut at the Metropolitan. De Sanna's protégée
found herself in very good company.

For the opera-theater season at the New Waldorf Theatre the following spring, Russell conceived an idea that, only imperfectly carried out
in London, served later in Boston to attract considerable attention. He
performed in tandem a play and its operatic setting, choosing Scribe's
and Cilèa's *Adriana Lecouvreur,* and Maeterlinck's and Février's *Monna
Vanna.* Emma Calvé was to sing the roles that Duse acted. The fine
scheme lost its force when the Public Censor prohibited *Monna Vanna,*
balking at the famous line: *"Vous êtes nue sous ce manteau?"* even
though the public could only guess at the nudity. Strangely enough, no
such prudery obstructed the dramatic production in Boston.

Russell's motives in suddenly turning impresario were perhaps not as
unmixed as he professed. Peering behind his euphemisms, it is possible to
discover that Russell shared the bias of his friend De Sanna in the matter
of casting certain soprano voices. De Sanna's candidate is not openly revealed by Russell, but his circumlocutions indicate Caruso's little known
sister-in-law. Russell's own candidate did not remain long in doubt. He
describes his first encounter with the woman whose loyalty, ambition, and
affections really provided the first link in the chain that led to the found-
ing of the Boston Opera House.

Consuelo, Duchess of Manchester, an agreeable American who frequently entertained King Edward, had as a brother-in-law Sir John Lister-
Kaye (it would not have been a proper Russell story without a leavening
of titles), who "had crossed from New York on the same boat as little
Alice Nielsen, a celebrated comic opera singer." He asked Russell to try
her voice and see whether she was not capable of doing better things.
"At that time it seemed to me that with study she might develop into an

interesting artist, and I arranged for her to sing for the Duchess of Manchester."

"The little Alice" (Russell invariably prefaced her name with a diminutive) met her future mentor at her own moment of decision. She was indeed celebrated, the darling of the operetta stage, a jewel in Victor Herbert's crown. In his *Serenade* and *Fortune Teller* she had made a reputation and a fortune for him as well as for herself, But just as she always chafed under management and eventually struck out on her own, so shortly after the turn of the century she determined to "better herself" and reach for a true star's orbit—the grand opera stage. Russell fell willingly in with her plans, not deterred by the rumor that her capital could be counted in six figures, and with alacrity signed her up for singing lessons. He also obtained her signature on a performance contract, so that when Sam Shubert desired to lure her back to the profitable musical comedy field, he was forced to go through Russell. Alice would sing opera or nothing in America, she vowed. Shubert reluctantly agreed. Thus Russell embarked on the voyage that was to lead him into the New World, far away from home.

Among his early pupils in Curzon Street had been a slim, dark girl, whose lustrous eyes began to haunt her teacher. Not much shorter than he, she nevertheless contrived to look up to him, an attitude that he found enchanting. Furthermore, she reminded him of his adored mother. Her raven beauty was matched by a sweetness of character, and her proud bearing suggested her noble Portuguese ancestry: Nina da Costa Andrade's mother was a descendant of the Marquis de Pombal who rebuilt Lisbon after the earthquake in 1755, the greatest Portuguese statesmen of modern times. Deeply in love with Henry, she married him in 1895. In 1896 their first son, Henry Tosti, was born. At about the same time Nina changed her name to Russell, she adopted Varese as a *nom de théâtre*. Her husband's friendship with Duse and with Maeterlinck brought Nina into intimate contact with the stage. A linguist and singer, she was one of the company that breathed life into Maeterlinck's plays in the poet's beautiful old abbey of St. Wandrille in Normandy, appearing with Georgette Leblanc, whom the world knew as Mme. Maeterlinck.

Shrinking from outward show, Nina retired more and more into the background. As long as her son Tosti could remember, his mother wore only one style of dress, which she had made for her year after year by Fortuny of Venice. A long robe, belted loosely if at all, the gown's only trimming consisted of a semi-transparent collar of lace or other soft material. Long-sleeved, either black or white, it served as evening as well as day raiment. Under her mask of meekness Nina concealed a passion for cleanliness, bathed three times a day, and would change from her skin out the moment she came indoors from any excursion, however brief. Her bureau drawers were crammed with heavy silk hose; she professed outrage at Georgette Leblanc's laundry, which regularly contained a lone pair. Nina wore no diamonds, only a fine gold chain with a miniature amethyst pendant or a string of delicate pearls, but her closet bulged with shoes—forty pairs at a time. She changed them a dozen times a day, as the fancy took her.

Herself disposed to fidelity, for to her, with her Portuguese-Jewish ancestry, the marriage vow meant literally "to the death," Nina soon discovered that her mercurial husband resembled more than one character in the operas he was now putting on stage. Waiting for her second son to be born, she came to the bitter knowledge that the child's father would in all likelihood never join the household again as a permanent member. The truth was that Henry quickly became bored with family life. He felt his place to be in wider, more glamorous spheres. Faithful after his fashion, he could be said to cleave to one woman—at a time. In the three years that saw Henry commuting over the Atlantic, touring with the San Carlo company, and establishing a beachhead in Boston, Alice Nielsen provided the lodestar of his affections, while Nina suffered loneliness and heartbreak. Into this vacuum came a young French musician, André Caplet; a deepening friendship with him brought solace to her bleak life. Boston insists to this day that the one condition this quiet woman exacted from her husband was that Caplet be engaged as chief conductor of the opera. Henry evidently withstood his wife's soft pressure the first year, but when plans became public for 1910–11, Caplet's name appeared in the conducting roster as chief of the French repertoire.

Those who are still alive to remember the Boston Opera years speak, possibly from hindsight, in half-amused, half-horrified tones of the far-away scandal; how much of the true situation showed itself to the Bostonians of contemporary days is hard to discover. That Boston, of all cities, should sit on such a powder keg without applying the match seems incredible, except that an odd mixture of the worldly and the innocent prevailed in that always insular community: those who knew or suspected would shrug shoulders and gossip only in secure company; the innocent wouldn't have known. Nina settled down near the opera house, placing her two sons in an adjoining apartment under the care of a tutor. Her rival lived only a few blocks away.

For the time, Henry had insured the exact balance of a precarious personal situation. His professional status seemed doubly secure, buttressed by the confidence and pride Jordan showed in him, the acceptance by Boston's most illustrious society, the readiness of the press to bestow on him the benefit of every doubt, and the smoothly functioning machinery of a company that bore his personal stamp in every department.

He expressed his satisfaction in an interview in the pages of the *Post* two months before the opening of the Boston Opera Company. The story was accompanied by a photograph of himself with his wife and two sons, Tosti holding a violin and Sheridan a cello. He confessed becomingly that while he loved "the very ground upon which my two boys tread," everything must take second place before the present job. He intended to sleep in his office and be at his desk by 6:30 A.M. This promised a somewhat sketchy private life, but then Henry was a dedicated man. He continued:

"I have my path marked out. I am willing to be enlightened, but my plans are all based on reasons, and every reason has been arrived at after much thought and deliberation. I am honest with myself, and while I invite honest criticism, no storm of adverse opinions can swerve me unless I can be persuaded that I have been wrong. And as such, the Boston public will have to take me. I am not an autocrat ... not a despot ... I do not aspire to be a grand opera Napoleon ... I am first of all a speculator. To me, directing grand opera is a work of love. I expect success but will not swerve from my ideals under any consideration."

This manifesto left no doubt in anyone's mind. Henry was boss.

4

"THE LITTLE ALICE"
(Alice Nielsen)

Philip Hale, Boston's illustrious music critic, following his custom of documenting in detail every important musical or dramatic event in Boston, was not slow to point out that Alice Nielsen had "been here" before her operatic debut with Henry Russell's San Carlo company. She had first entranced the Hub as Annabel in Reginald De Koven's *Robin Hood* with the famous Bostonians at the Tremont Theatre. The date was April 27, 1896. Another role that same season was Anita in Oscar Weil's *Wartime Wedding*, on May 14. The following season she had played Yvonne in Victor Herbert's *Serenade*, on September 20, 1897, and on March 13, 1899, she had graced *The Fortune Teller* in her own company at the Boston Museum (not to be confused with any museum of art).

By 1899 she was ready for a triumphant homecoming to Kansas City, Missouri, which adored her, making much of her success in a full-page newspaper tribute. Kansas City could not claim to be her birthplace, which was Nashville, Tennessee, but the Missouri metropolis had given a welcome—somewhat lukewarm, to be sure—to the Nielsen family when Alice was eight. Her father, a Dane who played violin and whose chief distinction seemed to have been a wound received in the Civil War, had died the year before. The mother, an Irish girl from Boston, settled in Warrensburg near Kansas City and attempted to stretch her late husband's pension into a living for a brood of daughters. Alice's memories of her youth retained the ugly color of the thoughtless cruelty of children, who made fun of her hand-me-downs and her bare feet. But the doggedness of the Dane and the spunk of the Irish combined early in her parents' daughter. When little boys set up their taunt of "Yah, Raggedy Ann, Raggedy Ann" in a grocery store one day, Alice hauled off and fired fresh eggs at her tormentors. "My first hit," she recalled.

Mrs. Nielsen scraped up enough money for lessons with a professor (who, after Alice became famous, sued her for eight thousand dollars— but lost). The determined little girl next set as her target the choir of St. Patrick's church, where in her cheap dress she sang "like a Florence Nightingale," as an enraptured but slightly muddled stranger wrote to Father Lillis after hearing her one Sunday. Despite the continued jealousy of other singers, she kept a precarious foothold there for five years. Only the organist showed any sympathy, quietly encouraging her in the ambitions that overshadowed her immaturity and lack of training. For him she felt gratitude that led her warm heart into one of its excessive gestures: she married him. His name was Benjamin Nentwig, but Alice seldom used it, and it persisted only in their son. Nentwig lacks appeal as a stage name, and that Alice was headed for the stage—she had already made her debut in *Patience*, at the Coates Theatre—there could be little doubt. Even as a private name, Nentwig endured only until 1898, when, in the midst of a calendar heavily planted with growing engagements, Alice paused long enough for a divorce. The marriage had revealed one incompatibility after another, chiefly a strong post-marital desire on Nentwig's part that the singer, now wife, should stay home and practice her new trade. Alice, although torn between her natural generosity of spirit and what must have seemed betrayal from her only mentor, saw no choice. She joined a traveling "concert company" in 1892, leaving her infant son Benjamin at home and flinging her still unformed gifts into the raw, coarse existence of a barnstormer. She was immediately billed as the "Swedish Nightingale," without even the appellation "new" to soften the arrant attempt to capitalize on a renowned reputation of half a century past. Alice was no Jenny Lind, nor for entrepreneur could she call on such an expert as P. T. Barnum. The company carried no fripperies, such as scenery or costumes, the girls improvising the latter and for the former draping the bare stages with bedsheets. More often than not, the "op'ry houses" of their small-town circuit boasted no dressing rooms, so that the girls would be forced to change virtually on stage, hanging the indispensable sheets across one corner. Behind this flimsy screen, in the glare of the unshaded lamp or baby spot, the harried prima donnas unwittingly provided a shadow pantomime for the audience, which yelled in appreciation. Niel-

sen and the contralto took turns shielding each other with full skirts spread
wide during changes.

When the boss showed presence of mind in absconding with the box-
office receipts—eight dollars—Alice would not give up. She dug into her
savings and what she had been able to squeeze out of her seventy-five
dollar salary, and staked the forlorn troupe to a western trek, thus establishing a pattern for future operations. In Denver, the prima donna came
under the eagle eye of the Pike Opera Company's manager, who promptly
preempted her for Yum-Yum in *The Mikado* and the leading role in
La Périchole. "The little Alice" was on her way.

She took her first big step in San Francisco, fabled theater town, where
opera troupes had prospered since mid-century. George E. Lask, the
manager of Tivoli, a favorite beer garden, easily persuaded Miss Nielsen
to change her affiliations. She rose from small roles to stardom and soon
joined The Bostonians, who bore an enviable reputation. An offshoot of
the celebrated Boston Ideals, its roster embraced every illustrious name
in operetta, headed by Henry Clay Barnabee, the beloved comedian who
also acted as manager.

Alice Nielsen became one of this attractive company. Edward N.
Waters, in his biography of Victor Herbert, says that she forced herself on
Barnabee, waiting day after day to see him and gain her objective, and
boasting with some complacency afterward of her unpopularity with other
members of the company. Not only did the leading lights look with dis-
favor upon her aggressiveness, but the rather imposing prima donnas
tended to resent the newcomer's "youthful figure, small feet, praiseworthy
ankles, and general daintiness." Her first part, Annabel in *Robin Hood,*
led to greater glory. Hoping for the exclusive right to the leading role in
Herbert's *Serenade,* she nevertheless had to yield to a previous claimant,
Hilda Clark, and take alternate performances. Alice cannily took her
turns to coincide with openings in Boston, Chicago, and New York,
thereby gathering in the first reviews.

Always with a bright eye for the future, "as restless as a canary and
as ready to sing," as Amy Leslie, the sharp lance of the Chicago *News*
staff, described her, Alice began to see glimmers of an even more exalted
position. She set her sights on study with Mathilde Marchesi, who had
launched Melba, Eames, and Calvé into operatic orbit. No hint of this
appeared in a typically simpering interview, quoting her as in search of
the quiet life all prima donnas in duty bound must profess to covet

above the tinselly glamour of their shallow triumphs.

After the success of Serenade, Alice became restive again. With the encouragement of Victor Herbert, for whom she could do no wrong, and the assistance of Frank A. Perley, who deserted The Bostonians to be her manager, she formed her own company to do The Fortune Teller, described as the musical success of the decade. Complementing the star were celebrities of equal prominence and even more experience—Eugene Cowles and Joseph Cawthorne, Marguerita Sylva and Marcia Van Dresser. The first and last frankly deserted Barnabee.

Amid its furor of success, The Fortune Teller struck an unexpectedly sour note during Alice's homecoming celebration in Kansas City. The Star acidly described Alice as "playing three roles, none of which is very clearly defined, and as she has little of the finesse of the art of acting, she is not very much assistance to a lame librettist" (Harry B. Smith). The avalanche of praise from other quarters must have overwhelmed any possible chagrin, however. She was called "petite and dainty as a Dresden doll with the voice of a lark," "a fairy out for a holiday among mortals."

The Fortune Teller tested its luck across the Atlantic in 1901. After a London season that came abruptly to an end with the opera's eighty-eighth performance (receipts did not justify the weekly expenditure of $5,750), a critic proclaimed Alice the best light opera prima donna America had sent over, but his approval could not save the venture.

Alice had reached another parting of the ways. Perley was quoted as ready to drop her, saying that "she cannot stand success." Even more damaging was his claim that a benefactor, Colonel Thomas Williams of California, had reached the same conclusion and was pulling out.

Henry Russell may have noted this tempest in the world of light entertainment, but it seems hardly likely, as he professed a loathing for operetta and musical comedy. Alice's higher aspirations had to crystallize before these two people could be of use to one another. Russell relates the outcome of Alice's first London soirée at the Duchess of Manchester's. The Duchess then and there asked the young American if she would like to sing for King Edward. Alice was overwhelmed.

"Although she had enjoyed unparalleled success in comic opera," Henry said, "she was really quite unspoiled. She assumed none of the airs and graces which distinguish certain successful stars, and the prospect of singing for a king seemed to appeal to her much as a fairy story appeals to a child."

After dinner on the great night, the King asked Nielsen to sing Tosti's "Goodbye." Lady Randolph Churchill, seated beside the King, began to talk in the second verse, and the King answered in his deep voice. Alice became flurried.

"It so happens [Russell resumes] that the third verse of 'Goodbye' begins with the words, 'Hush! the leaves are falling.' Alice aimed the word 'Hush!' so pointedly at the King that he was startled into silence. As soon as the song was finished, he got up and walking toward Alice said goodnaturedly: 'Miss Nielsen, I really deserved that. I hope you will forgive me for talking.' "

Alice did not have to resort to "shushing" in order to gain public attention, for she made a favorable impression, if not in any way a sensation, during Russell's Covent Garden season. We find her telling about it in a later interview, companioned by Henry. Henry began, presumably on the premise that what he said in California would not be reprinted elsewhere.

"I had relations with what is called London's 'Smart Set,' and when I announced a little season with Alice Nielsen and Caruso (the idol of the English public, although I could never understand why), a great many people seem to regard me as a madman."

Alice interrupted with a corrective slant on values: "But Caruso was an angel. He . . . coached me all through *Bohème,* then he made me take the bows."

Henry continued: "I went to Victor Maurel and told him, 'I have a little American who will sacrifice $130,000 to art and wants help.' Maurel had been kept out of London by a foolish opera syndicate, but he consented to sing Rigoletto for me—his first in ten years."

"He, too, retired to let me take the applause," Alice interjected. "He put his arm around me and almost carried me to the footlights."

Russell again: "She sang 'Voi che sapete' for D'Annunzio and Boito, and Boito said that only two others had ever really sung it like that: Patti and Melba. Boito [who was working on his seemingly never-to-be-finished *Nerone*] promised her the part of the Christian Maiden."

A curious discrepancy presents itself in the accounts of Alice's financial position at this time. Henry openly acknowledged in the California interview that it was her $130,000 that financed at least part of the Covent Garden venture, which he said left him with scarcely enough to maintain his family (almost his only mention of them in his book) for two months.

This sets strangely with his allusion to Alice as the recipient of a great London lady's philanthropy. "Mrs. Lionel Phillips overheard a girl with a beautiful voice singing in my studio. I explained that this was a young American anxious to study for opera, but who was forced to accept exhausting engagements in order to support her mother and family. These efforts, I added, would probably ruin her voice." The result was a cheque for a thousand pounds. Alice revealed that she had been the recipient of the gift, but attributed it to a slightly different reason. "I had turned down a contract for five seasons at three thousand dollars a week in order to study," she said in California. "When Henry Russell told Mrs. Phillips, she sent me the money."

Alice also benefited from Henry's association with Eleonora Duse. She claimed to have been present when Henry gave the actress her first lesson in breathing. Duse in gratitude taught Alice how to act—"I was her only pupil," Alice is quoted as saying.

"I was so scared I turned white. Duse said: 'Good. She turns pale. For *Traviata*.' Then when I was doing my bravest gesticulation, Duse commented: 'Pugilisto! That's exactly like a pugilist.' Duse is a dear and so beautiful," Alice wound up rather lamely.

The actress also appeared as the benefactor of "one young artist who was failing through lack of assistance," although possibly this was not Alice. Revealing her own warm heart and conscience, Duse wrote to Henry: "To the 'Secure Hand,' this is my prayer to you—to beg you to invite the little distant friend to come here. She must not suffer any more, nor, through her suffering, make others suffer uselessly and unjustly. I enclose a first-class train fare from Milan to Paris. I wish I could send her more. In order to help me, true and faithful Russell, I must be certain that no one else suffers. It would be unjust."

Another time she wrote: "Please invite the little one in my name, because I want to hear her beautiful voice. It is a force which helps one to dream and protects from life's daily realities."

"The little one," meanwhile, was still missed in America. The managers Sam and Lee Shubert, who leased the new Waldorf Theatre to Russell for his opera-drama series, approached Alice with tempting propositions, but ran headlong into her five-year contract with Russell. Alice would sing opera or nothing. The shrewd Americans, balking at the cost and uncongeniality of a production of Rossini's *Barber of Seville* (Russell's first suggestion), finally settled, but grudgingly, for Donizetti's *Don Pasquale*.

Russell claims that their fee precluded the engagement of good singers to surround Alice, but at any rate, the company ranked lower than second-rate and met a freezing failure at the Casino Theatre in New York when it opened in September, 1905.

"The New York critics broke my heart," admitted Nielsen in San Francisco, midway in a harrowing tour of one-night stands. Her Irish blood fired, she refused to accept defeat. By the time she reached the West Coast, her irrepressible spirits were high again. She confessed herself to be the happiest woman in the world.

"Why? Sift it all and you will find it's because of Mr. Russell. He is an artist—gave up pupils, even royal ones, to go to Duse. He is a genius—you should hear him at the piano. How he plays Wagner, and not a drop of German blood. He has been to me like—like a knight—like Lohengrin! My life today looks like a beautiful fairy tale."

Her sister Hortense, whom she had brought on the tour as companion-chaperone, chimed in in agreement with everything Alice said. *She* had tried to get Henry under the mistletoe, Alice said mischievously, but did not reveal the outcome. Both girls were in high fettle, and the words flowed gaily like soap bubbles. When her "Lohengrin" sternly forbade her to drink cream in her second cup of coffee, Alice naughtily defied him and drained the rich mixture.

She was, as a later Boston interviewer discovered, "ingenious, tactful, fresh, spontaneous."

So we see Alice as the Boston adventure began. A mobile face, with its wide, laughing eyes, sweet mouth, and the beauty spot on the left cheek that completed her piquant femininity; brown hair parted in the middle and wound behind the ears in becoming little knots; petite, yet softly rounded in figure, graceful, quicksilver in movement and glance. Cobina Wright, the socialite singer, granted Alice the most beautiful legs in the world—always excepting her own. Resourceful and courageous, she had quelled a panic in Chicago when fire broke out, stepping in front of the lowered curtain and signaling Maestro Conti for "The Star-Spangled Banner." Demure and filial, she brought her mother Sarah to live with her in an apartment on Hemenway Street, across from the New England Conservatory and near the Opera House. Whether she played a material part in selecting costumes and properties for the new company, as one account credits her, she undoubtedly held a consulting brief. Life was, indeed, like a fairy tale.

Act I

5

GRAND OPENING

Boston's greatest operatic day, November 8, 1909, dawned chill, with sullen clouds promising unwelcome showers. By nightfall, the unpaved streets around the new Opera House oozed slippery mud, while the few pavements themselves "were not exactly such as suit embroidered slippers and pumps," the *Transcript* remarked. As early as six o'clock, traffic plans, carefully spelled out in the newspapers several days in advance, fell into disorder. Huntington Avenue had been marked off for foot passage and for those who arrived in clusters on the lurching articulated trams, as Boston called its streetcars. Vehicles received their instructions to enter from St. Stephens Street at the back of the opera house and to unload on Opera Place, the new street cut through between Huntington and St. Stephens. The order of these vehicles stood firmly prescribed: the Taxi Service Company, Boston Cab Company, and Kenny & Clark (most popular public conveyor with Back Bay socialites who did not keep cars or carriages) to proceed on the west side of Opera Place; all others on the east side. Rival companies soon put an end to any system; jockeying for position, the cabs and private carriages and autos clotted Huntington all the way back to Massachusetts Avenue, and, to the west, became hopelessly implicated with traffic bound for the new Museum of Fine Arts opening, by some calculation or miscalculation scheduled at the exact same hour as the new opera.

Twenty police officers strove to untangle the jam of almost one thousand conveyances, but three frantic hours went by before the last passenger alighted at the door. The curtain had long since gone up at its ordained hour of seven forty-five.

Crowds gathered ("as sometimes at Covent Garden," said the sophisticated *Transcript*) to marvel at the unusual spectacle. As many as sixty or eighty spectators added to the police problem on Opera Place, while a crescent of two or three score stood patiently about the main doors, although showers smeared the streets with a thin layer of mud. Incandescent lamps of a thousand watts, shining through the gentle rain, were transformed into "an iridescent cloth of gold," remarked the *Post*, through its sanguine young critic, a protégé of the *Herald's* Philip Hale named Olin Downes.

Discounting the weather, which luckily remained warm throughout the downpour, early comers had left their carriages to stand on the steps in their furs, their diamonds, and their decolleté. The doors opened a trifle late, for the house still needed a few stitches—sewing women worked feverishly on the velvet coverings for the massive ropes dividing passages, while in the upper balcony lobbies, cement had barely dried underfoot. Not only had labor troubles plagued the venture from the start, but on March 27, just before midnight, an explosion that resounded from newspaper row on downtown Washington Street to Brookline had rocked the opera house shell, opening a great hole six feet in diameter in the front façade. Engineers called it a bungled job of dynamiting, for no structural damage resulted, but the necessary delay harassed contractor George W. Harvey. The mystery of the dynamiters never was solved, although the detective, "Never-Fail Burns," continued to maintain that the Boston explosion was but one in a chain of such incidents perpetrated by the notorious McNamara brothers and Ortie McManigal, including the bombing of the Los Angeles *Times* in 1910.

Once inside the new edifice, the nightmarish confusion of the exterior scene vanished into dreamlike order and beauty. Even the latecomers hardly disturbed the vision, so cleverly was the plan of entrances arranged. Entirely homogeneous, all of a richly woven pattern from the rail of the orchestra to the highest perch in the side loges, the audience conquered its self-consciousness with native breeding, and, breathing an air of solidarity, of good taste and perfect confidence, settled down to patronize the exotic art of opera.

"The wandering tribes have arrived at the banks of Jordan," wrote Louis Elson in the *Advertiser*, seizing the occasion to pun on the opera's

Maecenas. "The missing muse is joined to her sisters, and at a bound Boston becomes, thanks chiefly to one man, an all-round metropolis."

The dream had come true: a handsome building devoted exclusively to the production of opera by a company not visiting but dwelling, as Philip Hale remarked. At last, "a building artistic in design, structure, ornamentation, equipment, in which the spectacle is not through necessity only on the other side of the footlights; for there is at last an opportunity for the display of fair women in gala costumes which in an opera house adds so much to the brilliance of the scene and performances; which gives to the opera certain—if the word is sadly abused—aristocratic distinction." Bostonians hitherto had taken the pleasures of the concert room tranquilly, normally, and steadily, an editorial in the *Transcript* pointed out, while opera had been for them a breathless, exotic, passing excitement. On this November night, it seemed as if grand opera, "that rather showy hybrid" of the historian, Dixon Wecter, long slighted in favor of the more austere delights of Symphony in the Hub, might stand enshrined in its proper niche forever. The note of hope sounded strongly in Eben D. Jordan's modest speech at the conclusion of the evening.

"I know by your applause that you are satisfied. You must be satisfied with this theater, because it is a most beautiful theater, and I think future generations of Bostonians will be thankful that they have the privilege of sitting in it."

Henry Russell went further, promising to establish "what I hope will be permanent—I might almost say an eternal—opera in the city of Boston."

No seat was reserved for Cassandra in this new temple to Apollo and the Muses. Even the sourest cynic could not have denigrated the aura of the well-founded permanence that surrounded the new undertaking. The structure itself, noble in simplicity of line and material, exuded a substantiality and pride that suited its occupants well. Too fancy a building would probably have put Boston off. Grand opera in itself would provide a brimming measure of the baroque, the rococo, the wildly fantastic. To contain this surging motley within plain walls was a stroke of genius. Parkman Haven knew his town.

"The first Unitarian Opera House," Arthur Whiting, the Massachusetts author and composer, neatly dubbed it. Philip Hale, quoting his colleague in the aftermath of 1915, thought that he referred to the "staid demeanor of the sitters in boxes and orchestra chairs, their family pews." The reference might just as well have applied to the chaste red brick and light gray limestone and white terra cotta exterior, which Lawrence Gilman in *Harper's Magazine* pronounced "in admirable taste and reticent beauty, rather than prodigal sumptuousness." A monograph published coincidentally with the opening of the house made clear that "from the beginning it was resolved that the new theater should be a thing of beauty no less than of use." The result, except for the obvious stage house and the less obvious glazed and colored bas reliefs under the main cornice symbolizing Music, Dancing, and Drama, by the local sculptor, Bela L. Pratt ("a la Della Robbia but finer," said one loyal critic), might have been any large, dignified public building, even a house of worship. The very restraint of the design forestalled future controversy.

The throng that animatedly peered, promenaded, and commented on opening night found the interior equally to its liking. Here too a characteristic understatement prevailed. The colors chosen for decoration were grays, ivory, and antique dull gold. A palette so muted might strike the usual urban operagoer, inured—even passionately devoted to—red plush and gleaming gold, as somewhat chilly. Indeed, the monograph hastened to add, "this has been relieved by the Burgundian red used in the box hangings and proscenium curtains and valances." Even such "relief" is subdued by the adjective "Burgundian"; furthermore, gold in the draperies was severely eschewed. A sky-blue ceiling with white clouds and a glittering chandelier gave the crowning touches. Not a pillar or post broke the view anywhere, all tiers being supported by cantilevers, or, as the monograph made plain, "in popular language, brackets firmly secured to the walls. This and kindred uses of strong, light material such as steel brought about the new and important changes."

Boston—everybody from President Lowell of Harvard to Mrs. John L. Gardner, including the 2,750 subscribers and guests who filled every seat —approved and, in a rather reserved way, expressed delight in the theater. "When the lights came on at the close of the first act, and people got what was really their first look, there were little soft waves of exclamation over the beauty of the place," according to one reporter. Still, the atmosphere remained "typically" Boston for a few moments. Then the ladies and gentlemen were introduced to an innovation—the promenade. Never before had a theater provided such ample lobby space for this form of entertainment.

Another innovation, the Palm Room, a dignified but cheerful chamber on the second-tier box floor, fitted out with "graceful chairs and round tables" (apparently no palms), was adopted after the first act as a smoking room, "men taking the hint from a cigar case in one corner and match safes on the tables." An elaborate soda water and ice cream fountain, "expected to be used by the women," remained neglected. Seeing the men alone, Jordan himself took command, escorting a group of his own guests there, thus breaking the ice. After the second act, practically every seat held a lady, and "college ices became the fad on an instant."

Back in their seats, the operatic pioneers took the opportunity for further observation before the second act curtain. No orchestra players were visible from the parquet or "baignoire" boxes at orchestra level, for the pit was sunk below the level of the floor. The carpeted aisles softened footfalls, while rather plain wooden seats, simply upholstered, opened and closed noiselessly (a virtue they lost later in their fifty-year existence). Ushers, in imposing livery, with chains about their necks like those in London's Covent Garden, performed their services in seemly, courteous, and intelligent fashion. H. T. Parker, the sage of the *Evening Transcript*, commented that the programs were of pleasant appearance, with a reproduction of one of Pratt's reliefs on the cover. He thought the practice of stating the opera's name and that of the conductor on one page, while deferring the cast to another, was infuriating. Those curious about box occupants were similarly frustrated, for the list appeared apart from the numbered diagrams. Still, the programs possessed a singular virtue: white gloves handled them and remained stainless.

The intermissions, though never tedious, were long enough to permit admiration of the dramatic sweep of the Italian Renaissance proscenium arch and, high above, of a decorated frieze that terminated at the capitals of the pilasters under the balconies. In three lunettes over the proscenium, names of prominent opera composers stood enshrined (presumably Wagner, Verdi, and Puccini). Although the audience neither noted nor particularly cared, they had read that the stage opening measured 48 feet in width, 39 in height; that the stage enclosure allowed 130 feet vertically for the movement of scenery, was as deep as the Metropolitan's and 20 feet wider. The whole admirable system was devised by Eugène Castel-Bert, the theatrical mechanist who had been responsible for the Metropolitan's own stage renovations a few years previously, notably the ingenious transformations in Conried's sensational production of Wagner's *Parsifal*.

Few of the absorbed onlookers would find their way backstage; Boston

for the most part (always excepting Mrs. Jack Gardner) remained in-
curious about the machinery that operated this vast enterprise, preferring
to keep a respectful, even slightly suspicious, distance. Still, it was good
to know that the artists' dressing rooms were the last word in modernity,
each containing shower and toilet (amenities the Metropolitan could not
boast), and that the administrative offices reserved for Russell and his
staff on the third floor were richly furnished, as befitted a proper opera
impresario.

Of more immediate concern to those in the auditorium was the obvious
fact that all this rich dignity, this unostentatious discretion, served as a
showcase for a jewel: the audience itself. Once again the comparison
turned to London rather than New York. The professions, the arts, finance,
men of affairs, of intellect and ornamental leisure gathered there, with
women of society, art, and the philanthropic life of the city beside them,
Parker noted approvingly. "The daughters who will succeed them are not
far away, with three ages—seven ages, almost—flowing together," a plain
manifestation of Boston society as a family affair.

"They sat," continued Parker, "as though to do so on opening nights had
been the habit of their lives, while perhaps within they wondered how
X across the way or Y around the turn seemed so used to it as well. After
all, we are not quite habitual boxholders and subscribers yet."

A visiting Englishman applauded the special quality of Boston audiences. Algernon St. John Brenon, writing in the New York *Telegraph*,
disagreed with Maria Gay, the flamboyant mezzo-soprano, who had
characterized the Hub's listeners as cold:

"New York is disturbed by a certain restlessness and indocility, a waiting
for points and purple patches and loud unmeasured outburst . . . if those
points are attained. Boston listens seriously, equably, giving the artist the
same courteous, careful hearing it would extend to a Huxley speaking
on a problem in biology, to a James Anthony Froude on the character of
Mrs. John Gardner's latest ancestor, Mary Stuart [a reference to Mrs.
Jack's claim to relationship with Mary of Scotland]. Above all, Boston
listens, not languorously as we do in England, but earnestly, seasoning its
admiration with a concentration of intellectual curiosity."

The opening night audience reflected many new facets in Boston's
socio-cultural existence. Aversion to conducting social life in public had
hitherto been only slightly lessened by occasional bouts with visiting
opera. Furthermore, public display of wealth or personal adornment went

against the Proper Bostonian grain. The worship of money, however, had long been equated with health and beauty; in fact, the New England conscience had never abdicated but only expanded its jurisdiction. Now an irresistible spirit of lush prewar times moved Bostonians in kind, if not in degree, especially among opera boxholders.

Many felt themselves at home all over the world. The Back Bay woman who said, "Why should I go anywhere? I'm already here," had given a little ground to the world traveler, the pleasure seeker on several continents—in a word, the cosmopolitan. Boston Thayers occupied stately English homes for a month or two; Searses, Dexters, Bealses, Cochranes, and Curtises commuted to Europe regularly. Eben Jordan, an ardent hunter, rented a succession of Scottish castles in the autumn.

Many also indulged in two expensive pastimes—boats and horses. Automobiles still rated as conversation pieces and objects for collectors' acquisition. Frederick Cunningham of Milton (a very special place in Boston geography), owned four, including two "electrics" for use in Newport. Prominent in the yacht set was Herbert Mason Sears, a staunch opera lover, who occupied Box 38 next to the Jordans and looked equally at home in a top hat or a Commodore's cap. John Singer Sargent depicted him on deck of the *Constellation*, which he bought from Bayard Thayer, owner of several distinguished racing boats. The bachelor treasurer of the opera association, Charles Hayden, who gave his name and a fortune to the New York Planetarium, liked boats, as did S. Reed Anthony, the broker, mill magnate Benjamin P. Cheney, Sr., and Mrs. Guy Lowell.

Less mobile than steam yachts or sailboats, but equally luxurious, the Larz Andersons' houseboat *Roxana* was a magnet for younger bluebloods. The diplomat Anderson had just been appointed Minister to the Netherlands at this time. His wife, the former Isabelle W. Perkins, descendant of old "Long Tom," the acknowledged king of merchant princes, Colonel Thomas Handasyd Perkins, indulged in pursuits that would have been classified as mischief by her stern progenitor—innumerable gaieties in Washington, Boston, and Palm Beach, where her fashionable taste won her the title of "dressiest."

In horsey circles could be counted another member of the Sears clan, Miss Eleonora, to this day prominent at shows and meets all over the world. A tennis tournament winner, Eleo, as her friends called her, also sat a polo pony in a style hitherto unknown to the frailer sex and tossed off hundred-mile hikes with insouciance. The Charles S. Birds were still

more preoccupied with equines. At one time they lived next to the auto-
cratic Somerset Club on Beacon Street and, with the lordly privilege often
accorded Boston nabobs, had a door cut between the houses so the food
from the club's hallowed kitchen could be sent through. Another First
Family lady, a Forbes who married a Perkins, the mother of Mrs. Robert
Herrick, and a cousin of Major Henry Lee Higginson of Symphony fame,
owned a house adjoining the Algonquin Club on Commonwealth Avenue,
termed by Lucius Beebe the handsomest club, with the best food and the
most admirable circle of gourmets. Mrs. Herrick's mother kept a carriage
and pair, but not ostentatiously. One day, seeing J. Montgomery Sears'
elegant rig pass by, Mrs. Perkins' daughter asked why the Searses had
two footmen and the Perkinses but one. "They have to; I don't," the
mother serenely replied. This was pure "Old Milton" speaking.

Jordan's horses had been famous until the first year of the opera, when
fire demolished his thirty-thousand-dollar stables at "The Forges," a showplace near Plymouth. He had collected many trophies and was pardonably
proud of his thirty first prizes over Thomas W. Lawson's four. Lawson,
the Boston promoter, was one of those picturesque eccentrics whose antics
form the golden nuggets in Boston's history. Superstitiously governed by
the number three, he bought No. 33 on Commonwealth Avenue; already
possessed of four children, he did not rest until he got six, a multiple of
three. His eldest daughter, Gladys, first married to Eben Blaine Stanwood
and later to Philip French, remembers that her father tried mightily but
in vain to secure Box 33 at the opera. The handsome Lawson, who put
all his knowledge of money-making into two books, *Frenzied Finance,*
and *Friday the Thirteenth,* died with less than he had lived with, but
he left a colorful legacy.

Luckily for Boston, which always needed a reason for outlay, opera,
Henry James' "great vessel of social salvation," came comfortably labeled
"culture." As long as it appeared to be in a good cause, Boston for once
let itself go in what amounted to an orgy of dressing up. This new finery
defied the legends that had so long encrusted the image of the Back Bay
female, notoriously modest in dress. It began to seem as if Boston women
had remained dowdy only because of lack of opportunity. No qualms
of conscience appeared to trouble the exquisitely gowned women in the
two rows of boxes on opening night. From Box 1, where Mrs. Horatio N.
Slater was adorned in yellow charmeuse (a "new silk that cost seven
dollars a yard," breathed one reporter), all around the circle, jewel-colored

silks, satins, velvets, and chiffons glowed softly under the brilliance of real gems.

Mrs. Edward D. Brandegee, whose elegance of carriage and slenderness of neck and waist Sargent praised on canvas, shone vividly from Box 17 in cerise velvet and diamonds. This was a year for tunics: the black lace over white of the wife of William M. Wood (Mill-owner "Napoleon" Wood, a true devil-take-the-hindmost industrialist) in Box 7; the white French appliqué lace over black of Mrs. John Longyear in Box 26. John Longyear was an expatriate from Michigan. When copper was discovered on his property, he brought his huge house stone by stone to be re-erected in all its ugliness in Brookline (it later became a Christian Science retreat).

Conspicuous in any crowd, the daughters of Alexander Cochrane were outstanding in beauty, dash, and taste, particularly redheaded Ethel, wife of the artist, Howard Cushing, in jewel-embroidered white, and Mrs. George R. Fearing, Jr., whose costumes always complemented her ash blondness. Mrs. Wallace Goodrich, wife of the conductor, draped old rose satin over a pale pink petticoat; Mrs. Frederick Converse, wife of the composer who had singlehandedly sold the boxes, sported the first of a series of one-color costumes, this time in cloth of gold.

That Mrs. J. Montgomery Sears should appear in black was a foregone conclusion. The reigning dowager still mourned the tragic death in an automobile accident of her only son in August, 1908. Joshua, Jr., known as "Monty," was considered the prize of society, having reached thirty-three without marrying. "Probably the best liked young man in Boston," one obituary stated flatly. Certainly the richest, paying the largest individual tax in the city.

The new freedom in dress seemed likely to lead women on to an appreciation of their physical advantages—or disadvantages, Philip Hale wrote. He also plumped for the increased attention to dress on the part of the Boston male. H. T. Parker harped on the same string, deploring the anomaly of the wife or sister richly arrayed, while the husband or brother sat beside her in working clothes. It seemed a miracle that more than a thousand men appeared in stark black and white at the opera opening.

Fashion reporters rejoiced in a buyer's market during the halcyon years of the opera. At first it seemed possible that one former snag might be avoided. It had become the custom to report a lady's identical costume once or twice only; then, if she wore it again, to ignore the lady. But what to do about Mrs. Jack Gardner, who ran a tiny gamut from "white satin and her fabulous pearls" to "black satin and her fabulous pearls"?

The opera years created a flurry, never equaled since, for Miss Driscoll of Boylston Street, who dressed "everybody who was anybody." Although Miss Driscoll herself died in 1930, the old firm with Lizzie Cunningham Riley and Emily Mahoney still carries on behind its gilt-domed canopy, but mourning the lavishness of the early part of the century.

Even in the light of today's high cost of living, Boston prices of 1909–10 command respect. Mrs. Slater's yellow charmeuse cost $375, the top of the average, which was estimated at $250 to $375, although a gown could run to $1,000 and higher if fur were used.

The opera had fifteen Mondays to go, as well as other nights when full dress was obligatory. In the depths of his frugal soul, the Proper Bostonian must have quivered.

If the happenings on the stage received slightly less attention than that paid by the audience to itself, the imbalance was understandable: *La Gioconda* held no surprise. Perhaps many of the audience had judged Christine Nilsson in Ponchielli's grandiose work as early as its Boston première, given by Henry E. Abbey's troupe during the Metropolitan's very first season of 1883–84. Russell's own 1907 December opening would have refreshed those memories. Lillian Nordica counted as an old friend and favorite; her acquaintance with Boston dated from her appearances as Leonora, Marguerite, and Desdemona with Abbey's Adelina Patti company in 1890 and even earlier ones with Mapleson at the Globe, when Hale noted that she had been billed as "Mlle. Giglio Nordica." Parker considered it becoming that as the foremost of the elder generation of American singers, she should be summoned to revive one of the parts that "invited the largeness of her style, the sweep, the intensity, the brilliance of her tones." She had struggled of late, he added, with the inevitable, the exacting years, but by sheer force of will, she conquered. "The memory is of Nordica in her golden and puissant prime strangely and suddenly renewed."

Hale reserved the lion's share of his opening night criticism for a newcomer, George Baklanoff, a Russian baritone who made a marked impression with his manly, brilliant, yet agreeable voice. The role of the spy, Barnaba, as Parker pointed out, invites intelligence, imagination, and executive skill. Baklanoff, with pale face, restless hands, and half-jaunty, half-furtive bearing, made Parker see and feel "the Venetian devil, who reached with a snaky hand, half-curling body, and face of satisfied malignancy to seize Gioconda's old mother."

Another newcomer, Juste Nivette, was an accomplished French bass in spite of Boston's Italianization of his first name to Giusto (the designation "le grand artiste français" appeared on his visiting cards). In the rich dress of a Venetian nobleman he might have stepped out of one of Van Dyck's Italian portraits. His elegant stage presence and rich and sonorous voice, with a Parisian feeling for emotional characterization, all guided by a sure stylistic sense, ensured his Boston success.

Russell's stalwart tenor, Florencio Constantino, who had headed the San Carlo troupe for several years, was obviously nervous on this occasion. Perhaps he felt that he bore more than his due share of responsibility, and must give to the public that cherished him the uttermost of his voice and powers. But, to excuse him, he had been toiling strenuously in Argentina and had not quite recovered. By his next performance, he had regained the fineness and variety of emotional and musical shading expected of him, and was himself again.

Another Boston favorite, Louise Homer, had sung Laura to Nordica's Gioconda in the Metropolitan's 1904–05 Boston season. The comely American contralto had, in fact, charmed the city ever since her debut as Siébel in *Faust* in 1901, appearing in roles as diverse as Amneris in *Aïda,* Venus in *Tannhäuser,* and Brangäne in *Tristan und Isolde.* Boston now found her to be in the full richness of vocal maturity, with a new breadth of style and dramatic energy. Her commitments in the strenuous Metropolitan season in and out of New York (she rushed down to sing Amneris in Philadelphia the night after the Boston opening) kept her away from Boston later; she returned for a single performance as Brangäne in 1912.

For brevity, however, Anna Meitschek's Boston career probably takes the palm. This Russian contralto profundo, who was said to have stepped in once for an ailing baritone in Nizhni Novgorod, sang the blind mother in *La Gioconda* on opening night. The Met's favorite Witch in *Hänsel und Gretel* that season, dashing about from city to city, she never visited the Boston Opera Company again, either on her broomstick or by Pullman.

No fault could be found with the other elements of the performance. The evening marked, in truth, the first time in long recollection when ballet in opera justified itself. The chorus revealed a tone admirable in quality, a pervading animation, and a comeliness of appearance. Under

Arnaldo Conti, the orchestra, recruited from outside the Symphony (which was still ununionized), showed frequent rough passages, but an elasticity of spirit and a characterizing energy that promised well for the season. The Venetian settings, painted by Stroppa in Italy, assisted by H. Logan Ried of New York, offered a taste of the elegance and opulence that were to characterize Boston's stage thenceforth.

By common consent, the acoustics of the new house won approval. Professor Wallace Sabine, the M. I. T. genius who had produced Symphony Hall's exquisite acoustics, also officiated for the Opera House. No dulling or deadening of sound occurred, either in musical passages or during speeches. Perhaps the sound was a bit too brilliant, or at least Conti misjudged it in failing to check the coarseness of orchestral tone.

Governor Eben Sumner Draper, beaming from Box 21, allowed himself to be quoted as sharing the pride of the entire city, indeed, of the New England states, in the achievement. "I am glad to see the public support this undertaking so generously," he concluded. "Isn't it wonderful!" Lieutenant Governor Louis A. Frothingham echoed his superior. "There was never anything to equal it!"

1909—The Boston Opera House, "handsome, artistic, chaste red brick, gray limestone, white terra cotta," the first Unitarian Opera House.

1958: "The big steel ball struck against the great brick wall—soon one could see ghastly daylight through the gaping hole of the stage."

Eben D. Jordan, Jr., who built the Boston Opera House in 1909.

Henry Russell, opera impresario, whose life, private and public, kept Proper Boston agog.

The *Herald's* Philip Hale, "an intellectual rectitude lay at core of his lightest thought."

H. T. Parker, "Hell-to-Pay," the terror of the *Transcript*.

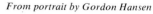

From portrait by Gordon Hansen

Donna, Russell's second wife; "their marriage was a success on its own terms."

Russell's sons, Tosti (elder) and Sheridan, in their first Boston days.

Museum of the City of New York

Alice Nielsen as Susanna in *Figaro*. She helped Russell start his opera.

Felix Weingartner, gentleman and scholar, right for Boston.

André Caplet, friend of Debussy, whose power grew as Boston opera leader.

Joseph Urban. "His life was baroque, his designs sent the spirit soaring."

Culver

Daguerre

Roberto Moranzoni. "Youthful energy, a perfect Italian, another Toscanini?"

Lillian Nordica as Gioconda, her Boston opening-night role.

Lydia Lipkowska, admired for her "pleasurable little ways."

Left: George Baklanoff's Scarpia—"a taint of fee-faw-fum." *Right:* Florencio Constantino. His "frank tenorality endears."

Vanni Marcoux. His Scarpia brought audible gasps and the threat of ban.

Mary Garden, the inflammable Tosca who incurred Mayor Fitzgerald's ire.

Mary Garden. Her Mélisande was "a wisp caught in the bleak winds of fate."

Mishkin

Giovanni Zenatello as Otello. He was one of Boston's most admired singers.

Dupont

Maria Gay, famous Carmen. She liked to sing with her husband, Zenatello.

Georgette Leblanc, assumed to be Mme. Maeterlinck, puzzled Back Bay matrons.

Lucille Marcel as Tosca, one of the roles she sang as Mme. Weingartner.

Opera News

Opera News   *Reutlinger*

Two of the great ones: *left*, Luisa Tetrazzini
as giddy Philine; *right*, Nellie Melba in a
moment of grandeur.

Dupont—Opera News

Emma Eames in her final
stage role, Verdi's unhappy
Desdemona.

Emmy Destinn as Minnie, Enrico Caruso, in one of his rare Boston appearances, as Johnson in *La Fanciulla del West*.

In Aubert's *Forêt Bleue*, Urban, Caplet (back), Aubert (center), Strony, and singers Bernice Fisher, Jeska Swartz.

Margarete Matzenauer as Brangäne. ". . . no such voice in recollection."

Olive Fremstad as Isolde. "Music in her throat had melting ardors."

Jacques Urlus, Boston's Tristan. ". . . voice kept its singing tone."

Frances Alda as Desdemona, "unexpectedly persuasive."

Leo Slezak, powerful Otello. "...excelled all," said HTP.

Giovanni Polese as Iago, "made a secure place."

Celestina Boninsegna, *Mefisto-fele's* Elena, an extremely puzzling singer.

Courtesy Ira Glackens

Ermini—Opera News

Carmen Melis, Maliela in *Gioielli*—"a birthright for such a character."

Zina Brozia as Gilda. She "left faintly agreeable, not lasting impressions."

Marceaux—Opera News

Rosa Olitzka as Amneris, recalling her versatility in "fugitive opera."

Lucrezia Bori as Cio-Cio-San, the role she never sang in New York.

Opera News

Frieda Hempel as Violetta, survived damage to a delicate nervous system.

Jeska Swartz, every Cio-Cio-San's Suzuki, admired in "trouser" roles.

Alfred Brown

Evelyn Scotney, "the surprise and delight of the evening," said HTP.

Maurice Renaud as Athanael.
"... as many Renauds as the
characters he played."

José Mardones as Alvise. For five
years unchanging, dependable,
serviceable.

Edmond Clément as Werther,
"romantic, sensitive, sentimental,
melancholy."

Ramon Blanchart as Amonasro.
Kind, courteous, faithful for five
years.

Charles Dalmorès, an impeccable tenor, once a horn player, always an athlete.

Anna Pavlowa as the Dumb Girl of Portici, with odd but beloved pet.

Family Portrait I: Ferrari-Fontana, Matzenauer and baby daughter Adrienne.

Family Portrait II: Lina Cavalieri and her bridegroom, Lucien Muratore.

Painting by Irving Wiles—Opera News

Jeanne Gerville-Réache as Carmen.

Moses—Opera News

Fely Dereyne as Carmen—"no coarseness."

Maggie Teyte as Oscar in *Ballo*.

Marguerite Beriza, each role individual.

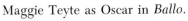

6

FIRST FLIGHT
(1909–10)

On November 14, grand opera had taken its place as a reality in the Hub, with a fighting chance for permanence. All the tentative steps that had teetered along on soft and uncertain ground were viewed with tolerance in retrospect; downright errors received absolution. Henry Russell and his administrators and artists buckled down to the long job ahead of them: to make fifteen weeks of almost continuous performances palatable to a relatively inexperienced public. The manager encountered almost immediately the danger inherent in the situation, a danger which had probably not occurred to him. Hardly had the enterprise been launched when the weight of Boston society's natural apathy to the theater began to drag it down; from then on, the battle consisted in heaving enough of this deadening ballast overboard to stay triumphantly afloat.

Faint signs of the approaching tournament between energy and inertia appeared after only two performances. In a review of the situation, the *Transcript* remarked that grand opera, a new pleasure for Boston, now shone forth not as a "gala," but a diversion, taking place in the due routine. The word "routine" gives the clue. The Boston Opera House rapidly assumed its place among other playhouses. Perhaps Parker intended a compliment, but a little reflection would have shown that Boston's theaters did not depend for their living on the good will and patronage of the thousand or more citizens involved in the new operatic enterprise. Furthermore, New York's transient public, on which theater business fed, had no counterpart in Boston; and no longer could an Italian sub-stratum be

51

counted upon as operatic seeding ground. Parker, indeed, seemed to sense that a struggle was inevitable. Nobody but a reviewer ever went to the theater because he ought to, he claimed. "Exhortation to dutiful attendance never swelled an audience by any perceptible fraction."

The first week's audiences established a pattern that was to remain almost unbroken. Mondays, traditionally the nights for show since Mrs. Caroline Astor chose them for balls "to go on to" after the Metropolitan performances in New York, continued to glitter with bejeweled box-holders; Wednesdays usually showed a falling off, although what remained appeared "seemly, ornamental, intelligent, and discriminating"—not necessarily synonymous with "fashionable." Thursdays and Fridays brought a mixed bag; Saturday matinees often saw the balconies full to the last rows. Saturday nights, set aside during the first part of the season as a showcase for young debutantes, fluctuated alarmingly. As the season wore on, the dichotomy appeared for the world—and the box office—to see. Subscribers' seats, accounting for the bulk of the house, were safe, although not faithfully occupied. The fringe simply would not sell, so that the higher reaches often gaped unpopulated. The "public" lacked interest. And when repeats began to show up in regular subscription nights, many Bostonians were heard to grumble, "Do we have to hear this opera a *third* time?"

But all this is hindsight. For the nonce, its head done up in the latest coiffure, its nose sniffing greasepaint—daintily, and from the civilized side of the footlights—its ears ringing with roulades, and its eyes dazzled by new scenic glories, the Boston opera audience moved almost as if under a hypnotic spell. All but the scribes and prophets and possibly the management remained too close to the immediate present to sense the future.

While outside critics might jeer at Russell's conservative repertoire, he had judged rightly that Boston would cleave closest to old favorites, with a mere surface sprinkling of novelty. Although most ambitious, Boito's *Mefistofele* and Meyerbeer's *Les Huguenots* failed to entice audiences. The trivial *Maestro di Capella* of Paer and the fragmentary scene from Rachmaninoff's *The Miserly Knight* passed without leaving a ripple, except that the latter proved a starring vehicle for Baklanoff. Verdi, Puccini, Rossini *et Cie.*, accompanied by a few Gallic *confrères*, sustained the weight of the fifteen weeks.

Nordica, whose first night Gioconda savored strongly of "Auld Lang Syne" rather than "Rock of Ages," paid another courtesy call in the same role later in the season. She had completed her service with the Metropolitan on December 16, 1909, singing Leonore in *Il Trovatore* in Baltimore as a part of that season's marathon tour. Gatti-Casazza could not win her back, if, indeed, he wanted her: the former bearer of the American crown at Bayreuth had passed her prime. Still, Russell could persuade her out of the retirement that encroached ever more threateningly on her shining career. The Maine girl owned to even more binding ties with Boston. She had entered the New England Conservatory at the age of fourteen, and there Jordan took an interest in her. Through her steady progress in companies headed by Mapleson, Abbey, Abbey and Grau (the Met itself), Damrosch, Hammerstein, and Russell, the prima donna held to an affection for the city where she got her start. Hale, who refused for years to allow Nordica in the sacred company of actors, calling her Donna Elvira a cardboard figure and accusing her of moving in lines instead of curves, would soften his quill in 1910, admitting her Marguerite in *Faust* on December 3 to be conspicuous for its originality of conception, effective business, and skillful use of song for dramatic purposes. Even the well-seasoned operagoer must have experienced new sensations, he thought. They saw an original impersonation, a Marguerite who dreamed and loved and paid the cost. This was a modern interpretation. She had more than merely committed her lesson to memory, a step forward Hale had noted in the nineties, when Lillian had come home from Bayreuth, the first American to be honored by the Wagnerian shrine. Her final performance in Boston would be as Isolde on March 26, toward the end of the 1912–13 season, when the years had pressed relentlessly on her voice and spirit. Yet Hale, at the last *Tristan*, would pay what was to be a final tribute to her voice, proclaiming it to be again in its highest estate in this Wagnerian glorification of love and death. On May 10, 1914, as the Boston company reached the middle of its triumphant Paris season, would come the news of Nordica's tragic death in Java after a shipwreck. Russell mourned her "as a friend and as an adorable woman."

Spaniards played a vital role in Boston's destiny, for in addition to the tenor Florencio Constantino, the baritone Ramon Blanchart, and the bass José Mardones, the company was enlivened by the presence of Maria Gay, one of the most famous Carmens of her day. In Barcelona, Gay had studied to be a sculptor, then a pianist, before her vocal potentialities were discovered. Constantino and Gay headed the cast for the *Carmen* of December 22, 1909, acclaimed as the ablest and most stirring of the season. Conceiving Carmen to be the wholly sensual and wholly selfish animal, a woman at home in tavern and cigarette shop, smugglers' den and bull-ring, Gay sustained this animalism without lapse, giving what Parker admitted was an unmistakable thrill to the watchers, including himself. Gay's Carmen reached its apex at this performance. "It will be impossible to think in future of Carmen without remembering Maria Gay," Hale commented. Her gypsy girl reeked of "the perfume of a savage beast."

Baklanoff's Escamillo and the Micaela of his Russian compatriot, Lydia Lipkowska, added further color to this peak performance. At last a true ensemble, constantly sought as an ideal by Russell, had apparently been achieved. Illusion dwelled in the settings, the orchestra assumed individuality and a finer quality of tone under the well-routined yet not always inspired Conti, while even the humblest character became momentarily vivid. The famous quintet of smugglers fitted into the action almost conversationally, instead of standing out as a virtuoso set piece. Even the tenor "vanished in the part." Hitherto a discreet and rather self-conscious opera actor, Constantino quickened to Don José.

José Mardones gave five years' solid service to Boston—in fact, "serviceable" was the level consistently ascribed to his efforts, although he ascended above the plateau in Boito's *Mefistofele,* where his voice colored his sinister interpretation of the Goethean devil. Russell preferred not to duplicate parallel roles—Marguerite and Helen, Martha and Pantalis, Wagner and Nereus—which gave more singers a chance, though it did not add to the unification of the plot, which embraces a scene in ancient Greece. His Helen in 1909–10 was Celestina Boninsegna, one of the most puzzling singers ever to flash across the American scene. Her reputation in Italy was secure, but her one season at the Metropolitan in 1906–07 brought her only two roles, Santuzza and Aïda, and little warmth of appreciation. Both had a place in her Boston repertoire, Santuzza seeming more in her particular range of ability than Aïda, because of its shorter melodic line and concentration of phrase. Tosca, too, suited her well. She tended to cut the longer Verdi line into short declamations, Parker opined.

Still, Boninsegna retains a special corner in the hearts of a few who recall her distinctive qualities. Max de Schauensee, critic of the Philadelphia *Bulletin,* quoted Riccardo Stracciari in *Opera News* in 1954 on the subject. The powerful baritone remembered Boninsegna as "the only one who could sing Aïda the way I thought it should be sung.... Her voice was so big and beautiful, sheer velvet, but she had no charm, no elegance of person, and when she appeared in her Metropolitan debut (I was her Amonasro), her ample form swathed in chocolate-colored underwear, the New York public and critics would not forgive her, despite a voice that was unique in this role. Besides, the Metropolitan had Emma Eames—*una bellissima donna!*"

A New York critic remarked: "She was a veritable Topsy to look upon, with her kinky hair, her rolling eyes displaying wide expanses of white, her plain dresses and slavish demeanor; there was not a trace in her of kingly descent. How, one thought, could Radames prefer her to the Princess?"

Boninsegna also had a part in *Les Huguenots*. In this opera the singers, all experienced and routined, reaped their rewards, although the opera itself kindled little excitement among the public or critics. Parker stated flatly that "the generation whose operatic experience began with Wagner and has gone gloriously forward with music drama" could barely endure Meyerbeer. The audience was listless and for the first time showed a tendency to drift away. In the *Advertiser*, Louis Elson quoted a German wit: "The Catholics murder the Protestants, while the Jews make music to it," to describe the opera. He found the performance not as brilliant as in the days of Abbey, Schoeffel, and Grau (who, after all, could call on Nordica, Melba, Scalchi, the De Reszkes, and Plançon for an all-star cast), but, as Elson sighed, " 'twill serve."

Except for Constantino and Paul Bourrillon, candidates at the top of the masculine range impressed more by numbers than worth. Bourrillon, a Frenchman, had, as Lahee quaintly puts it, "begun life" as a bicycle rider (anticipating the similar background of Ezio Pinza), working up to the championship of France in 1898. The handsome, mustachioed athlete made the mistake of singing the Flower Song from *Carmen* one night while waiting in the rooms of his friend Maurice Renaud. The great baritone overheard, so the legend goes, and hustled Bourrillon around to a top teacher. He had to study only one year to reach the stage, even that of so exalted a theater as the Paris Opéra Comique. His Boston debut as Gérald in *Lakmé* elicited phrases such as "comely, well-schooled, fascinating baritone quality, admirable ardor, and intelligent skill" from Parker, and a more restrained "favorable impression" from Hale.

Bourrillon continued to exert appeal in all of his roles except Faust, which Parker found too tame. Otherwise Russell seemed to pursue a course almost of desperation, hiring a gaggle of tenors where two first-class ones might have sufficed. Among those given a half-dozen assignments or more, only Christian Hansen, a young Dane who had previously lumbered through a few German opera houses, commanded much respect. Like many youthful singers, he was inclined to emit for all he was worth, but Hale thought he possessed the stuff of a heroic tenor. He was conceivable as Radames, the rude soldier, if hardly as Radames, the romantic hero. His essay at Lieutenant B. F. Pinkerton surprised everyone by its intelligence and quality. No doubt the tenor benefited from a revitalized spirit in the leading lady, Alice Nielsen.

Nielsen, against medical advice, had insisted on singing Cio-Cio-San for the first time in her life on December 8; she had come close to disaster. Now recovered, with her powers "undimmed and dependable," she kept up a standard of sensuous beauty throughout the Japanese maiden's woeful tale. Excuses for the "scrappy, jerky" first performance were not needed at the second: "Conti had learned the score." (The well-routined but not invariably inspired conductor suffered under many such barbs.)

Hansen participated in the ill-advised *Lohengrin* after the mid-season tour, Russell's only attempt at Wagner the first season. He sang in German while Mardones, Dereyne, Claessens, and Blanchart surrounded the Swan Knight with a blanket of Italian. This *Lohengrin,* incidentally, provided the third occasion of the season for bringing into play the kind of statistics relished by the press: two performances by the same singer on one day. Raymond Boulogne, a robust French baritone whose Marcello "would have painted everything red," and whose father in *La Traviata* confirmed Coquelin's contention that Germont was no *père noble* but a *bon bourgeois* in distress, encompassed a Marcello one November Saturday afternoon and an Amonasro that night. Francis Archambault also doubled in one day as the King in *Aïda* and Sparafucile in *Rigoletto.*

Blanchart rounded out the trio of tandem performances with the *Lohengrin* Telramund in the evening, after a matinee *La Traviata.* The Spaniard's ideas of Germont *père* forced Hale to think of possible revisions to the libretto. "Blanchart's looks of solicitude and commiseration, his so impassioned kisses imprinted on Violetta's resisting hands made one wonder if, his daughter safely married and Alfredo out of harm's way, he might not return and offer further consolation in the shape of his own benevolent person."

Other tenors won a few passing kind words. Carlo Cartica, a good-natured, fat fellow, emitted flashes of power in rather routine and mature impersonations of Radames and Manrico (minus the high C), but he was eclipsed as Edgardo by Eugenia Bronskaja, taking over Lucia's role in place of Lipkowska. Bronskaja had remained a Russian riddle for the first fortnight. Her name appeared in the roster and even in the newspaper advertisements as Nedda in *Pagliacci,* but the lady had not showed herself on the stage. Parker found her out at a Sunday concert on November 21. "At last Bronskaja emerged from the mists that enwrapped her and proved to be no other than Mme. Makaroff, the coloratura soprano who was singing in September at the Academy of Music in New York. She is evidently experienced, but with a voice somewhat worn; still she keeps facility and glitter in showy music." Bronskaja did not receive a role in her own right until Christmas afternoon. However, her pleasure in Parker's compliment on her practiced skill as Micaela must have been dimmed by a storm that shook the city. Twelve inches of snow fell, and the tides ran their highest since April 16, 1851, when Minot's Light was destroyed. Russell took pity on the soprano and penciled her in for Micaela again two days later. The New Year brought better opportunities: three Musettas, two Marguerites in *Huguenots,* another Micaela, and one Gilda, but someone else invariably stole the show: Nielsen and Constantino or Lipkowska and Jadlowker as the lovers in *Bohème;* Gay or Dereyne as Carmen; Baklanoff's superb Rigoletto. At last she was able to turn the tables. Lipkowska pleaded indisposition for *Lucia* on February 26 just before curtain time. Bronskaja showed her mettle in this crisis. She had never sung the role before but, as was the natural right of every coloratura, had learned the Mad Scene. It became an experiment to test how many set pieces she had memorized. Parker commented that as stage folk say, she had to "fake." A kindly stage director ordered the amputation of the second act right up to the Sextet; Bronskaja plunged in courageously. "It was no diminution of her glory that vacancies occurred in the final duet of the first act," Parker continued. "Her skill in stage routine and resource in relating the voice to the orchestra accompaniment" carried her through with "hardly a jar to illusion. It was gallantly done."

Bronskaja earned another distinction in her single Boston season. She was one of a half-dozen singers chosen by Russell to make a set of recordings, superb for their time. The astute Boston manager had signed a contract as Consulting Director with Columbia Records. He immediately enlisted Boninsegna, Bronskaja, Bettina Freeman, Constantino, Mardones, and Blanchart, who immortalized themselves in a wide variety of arias, duets, trios, and other ensembles up to the *Lucia* Sextet.

Russell's grandiose scheme for presenting new singers began to deflate after the first few weeks, and when the season had resumed in February after the tour, all pretense at Saturday night showcases for newcomers collapsed. Several promising young folk blinked in the limelight momentarily; none stayed the course. Without question the most attractive was a delicately beautiful girl, tall, fair, and slim, named Viola Davenport. A Massachusetts native, the only child of a superintendent of schools, she persuaded her reluctant father and four schoolteacher aunts that tutors in Paris offered a fair substitute for an American college. Jean De Reszke predicted that although a coloratura at the moment, she would one day sing Elsa; Oscar Hammerstein waved a big cigar and pronounced hers a promising voice. Still, these encouragements brought no contracts. Russell appeared providentially, with the suggestion that Viola go straight to Boston as a member of the new Opera School. She made her debut as Lakmé on the second Saturday night. All the critics agreed on her charm and her vocal abilities. In eight inches of close-packed type, Parker pontificated on the individuality of her voice, its expressive coloring in the "water-color music," and the modest attainments that "are many fold more important than the excellences or the blemishes of her bravura." Hale also dilated on the newcomer's good beginning as an actress, amateur of course, but knowing the value of repose and carrying herself well. "She has learned something of the expressiveness of the hand—hers does not look like a bunch of radishes." The only debutante to be accorded two Saturday evenings, Viola again gave clear proof of her fitness for her profession as Gilda in *Rigoletto*. Olin Downes remarked in the *Post* on her freshness and expressive capacity, also noting that her costume in the third act seemed not as becoming as the previous one. Many years afterward, Miss Davenport explained. The costume, a long, white trailing nightgown, had not been tailored expressly for her and fit her badly. Halfway through the emotional scene with her father, while confessing that the Duke had actually had his way with her, the gown fell off one shoulder. Her frantic struggles with the loose, slippery frills reduced her to genuine tears, which only heightened the effectiveness of the scene. Yet Miss Davenport ended her public career right there; not because of the contretemps, but as a result of a struggle between professional ambition and personal desires. If Russell had held out more promise to her, she might have continued. She yielded to the ardent suit of a young automobile dealer, who pursued her to Paris that summer and persuaded her to become Mrs. Alvan Fuller. Conti and Bourrillon among others urged her return to opera in vain. When her husband ran for Congress, she accompanied him to Washington, returning to Boston in 1918. Fuller was elected Governor in 1925 and played a controversial part in the Sacco-Vanzetti case. His wife became one of Boston's *grandes dames,* retaining until her death in 1959 a lively and affectionate absorption in the city's musical life.

Other native debutantes such as Elfrieda Schroeder as Nedda and Elena Kirmes as Santuzza prompted a gentle reminder from Parker that America was not as yet the most fertile soil for operatic development: "The language of operatic tones and gestures does not pass as current in American drawing rooms." To balance these ephemera, Russell counted on several veterans. Fely Dereyne, a bouncy French soprano, was still a young woman when she joined the Boston Company but had already earned her spurs as a member of Russell's San Carlo troupe, with which she made her American debut in New Orleans. Later she appeared with the Montreal Opera, and just before the Boston opening, her name appeared on the Metropolitan roster for a season. Her Marguerite pleased Hale by its simple grace and dignity of maidenhood—this was a Marguerite who did not anticipate her fall. She sang with almost too much beauty of tone in her lone attempt at Carmen, with not enough coarseness to prove she was living the part. Her Musetta was thought to be a good soul; she would not go deep but would wear well. Her Tosca radiated beauty and sincerity, according to the *Globe.* In the unfortunate *Lohengrin,* her voice stood out as fresh, sympathetic, and colorful. Altogether a capable lady, and more than capable in lighter roles, she graced the company for four seasons.

Two genuine old-timers enjoyed an Indian summer for one brief Boston season. Rosa Olitzka bobbed up to do an Amneris and an Azucena, recalling to Parker the "fugitive opera" in Mechanics Hall when Olitzka sang everything from Siébel and the Shepherd in *Tannhäuser* to Ortrud, Brangäne, and assorted Valkyries. Her method, Parker remarked dryly, was not one "that behooves the nurslings of our opera house to copy." Of even more ancient vintage, Guerrina Fabbri seemed indestructible. In the dim past, she had toured in 1889–90 with Abbey's company that starred Patti. She was an ideal Azucena or good in any trouser role, but somewhat ungainly as Nancy in *Martha.* In 1891–92, she sang Nancy to Patti's Martha. Boston also heard her that year as Arsace in *Semiramide.* Now she came out of the mists of nearly a decade to take up Azucena and La Cieca once again. Perhaps Russell was inspired to bring back this old trouper by her re-emergence in late November as a replacement for Homer's Laura in the Metropolitan *Gioconda* performance in Philadelphia. Fabbri could sing Laura as well as La Cieca. Her voice still held rich notes, and few more frenetic Azucenas existed.

Claiming longer service with the Boston company, if of less stature than the aging Olitzka and Fabbri, two mezzos remained: Maria Claessens (four seasons) and Elvira Leveroni (five). Claessens, "the changeless," never provoked complaints and never inspired warmth. Leveroni impressed Parker as a secondary singer having a "gay little try" at Amneris, the most important part that fell to her lot. The Metropolitan inherited both ladies, Leveroni showing up in New York as late as 1921.

With Gay, Blanchart, and the pair of *comprimari,* Ernesto Giaccone and Attilio Pulcini, the five-year club counted for completion on three others: the venerable buffo, Luigi Tavecchia, who created an individual from each role; the baritone Rodolfo Fornari, who excelled in comedy roles, especially Rossini's Figaro; and the attractive mezzo-soprano Jeska Swartz, who soon appended her married name, Morse. One of the few singers remaining who can recall from personal experience the great days of Boston's five-year operatic boom, Jeska Swartz-Morse belongs to the present as well.

7

TWO RUSSIANS
(Lydia Lipkowska and George Baklanoff)

It seems a tribute to the international character of the Boston Opera Company that a pair of Russians should carry off top honors in the first two seasons. With all deference to Nordica and Constantino, Maria Gay, and above all, to the cornerstone of Russell's edifice, the gentle and appealing Alice Nielsen, it fell to Lydia Lipkowska and George Baklanoff to come nearest to the public's idea of what opera singers should be. Not only did they look the part and measure up to the highest artistic standards Boston could set, but their respective backgrounds reeked of the kind of romance that only Imperial Russia could furnish at the turn of the century and that the press took the keenest pleasure in exaggerating.

Boston soon learned that Mme. Lipkowska had been born either on her father's estate in Poltava, Southern Russia, or as a pauper of humble origin, place unmentioned; that she graduated from high school at seventeen and immediately entered the St. Petersburg Conservatory; or, more appetizingly, wandered the streets of the city plaintively singing folk songs until a rich nobleman heard her beneath his window and decided that her talents should be cultivated. The accounts also disagree on her debut in St. Petersburg (1906? 1909?) as Gilda in *Rigoletto*. A reigning favorite from that time on, she was nicknamed "La Petite," by reason of her tiny, slender figure, so happily contrasted with the usual barricaded coloratura. The *Transcript* dwelt on her delicately modeled features in a Madonna-type face; her soft, clear blue eyes (brown, according to the *Traveler*), and her smile, half of pleasure, half of melancholy.

For her second and final season in Boston, the Russian beauty arrived with her seven-year-old daughter, Aldenna, complaining of the Dutch food on the *Nieuw Amsterdam*, but quickly recovering under the ministrations of her own chef, Edmond Nowatowski. The story got about that her husband (a Russian nobleman?) opposed her journey, but the Tsar interceded in her favor on condition that she take her daughter along. Established in an eleven-room apartment, she was "surprised" by a *Globe* reporter, who, admitted to the parlor (with piano) and the dining room (with samovar), painted a picture of her domesticity that satirized all such interviews, whether or not intentionally.

"The sedate young matron makes a real home, chiefly supervising the education of her daughter." An American governess (who divulged the existence of another Lipkowska infant, presumably left behind as a hostage), a maid, an errand boy, a French waiter, a chambermaid, and the famous chef assisted the prima donna in her simple housekeeping. Of course she claimed no prowess as a cook, although she found time in her busy schedule to give orders to the chef. She might also have been an interior decorator. Why, she drove nails for the pictures herself, and arranged all the little things, directing the placing of furniture—naturally she was not strong enough to do it with her own hands. Despite her fragile form and wistful air, she showed her fondness for romping and dancing to the talking machine. Finally, she was induced to reveal her secret recipes for *kulebiak, betka,* and *borshch.* A photograph showed her at the piano with her daughter and the chef—all reflected in the mirror, a favorite technique of newspaper cameramen.

Another interview placed her in a somewhat different light. As the unconventional artist, she banned the wearing of stockings—"Oh, not when visitors are around, of course. That would be somewhat shocking!" Most women knew the value of a tightly drawn stocking as a weapon of coquetry. Lipkowska scorned such wiles. A third journalist proclaimed her to be a suffragette—but not so advanced that her womanly qualities were dimmed. Still another discovered her to be an ardent advocate of fashionable dress. American evening raiment seemed very strange to her (a hint that Boston women had still not reached a new low in decolleté). The street costumes, however, appealed to her as "simple, satisfactory, adorable!" At the Boston opening, she appeared in a pale green silk gown, wearing diamonds and pearls, and around her hair a wide ribbon, a style already known as the Mme. Lipkowska coiffure.

After one of her comments in January, 1911, it would not have been surprising if her popularity waned perceptibly. She said, "There is less individual freedom here than in Russia. Boston is so provincial and so quiet. If it were not for my art, I should die like a fly in autumn."

Lipkowska later reappeared in America under unfailingly romantic circumstances. Caught in Odessa during the Revolution, she was rescued by a French officer, Lieutenant Pierre Bodin, who smuggled her out in peasant disguise, taking her as far as Constantinople. Then, with six fellow officers disguised as Russian sailors, the doughty lieutenant put back into Odessa in a felucca with a Black Sea pilot and brought out the lady's daughter, by then fifteen (no mention of the other daughter, or of Lipkowska's first husband). The singer married her knight errant in Paris soon afterward and brought him to New York. There she played in *The Merry Widow* for a season and planned to sing *Snegurotchka* in Chicago.

While her private life continued to preoccupy the more superficial columnists on the dailies, the serious music critics went about evaluating her talents. It was inevitable that her Lakmé, the first of seven roles in the season and the one she sang most often, should provoke comparisons with Marie Van Zandt, the American for whom Delibes wrote the opera. The critics evidenced a soft spot for the new Lakmé's charms. "She had but to clothe herself in Oriental dress," breathed the ensorceled Parker, "and ply the dexterous external routine in which she was trained; for the rest, her transparent personality, when once the music and play had stirred it, amply sufficed." As Violetta in *La Traviata* Parker thought her a girlish amorist. "No wonder Paris and St. Petersburg liked her for her 'little ways'—the more welcome on our reticent Boston stage." Hale went so far as to call her "cuddlesome," and, borrowing a word from the King James version of the Bible, "desirable."

Along with this personable exterior went a voice of natural charm, lightness, clarity, and trained agility; neither metallic nor mechanical, never hardening to mere glitter. Tiring a trifle by the time of her first Gilda on December 2 (understandably, as the performance took place the night after a *Traviata*), she departed from pitch, and still felt the effects at another *Traviata* on December 6. Her Lucia brought garlands from Hale for acting without exaggeration and secure coloratura without labor. Parker added that Lucia's dress for once was becoming to romantic Scotland, rather than being the newest in French frocks.

Some of the bloom had worn off the petal after the tour. Her Rosina on March 16 prompted a disillusioned outburst from Parker. She treated the character as a child, he complained, a child that belonged in a middle-class nursery in England. She missed all the implications, and even sang in a slovenly Russian fashion rather than with Italian discipline. Perhaps she had pleased the public too well for her own good and progress. Now her "pleasurable little ways" did not accomplish an operatic impersonation. She sagged from pitch, pushed her upper tones, blurred her scales, and let shrillness thin her voice. Then Parker's initials disappeared from Lipkowska reviews. Even her one new role in her second season, Massenet's *Manon*, was covered by an assistant, who gave her credit for creating a picture and singing exquisitely, but granted her no penetration into even the shallows of this girl to whom "good faith was not as strong as a delight in brocades." As a final straw, she did not even suggest seductiveness. Hale applied balm to the wounds. He said that her voice as Violetta showed the peculiar quality of delicacy and carrying power of a Cremona violin, not excluding warmth. "Nor any fairer, more exquisite apparition [is there] on the stage of the Boston Opera House."

The Russian prima donna seldom met her compatriot, Baklanoff, on stage. *Carmen*, one of the three operas in which their names were bracketed, allowed them no conversation. In *Rigoletto* and *Lakmé*, theirs was a father-daughter relationship. Offstage, rumors of a romance ran strongly.

The public never wavered in admiration for Baklanoff, the burly, broad-shouldered Russian with the captivating personality. In his first season, eight leading roles gave scope for his versatility, aiding his rapidly burgeoning development as a singing actor. His voice, for which he had given up the study of law in St. Petersburg only a few years previously, already served as a powerful and resonant instrument, rich in tone and smoothly manipulated. Now it remained to be shown what he might do with the complicated characters created by Italian and French librettists. After his cruel and sensual Barnaba in *La Gioconda*, Amonasro in *Aïda*, a different portrait, challenged him. Parker evoked the memory of Victor Maurel, rating the newcomer as less savage an Ethiopian King, more elderly and reticent. He approved. But Baklanoff's next impersonation left him cold: "He is still at the beginning of Rigoletto." Hale, on the contrary, believed Baklanoff's Jester uncommonly good. Still, his histrionic abilities being in question, the baritone had to sharpen his teeth on

London before being accepted by the *Transcript* the following season in the title role of Verdi's opera, and then only by an assistant to Parker. However, both critics joined in hallelujahs for Baklanoff's first Escamillo on December 22. In the dashing Toreador, Baklanoff found a hero to his liking. He sang the bravura aria, and he got the girl—at least he was the last to enjoy her favors before her untimely demise. Handsome, "not a Spanish dandy off a raisin box but a reticent, slightly sombre, and deliberately mysterious matador—a man, not a quarrelsome fop," Escamillo dominated the stage. Hale granted him "the best here in many years, the first (not excepting the early favorite, Del Puente) who comprehends the character of the Toreador Song, by singing the second verse directly to Carmen."

Baklanoff achieved one further *tour de force* near the end of the season. Russell conceived as a novelty the excerpting of a single scene from Rachmaninoff's *The Miserly Knight* (billed as *Der Geizige Ritter*). The baritone's personal success rather than the lasting quality of the music kept it in the next season's repertoire as a companion piece on various double, even triple, bills. He added to his kudos by singing two roles on one late March evening as a sort of good-by gesture, capping Rachmaninoff's stingy knight by another characterization equally unappetizing —Tonio in *Pagliacci*. Parker found him a curiously original and clever impersonator, his makeup a decided innovation. His wig straggled sparse and sandy over a burlesque nose; a short jacket barely began to cover a heavy paunch; his pants hung slovenly and baggy. Employing no gestures in the Prologue, he conveyed by his appearance and facial mien the doltish, cruel, and sensuous clown. His fine restraint avoided the coarseness of actual burlesque.

While Baklanoff's Scarpia never attained the stature of other men's in Boston eyes ("a taint of fee-faw-fum" pervaded it, according to one critic), the Russian's Valentin in *Faust* continued to breathe manhood and fire into a stuffed effigy. He held his own in all of his roles into the middle of the second season, adding an Iago that was highly praised. Then, scheduled on December 14, 1910, for the juicy part of Ramon in Laparra's *La Habañera*, a Spanish horror piece that Russell had captured as an American première, Baklanoff exercised his right to be captious. A letter from Russell, made public on December 14, the day of the performance, tells the story, as well as revealing Henry's seignorial style:

The full dress rehearsal of *Habañera* was set yesterday at 1 P.M. Invitations had been sent to the press, the directors, and their wives. At a quarter to one, I arrived at the stage door and went immediately, as is my habit, to the regisseur's office to find out if all was in readiness. I found Baklanoff standing in the corridor talking to Conti, Caplet, and Menotti [two conductors and stage director]. He was not dressed. I immediately asked why. His answer was brief and to the point: 'I shall not sing today nor tomorrow unless you let me sing Iago next Saturday.' I replied quite calmly that he know perfectly well I had arranged that he sing *Tosca* in Chicago with Carmen Melis next Monday, and in exchange Sammarco would be here Saturday afternoon. This arrangement had been completed several days; no changes could be made. Without a moment's hesitation, Baklanoff turned his back on me and left the theatre. Nor did he make any attempt to return. I sent for Ramon Blanchart, who was eating lunch. He courteously and kindly ran around to the opera house and took up the role, with no opportunity to rehearse, only having studied it last summer.... Without Blanchart, we would have had no performance; a performance of a complicated opera is not possible without a dress rehearsal. A child can see that if the director of an opera house consents to compromise with an act of open revolt, discipline would be permanently undermined....

Russell proceeded to fine the offender (some said as much as five thousand dollars, but the sum of two hundred or so is more likely) and to suspend him from the company. Although right lay undoubtedly on management's side, Baklanoff lost no popularity with the public, which showed every evidence of delight at his return a month later, when he could have been considered properly punished. He said farewell to the company on March 6, hand in hand with Lipkowska in *Lakmé*.

If the virile Russian baritone had consulted a crystal ball, he might have modified his haughtiness. Sammarco took over Iago at the matinee after the *Habañera* incident as scheduled, but another performance of *Otello* came along a week later, and Baklanoff cheated himself out of a Christmas gift. Blanchart, the conscientious, got this part too, though the years had dulled his voice beyond even his practiced skill to conceal, remarked Hale, and his tones wobbled and were as "a reed shaken by the wind." Indeed, Baklanoff, who had perhaps been incited to rebellion by the *Transcript's* comment (unsigned) that his own personal vigor and artistry had forced Iago into the frame alongside even Slezak's overwhelming impersonation of the Moor, never got to sing the role again with

Russell. Giovanni Polese, who had sung with Oscar Hammerstein's Manhattan Opera, came to Boston as Iago in a debut on January 2, and he immediately made a secure place for himself. Now Russell could occasionally command the distinguished services of Antonio Scotti and Pasquale Amato from the Metropolitan, as well as those of the somewhat boisterous and not very characterful Carlo Galeffi, to hold as a threat over the rebellious Russian. Nevertheless, in his final two months Baklanoff retained Escamillo, Tonio, Amonasro, Rigoletto, Valentin, The Miserly Knight, Barnaba, Scarpia, and Nilakantha (one each), decidedly no meager portion.

When Baklanoff arrived for his second season, he told a tale of robbery in Russia by thirty peasants, whom he later defended. The reporter thought it funny that the man who had pleaded the cause of the miscreants so ably that they were released should play the part of the persecuting sheriff in *The Girl of the Golden West*. Just as he refused to stay banished from Boston, so did he pop up smiling from far more perilous adventures. The aftermath seasons of Max Rabinoff's Boston Grand Opera, 1915 and 1916, found him, all six feet three clad in azure blue pajamas, his boyish face freshly shaven (in the words of the Boston *Post*), a completely different man from the one who had participated in the 112th Regimental drive that captured Presmyzl. The war had caught him in Italy. Assuming the disguise of a woman he slipped home through Turkey, which presumably was accustomed to veiled ladies of Amazonian proportions. After his baptism of fire, fear left him, he confided, to be replaced by blood lust. "I want to kill, kill, kill!" (He still spoke "restaurant" English, the reporter noted, possibly accounting for the use of the present tense.) Happily this emotion proved only transitory, and the hero was restored to his own sunny disposition. At the very last of his war experience, he knew true horror. Trapped in a tree all night by Austrian artillery, he saw the morning light break on a scene of destruction, himself the only living thing—except the tree—in a panorama of death. A bursting shell finally invalided him out of the Army. How stupid, how grossly inefficient the Russian government that reported him dead in Germany! And what about the American government that interned him temporarily on Ellis Island in the twenties? No comment.

Confounding all his detractors, Baklanoff lived vigorously until 1938, in and out of scrapes, in and out of opera companies. His main port of call was Chicago, where he sang with Mary Garden in *Monna Vanna*,

Carmen, and other operas that showed his art to have matured richly. One of his final distinctions in America was singing the title role in the "original" version of *Boris Godunov,* performed with Leopold Stokowski and the Philadelphia Orchestra in 1930. He continued for several years as a pillar of a Russian opera company in New York, sonorous and lively to the end. Lipkowska followed him at least as far as Chicago and outlived him by seventeen years.

8

TO THE ROAD!

In January, 1910, the newspapers and magazines took note that never before, in their own perennial phrase, had so many—four hundred—embarked in so large a caravan—thirty cars making up two special trains for the Boston Opera Company's extended American tour. Even the Metropolitan at the turn of the century and again in the forties and fifties could not match these impressive totals. Fourteen cars were required to convey the opera scenery—one a dismantled passenger car to accommodate the overlong backdrops—and three baggage cars for personal luggage. Orchestra (eighty), ballet (fifty), and the American girls (variously estimated at twenty to fifty) whom Russell had introduced into the chorus (total 125), rode in style in six sleepers, links in the first section of the passenger train. The foreign choristers of both sexes were relegated to three coaches, every car a smoker, the *Globe* commented, with the heads of women encircled by acrid clouds from the cigars and cigarettes of their male traveling companions. Chorus reform had not yet entirely taken over in Boston. The double standard prevailed, with one set of rules for the natives, another for the foreigners. By contract, these singers, chiefly from Italy, came over with passage and transportation paid by the management, which consequently fixed as low a figure and standard of accommodation as the traffic would bear. The worm had already turned at the Met, where a chorus strike in 1905–06 had caused a couple of very odd performances, but resulted in Pullmans on the road and a raise in weekly pay to the munificent sum of twenty dollars. In 1912, Russell still paid his chorus singers in total about the same sum per week that one distinguished guest conductor received—three thousand dollars. Union protection for chorus and ballet still lay in the future.

In the second train rode the upper echelons of management and artistry, spread out over elegant drawing room cars, each with seven staterooms, a buffet, and a diner. Chefs of several nationalities and several interpreters served cosmopolitan palates and tongues respectively.

Careful to list the occupants of each car, the *Globe* report nevertheless showed some discrepancies. If all cars were of the drawing room type, a great deal of doubling-up must have been the order of the day—and night. Without further comment, the roster was printed: In the first car, Russell, Constantino, Boninsegna, Claessens, Lipkowska, Conti, Nielsen, and Goodrich. In the second, Baklanoff, Mr. and Mme. Boulogne, Bourrillon, Otto H. Kahn (his presence a good augury), Fred Pond (resident manager), Luzzatti, Kolombin, Archambault, Mardones, Giaccone, and Mr. and Mme. Muschietto (he a stage manager, she the ballet mistress). The other cars repeated the pattern of assorted singers and officials.

Expenses, it was agreed, would run forty thousand dollars a week. At a three-dollar top, Russell had his work cut out to show a profit. No figures are available except in Chicago, where the fortnight's take was given out as eighty-two thousand dollars, which allowed a slight margin in the black.

The tour opened in Pittsburgh on January 3, for eight performances in the Nixon Theatre. Pittsburgh, with a tradition of annual Metropolitan Opera visits from 1898 (excepting only the season of 1906–07), had attempted to wrest the Metropolitan management from the control of New York millionaires in 1903, offering as a candidate its local impresario, George W. Wilson. Wilson never had a chance, although home-town papers loyally stood by him until the inevitable triumph of Wall Street became clear. Under its new director, the German actor-manager Heinrich Conried, the Met continued to patronize the Steel City.

In 1910, traveling opera flared to its zenith, then burned out within three months. The Met's short season of 1910, following, in April, Russell's January incursion, upset everybody. Pittsburgh felt itself victimized by the split tour, instituted once and once only to meet the ballooning threat of Hammerstein's dominion. While Chicago basked in the presence of the company's Right Wing, the Left Wing played a "rather disastrous" engagement in Pittsburgh. The Met never returned.

It would have been consoling for Russell to believe that the excellence of his troupe had created in Pittsburgh a dissatisfaction with the older company. But the evidence hardly supports such an assumption. Russell's elevation of the ensemble principle by suppression of the star system received respectful, if not exactly rapturous, attention. This was an old and recurring story. Pittsburgh had recently lived through Conried's similar avowal and his ultimate subjection to the comet-like Caruso. Politeness wore a trifle thin after the matinee performance of *Lohengrin*. This was the first time the company had tackled Wagner. With the insouciance of earlier days, before performance in the original language became the norm, the Bostonians, with the exception of the Swan Knight himself, delivered their burden in Italian. To add to the distress, Lillian Nordica did not sing; one Sara Anderson was pressed into service. The real ovation was reserved for Howard White, a Pittsburgh boy, a former lawyer, who sang his first King Henry.

La Bohème brought Alice Nielsen's first local appearance in grand opera and the revelation of Florencio Constantino's real métier as a lyric singer (he had assumed the dramatic roles in *Aïda* and *Carmen* uneasily). *Madama Butterfly*, however, failed to please Miss Mix, the *Post*'s discerning critic. Lieutenant Pinkerton's character seemed obnoxious; Goro, the marriage broker, was out of place in grand opera; the appearance of Kate was vulgar; and the whole thing went to pieces at the end. The child Trouble screamed—the Met's Trouble had also misbehaved the previous year in spite of Farrar's soothing ministrations. "Why was the opera ever written so that the presence of the child is imperative?" Miss Mix asked in exasperation. "One can see why it is not a success in Italy." At least Nielsen did not totter about the stage with her hands dangling before her like kangaroo paws, which some misguided Occidentals felt was obligatory in interpreting the Japanese maiden.

Maria Gay's realistic Carmen, "openly coarse and vicious," made a hit, despite memories of Calvé and the less flammable Olive Fremstad. "Her kisses were the real things. They could be heard as well as seen." George Baklanoff's impressive Rigoletto also received a cordial word. But the chief attraction of Pittsburgh's week, as of St. Louis's, proved to be the unknown Orient in the seductive shape of Lakmé. Society, with every box "in requisition" and jewels gleaming, turned out as fully as the rival attraction of the Cotillion permitted, and applauded generously the opulent settings and attractive cast. Many, however, reserved their patronage for the second performance, when Russell provided an additional fillip in the form of a "classic" dancer, Thamara de Swersky. Audiences had still not learned to be content with trifles like *Lakmé* and *La Bohème,* and complaisant managers hastened into the breach with afterpieces that occasionally made odd bedfellows indeed. The day was not long past when Nellie Melba, her hair streaming, her eyes wild, would step out of character as Mimi and take on Lucia's madness in order to give the customer full measure. Russell resorted to ballet, a happy compromise—at least in the eyes of Pittsburghians and Chicagoans. Edward C. Moore of the Chicago *Journal* likened Miss de Swersky to "a woodland elf, the pagan embodiment of the joy of life and grace." Many years later, in his book *Forty Years of Opera in Chicago,* he remembered the incident more circumspectly, calling Miss de Swersky the first of an epidermic school of dancers—abundantly so.

The farther Russell penetrated into the heartland, the greater grew the resistance to paganism as exemplified by Miss de Swersky's gossamer flights. Cincinnati's critic acknowledged the audience's enjoyment of the Strauss waltz in *Fledermaus,* for which the dancer draped herself in partially concealing mouse-colored veils and movable wings, but professed to be puzzled at portions of Grieg's *Peer Gynt* Suite, in which the lady appeared "possibly in her right mind but hardly clothed." The costume, if you could dignify "a few shoulder straps and girdle of iridescent fringe" by the name, recalled Salome rather than the northern Anitra.

Indianapolis provided the stone wall against which Mlle. de Swersky's wings fluttered and broke. Even though Guernsey Van Riper showed in the *Star* that the Strauss waltz brought the delight that Strauss waltzes invariably awoke in Indianapolis breasts (Isadora Duncan had won a triumph in the same sort of vehicle the previous year), the cold, Puritanical reaction of the *News* probably represented the majority opinion. The people "gasped, sat open-mouthed at the daring, and when the first dance was over, there was scarcely any applause, which spoke well for the audience," read the priggish report. This Jeremiah concluded: "One wonders what kind of a woman it is that will bare her body and exhibit it to public gaze. Art? One kind, perhaps, but there are some people brought up with ideas of modesty that will be willing to have this branch of their education undeveloped."

The writer's scruples did not forbid a deep appreciation of Lipkowska's charms, however. "It was not difficult to love her," either for the stage

Gerald or the real Hoosier. Furthermore, the organization itself, one which could go with certainty and confidence into the most cultured city, had charmed both critics and the audience which filled English's Opera House to the last seat. The single Indianapolis show had been a success after all.

Russell's severest test came quite naturally and expectedly in Chicago, the tour city most inclined to be blasé, its long-assured position as the railroad center of the country making it the required stop for all migrant entertainers. Chicago's beautiful Auditorium, dedicated by Adelina Patti and Henry E. Abbey's touring company in 1889, had opened its doors hospitably to one troupe after another, lacking an operatic occupant to call its own. Russell's January fortnight anticipated by only a couple of months the news that Chicago would indeed acquire its own company after the sundering of Oscar Hammerstein's empire. Overtures to the Boston manager were doubtless still made behind closed doors; Chicago could not forget that the sterling imprint of the San Carlo troupe in 1907 had stimulated revolt in one faction at least against the Metropolitan's ever more careless treatment of its tour commitments under Conried. At that time, Russell might have had the job of shaping a Windy City ensemble. He was still received with confidence.

The Boston ideas of discipline, concentration on all forces instead of merely on the prima donnas, and attention to staging and scenery drew an ever increasing public during the two weeks of the tour; the marvel of opera for opera's sake seemed at last attainable. At least three influential writers, W. L. Hubbard in the *Tribune,* Glenn Dillard Gunn in the *Inter-Ocean,* and Felix Borowski in the *Record-Herald,* joined his camp. So impressed, in fact, was Mr. Hubbard, that he turned up two seasons later as Russell's publicity manager. The critic's estimate of Russell as "above all things sincere" cannot have hurt his prospects, although his paper simultaneously carried an editorial jeering at Boston's circumspect ways. "After 11 P.M., Boston has all the decorum of a lethal chamber. All one can hear is the watchman's rattle, until the well modulated voice of the dignified chanticleer awakes the town once more to life."

The expanded Chicago visit allowed the addition of *Faust, Les Huguenots, Lucia, Traviata,* and *Trovatore. Traviata* especially impressed the writers as being as beautiful in every respect as one could wish. Hubbard admired the production, which Russell had put back in time to 1790, with white wigs and all the eighteenth-century trappings.

Accepting Russell's innovation at face value, the critics reviewed production as much as individual performance, and used genuinely kind words for the chorus, with its fresh-voiced Americans; the orchestra, finely trained and performing expertly under Conti, Goodrich, and Luzzatti; the settings, especially the opulent Egypt of *Aïda* and India of *Lakmé;* and the hitherto unknown singers of first and second (if not entirely stellar) rank, who came as strangers and departed as friends. Promises were faithfully kept (a dig at Conried, who had never delivered *Salome* in spite of annual assurances), and the management had been smooth and courteous (another snap at Conried's imperious manners, which had not ceased to rankle, although the leonine German had been gone two years). Due credit fell to the local manager, F. Wight Neumann, an experienced hand at Auditorium attractions.

Needless to say, individual singers were not neglected in this estimate of a possible millenium. Constantino's splendid art, Lipkowska's pictorial and vocal triumphs, Baklanoff, who rivaled Scotti in his prime, Nielsen's advance from *The Barber of Seville* and *Don Pasquale* to *Bohème* and *Butterfly,* and Gay's seductive Amneris and rowdy Carmen won complete approval. Boninsegna's "excellent gifts and attributes" were appreciated more sincerely than in any other city, including Boston. The tall soprano must have relished Gunn's description of her voice as "pure, true, with ample volume, produced with ease and controlled in all varieties and shades of vocal nuance." Hubbard, while agreeing that the instrument had power and resonance, control and accuracy of pitch, objected mildly to the "white" production favored by Italians, which resulted in leanness of tone in the middle and low registers. The Chicago *News* alone found her acting graceful enough to distract the mind from her outside proportions. Her Valkyrian size disturbed other critics. Amneris should have been a giantess to match Aïda, Hubbard thought.

Marguerita Sylva's first appearance with the company as Marguerite in *Faust* was dutifully labeled "praiseworthy," a lukewarm adjective for this vibrant creature, who was later to earn from Philip Hale the nomination for the most distinguished and vivid Carmen in Boston since Calvé's first. She also sang Nedda in the final *Pagliacci.* Bourrillon, who had been dogged by a virus since the very first *Lakmé* in Pittsburgh and had been replaced by Kolumbin as Gerald and Faust and by Leliva as Don José, finally made a token appearance in the final truncated *Lakmé* (combined with *Pagliacci* for good measure), without doing himself complete justice. He recovered to sing all three French roles before the tour ended.

After its single *Lakmé* in Indianapolis, the company opened in Cincinnati with *Carmen*, revealing new beauties in this all-too-familiar score. *Lakmé* (and de Swersky) packed Music Hall the next night, prompting Nina Pugh Smith to a confidence in the *Times Star:* "Cincinnati is said to be the despair of artists, and of managers. That is merely because Cincinnati is but imperfectly understood by singers, players, and those who promote their interests. A relation of confidence once established is not broken by us, and we have most fortunately established such a relation with the Boston Opera Company.... It is pleasant to reflect," concluded Miss Pugh, consulting her clouded crystal ball, "that Music Hall will in future welcome the Boston Opera Company."

St. Louis, the western extreme of the tour, had always showed itself notably febrile in the tone of its newspaper reports. In the earliest days of the Metropolitan Opera's tours, management and singers writhed helplessly under the wicked assaults of a gossip columnist in the *Globe-Democrat* who never missed a chance to label a favorite tenor as a lush or a famous general as a lecher. A schizophrenic preoccupation with the status of its culture appeared periodically in this city's press.

Of Russell's St. Louis repertoire, only *Lakmé* offered fresh material for audiences and critics, impressing critics with its brilliance and color. It is to be feared that Mme. Lipkowska's charms somewhat blinded the *Republic's* critic, one Sheridan, to the other elements of the opera. Her physical condition to him seemed firm as a trained gladiator; her brow one to which poets must have written sonnets: "... low, broad, beautiful, with great spaces between the eyes that denote serene courage." This poet in his own right effused further: "Lipkowska makes the very prettiest love we have ever seen made on the stage! She flirts and dances and whisks and whispers and turns and twists and frolics and fondles like a young white greyhound about her master on a green sward; she cooed and wooed and sued and rued," and so on in a confusion of alliteratives.

After the Cincinnati *Bohème* on February 3, the three sections of the Boston Opera Special pulled out, the scenery that was no longer needed was shipped directly to Boston, while enough company to give three operas in Springfield, Massachusetts, went on about its appointed round.

Springfield displayed immoderate enthusiasm for Boston's visit, revealing itself as flattered at being elected to the high company of larger cities on the itinerary. Russell's unstinting productions drew fulsome appreciation, for Springfield considered itself to have been shabbily treated by earlier migrants. Russell was doubly welcome for choosing from among his season's repertoire such sure-fire and yet to Springfield rare items as *La Bohème, Cavalleria Rusticana,* and *Pagliacci.* The singers received universal approbation.

At the close of the home season, while pluses and minuses were still being totted up on the scoreboard, Russell shepherded his company to Providence and New Haven for seven performances. Fely Dereyne's Carmen, almost too agreeable to please Philip Hale, nevertheless titillated both smaller cities, while Nielsen and Constantino in *Bohème* satisfied the romantic yearnings of Rhode Island and Connecticut. Bronskaja added a new note as Providence's Gilda in *Rigoletto,* while Nielsen's Violetta, which she had not sung in two years, symbolically closed the tour and therefore the season. The original inspiration for Russell's American ventures, the "Little Alice" had by her rare gift, in Parker's opinion, restored to the old Italian opera music the emotion and significance of characterization that go hand-in-hand with its tunefulness—fitting musical conclusion to a remarkable chapter.

Russell would sortie to New England cities again in the years to come —Springfield and New Haven being favored—but the audiences farther afield never again experienced Boston's particular brand of opera. Perhaps it was just as well, Parker remarked. Tours at best could be exhausting, precarious, and uncertain of revenue. This one heightened Boston's prestige but hampered work at home. "Opera companies in best estate are stationary and not migratory," concluded the sage of Boston's *Evening Transcript.*

Act II

ILSA

9

SECOND SEASON
(1910–11)

Boston's second year of opera posed a peculiar difficulty in that while novelty had fled, habit had not yet taken firm hold. Henry Russell took a daring step away from previous experience at the beginning of the season of 1910–11 in Boston's new opera house. He raised ticket prices. The three-dollar top that had set Boston apart from any other major opera company and had inspired Chicago critics to demand the same from their new troupe had vanished like Boston's dream of reducing real estate taxes. Russell considered himself in the right. After all, as Oscar Hammerstein had insisted: "There is no such thing in America as cheap and *good* opera." Those who most resented the higher prices insisted at the same time on higher standards. The new five-dollar rate would, Russell promised, enable him to pay for more illustrious singers, for whom the demand always existed.

Philip Hale justified the innovation of higher prices on the ground that Boston could not be patient if its opera house served merely as a dumping ground for inferior singers who "do not please the New York public and yet are under contract to the Metropolitan." Parker went so far as to use the word "foisted" to describe the exchange with the Metropolitan. Uneasiness crept in on both sides. Lipkowska and Constantino (and Baklanoff on one tour performance) had not aroused wholehearted admiration from the Metropolitan's critics, while the capricious demands for their services had forced Russell several times to reshuffle his schedule very embarrassingly. Frances Alda, Jane Noria, and Herman Jadlowker did not quite match up, although Louise Homer gave good value.

Parker remarked resignedly after Alda's first of four appearances that in a sense it was inevitable: "Where goes Gatti-Casazza, there goes she. Generous are the operatic fates that watch over her." The New Zealand soprano had just married the Metropolitan manager. Alda herself describes this situation in her entertaining memoirs, *Men, Women, and Tenors.* She overheard Otto Kahn say to Russell, "Perhaps it would be better if Alda didn't sing in this house just now." The spirited soprano flung into their presence with the words: "I suppose it would be all right if I were his mistress! I resign right now!" The Boston appearances soothed the ruffled feathers of the bride, who refused to sing under her husband's management for a full season, except in Atlanta, which asked for her.

Jadlowker, although well formed enough to wear Faust's doublet and hose without looking like a tailor's dummy, and resembling a gallant young squire out of Goldsmith when he sang Alfredo, nevertheless seemed a trifle Teutonic for these Latinate gentlemen, and furthermore he sang *La Traviata* in German. The occasional boom of a ten-pound *"gung"* or *"keit,"* a *"Was hast du?"* or *"Ich liebe dich,"* in Parisian surroundings understandably nettled Parker. Jane Noria, the Boston Gioconda in December 1907, had fled from Russell's San Carlo company to the Met, but Russell still thought enough of her to engage her for two performances. Her Santuzza drew comparisons with Duse and Aguglia, for "her face spoke volumes," although she sang out of tune. But her Marguerite struck Hale as wrong from the start. The moment she saw Faust she made goo-goo eyes, was ready to fall on his neck; there was no need for Méphistophélès or any electrified flower bed.

The Metropolitan redressed the balance in favor of Boston in 1910–11, sending more than a dozen top (or near top) artists, led by Destinn, Slezak, and Amato. The influx remained fairly steady for the rest of Russell's Boston life. Otto Kahn used his good offices time and again to bolster Boston's casts, out of friendship for Russell as well as with intent to keep the three-city web between Boston, Chicago, and New York alive. But Boston had to pay for this added accumulation of star dust. Taking it out of the public's pockets through the box-office window is usually the last resort of an opera management, which prefers to keep its begging hand behind the scenes in private purses. These, however, had already yielded tithes in box fees for three years and could be asked for only partial readjustments.

Emerson wrote in 1845: "One would like to see Boston and Massachusetts agitated like a wave with some generosity, and for learning, for music, for philosophy, for association, for freedom, for art; but now it goes like a pedlar with its hand ever in its pocket, cautious, calculating." Had Boston really changed? Perhaps. Hale ventured cautiously the opinion that now a general, genuine, and deep interest in opera had been born, not confined to the boxholders and other subscribers, but manifest throughout the city and suburbs. Furthermore, it would be good to see the lyric art practiced at decent and regular intervals, with no such debauch as in a recent week, into which fifteen performances by two companies had been crammed, to be followed by a state of depression and apathy. The Met's battles with Hammerstein on Boston ground always produced this glut.

The business of drawing for seats, always long and tedious, showed Monday the most popular night, to no one's surprise. Wednesday ran second, with Friday nights and Saturday matinees neck and neck in last place. The first name to be read was that of Francis W. Dana, whose proxy selected two end seats in Row B in the balcony at three dollars. George Macomber next chose R 1 and 2 on the floor for Mondays. Slowly the house began to fill.

Splitting subscriptions in half may have upset boxholder's habits, but very few dropped out. Nine-tenths remained faithful during the entire life of the Opera, although some changes occurred in the lineup as the possibility of sharing the responsibility opened the lists to new names. The *Transcript*, which noted such details, remarked that the division produced the same haunting puzzle as the Metropolitan's of odd Wednesdays, even Fridays, and alternating matinees. Among the notable shifts, Mrs. Franklin Gordon Dexter, an Amory and a descendant of John Singleton Copley, rose in majestic wrath and moved from Box 5, where Mrs. John L. Gardner had turned a cold albeit beautiful shoulder to the older lady. She found refuge in the upper tier with Charles Hayden, and remained there on Wednesdays and Fridays.

Late in October several artists arrived from Europe and were given a Halloween welcome. Fely Dereyne brought her sister Ida and, from Buenos Aires, a little kitten named Poiluchun in a jeweled cage; she didn't declare it to customs. Jenka Czaplinska, the new Polish contralto, brought her mother; Leon Sibiriakoff, the six-foot-six Russian bass who would roar lustily for a single season (and in Russian, regardless of the opera), came equipped with wife and son. After his December 9 *Barber of Seville,* his eighth performance in three roles, Sibiriakoff disappeared, although so robust that it seemed hardly possible for thin air to swallow him up. It was whispered, said the *Transcript* later, that he had been grossly impertinent to the manager's wife, but this was only one of the rumors that added gaiety and broadened the social horizon. In 1925 he was spotted giving a recital in Paris. The stalwart bass at his best moments recalled to Parker the eminent Chaliapin, "whom Teutonized New York so misjudged" on his first visit.

In blueprint the prospects for the new season looked worthy enough, although it is probably hindsight to see politeness rather than wild enthusiasm in the public estimates. That the saintliness of Debussy's *L'Enfant Prodigue* would be passive as well as pretty, while Raoul Laparra's *Habañera* piled gruesomeness on gore so that *Cavalleria Rusticana* faded to a pastel; and that Frederick Converse's *The Pipe of Desire* and *The Sacrifice* should evoke neighborly handshakes rather than heartfelt applause could possibly not have been foreseen, although in the latter instance one suspects that Russell paid too heavily for his gesture to Back Bay's own. Of his fresh material, only Puccini's *Fanciulla del West* paid off. Though not a genuine smash hit, it generated enough fire in its première on January 17 to warrant an almost weekly repeat until season's end. The Metropolitan had ushered in the world première on December 10, with Toscanini, Caruso, Destinn, and Amato, accompanied by fanfares for the composer, who journeyed across the ocean and remained for the duplicate performance in Philadelphia ten days later, passing up the opportunity to hear a different cast—Melis, Constantino, and Galeffi—in Boston. At two performances, Boston was treated to the original Chicago heroine, Carolina White, who made a deep impression both as singer and actress.

Russell persisted in the overconfident belief that Boito's *Mefistofele* would win its way into Boston's hearts. The long, sprawling opera was becoming a *spécialité de la maison*, Parker remarked. It hardly belonged in the opening or closing spots, however, even though the interminable intermissions that had dragged out each of the first season's five Mefistofelean evenings had been shortened so that this year's opening curtain could rise at the civilized hour of eight. Outside Germany, Parker opined, there is no audience so prompt as Boston's; still, a seven forty-five curtain arouses no zest. And as the mood of the audience is no small part of the battle, and as working men showed up in numbers, the change was all to the good. Even so, latecomers continued to straggle in all during the first act, and the iron rule of not seating them was tacitly ignored.

Had Boston already become blasé about opera? Arthur Wilson wondered in the *Globe*. No crowd stood outside to watch the opening night glories on November 7, even though the weather stayed crisp and clear. Inside the substantial brick walls, the scene was once again all gaiety and light. The second intermission, favored for visiting, promenading, and general observation, found the main foyer on the mezzanine resembling the Boylston Street Bridge after a Harvard-Yale game, while the Palm Room (still with not a single palm) filled with those who thirsted for conversation and temperance drinks.

Backstage, all had not been so orderly. The new costumes from Italy nearly didn't arrive because of a railway express strike. Finally they were loaded in bond on a Metropolitan steamship from New York. Only the courtesy of Charles B. Osgood, who spent all Sunday at the opera house inspecting and determining the duty, enabled the ladies and gentlemen of Boito's Heaven and Hell (and Frankfurt-am-Main in between) to appear properly garbed.

Three new singers commanded attention. Carmen Melis, who had sung the year before in one of Mrs. McAllister's elegant musicales, and whose opulent, dark Italian good looks and free, amply colored voice recommended her to the opera stage, sang Helen of Troy. Her photograph in the role showed a long chin and big nose, which "somehow blended into beauty." Her hair was drawn down in two wings, secured by a bandeau across her forehead. Sibiriakoff's "beery bass" challenged the unseen angels in the heaven above. Robert Lassalle, son of the mighty baritone, Jean, who had consorted happily with the two towering De Reszkes as an equal in the golden nineties, unhappily did not live up to parental standards. His tenor voice, reedy, wiry, *sans* body, *sans* warmth, *sans* anything of sensuous charm, hoisted for tones when not spreading them, Parker fulminated. Furthermore, even allowing for the fact that he had been called only a week before to substitute for Constantino, who was detained in South America, his stage experience seemed unworthy of even a French freshman. Back to Paris he should go!—and did, but not until he had been cast in three French operas and *Cavalleria*. Russell intended poor Robert for *L'Enfant Prodigue*, where, indeed, he appeared more at ease, although his voice still retained its wiriness. Only Wilson had a good word for him at first blush. Conti's orchestra furnished further shortcomings, "tireless vociferation of brass and whacking of bass drum."

Ambassadors from various other companies honored the occasion, quite amiably spied out the land, and presumably bore good reports homeward. William J. Guard, the wily press agent, who had undoubtedly learned a trick or two from his previous boss, the galvanic Hammerstein, now applied his notable wizardry to the Metropolitan's public relations. He alone of the entire company looked the part of an artist, with his straggly goatee, string tie, and broad-brimmed, jauntily tipped black felt. Thomas Quinlan, representing Thomas Beecham (not yet knighted) praised the Boston acoustics and impresario in equal measure. George Maxwell, the ubiquitous American representative of G. Ricordi, lent a certain note of authority by his presence. Ricordi's had been hand in glove with opera producers as a matter of course and consent for many years of mutual understanding. How iron the hand, how velvet the glove, depended on the point of view.

Blue had taken over as the color of the year, one reporter asserted, citing the preponderance of blue shirts at the ball park the previous summer and the cerulean tints of the gowns of the brilliant audience. Against this heavenly background, Mrs. Nathaniel Thayer's purples and lavenders, the startling white satins of Miss Fanny Mason and Mrs. Bayard Thayer, and the pale pink chiffons affected by several debutantes, picked out notes of contrast. Transparent tunics still gave range and variety to materials and trimmings, which glittered and shimmered even after house lights dimmed.

When the last salvo of applause quieted, a hundred ladies and gentlemen embarked for the Lenox Hotel, the chief operatic caravansary, where the Jordans and Russells entertained at what a society editor stiffly termed an "Early Morning Dinner." A few speeches from the expected sources, a little singing from the artistic lions and lionesses, and a delicious collation gratified Ameses, Amsters, Fearings, Mittons, Searses, Chadwicks, Thayers, Stones, an Anderson (Mrs. Larz), Peabodys, Shaws, a Hunnewell, a Boardman, and a few dozen members of the opera company.

The first of Russell's clever juxtapositions, manifested several years before in London as stage-vs.-opera exhibitions and later to take the form of the pairing in one day of two casts for *Thaïs*, aroused mild interest in 1910, when on two consecutive days he staged Massenet's *Manon* and

Puccini's *Manon Lescaut*. But by all counts the highest point of repertoire and performance came in the very first week with Verdi's *Otello*. The towering masterpiece had not been heard in Boston since a production in English by Henry W. Savage's Company seven years past. Boston had dearer memories of the rare performances by Abbey in 1889–90, with Tamagno, Albani, and Del Puente; by the Metropolitan in 1894–95 with Tamagno, Eames, and the fabulous Maurel; and in 1901–02 with Alvarez, Eames, and Scotti. This latest trio, even including Alda, who showed "unexpectedly persuasive qualities of voice and acting in the finale," ranked with the best. Parker brought out his finest flourishes and most elaborate sentence structure to describe Leo Slezak's Moor, which for him excelled all others in his memory. Slezak never allowed the narrower channel of acting and appearance to cloud the "superior puissance" and resonance of his tones. He could thunder imprecations, swell his way through thick ensembles, yet show finely intense lyric beauty, mournful and shadowed tenderness. Wilson reserved his unqualified love for a later embodiment of Verdi's and Shakespeare's hero. Giovanni Zenatello stepped into the Boston frame as Otello on December 17 and at once into a new ambience. His new finesse and control in all departments fitted him for the accolade of "singing-actor," while the voice, never losing its intrinsic melodiousness, gained a new poignance and intensity. He lacked only the sheer physical bulk of the character, but compensated by alert, elastic movement. Wilson attributed this growth and deepening in intelligence and artistry to the goading of Zenatello's wife, Maria Gay, who taught him in one summer an entire new approach. She believed that beauty of vocal timbre was seated in language, and she forced him to consider his diction, as well as refining his voice by making him hum constantly. Whatever the method, it produced startling results. Zenatello rapidly became the pillar of Boston's Latin wing, supplementing and in many minds outstripping Constantino.

Otello enjoyed five performances in this season and returned each year thereafter, always a vessel for Russell's vintage wines. Zenatello continued to dominate the title role, only once in illness giving way to Slezak. Emma Eames said farewell to her illustrious career as Desdemona in 1911–12; Luisa Villani appeared once on March 11, 1914. Carmen Melis displayed one finely tempered Desdemona, equal to Zenatello, before Lucille Marcel arrived to take over the role under the leadership of Felix Weingartner.

Certain singers remained fixed stars, as is true in any of the world's opera houses. Zenatello grew to that stature in Boston. How much Russell depended on the tenor would show in 1912–13, from late December through March. Zenatello seldom absented himself and sang every other day or so for a total of twenty-seven performances of a dozen roles, more than any other leading singer except his wife, Maria Gay, who beat him by four performances but in a more limited repertoire of eight roles. More important than the bulk of Zenatello's achievement was its quality. He made vitally attractive the French heroes, Julien, José, Faust, and Samson, whom he turned into creatures of flesh and blood, serving them as no other Italian except perhaps Caruso has done. "His look is high, his stride heroic, his manner that of a man still young, yet conscious of great destiny"—a comment appropriate to any of his more bravura roles.

His rather stormy transition from Hammerstein to Russell had involved a lawsuit for breach of contract when Oscar I sold out to the Metropolitan. The Met did not choose to pick up Zenatello, being satisfied with its own large stable of tenors: Caruso, of course, leading the list. Zenatello settled down rapidly in Boston, under the restraining influence of his solicitous spouse, and was chosen by Russell to top off the last two seasons in *Jewels of the Madonna*. Because Zenatello never sang at the Metropolitan (although Hammerstein lent him briefly to Gatti in 1909 for a half-dozen replacements of Caruso on tour), he has perhaps never received the recognition to which these years in Boston and subsequent service in Chicago entitled him. He and Mme. Gay later achieved a measure of fame as esteemed teachers and the discoverers of Lily Pons.

Possibly even happier than Russell and the public at Zenatello's presence was Maria Gay. The plump, bouncy Spaniard, in real life as vivacious and down-to-earth as her Carmen, had joined forces with the tenor in his first season at Oscar Hammerstein's Manhattan Opera. Maria sang with the Met the following season. She had been in Boston alone in 1909–10; now her Giovanni was by her side and she rejoiced. Somewhere along the line the two were married, as Henry Lahee put it delicately, "after a romantic courtship of two or three (or four) years, during which she had been associated with him in opera." Arthur Wilson, who came to know the couple well in Boston, insists to this day that when told they should be married to satisfy Boston's sense of propriety, Maria exclaimed, "Oh, alla right—we getta up and go to minister." Encouraged by the spectators, Gay allowed her Carmen to slip little by little into over-extravagant reality, as Calvé had done before her. But, as one observer remarked, she was an elemental force, and it would be as idle to demand accountability of her as of a wild cat. Her Azucena, Amneris, and Santuzza, the first break in a long file of Carmens, still smacked of the wild gypsy.

Spurts of excitement continued to stir the faithful during the initial fortnight of the season. The first Saturday matinee brought Melis as Tosca and the debut of a young Italian conductor, who would revitalize the conventional repertoire. Roberto Moranzoni, now thirty and fresh from the Teatro Costanzi at Rome, seemed all youthful energy, even to the tossing hair and extravagant gesture, loving an energetic pace, alert to telling contrasts, but not forgetting the less obvious qualities of a conductor. He felt and seized the individuality of instruments and voices; could attain the thick richness and ample breadth of Italian instrumental song; led significant melodies skillfully out of the welter of "verismo" music, but did not distort nor inflate to gain effect. He clothed dry bones of older Italian music with new flesh and blood. In short, according to Boston estimates, a perfect Italian conductor. Parker believed he had discovered another Toscanini. All eight operas he conducted pulsed with new life. It was rumored that Tito Ricordi, who was suspected of manipulating casts all over the world, had placed Moranzoni conveniently in the path of Russell, hoping Russell would bypass Conti for the new *Girl of the Golden West*. If so, the conniver succeeded only partially. Conti conducted the entire layout of the *Girl*, while Moranzoni fell heir to it only the next season.

This new abandon introduced by Moranzoni admirably suited Melis's idea of Floria Tosca. Reticence was not precisely Tosca's virtue, any more than it was the Roman singer's. In fact, the only true Tosca is a real Italianate one, Parker conceded, unfurling one of his chains of pungent words—hot and gusty, alternating affection and jealousy, playfulness and pique, self-torture and resolution. Melis's Latin beauty, and the Latin beauty of the flesh, served this idea eminently well. Assaulted by Baklanoff's gusty Scarpia in the matinee performance, she met a real old master in Maurice Renaud at the second hearing November 21. The French baritone was then forty-eight, and had attained renown in Europe and with Hammerstein and the Metropolitan, inspiring columns of baffled yet rapturous conjectures about the reasons for his greatness. The sheer force of his vocal and histrionic art built his solid success, without factitious information, sensation, or idle gossip. Very little trivia about Maurice

Renaud ever appeared, no tidbits about his personal life or habits. "No operatic 'personality' as Jean de Reszke nakedly was, or Mary Garden insistently is," said Parker, there were as many Renauds as the characters he sang. The man split himself into them like the germ of the biological process.

Broad-shouldered, deep-chested, boyish, with a twinkle in his eye, a fascinating smile and manner, a moustache turned up at the corners; this was how this paragon appeared to a writer in *Theatre Magazine*. "Renaud moves with strength, ease, and the semi-indolence of a cat," the lady reporter continued. "He is Southern French [Bordeaux was his birthplace] to the finger-tips, with one exception—repose of manner. His hair is white, curling crisply, his brows startling black, his eyes light blue-gray." Renaud expressed his dissatisfaction with certain operatic conventions; the stiff *coulisses* (wings) and painted skies, the anachronisms all too often allowed in costuming.

He had made his New York debut in 1906 with Hammerstein as Rigoletto. Grau had hired him before the turn of the century for the Metropolitan, but the Spanish-American war caused a postponement. His contract, renewed in 1903 for five hundred dollars a night, was abrogated by Conried, who showed a *kolossal* disregard for anything French, whereupon Renaud sued Grau, winning fifteen thousand dollars, an unusual victory in those days of a constant procession of such suits through the courts. Hammerstein, though resentful, was forced to raise his fee to eight hundred dollars. The Frenchman was once asked to sing an extra performance. With typical thrift he answered: "Renaud was not contracted to do favors."

His Scarpia fascinated critics, though it is to be suspected that the subtleties passed over the heads of the rather small, not very demonstrative Boston audience. This Roman police chief wore dead black, with snowy white lace jabot and cuffs. The full face seemed pale, without the flush of the practiced voluptuary; the nose was a beak. The eyes, one of Renaud's most adroit and fruitful histrionic means, showed large, clear, cold, searching. With them he kept Scarpia in the picture during Tosca's singing of "Vissi d'arte," a practice that cannot have pleased Melis, if indeed she knew it. This Scarpia's chief motivation was a cruel voluptuousness, kin to medieval and Renaissance characters. His spirit was like Paradise Lost, his torture both hot and cold. "Oh, this was as vivid and racking a performance of *Tosca* since it first came to the stage!" Parker exclaimed. Neither Ternina and Scotti, nor Geraldine Farrar in her frenzies the past year, surpassed it.

The outlines of a "grand plan" in Russell's thinking began to show as the second week coursed by. The Italian wing had already been established with Moranzoni and the faithful Conti, who would stay on for another season. Now the French fences were to be mended to enclose a defined territory, instead of the polyglot sprawl of the previous season. Enough French operas had been sifted into the list to justify the separation: the old familiar *Faust, Carmen,* and *Lakmé,* Massenet's *Manon,* and the two real novelties, Debussy's *L'Enfant Prodigue* and Laparra's *Habañera.*

André Caplet made his debut as the new Gallic conductor with *Faust* on November 14. Whatever the personal and private urgencies behind the façade of his engagement, the young Frenchman addressed himself soberly to the task. Although Parker was to grumble even a year later that Caplet, like George Henschel in the Symphony's maiden season, was learning his trade as he went along, his musicianship never could be challenged. No less a personage than Claude Debussy vouched for that. The impressionist trusted Caplet with orchestration and plainly mourned his defection to America in times when, he claimed, he was needed most.

Within the Boston operatic family, Caplet met resentment at first. He seemed surly and withdrawn, perhaps the mask for a truly inward-looking character that later turned to mysticism. The clearest contemporary picture of him is provided by Alexander Smallens, who became an assistant conductor in 1911. Caplet spoke no English and would greet a morning *"Bonjour!"* with a sniff; a noonday *"Bonjour!"* with a sob. Like any imperious leader, he expected perfection, and he met any halfway measures with scorn and fury. One night in a famous death scene, the usual chain of assistant conductors was set up to relay signals for an important bell chime from the depths of the stage. Smallens, posted at the crucial point, depended upon his confederate, Charles Strony, who peeped at Caplet through a hole in the scenery. Strony, a gay young blade, forgot his duty as five personable nuns gathered around him to sing a few measures. Smallens, hearing what he thought was the appropriate music, rang the bell, but too late. After the performance, Caplet strode backstage, glaring. Still not speaking, he turned away, leaving the verbal chastisement to another assistant, Walter Straram. In true French style, Straram obliged: *"Qui a sonné comme un [sacré] cochon?"* At the end of the fifth season, knowing he would not return, Caplet asked Smallens to dinner and showed some of the charm that undoubtedly endeared him to a few intimates. "You told the truth," he complimented the brusque Smallens, speaking of the bell incident. "It takes a man to tell the truth and to take it."

At the end of the war, in which he insisted on active service in spite of his age, Caplet was wounded and gassed at the Battle of Champagne. He then sought spiritual paths. The death of Debussy in 1918 greatly shook his already waning strength. His final compositions bore religious titles: a Mass, "Mirror of Jesus," and "Prayers," and showed a strong streak of mysticism. He died after a bout of *la grippe* in 1925.

In his first appearance, Caplet revealed typical Gallic qualities. He labored with the orchestra to obtain that finish only a Frenchman could attain for the music of another Frenchman. He smoothed, he polished, he elaborated the *Faust* score until the orchestra gave out a rarely beautiful tone. In *L'Enfant Prodigue* two nights later, he subjected the men to a long-needed training in transparency, euphony, mellowness, delicate variations of color, gradations of force, supple rhythms, finesse of accent, subtlety, suggestiveness, and charm (who else but Parker would string such a verbal necklace?) In *Carmen* the next month, the orchestra compelled attention for its flowering with new voices of melody, while the old melodies sang as if new.

As the first novelty of the season, *L'Enfant Prodigue,* Debussy's Prix de Rome cantata, bore a great deal more attention than its slender scaffold could properly support. Its music showed precognition of the matured composer in certain instrumental phrases, but its set pieces smacked all too closely of the melodic graces of Massenet, of whom Debussyites liked to speak spitefully. In effect a concert in costume, the piece shared double and triple bills variously with *Pagliacci, Cavalleria, Hänsel und Gretel, The Miserly Knight,* and full-length ballets. Evidence of careful preparation showed in its mounting. On the backdrop, an arm of Lake Genezerath (Gennesaret), deepest Oriental blue, caught the reflection of a white-walled town on the opposite shore; the sky added pinkish tints. In the distance, a few crumbling columns on a shadowed hill; in the foreground, the suggestion of another ruined temple. Below, a second village descended to the nearer side of the lake. Tall palms stood in intervening spaces, and a few tufts of darker vegetation showed here and there. The lighting matched the scene in imaginativeness.

The space expended on this description of a painted canvas suggests that little else on the stage clamored for attention. The singing lacked distinction, for all three voices—Alice Nielsen, Robert Lassalle, and Ramon Blanchart, seemed dessicated. When to please Caplet *L'Enfant* was revived the next season, two Frenchmen played father and son (Riddez and De Potter), and Maria Gay's big, lush voice coped with the high B of the mother's wailing "Azael!"

All the while, Caplet prepared for *Habañera* with grim thoroughness. Baklanoff's breach of discipline, which kept him out of the cast for good, gave the young conductor some bad moments very close to curtain time. The extra efforts expended by everybody, especially the conscientious Blanchart, who replaced the naughty Russian at the final dress rehearsal, produced a good show, remarkable under the circumstances. The simple designs, somber and shadowed, made their own impression. The audience sat breathlessly through the brief three acts of mounting horror, while Ramon murdered his brother Pedro for love of the luscious Pilar, then swore to avenge his brother's death. This blasphemy brought out the ghost of Pedro, visible only to Ramon while the villagers danced the Habañera with abandon. In the cemetery, Ramon at last confessed his crime to Pilar, who dropped dead on the tomb of her lover. This grisly story dominated the music that set it; harsh, bitter, but with delineative force, Laparra's expressive score nevertheless showed individuality. In 1911–12, the opera made a perfect vehicle for the tempestuous Maria Gay, who enjoyed its excesses far more than the graceful Fely Dereyne had done at its first hearings.

Attention to the German repertoire was paid only in token, with *Hänsel und Gretel,* but for an appreciable moment, it seemed as if Russell might establish an American wing. That he chose to try it with the works of a single composer, and a member of his board at that, created in some minds the faint suspicions of patronage, though Boston generally professed itself happy to honor its own prophet. Dear Mr. Converse was so well liked. The justification for Russell's choice of one of his works, *The Pipe of Desire,* lay open to view: it had been accepted and performed as the first American work ever to gain the Metropolitan stage as recently as March 18, 1909. Whatever its reception in Manhattan, it deserved a wider hearing in Boston than the comparatively private ones on January 31, 1906 and again in March in Jordan Hall.

With the advantage of this comfortable background and preparation, the Boston performance on January 11, 1911, afforded considerable satisfaction to all concerned. Parker came to the conclusion that *The Pipe of Desire* belonged in the category of finer things at the opera, even though it could claim Americanism only by virtue of having been written by a native. The scene was the forest of nowhere, the time, merely spring, the personages fantasy, the music allegory, the design fanciful and symbolic. The music, while characteristic of Converse, showed no other token of American origin.

Interest focused chiefly on the orchestra, so that Wallace Goodrich's contribution became crucial. The young Bostonian, a colleague of Converse's, threw himself into the venture wholeheartedly. As a reward, he could treasure the *Transcript*'s remark that it was hard to recall when the orchestra had played with such sensitive tone, such feeling for the music in hand.

This first rather tentative essay into the realms of native speech—tentative because of the leading singers only one, Riccardo Martin, boasted American birth—met with the usual inconclusive reception of such sorties. All the singers seemed to be groping, both for meanings and vocal paths. Martin, whose Americanisms had passed scrutiny in the naval uniform of Lieutenant Pinkerton, came in a poor third to the Spaniard Blanchart and the Frenchwoman Dereyne for clear diction. *Pipe* was laid to rest gently after three January performances, in tandem with either *Cavalleria* or *Pagliacci*.

When a second Converse opera showed in the horoscope, interest picked up. A full-length drama that looked promising; *The Sacrifice*, Converse called it. Russell scheduled a clear track for four performances in March after all other novelties had paraded by and only repeats would surround the newcomer. Full-dress precautions included a souvenir program and a campaign of education in the daily press. Hale cannily printed blow-ups of pages of the score on a Sunday before the March 3 première, thus dodging a detailed analysis. The *Globe*, with two ears to the ground, prompted by Jordan's large stockholdings and Converse's relation by marriage to one of the two Taylor brothers who had inherited the paper from the founder, scented a lagging enthusiasm on the part of ticket buyers and got up a special issue, even including Hale's pictorial spread from the *Herald*.

The story of the 1846 struggle between the United States and Mexico in California promised passionate action in the good old Italian style—a Mexican spy and his lady friend, an interfering American captain, jealous as well as military clashes, and a final sacrifice à la Sydney Carton on the part of the American, leaving the lovers happily reunited at his grave. But the conventional music did little to enhance the drama. America's entry in the Boston opera sweepstakes ran quietly into the shadow of obscurity. Hale remarked that Converse's second try showed an advance on his first, but advised him not to be in a hurry to make a third. Converse disregarded the critic. His *The Immigrants* lay in readiness for Russell's abortive sixth season, and was swept into oblivion along with other dreams.

One new rule boded ill for the happiness of certain singers, who turned towards an audience beating its hands together as trustingly as a flower faces the sun. "No encores," said the management. And, "no applause, please, during the action." The full impact of this ukase hit the *Rigoletto* quartet at the second performance on November 9. The singers waited like well-admonished children refusing a second helping while the audience signified its pleasure. Then Goodrich picked up the beat. Although Constantino once stepped out of the frame as usual to bow acknowledgment, the encore nuisance was definitely abolished.

Early in December, Boston rather self-consciously examined what it was doing for grand opera, in a symposium of eight authorities published in the *Globe*. Leading off, William H. Leahy, secretary to the Mayor, declared that the "White Orchid of Art" view was highly exaggerated. Boston's audiences might still be a trifle reserved, as if uncertain of their own authority and afraid of exuberance and tumultous rapture, yet where else could be found a spirit more receptive, a purer taste, a temper more hospitable to all contending schools?

After several sober estimates of the situation by critics and educators, Nathan Haskell Dole, author and "music connoisseur," offered the prophetic statement that public interest is healthier than subvention, "whether rained down democratically or squirted through the nozzle of royalty." He foretold government support, in terms that have remained familiar and applicable, seeing the time when instead of wasting a million on big steel cruisers destined for the junk heap, we will find the money requisite for beauty. But his tolerance went only so far: in a peroration that undoubtedly cheered Converse, he thundered that he would stimulate artists not to write "exotic, mephitic, erotic, Semitic operas of seduction, adultery, or incest, but instead good wholesome operas written in English by real American poets and set to music by composers of the first class."

Simultaneously with Boston's second season, a new era opened for Chicago. The Windy City, in fact, beat Boston to the opening curtain by four days, launching its brave new enterprise on November 3, 1910, with *Aïda* in a renovated auditorium, golden and glowing. The backers of "permanent" opera, basking in the self-congratulation they deserved, exulted along with manager Andreas Dippel in the successful beginning.

Before the Boston season had advanced more than a few weeks, Symphony Hall, the opera house's cultural twin on Huntington Avenue, experienced a cyclone that figuratively blew off its top and literally lifted the lids from the ladies in the audience. Opera patrons, troubling the sight-lines at night with nothing more obstructive than a graceful aigrette or a languid feather, became a menace at Symphony matinees to the view of Max Fiedler and his dignified cohorts at the elect Friday matinee "public" rehearsals. Mayor "Honey Fitz" Fitzgerald, always vigilant in pursuit of his constituents' comfort and convenience, issued a request early in November, at first courteous, then threatening to revoke the Symphony license, reminding the ladies that their headpieces constituted a public nuisance. The newest 1910 models aspired to heaven—or Symphony Hall's ceiling—with bowl piled upon bowl, topped by feathery geysers; while desperate architects contemplated widening doorways to admit the swaying platforms atop milady's elaborately coiffured heads.

The Symphony management passed a law, printed it in the programs, and reinforced injunction by placards in the lobbies. After some panic in the distaff ranks, peace and bareheadedness reigned at last; no strong-arm tactics had been needed; no employee showed hatpin wounds. Symphony Hall's triumph echoed around the musical world.

Grand opera appeared to have sent down firm roots into Back Bay's filled ground. Although the deficit had mounted, the opera house now stood as an institution in which all inhabitants should take pride, Hale thought. It had broadened musical knowledge and developed critical and discriminating taste. Furthermore, an audience brought together in enjoyment, though some sat in boxes and others in a gallery, fostered a strong democratic tie. And finally, the commercial effect meant a great deal at a time when "croakers insisted that the city will soon be only a way-station." As for the fate of the city's newest cultural structure, a *Globe* headline, over a review of the season, gave sober promise: "Opera's Permanence Seems Assured."

10

QUARTET IN ALT

Two pairs of prima donnas, each completely representative of different eras, afforded Boston an education in the operatic art—two glories of the past: Nellie Melba and Lillian Nordica; and two auguries of the future: Emmy Destinn and Mary Garden. Not only the gulf of years separated the two mettlesome teams; a whole new style emerged between their zeniths. Melba at one pole and Garden at the other, with Nordica and Destinn midway between the two opposite ends, formed a firm chain of progression from the old bel canto to the new "singing actor." The differences between the two extremes lay not only in vocal approach, but also in the singer's person from head to toe. It could even be said that as the new ideas of dramatizing an opera part took hold, the singers' feet were freed from the floor. Melba might stand rooted as her crystalline voiced soared in all the gymnastics required of it, Nordica remain the stately figure; but Garden could fling herself impetuously across the stage while her throat emitted any sounds that the action called for, musical or not. The fact that she sang at all confounded many, who could not see the Divine Mary's unquestionable musical gifts for the surrounding staginess.

For supreme artistic singing, the season's blue ribbon would have fluttered to rest on the ample shoulder of the Czech soprano who had already won favor in New York as a member of the first team, along with Toscanini, Caruso, and Homer. Emmy Destinn was her stage name, borrowed from a teacher and greatly to be preferred over the surname of Kittl to which she was born. She made her bow with the Boston company as Madama Butterfly on January 6, 1911, and at once ascended to a high and holy place in critical estimations. The voice, of individual quality, not enormous or highly resonant, showed a texture unusually fine, even, and sensitive, its subdued warmth and plaintiveness bringing to Parker the shadowy suggestion of a clarinet. It was always the Destinn voice that commanded; second to compel interest, the figure and presence conveyed less, even conventional, meaning, although subtle facial expressions always came to the aid of characterization. She had already shown herself to be the supreme Verdi singer, as the Met's Aïda in Boston on March 28, 1910. Her other parts in New York included a wide range of styles and nationalities: the Italian Tosca, Nedda, Santuzza, Butterfly, La Wally, Mistress Ford (*Falstaff*), Ricke (*Germania*); the German Marta (*Tiefland*), Marie (*Bartered Bride*), Eva, and an unexpected Gerhilde in Philadelphia (stepping in for Leonora Sparkes). Restlessly she complained a season later, even after she had added Puccini's Girl and Wagner's Elsa and Elisabeth, that the Met's demands nowhere near met her capacity—and desire—for work. Barely an eighth of her repertoire of eighty operas had been tapped; her time seemed wasted with only two performances a week. Lahee commented mischievously that perhaps Miss Destinn was suffering from the precedent of singers, who, paid by the week, elected to sing as seldom as possible; while those on the single performance rate cried hungrily for action. "It is wonderful," he concluded, "how often singers are in condition to sing when each appearance adds to their income; and per contra, they are delicate, fragile things when they are paid by the month or the season." Boston hardly offered the amount of work the singer demanded, but Boston paid her the compliment of feeling electrified at each new revelation of a role, from Puccini's pathetic Japanese or Minnie to Mozart's Donna Anna or the grand Gioconda.

Mary Garden had been introduced with flourishes of trumpets by Oscar Hammerstein several seasons previously, and seismographs had almost broken down from the shock of her Mélisande, Thaïs, and Jean in *Le Jongleur de Notre Dame*. But she had never sung Marguerite in the United States before. Russell's choice of the virginal maiden as the role in which to introduce Garden to the company proved a master stroke. Hale reminded his readers that those who looked for extravagance forgot that Garden had brains and composed a part with the utmost care. Her Marguerite could not do anything commonplace or mean. She gave

Marguerite character from the first entrance, unconventional, natural, effective. She was neither shy nor coquettish nor sophisticated. No petty business, no aimless wandering cluttered the beginning of the garden scene. The Jewel Song revealed character; the love scene truest art. Her face lifted to Faust showed pure, youthful, adoring love. Still more remarkable was the church scene, where no passionate outbursts nor imitations of the mad lady of the village marred the simplicity. Her points were made quietly, with ever changing facial expression, even at the most dramatic moment of Valentin's death. Judged by ordinary rules of song, she showed faults: in her attack, not always decisive; in the slurs from high to low and vice versa; in an inclination to drag in expressive passages. But how could these faults be weighed against her many excellences?

Round the circle, from bel canto to expressionism and back again, leads the spectator to the indestructible image of Nellie Melba, who graced two Boston seasons with rare appearances set like pearls in delicate, old-fashioned mountings. When she sang Mimi on December 15, 1910, it was nine years since her last Boston opera appearance, although she had uttered pretty sounds in the Mad Scene from *Hamlet* but a fortnight previously with the Symphony, albeit burdened with a cold.

The Diva's relations with Russell, since the early days when Russell's brother Landon Ronald served as her accompanist, partook of that off-again, on-again quality that so often disfigures an association between two imperious temperaments. The current had been "off" for a considerable period when Russell, to his surprise, as vouched for in his memoirs, received a mysterious message from Melba through an intermediary, Mrs. John L. Gardner, always the singer's champion. Its burden: the soprano would like very much to sing at the Boston Opera House, except for the fact that Russell directed there. The manager attributed Melba's sudden capitulation at least partly to the frequent presence in Boston of Frances Alda, who in addition to being a younger rival for the Antipodean championship of the opera world, had shown the initiative and gumption (and to Melba, some suggested, the gall), to marry the director of the Metropolitan Opera. Always the businesswoman, Melba melted somewhat at the temptation of fees that might reach as high as twenty-five hundred dollars, Russell hinted. Whatever the hidden motives and backstage maneuverings, one night Melba arrived at the opera house "and found herself in the anomalous position of singing under the direction of a man to whom she did not speak." Russell insists that he initiated the ice-breaking that brought on the thaw. No matter: Melba sang, as she was to continue to do under this hate-love relationship far into the twenties and on another continent as well.

As if to confirm that the old, familiar ways are best, Boston showed up in numbers and social brilliance superior to opening night's for the *Bohème* on December 15 that conveyed Melba's Mimi back to an adoring world. The circumstances that Melba, and Melba only, drew them accounted for the rustle of their silks and satins as they slipped into their seats during the Bohemians' horseplay around the garret stove. When the timid knock came to Rodolfo's ears, as to theirs, a loud sigh of anticipation shuddered over the dark house. And in answer to the poet's "Chi e la?" the shy figure appeared in the doorway, signaling the expected outburst.

As the evening passed, that unique voice seemed to grow in beauty: there was, as Hale remarked next day, none like it for quality. "It is golden," he wrote reverently; "it is also emotional." Here other opinions split away sharply from Philip the Great, who remained almost alone on his eminence as believer in Melba as an expressive singer, even apart from acting. Parker maintained his position that one "may not by taking thought acquire histrionic temperament," and Pitts Sanborn in New York, comparing Tetrazzini to Melba, noted spitefully that "there is reason to suppose that Melba has not lacked temperament, but she never related it to her singing."

On this winter evening, a quality of virginity had been restored to the prima donna, at least in vocal realms. Perhaps the division had always been between the acting that can be accomplished by voice only, a point constantly emphasized by early critics, and that which must be conveyed by bodily presence, magnetism, gesture, facial mobility, and the expression that looks out from the eyes. Melba's voice to Hale seemed possessed of the frank, fresh, virginal accents of girlhood—weighted, to be sure, by the bloom and fullness of a woman who has lived. Apparently Melba could have it both ways. Her lower and middle tones showed a richer body than even twelve years previously, when she first sang Mimi in Boston with the Ellis Company on January 25, 1899. The voice sufficed for Parker too. "We go for interpretation to Farrar or Renaud; for singing to Caruso or Melba."

Around this quartet of divas revolved the lesser planets—men. Sparked by Mary Garden's flame, the entire performance of *Faust* came alive. Of no small assistance were the two Frenchmen, Charles Dalmorès and Léon Rothier, who partnered the soprano, and the third in the pit. Caplet, in fact, made the orchestra a new character in the opera. Rothier's rich voice gave Méphistophélès a songful aspect. Dalmorès, who came to Boston by way of Hammerstein and Chicago, having survived one of the usual manager-singer lawsuits (he escaped a subpoena by masquerading as a ship's cornetist), boasted an impeccable musical background, having played horn under Colonne between the ages of seventeen and twenty-three and, at the latter ripe eminence, winning an appointment as professor of horn at Lyons. His efforts to climb out of the pit onto the stage won only ridicule at first, but a fellow professor who had been a bass at the Théâtre de la Monnaie in Brussels gave him encouragement and instruction. At his debut, accomplished at twenty-eight in 1899, the good citizens of Rouen instructed the captain of police to hold up the sign, "Approved," according to their method of judging an artist.

Hale acknowledged the tenor's artistic qualities, and pronounced him manly, chivalric, a tender lover as well, picturesquely costumed without disfiguring whiskerage. His consummate skill both in amorous and heroic measures showed song and action to be inseparable. Parker agreed, speaking of Dalmorès as a figure of romance, with a tenor's grace.

Dalmorès well knew the value of publicity as well as of solid merit. His cunning evasion of Conried's minions of the law made all the papers, and he roused considerable to-do with a boast that he would exceed the thirty-second kissing scene enacted by Edward Johnson (the young tenor who one day would accede to the Metropolitan roster and eventually to its management) in the operetta, *Waltz Dream,* Broadway's most enchanting musical show circa 1908. Dalmorès named Mary Garden as his partner in the osculatory exercise, the opera to be *Louise.* If he made good his promise in Chicago or New York, Boston heard nothing of it. The couple never sang together in *Louise* with the Boston Company. In any event, one imagines that Miss Garden would have had a say in the partnership.

With all his flamboyance, Dalmorès is remembered best for his seriousness of artistic purpose and his high accomplishments as a singing actor. He expressed the belief, which has steadily grown more accepted, that musicianship is a vital if not the first necessity for a singer; that he must not live exclusively in the narrow little world behind the footlights. "Every symphony I have played has been molded into my life experience in such a way that it cannot help being reflected in my work," he declared.

Garden's single appearance as Massenet's Manon in 1910–11 fell out-side the frame in which Russell exhibited his two Manons in tandem. This occurred on February 20 and 22 respectively, with Lipkowska and Edmond Clément as Massenet's lovers; Melis and Amadeo Bassi as Puccini's. The only common denominator was Rodolfo Fornari, the bari-tone who had been found useful in comparatively light roles, as Lescaut. Bassi, who had seen service with Hammerstein, sang some performances at the Metropolitan in this very season and later joined Chicago's tenor ranks. This Des Grieux marked his Boston debut. Occasional spurts of brilliant singing did not quite compensate for the reediness Parker de-tected in his voice, and the labored and unsympathetic acting attributed to him by Hale in the only other display of his talents, as Johnson in *Fanciulla*. Parker, in fact, spent more space than perhaps he deserved in describing the tenor's besetting trick, one step forward at each swelling progression of tone, a click of heels, then another step, until he landed at the prompter's box, crying his passion, not to its object, but to the house.

Clément on the French side of *Manon* fared much better. The reputa-tion of this distinctive artist, unspectacular yet richly varied in expressive-ness, had preceded him from the Paris Opéra Comique, where he had basked in security and fame for two decades. A short-lived experience with the Metropolitan the previous season, when virtually two companies were maintained to fight Hammerstein's French fire with flames equally Gallic, had added few leaves to his laurel wreaths. Boston (and later Chicago) opened more congenial doors, and Clément enjoyed particular *réclame* especially in his second and third seasons. For the moment, Hale remarked that this was the purest bel canto singing, not heard from tenors since Bonci's advent. Companioning this exquisite Frenchman and Miss Garden in the final *Manon* of the season was Dinh Gilly, who had made his American debut in *Werther* alongside the tenor at the Metropolitan's New Theatre venture in November 1909, with Farrar for a heroine. Gilly, whose name was frequently linked with that of one of the quartet of prima donnas, soon earned the nickname of "La Forza del Destinn."

Swept along in the wake of Melba's *Bohème*, a new young Irish tenor had proved his mettle as a vocalist from the moment of his debut with Hammerstein in New York, November 10, 1909, as Alfredo in *La Traviata* with Tetrazzini; he had also made a hit at his Boston debut opposite the plump prima donna's Lucia. He seemed destined for a continuance of this brilliant partnership—some called it competition—all through the season, and escaped it only to join with Melba at the Metropolitan the following year. But the name of John McCormack soon needed no other alongside it to draw admirers. Later on critics and worshipers at his concert shrine found it hard to credit the perfect interpreter of "Mother Machree" with the accomplishments in Verdi, Puccini, Donizetti, and above all Mozart (in which he would later excel) that studded his early decade in opera with Hammerstein, Russell, Gatti-Casazza and Campanini. Boston's own opera company welcomed him first as Turiddu opposite Melis on December 2, 1910, with a repeat on December 5 and an intervening *Bohème* on December 3 with Nielsen. Being human, the *Transcript* thought, he sang a better Rodolfo to Melba's Mimi. His voice chimed in sympathy with hers; he too possessed that exquisite quality, Hale thought, a purity that is warm, a sweetness not cloying. His fine vocal art produced memorable moments when an unconscious technique seemed merely natural, inevitable vocal expression. As an actor, he stood about equal with Melba, according to his own admission, which left the drama of Puccini's opera pretty much to the orchestra and to Marcello and Musetta. Fely Dereyne, as restless as a fish swimming in a kettle, found a new artist-suitor this evening, the dapper, curly-haired, dimple-chinned Mario Sammarco. This personable Italian baritone only showed his art to Boston in two performances, this *Bohème* and an Iago in *Otello* two days later, but he left an impression of practiced skill in the use of his rich, agreeable voice.

With their attendant cavaliers, this quartet of sopranos—Melba, Nordica, Destinn, Garden—summed up Boston's second opera flowering: Mary Garden like an arrow pointed inexorably to the future; the other three gradually retreated into a past where only the sounds that came from a silver throat mattered. As a final picture, we see two of them, stately as queens, in *propriae personae*, gracing rival boxes in Boston's diamond horseshoe. Down at the lower right, Melba, tall and straight, dressed in creamy white mousseline with pearls, sat with her friend Mrs. John Gardner in Box 5. Set like a jewel in the center of the upper circle, Lillian Nordica gratified her patron-hosts, the Eben Jordans, in Box 37, her white chiffon banded with sable, emeralds glittering at throat and breast. While these two still trod the boards or showed themselves on the other side of the footlights, even though they might not be speaking to each other, the golden age of opera still lived in Boston.

11

TWO SCRIBES
(Philip Hale and H. T. Parker)

The Boston Opera Company was fortunate, as it proved—although Eben Jordan, pounding his hand on his dining table, scarring the wood with his heavy ring, while digesting the daily crop of newspaper reviews, might not have agreed at the time—in coming under the scrutiny of two of the most sagacious music critics of all American time. While New York currently boasted four whose names are even now mentioned with varying degrees of respect, Boston's titans need bow to none. Philip Hale's reign over the "artistic" pages of the *Herald* was absolute from 1903 to 1933; Henry Taylor Parker was immovably entrenched in his corner of the *Evening Transcript* from 1905 to 1934. Both men commanded the attention of the international music world, and both accomplished prodigious feats in evaluating the theatrical scene as well.

Perhaps the measure of the complete authority of these two prophets is their identification by initials or nickname. No New Yorker ever knew any other appellations than Henry E. Krehbiel, Henry T. Finck (his middle name was the exploitable Theophilus, but no one dared), William J. Henderson, and Richard Aldrich for the respective reviewers for the *Tribune, Post, Sun,* and *Times.* Boston, however, little given to sobriquets, never doubted the identity of "Philip the Great" (occasionally "Philip the Terrible," and more intimately "Phil"). As for "H. T. P.," wrote David McCord in *Theatre Arts Monthly,* "these letters in Boston are as insidious as 'G. B. S.'" Parker's initials were inevitably expanded to "Hell-to-Pay," which doubtless gratified him in certain moods.

Boston's star critical duet sang any way but harmoniously; in fact, their natures, their backgrounds, and their written opinions clashed as dissonantly as the forbidding new "atonal" music just starting to set people's teeth on edge in Vienna. Hale's *curriculum vitae* marched openly along from birth in Norwich, Vermont, through private school in New York City, to Yale (where he twice suffered expulsion but managed to pass his exam after five months' absence) and thence to music, which he chose after fulfilling a promise to his father to read for the law.

Not so Parker's. "His days were confounded, it seems," wrote McCord, "between New England where he was born, England, where he went to school, Harvard, where he ranked with the class of 1890, New York, where he began as a critic, Boston, where he lives, and Germany, where he intends to die." At every point in this shuttle between goals, Parker absorbed the arts and cultivated his own idiosyncrasies.

Hale, who studied organ, piano, and composition in Germany and Paris and practiced as an organist and chorus director, represented the professional, a status which Parker furiously envied but could never attain. It has been said of H. T. P., even by his stoutest admirers, that he was virtually a musical illiterate, unable, for example, to tell the difference between a major and a minor chord and certainly lacking the ability to read notes. Still he knew music "from the outside, if not from the in," acquiring a corpulent body of information. Furthermore, his instincts were sound, more so than Hale's, and he labored under fewer blind spots. His graduation to criticism had come through journalism. The city editor of the New York *Globe*, "knowing Parker hung around the right end of theaters," sent him to cover *Cavalleria Rusticana* in place of the paper's regular critic. Thereafter music and theater fell under his scratching pen to the end of his days.

Whatever planets in their courses conjoined in the year 1854 to bring forth at least three brilliant music critics—Hale, Finck, and Krehbiel— a dark star presided over 1934, when the lives of both Hale and Parker were cut off. Parker went first, expiring in harness as he would have wished, felled by pneumonia incurred in the labor of bringing the Metropolitan Opera back to Boston after its long absence. "Honest opera returned last evening," the *Transcript* proudly proclaimed on the afternoon of April 3. But these were only Parker's sentiments, not his words; the diminutive fire-breather had died four days previously. Hale lingered six months after his arch-rival. He had ceased active work the year before, and with his wife (Irene Baumgrass, whom he had married in 1884 when both were students in Berlin), he moved into the very stronghold where Parker had held forth for years—the staid Hotel Vendome on Dartmouth Street and Commonwealth Avenue. This hostelry has been dubbed by the more irreverent set as "God's Waiting Room," because so many of Boston's more or less affluent elders choose it as an antechamber to Heaven.

Today's critics, with drastically curtailed space, would blanch at the amount of sheer labor these earlier Boston men undertook as a matter of course. Parker could fill three twenty-one-inch columns of closely set seven- or eight-point type with an opera review and still count on a column for concerts or theater; while Hale used one word to his colleague's five, yet matched him in consumed space for his more varied output. McCord estimated that H. T. P. through thirty years had turned out (and seen printed!) the equivalent of three hundred full-sized novels, or close to a novel a month.

Hale's scrapbooks reveal a comparative prolixity, yet the bulk of his *oeuvre* and his everlasting claim to fame will remain the program notes for the Boston Symphony, which he began in 1901 and continued until his retirement. Olin Downes, forever his disciple, in spite of later renown as *the* music critic of *The New York Times*, wrote: "If only one work could be saved from the English literature on music, we would vote for the preservation of the thirty-odd volumes of program notes which Mr. Hale has compiled."

The newspaper hand in those days—as in these—also did Sunday pieces, magazine articles, and coverage of out-of-town events, but everywhere in larger proportion. Furthermore, each of these two men supervised what his assistants wrote and remained sole arbiter of the overall contents of his department. His functions have been split in at least two parts in Boston as in other metropolises today.

Parker's was the only description of the "social" side of Boston life the *Transcript* permitted. This mirror of all that was good, true, pure, and beautiful in Boston never demeaned itself to the "social column" level, subscribing to—or perhaps having promulgated—the tenet that a real lady's name appeared in the public press only three times: at birth, on her wedding, and after her death. Charles Alexander, for many years head of the department that would be called "Society" in any other paper, was the original of the story later attributed to *The New York Times*. Covering a First Family funeral, he was admitted by a maid, who announced to her sorrowing mistress, "There are some reporters to see you, Ma'am, and a gentleman from the *Transcript*."

Let other and lesser sheets scramble for low gossip; the *Transcript* printed only what Proper Bostonians believed was fit to print, whether from conviction, or as Charles W. Morton has recently suggested in the *Atlantic Monthly*, from a peculiar kind of inertia. This left the field wide open to less dainty—or as some preferred to say, less snobbish—journals, who made the most of it. The *Globe* used the tame and not altogether representative heading of "Table Gossip" for its hundreds of anonymous daily and Sunday items, while other papers often allowed by-lines or catchy pseudonyms to its "lady reporters," several of whom did a flourishing interview trade as well.

Hale's talent and knowledge spread far beyond the boundaries of music and drama to cover human life in its highest and lowest degrees. The anonymous author of a column called "As the World Wags," he let his fancy roam over the world, quoting appositely from quaint and ancient authors such as Artemus Ward or Sam Johnson, or reaching forward to Gertrude Stein. An intellectual rectitude lay at the core of his lightest thought, as a resilient spine upholds the delicate fronds of a feather.

Bostonians waited eagerly for the adventures of Herkimer Johnson, an alter ego Hale created to comment on men and affairs. This eccentric philosopher was devoted to writing a great work to be called "Man as a Political and Social Beast," to be published in elephant folio and by subscription only. The fate of this tome concerned Boston for many years. Thus Hale gently comported himself, to the delight of his public. His humor, clean and bright, seldom curdled to satire, but he could demolish a fledgling pianist, who should never have been allowed at the starting point, with four words: "She consumed valuable time."

Once in a long while, Parker would limit himself to comparable succinctness. He wrote a tiny paragraph about the recital of Ganna Walska, the Polish-American dilettante, making clear that the lady possessed limited vocal resources and ending with Ethel Barrymore's famous line: "That's all there is; there isn't any more." He could be epigrammatical as well. After the discovery that the conductor Henry Hadley had been in the middle of a Boston Symphony-versus-union scrap in 1920, Parker tossed this off: "A kinder fate would have given Mr. Hadley less talent for publicity and more for music-making."

Hale loved to jibe at his New York colleagues and found occasion to do so when a Manhattan paper listed the attendants at church "as though a reception at some lion-hunter's residence or floorwalkers' ball." Was this disgusting? he asked himself. No, for it might encourage church-going. The thrust went a little deeper than appeared on the surface: Hale may have been twitting the Boston papers for their respectful listing of the guests at every first-class funeral.

When W. J. Henderson gravely prognosticated in the New York *Sun* that Boston's new opera would make inroads on Symphony loyalty, the two Boston critics reacted characteristically.

Hale dismissed the threat with mockery: "Will the Boston Symphony Orchestra be as one playing in the wilderness? Is it possible that Symphony Hall will be a desolate house in which wild beasts of the islands shall cry? that owls shall dwell there and satyrs shall dance there; that her time is near and her days shall not be prolonged?"

Parker took the challenge literally. He huffily retorted that Bostonians had found enough interest in the Metropolitan in 1907–08 and in Hammerstein's company in 1909 to fill the Boston Theatre for nearly every performance, without damage to the Symphony audiences—which rather missed the point.

In a city that always boasted a high tolerance of eccentrics (taking its cue possibly from the original English model), Hale and Parker, the latter especially, belonged without question or quibble. Even when *The New York Times* offered Hale a much higher salary than he received from the Boston *Herald,* he refused, believing that Boston air nourished the individualist as New York's tended to submerge him. Parker displayed more idiosyncrasies in manner and dress—McCord described him as a "small, fierce-eyed individual, of graying mustache and adequate age, tweedish clothing, Habig fedora, huge bent bamboo cane, and a German cavalry overcoat made for him with belt and saddle-split by a military tailor in Wiesbaden"—but Hale's personal badge, a flowing bow tie of either red or black, in later years occasionally enlivened by polka dots (some said depending on his charitable or uncharitable mood), distinguished him as surely. Both men "dressed" for the opera: H. T. P. in a red-lined opera cloak of what McCord calls a "Parker sack"; Hale in white tie and tails, a slim, tall figure, reminding his young assistant, Elinor Hughes (now drama critic of the *Herald*), of a grand duke. Parker perched like "a small and bitter gargoyle above the Brahmin sea," wrote McCord, in the first row of the first balcony of Symphony Hall, almost invariably alone in one of the conventional pair of critic's seats. Hale, usually accompanied by his wife, occasionally by a crony, reigned serenely a few rows behind. Parker had a habit, "a Continental method, and rather objectionable," said McCord, of applauding by bringing his cane into sharp contact with the floor. "An accurate myth relates that once he brought it down on the toes of Mrs. Jack Gardner, with whom he was sharing a box. The fireworks which followed will surely survive them both."

The inviolate perquisites and privileges of the men on the aisle have been periodically and abortively challenged by some theater manager who bars his door to an offending scribe, or by some businesslike impresario or sponsor who can't get it through his head that a valuable seat should be occupied by a freeloader's overcoat and hat instead of a warm, breathing—and paying—body. Eben Jordan learned his lesson before the Boston Opera curtain went up. The incident was recalled in a letter to the Boston *Herald* many years later from Arthur Wilson, who had come to Boston first with Russell's San Carlo opera in the press department and filled the vacuum in the *Globe*'s entertainment pages when the opera house seemed likely to open without a music critic on the paper so long and intimately connected with Jordan. Wilson proved to be no tame pet, to the surprise of both Jordan and Russell, but reviewed "according to his lights," which included a knowledge of voices and an honest approach to quality. The closing of Thompson's Spa, a newspaperman's snuggery across the street from the old *Globe*, occasioned Wilson's letter. In the days just before the opera's opening, he saw H. T. P. and Charles Howard (drama editor of the *Globe*) in earnest conversation at Thompson's, "Mr. Howard listening with that informed gentility ever characteristic of him, and H. T. P. more agitated by the second, and presently arriving at such a feverish state, his head bobbing with rhythmic precision and mounting vigor, and the ash from his ever pendulous cigarette spraying his food, that he had all but fallen off the stool on which he was sitting. Charley Howard later told me what the spark was that ignited the outburst.

"The new Boston Opera House was about to open. Mr. Jordan had sent word to the newspapers that he saw no need or reason to send two tickets (fixed custom in the theaters since coinage of the phrase 'Two on the aisle') for the critics for each performance. Mr. Jordan said when he sent a buyer on a mission for his store, he did not include transportation or accommodations for the buyer's wife."

The merchant's generosity in larger matters soon filtered down as he became disabused of any parallel between the mercantile and the amusement worlds. Parker, though indignant on principle, needed the extra seat less than any of his confrères. So seldom was it occupied that when he turned up on rare occasions with a female companion, the knowing part of the audience could hardly credit its vision. One observer remembers the stately procession through the foyer: Parker leading by the edge of his pince-nez, doubled over in the posture that silhouetted him unmistakably, talking, talking incessantly (for once *mirabile dictu* minus his cigarette, to which McCord attributed propulsive powers as fuel), never looking (it would have had to be upward and a little backward) at his companion, who towered two heads above him. She, imperturbable and silent, stalked at his side, looking straight ahead, never at Parker, never smiling. Parker never introduced her to anyone; she remained one of the minor mysteries surrounding the small oracle. More often he was "publicly alone," said McCord. "If you should dare to address him, he will answer briefly, cigarette in mouth, his head bobbing emphatic emphasis behind a cloud of volcanic ash. His manner does not suggest long interviews. An infallible ability to make his first comment sound like his last produces an awkward silence not easily broken by anything short of departure."

The record does not show that Parker was publicly thanked for his contribution to any artist's career, though he may have pointed out the path to many an aspirant. However, mixed with the awe in which Hale was held by the contestants parading over Boston's stages was an occasional ray of gratitude. Philip the Great seems to have managed to a degree to maintain a friendly relationship with a few of the artists he reviewed; his Olympian heights allowed him that latitude, generally denied one who sits in judgment on his fellows' attributes. He even attended "parties," a dispensation Parker never allowed himself. Marguerite D'Alvarez's thanks are shown in her autobiography; to them may be added the appreciation of the pianist George Copeland, who came back to Boston after the freedom of Spain and Italy to incur the danger of atrophy in his father's shadow—Copeland Senior seemed the "latest George Apley" to his son. Hale, at first unconvinced of the pianist's artistry, allowed Mrs. Jack Gardner to bring them together, and thereafter listened to Copeland with understanding and pleasure. He gave some good advice: "I'll drive you out," he threatened. "You mustn't be localized like so-and-so" (naming a Boston pianist who remained a medium-sized frog in a small puddle all of his life). "I learned more from Philip Hale than from any teacher," vowed Copeland.

Still, Hale could be heard to say that the more he heard music, the more he hated it, perhaps sincerely, or perhaps only from the mischievous desire to shock. At that, a successor often quoted him as vowing that he wearied of concerts long before losing his taste for drama—if, indeed, he ever did.

Critics today as yesterday in their little nests seldom agree (which either invigorates or infuriates their followers), but today they maintain total silence in their professional showcases about the persons of their competitors. In other and more carefree years, this rule of tacit togetherness occasionally was rent wide open. A dislike of almost Dr. Fell-ian proportions grew up between Parker and the young Olin Downes. The elder man once leapt into print against the younger, reprinting Downes' paean to Toscanini for his "revelatory" performance of the Prelude to *Parsifal,* and adding: "Then came the ominous recollection of [Karl Muck at] Bayreuth." He went on to quote verbatim Downes' awkward attempt to crawl out of what amounted to *lèse majesté* in those days.

However much a monkey he may have made of his junior, Parker lost the last word. The post of music critic on *The New York Times* fell vacant in 1923 when Richard Aldrich retired. Aldrich sought Hale, who declined but in turn recommended Downes. The young Olin went from seventy-five dollars a week in Boston to an eventual ten thousand dollars annually in New York. This was almost more than Parker could bear. He confided to Warren Storey Smith, who had become his assistant in 1919 and in 1924 would succeed Downes on the *Post:* "Downes won't last. He's always late with his copy, and no one can read it anyway."

This from Parker seems a plain case of black pot and kettle. Notoriously the *Transcript* critic clung to his own crabbed hand long after lesser men had taken to typewriting. Only the *Transcript* would have tolerated it. Perhaps fewer than a dozen people could puzzle out his longhand; the paper kept a typographer long after his retirement was due merely because he could confidently set Parker's copy. Even then, "the types" sometimes betrayed him, and strange exoticisms emerged in the early editions. Parker caught one of these at the galley-proof stage, by Smith's account. His "fire charm" had been translated as "fire alarm." Every so often, McCord relates, "an undertone of talk about a typewriter ends with a sample of Parker's worst sent up to the chief. But he looks at it, and without reading it says: 'Anybody can read that!' and there's an end to it."

Hale also was attacked by H. T. P., who called down curses on "old men at Symphony Hall," referring to a review of Mahler's *Lied von der Erde*, which Hale lightly said contained "melodies in folk-song vein." Parker complained of "clichés old men remember whether or not they fit the case in point." He was, after all, some fifteen years Hale's junior.

Neither was Hale immune to the temptation to criticize a confrère (though in private). "Who's the damn' fool on the *Globe*?" he asked. It was Penfield Roberts by that time, and the opinion in question was a diatribe against what Koussevitzky, "the terrible Russian," had done to Rimsky-Korsakoff's *Shéhérazade*. Why, Koussevitzky had made it sound like a page out of Arabian Nights, fumed Roberts, ignorantly preferring Muck's "impression of stylized figures on a Chinese vase."

Hale's Germanophobia extended beyond Wagner even to Bach, whose music he described as "counterpoint by the yard—you can begin anywhere and end anywhere; a sausage factory." He was, of course, known for suggesting a sign in Symphony Hall, to read: "Exit in Case of Brahms." Later in life he mellowed somewhat and must be credited with warm and perceptive reviews of Richard Strauss' *Salome* and *Elektra* at a time when other pens dripped horror and vitriol. Parker, on the contrary, appreciated even the exalted intricacies of Bruckner and Mahler, and was one of the first honorary members of the Bruckner Society.

The temptation that assails the best of critics on occasion—to write a review before the event and take a chance on confirming it by telephone or perhaps not confirming it at all—once nearly led Hale into trouble. In his scrapbook for the year 1912–13, a review of the fourth performance of *Louise*, spelling out each character, is marked "Fake!" in Hale's own handwriting. It plainly bears his printed signature. No one will ever know what circumstances dictated the deception. Things sometimes get too much even for a large staff.

As writers the two men differed greatly. Parker himself thought that his singular style went back to Latin and to the best of Francis Parkman, but its peculiarities defy accurate comparison. "Architecturally, each review comes smartingly to the point," McCord explains, quoting Parker as saying: "I like the slow building up of the argument, bringing the thing into focus." This sense of slow, cumulative motion, as of an animal stalking its prey, gathering its forces, then pouncing in one lightning stroke, is reminiscent of Henry James in essence. The reader is compelled to traverse paragraphs that begin and end at the same relative points; only the language, the similes, the adjectives, are different. To quote Parker therefore becomes a question of alternative methods: either quoting him entire, a sheer impossibility, or choosing which set of descriptions one finds most apt and telling. He does not "excerpt" as well as Hale, with the latter's open progression of thought and brevity of sentence. Hale's mind clearly worked through his lean, pointed prose. "Terse, idiomatic sentences were characteristic of the clarity of his thinking and the quick and penetrating processes of his mind," Downes wrote after his death. Innumerable examples of this felicity of expression can be found in his opera reviews.

The bon vivant, the traveler who "by synthetic accident of foreign clothes, tri-lingual facility, and the Continental manner is assumed in London to be a Frenchman, in Paris a German, and in Berlin an Englishman," who journeyed alone and the faster for it into legend, Parker remains unique. As McCord predicted: "Not until one tries to fill his shoes will Boston realize the cosmic particle she harbors."

Equally lofty on a pinnacle of scholarship, genuine humanity, and sheer musical competence, the proud Hale, twice honored by academia with honorary degrees, selected for a scholarship award of Sigma Delta Chi, professional journalistic fraternity, dubbed by Carl Engle, the musicologist and editor of *Musical Quarterly*, the "Eaglet of Seventy" in 1924, flew his banners brilliantly into the third decade of the century.

The two men, so different, each the salt of the earth (which too often found its way into the wounds of the lesser talents put up for their judgment), gave Boston a character no other city could boast. Giants there were indeed, in those days.

Act III

12

ALL GAUL
(1911–12)

Even though the crowning achievement of *Pelléas et Mélisande* did not occur until January, a distinctly Gallic atmosphere pervaded the Boston Opera Company's third season from the opening strains of Saint-Saëns's *Samson et Dalila*, on November 27, 1911. Italy offered only one new contender this year, Alberto Franchetti's *Germania*, a thickly political drama which the Metropolitan had introduced to America two seasons previously as a vehicle for Caruso, who had created the role of Frederick Loewe at La Scala in 1902. Zenatello sang the Teutonic hero's part in Boston with his usual fine discrimination. Melis and Amato (later Polese) completed the amorous-cum-political triangle. The opera won grudging praise for its spectacular qualities (Russell had borrowed the Met's scenery, which came originally from La Scala), but Hale expressed the wish that some other Italian had written the music. Franchetti, he said, was rich in the world's goods, but poor in musical invention, another instance of the divine average.

Numerically the French works were outranked eleven to fourteen by the Italians, while two from the pen of Debussy (in addition to *Pelléas*) struck very delicate notes indeed, yet the introduction of *Samson*, and of *Mignon*, *Thaïs*, and *Werther* to the repertoire, while *Carmen*, *Faust*, *Habañera*, and *Manon* held their place, showed Henry Russell's clear intent to favor the French tricolor, particularly in the realm of novelty.

Perhaps it was the static qualities of *Samson et Dalila*, always caught between the two stools of opera and oratorio, that delivered Boston's

115

third opening night over to comparative dullness. Or it may have been only the natural reaction, a sort of "third time's a charm" effect. Little had changed in the appearance of the house, except added posters neatly framed beside the doors, several new mirrors in the cloakrooms, and more signs about the warning bells. The two intermingled lines of intermission promenaders in the grand tier foyer barely moved, so great was the crush. Although sumptuous as before, the toilettes appeared more matronly. The enthusiasm, too, seemed middle-aged, the throng apparently deciding to assume its most austerely formal aspect, from which no happening on the stage could jar it into spontaneous self-forgetfulness.

Few tenors could create the illusion of the strong-gentle Samson, Philip Hale believed. He remembered Antonio Ceppi, a man of giant frame, who gave the impression of tossing vocal cannon balls before his great voice became tamed. Francesco Tamagno, the first operatic Samson in New York, with the Metropolitan in 1895, radiated great strength. The slighter Zenatello could not measure up in robustness, although his virile voice suited the music well. He gave way only once in the half-dozen performances; in February he seems to have had a short respite from the rigorous schedule that prescribed thirty-two performances of twelve operas for him, including the new *Germania*. The one-time substitute in *Samson*, a relatively inexperienced tenor named Ferdinand De Potter, plodded through two seasons very much under the twin shadows of Edmond Clément and Zenatello.

It fell to Maria Gay's bad luck that after working hard to subdue her natural boisterousness and divest the role of Dalila of "Carmenisms," she should be totally eclipsed by the sensuous charm of Jeanne Gerville-Réache, who unveiled a Dalila at the final two performances that has never been forgotten. She had sung it with Hammerstein in New York, but this was Boston's first acquaintance with her Philistine siren. So great did Hale think her interpretation that he placed it in a precious gallery containing only Jean De Reszke's Roméo, Milka Ternina's Isolde, Fernando De Lucia's Canio, Emma Calvé's early Carmen, and Victor Maurel's Iago. It seemed reasonable to ask that the temptation which betrayed Samson be at least intelligible to the spectators. This Dalila's voice alone would lead Samson astray with its sumptuously beautiful low and middle tones, a texture that one worshiper compared to soft and yielding pile. But in addition, her facial expression, her gestures, attitudes, nuances of sensuous excitement, intensity of passion, made her irresistible to Samson, as well as to the critics, and, without much doubt, to at least a portion of the Boston audience. This lovely French contralto also sang two Brangänes and then vouchsafed her treasurable art to Boston no more, although she responded to an emergency call, substituting for Gay as Carmen in New Haven, a thankless bit of kindness, for the college town refused to admire her. What New Haven didn't know was that this latest gypsy, quietly married to Dr. G. Gibier-Rambeaud, director of the Pasteur Institute in New York, had gallantly answered Russell's distress signal in spite of being in an interesting, not to say, delicate, condition. She claimed that her Don José, irked by the absence of his own spouse, mishandled her on the New Haven stage. Zenatello and Gay, fiercely loyal and loving, preferred to act together in their favorite roles. When Gay drew Clément for two Carmens this season, he vowed that never again would he be her José: she was the rough one. He kept his word, for Calvé was assigned to the final performance, after Gay and Zenatello got together just once. But under the circumstances, it is easy to excuse Gerville-Réache for a certain reticence in her stage action. She died shortly after, in 1915 at the untimely age of thirty-three. At the height of her triumphs, she passed along some unusual advice to young lady singers: begin modestly, even in a musical comedy chorus if you can't get European training, and do not conceal your laziness under the mark of pride.

Dinh Gilly, the Algerian baritone who had appeared the previous season in *Carmen* and *Manon*, sang the High Priest at the opening only, being succeeded by the unloved Jean Riddez. Gilly's voice seemed greater in volume this year and his diction remained a constant delight. The final performance of the opera called on Maurice Renaud's impressive art. As if stepping out of a canvas by Rembrandt, an old man with a white beard like Moses', a grave and yellowed face, fiery and deep-set eyes, shaggy black brows, the lights and shadows of storm playing around his formidable figure, Renaud characterized the Priest by bearing and appearance alone. Mardones' Abimelech never changed: a personage so in the oratorio spirit that the only appropriate costume seemed a swallowtail coat and white cravat. Edward Lankow, at his debut as the Old Hebrew, showed a true bass voice of noble quality, reminding Hale of Plançon, especially in its upper range. A press agent had sought to shroud the young American in mystery, but Hale revealed that he had taken the name of his teacher and foster mother, Anna Lankow, for work abroad, and that was all there was to know.

Regardless of its other components, *Samson et Dalila* offered a spectacle that should have crowded the house on its own merits. The real beauty of staging and costumes filled the eye at every turn. Boston's technicians, backed by the German designers, succeeded overwhelmingly in the crucial scene of the temple's destruction. As Samson pushed mightily against the pillars, there was a moment of sudden darkness, during which the crashes and shrieks died into wailings, the air seemed filled with falling pillars, beams, dust, debris, and din. As the clouds cleared, the ruins showed ghastly in the glare of a pale light.

Only the ballet shattered the illusion. The dancers' technique showed insecurity, and it would have been well to eliminate the "Kiralfy Kick" (a timely reference not clear today), thought Hale. Dolores Galli, the première danseuse, showed skill and deserved more applause than she got, but Maria Gay should have displayed less valor and not attempted a *pas seul* in the priestesses' dance, which hardly offered the opportunity for a mild *danse du ventre* on the part of the leading lady.

As if to partake of two worlds, Caplet showed *Samson* in its sober oratorio dress for one act at a Sunday concert in December, where Maria Claessens offered little competition to other Dalilas.

Three Massenet operas in any one year at any opera house outside of Paris added up to a virtual Massenet Festival. The Metropolitan then and later never ventured beyond two at a time—a *Manon* and a *Thaïs* or *Werther* or *Navarraise*, a *Thaïs* and a *Don Quichotte*. Chicago, in the regime just beginning, favored all of these, plus *Cendrillon* and *Le Jongleur de Notre Dame*, the last-named a heritage from Hammerstein, who even produced *Hérodiade*, *Grisélidis*, and *Sapho* in a season with three others more familiar. Excitement over Massenet's melodies died down after Garden's impersonations no longer breathed life into them, so that *Manon* remains the one consistent visitor in American repertoires. Russell came out with a triptych in 1911–12, comprising *Thaïs*, *Werther*, and *Manon*, the first two new to the company. The French composer never outranked Verdi, of course, who was represented by six works this same year, but he came close to Puccini's four.

Hiram K. Moderwell, spelling Parker on the *Transcript*, tossed off a contemptuous word or two about *Thaïs*, insisting that it belonged to the category of operas that were made by degrading books. The music, better than most of Massenet's to his mind, still did no justice to Anatole France's *Thaïs*. Hale, touching on the edge of a famous literary controversy, remarked cynically that France might have said with Charles Reade (who had been accused of plundering Erasmus and others for *The Cloister and the Hearth*): "I milked a hundred cows; the cream is my own." At least the Boston critics pronounced no moral judgment on the opera as Henry Krehbiel had done in New York.

Considering this opera to lie on the dark side of Massenet's talent, Hale thought that only Mary Garden and Maurice Renaud might make it tolerable, even engrossing. Fortunately for Boston's relatively inexperienced audience, cuts were made in the score. Not the Divine Mary, but a singer of tinier lyric achievements (although her attractions were said to be considerable as a coquette), inspired the introduction of *Thaïs*. Zina Brozia, who had sung in Brussels and Paris (and who was recommended to Russell by Max Léon, a French banker and a European member of the Boston Opera board of directors), made her Boston debut as the Alexandrian courtesan, leaving faintly agreeable, if not lasting, impressions. She conceived the character as a *petite femme*, amiable, amorous, vexed as a child when the Monk did not at once fall at her feet, easily persuaded to abandon the world when assured that she would be beautiful forever. She did not rely on undue bareness to excite admiration and compel applause. Still, as Hale pointed out, while a prudish Thaïs would be grotesque, one who put her trust wholly in her curves would soon become a bore.

Mme. Brozia was the sole Manon of the year, a role better adapted for her somewhat bourgeois charms, which extracted some passionate moments from the scene where she exhorts Des Grieux to return to the fleshpots from the monastery. She fitted well with the American conception of *Manon*, Parker thought, dismissing the opera as Laodicean, one that never blows hot and never quite blows cold across the auditorium. Perhaps some day, he sighed, a vivifying performance would arrive. Meanwhile, Bostonians, as other audiences, had to be content not to see the Cours La Reine scene, which even Mary Garden wished to omit, unkind wags averring that she would find its music too dramatic for her scope.

Neither Brozia's Mimi, who asserted an aura of poverty in a gown of flame-colored changeable taffeta (although she revealed vocal excellences hitherto unexpected of her), nor her Marguerite, who reached heights of sophistication unparalleled in the house (the jewels may have seemed "rich and rare," but assuredly presented no novelty to this mondaine), won her a return ticket to Boston. As the half-goddess departed, the real thing came in. Mary Garden finally appeared as Marguerite, at the opposite pole from the "shallow flirt" Brozia had portrayed; she also stepped into two *Thaïs* performances to bestow largesse on that part of the world that considered her to be the one and only after Sybil Sanderson, the American girl with the "Eiffel Tower notes," for whom Massenet wrote the opera. But to Hale's chagrin, the diva failed in her mission. He could find no reason why Athanael should be disturbed by this female. Garden's exhibition might have suited a church fair or any New England town hall. The prima donna's art had always expressed sensuality without vulgarity—Swinburne's "noble and nude and antique"—but this reticence carried discretion to the point of ennui.

Russell cunningly took advantage of the simultaneous presence of a half-dozen reliable French stars to put on one of his stunts, similar to the juxtaposition of the two *Manons* the previous year. He scheduled a Saturday matinee and an evening *Thaïs* on March 16, keeping the orchestra, under Caplet, and the secondary singers as the fulcrum on which teetered the respective virtues of Garden, Renaud, and Clément and those of Melis, Riddez, and De Potter. Only a look is required to divine where the weight lay. The matinee carried the day. It is perhaps unfair to compare Garden, the incomparable, with Melis, who nevertheless had found Italians warmly approbative of her Thaïs, and who in Boston satisfied reasonable curiosity about why she could be the idol of Alexandria. (Hale suggested that the two early performances might have benefited from her presence rather than Brozia's, and Arthur Wilson of the *Globe* found moderately heated words for her face, jewels, and upper voice.) But the evening males were not to be mentioned in the same breath with the afternoon's. Renaud's Athanael belonged to the ages while Clément brought well-nigh inexhaustible resourcefulness to the thankless role of Nicias. Even showing the fatigue probably induced by too much singing (he had given sixteen performances of seven roles to date, as well as an exacting song recital), the tenor sustained his elegant bearing. Against these two *exquises,* the evening's heroes—Riddez, whose voice lacked every saving grace and who barely defended his franchise as an actor, and De Potter, who seemed not to have ripened in either voice or action—could not hope to prevail. Both must have chafed at the enforced comparison.

Critics and spectators at the various showings of *Thaïs* uncovered minor nuggets, which gilded several news columns as well as Back Bay dinner conversation. It was with the December 6 performance that the predictions of an exalted career for Evelyn Scotney first arose. As La Charmeuse, a voluptuous dancer, she was the surprise and delight of the evening (Parker's very words), showing promise of an interesting coloratura voice. Hale, though dismissing the shenanigans at Thaïs' party as more suited to operetta, later appraised the Australian's voice as an unusual one, extraordinarily pure and crystalline in its upper reaches, excellent in florid passages, and possessing a trill uncommonly good for her age. But a peculiar childish quality in its middle tones began to bore and irritate him toward the end of the season. Russell capitalized on the public's interest to give Scotney the three leading coloratura roles, Lucia, Gilda, and Violetta. From the second-string critics, and from Olin Downes, who by this time had excavated a secure niche for himself as the *Post's* musical authority, nothing but praise showered upon the handsome girl. When she took her turn at the same three roles the following season, Downes found that she had developed even further. An occasional piping, childish note still occurred, but less frequently in a rounder, more sensuous tone.

Thaïs also furnished a showcase for the talents of an enchanting pair of young singers. At that stage of their development, Bernice Fisher and Jeska Swartz would be called "starlets" today. The petite blond soprano and the equally tiny brunette mezzo had graduated from the Dew Fairy and Sandman respectively to the leading roles in *Hänsel und Gretel*. Fisher, whom Russell had discovered during the company's visit to Chicago, also progressed from Frasquita to Micaela between the *Carmen* of 1910–11 and that of 1911–12, a decided step upward. It was good to see Micaela as a wistful and timid child, not as a mature opera singer conscious of condescension to the part, said Parker, complimenting her. Fisher had also embodied one of the sympathetic characters in each of Converse's two operas, and exemplified the perfect Yniold in *Pelléas et Mélisande*.

Jeska Swartz carried the responsibility of a steady, well-favored member of the company on her gently sloping shoulders—or perhaps more justly, on the prettiest pair of legs in sight. Diffident to a degree, the youthful Albany singer found herself, to her embarrassment, constantly in demand for "trouser parts," and so began with a *Rigoletto* Page, later attaining a Siébel in her first season and retaining both roles for several years. Hänsel and Frédéric in *Mignon* also fell to her. She donned skirts with relief, even for the lesser opportunities of Kate Pinkerton and the Javotte of *Manon,* but by her third season, she had been allowed to assume the kimono of Suzuki. She reverted to type in the short pants of Le Petit Poucet in *La Forêt Bleue,* the novelty of 1912–13. Then *Thaïs* offered further consolation in costume. As Myrtale, one of the two slaves of the wealthy Nicias, Swartz appeared at the first performance in clinging drapery that virtually vanished in certain lights. As her partner, Crobyle, Fisher is supposed to have thought Jeska's display indecent. Whether it was a prank on the electrician's part, or a deliberate piece of stage business, Myrtale got all of the limelight—from behind. One newspaper, always willing to blow up a trifle into tasty headlines, reported that "Songbirds Row over Near-Nature Gown," attributing righteous indignation to the dainty Fisher.

Both girls displayed a capacity for true and enduring friendship, a rarity in the opera rosters of yesterday and perhaps even today. Swartz affectionately called Fisher "Peanut" and teased her constantly. Before the curtain, no matter what the opera, one would murmur to the other, "You love me, Hänsel?" and the other invariably replied, "I love you, Gretel!" Swartz often became the victim of rather cruel teasing from Russell and his business manager, Ralph Flanders, who sensed a susceptible subject. Russell could unnerve the prim little mezzo by calling after her, as she left his office, "Your blouse is unbuttoned in back!" She would blush and fumble and hurry out the door, but beard him just as fiercely and independently the next time. Russell finally acknowledged her matured talent: after her Suzuki he said: "Little Swartz, you are an artist—like a figure on a fan—I have to recognize it."

Thomas's *Mignon* brought solace to the graybeards, who, as Hale noted, thought *Lucia* rather too showy, and *Trovatore* and *Rigoletto* rather too robust. They liked *Traviata,* these Boston oldsters, but it took either *Mignon* or Flotow's *Martha* to stir them genuinely. They met at intermissions and compared the performance with those in the seventies and eighties. They had, after all, heard Nilsson, Kellogg, Roze, Cary, Hauk, Farrar, and even one ill-fated attempt by Calvé. Tonight, *Mignon* seemed not quite the same. It wasn't that any wrong attached to Fely Dereyne,

Edmond Clément, and Léon Rothier—and certainly none to the breezy Luisa Tetrazzini, who was appearing as Philine for the first time in America (incidentally singing in Italian). No: it only seemed that even *Mignon* could not escape the new operatic trends. Such excellent scenery and fine chorus singing certainly were not expected. And as for the acting! Dereyne's Mignon was a charming, sincere, living being, not a classic tradition. Frédéric in the person of Jeska Swartz both sang well and kept within the action. Whoever had previously thought twice about the text? Yet here was Clément, with his perfect diction and an appearance so authentic that even the youngsters were impressed. One old lady was heard to quaver: "We never really thought of how they looked or behaved; we only cared how they sang."

Only Lothario (Rothier) quite reassured this portion of the audience (also winning Hale's vote for inclusion in his gallery of operatic bores), since even Tetrazzini for once touched Philine with little strokes of acting. Backstage she had giggled at Swartz's Frédéric: "This leetle boy is supposed to be in love with me? Like a peanut next to a mountain." And had gone most good-humoredly through the stage director's final instructions. This genuinely traditional prima donna gave the galleries their meat, however, throwing brilliant notes at them during the waltz and what Hale called the hopelessly old-fashioned, dreary Polonaise. The distinguished critic maintained a lonely eminence in this opinion; the tide of public approval ran against him.

One more new French work of impressive proportions remained to the season—the *Werther* that completed the Massenet trio. The opera house did for this first Boston performance all that could be done, except provide a curiosity and liking for such a piece written in such a style. It was obvious to Parker that few cared for an opera that runs steadily in a vein of sentimental longing and melancholy and that sets no more than a pretty little genre picture on stage. "Usually we like our opera big and hot," he concluded wryly.

Still, to many the settings appeared charming, with suggestive German touches of homely clutter, then of appropriate mistiness, and of the mournful solitude of Werther's bare lodging, where he prepared to make an end to passion and to himself. The choice of Maria Gay for Charlotte could possibly be justified on the grounds that the intelligent singer-actress always stood ready to learn, and indeed proved that she could, displaying a surprising tenderness and nuance in her big voice, and needless to say, full opulence where it was required. Skillful facial disguise and costuming made her Charlotte fairly plausible, if somewhat full-blown. But no fault could be found with Clément, who fully satisfied the imagination as Werther. The Met had not sent its 1910 *Werther,* with Farrar and Clément, to Boston, so this was the city's first opportunity to judge one of its favorite tenors in a new role. Presenting a truly romantic figure, with curly blond locks, a full, melancholy face, sorrowful and sentimental glance; ruffles at his wrists, his flowing tie and sugarloaf hat the very essence of poetic dress, he stirred the gentler emotions. The baritone quality so pervasive in his voice added sensitive and shadowed color.

For three of the five performances of *Carmen* that Clément graced during the year, he was privileged to plunge his dagger into the breast of the most famous Carmen of all time: Emma Calvé. The aging diva (she was fifty-four, but would live to eighty-four) emerged from her preoccupation with concertizing to confer an added cachet to Russell's company as she had done for Hammerstein in 1907. Hale's recapitulation of the situation contained the most poignance, for the critic had followed Calvé from the first fullness of beauty, the first vividly dramatic portrayal in 1894, through the success that Victor Hugo said is hideous, and that certainly had proved injurious to her—and then back again to this resurrection of very nearly first principles. Her early Carmen was broadly conceived, yet abounded in subtle detail. Then, as exaggerations accrued, her spontaneity turned to capriciousness, her plastic art stiffened into caricature. She blatantly flouted the dignified conductor, Felix Mottl (who never should have been assigned the opera anyway) in rhythms and movements, so that he frantically semaphored to her from the pit in scene after scene, only to see her laughing openly in his face when she attempted a high note and missed. The last act often resembled a rout on stage rather than a bullfight off; many an exasperated tenor wished his rubber dagger were real steel.

Now what could Boston expect? Here she was, making her entrance with some of the old swagger. Yet there crept in a singular lack of ease— she had, after all, not sung the role for several years. Her intonation was uncertain; her stage business meager. She took odd liberties with the music and text. Yet the peculiar and unique timbre of the voice remained; the incomparable diction remained; the unique vocal art remained.

In the second act, she became more herself, and at the same time, more Carmen. She colored her tones with irresistible dramatic effect. The spell held till the last. The voice still was the wonderful instrument of expression; it still caressed, enchanted, played at will on the nerves and heart. This was Calvé's Carmen in the year 1912.

That young people were drawn by the diva's magnetism was attested to by the number of librettos sold. Old-timers knew the story by heart, and the libretto boys counted it lucky if twenty copies went. This afternoon, the house fairly rustled with the turning of leaves. Tributes flew straight to the prima donna's feet—only a very, very small part of this audience dared to love singers of its immediate time, Parker thought scornfully. But those who did actually rejoiced in one fresh voice—Bernice Fisher's as Micaela. The performance as a whole lacked polish. Then at Calvé's last appearance, a special Wednesday matinee, the prima donna tended to whoop it up, possibly because of the finality of this performance. The overwhelming energy she put into the gypsy dance forced the tempo ahead until it was almost twice as fast; everyone followed to a delirious close. The music stood the acceleration admirably, but poor Riddez' Toreador Song sounded afterward more like a lullaby than a rousing apostrophe to bravery.

Carmen settled back into a comparatively more artistic frame with its last hearing on March 27. The audience may have expected still further shocks from Mary Garden's first try at the role in Boston. If so, they were disappointed. Garden possessed the intelligence, the wit, and the determination to forge her own interpretation out of her vast resources. Her Carmen resembled no other in memory. It was remarkable as much for what she did not do as what she did. Her virtues of omission: no violence to Bizet's music headed the list. Her gypsy was not tough, vulgar, rowdy, noisy, chattering, nor shrewish. She did not tear, scratch, nor bite. Shorn of cluttering detail, this Carmen nevertheless drew on a wealth of nuances. Sensual and stony-hearted, she was a fatalist, not a coward. The ruin of one man, the death of another—indifferent to her. Garden had her own way with Carmen's costumes, too: shining blue stuff and a red shawl in the first act, multicolored flaring skirts in the second (recalling Zuloaga's picture of Lucienne Bréval), white mantilla and glossy bodice and skirt in the fourth. Nothing to make the audience sit up and take notice, said Parker, but very much in character.

Almost as miraculous as her bodily presence, the voice never seemed more mellifluous. Only once before in memory, in the *Thaïs* with Hammerstein at the Boston Theatre several years before, had she sung as well, thought Parker. Hale summed it up: None in his recollection—and he had seen many—had expressed so much by mere facial play. This was one of the most artistic and engrossing Carmens since Galli-Marié's creation in 1875.

Somewhat less attention focused on the José of Dalmorès and the Escamillo of Hector Dufranne, both new to Boston. In his only appearance of the season, the tenor seemed tired, with little tone at his command; consequently he sought to compensate by declaiming whole passages. Dufranne's large voice had thrown its hard sonorities into Hammerstein's *Pelléas et Mélisande* some seasons previously; he would sing Golaud in the final Boston *Pelléas*, when his perfect diction and admirable character-ization gave Hale pleasure. The lesser roles in *Carmen* upon which the excellence of the ensemble depends—"ensemble" had become a watch-word this season; Russell had preached on the subject many times, until the critics grew rather sensitive on the point—let the structure down badly. This seemed one instance of the triumph of preaching over prac-tice. Complaints arose especially about the pair of gypsy girls, Frasquita and Mercédès.

Boston became accustomed this season to a procession of heroines in the old stand-by *Faust*. Brozia had hardly vacated the role when an American stepped in—Elizabeth Amsden, who had made her debut in a Sunday concert but went on to higher things. Close on her swaying skirts came Lucille Marcel, who in turn was succeeded by Mary Garden. Doubt-less, Garden was hard to follow, yet Dereyne essayed on March 9 her first Marguerite since her Boston debut in 1910, and brought the scales back to balance with her simple grace, neither coquettish nor prudish. Her Faust was Herman Jadlowker, who thus rounded off his services to Boston in the role in which he had made his American debut at the Metropolitan and returned to his position in the Berlin Opera.

Dereyne, as well as Garden, put up with the conventional deviltry of Rothier, but the other three ladies were treated, along with the audience, to a remarkable new Méphistophélès in the person of Vanni Marcoux, who had made his debut in *Pelléas et Mélisande* in January. Edouard De Reszke in comparison seemed commonplace; Plançon was superior as a singer, but his dramatic conception not so vivid, picturesque, and varied. It was always a mistake, thought the critic, to go out of the operatic frame and try to revert to Goethe. Marcoux first showed himself as the friendly companion, the man of the world, and at the Kermesse, the good fellow. Struck to sobriety at the sight of the soldiers' swords raised and reversed like crosses, he did not writhe, mow, and gibber; standing erect and still defiant, his face revealed anguish, his knees turned to water. Then he quickly recovered his *sang froid*. He indulged in no buffoonery with Martha; his mockery in the serenade was sinister, not boisterous.

As for his ideas of costuming, he was not the first to discard the scarlet of tradition, for Maurel wore black in Paris. Marcoux appeared first in black doublet and hose, slashed and pointed in iridescent green. His cape showed flashes of dull red. For church and the serenade, he was swathed in a full mantle of black velvet. The prison costume was mouse-gray. His face beardless, his neck bare and sinewy, a close-fitting cap cut away for his ears and peaked in front to reveal a tongue of red hair, he was a figure to excite apprehension and terror. "Some of us," said Parker, "saw and heard for the first time the Méphistophélès *Faust* really contains."

Marcoux's presence, along with Garden, Destinn, Tetrazzini, Clément, Urlus, and Renaud, built into the company for the first time the nucleus of supreme talent that acts as a lodestone. Without it true superiority is evasive and uncertain. Marcoux received a warmer welcome in Boston than any other singer in many a day. A wave of disappointment swept the patrons and press when he was announced for only a few performances, in *Pelléas* and *Faust*. Gladly Russell signed him up for a *Barber of Seville* and a *Tosca* and quickly made sure that he would return another year with a great deal more to do.

Marcoux had first appeared as an uncommonly intelligent and pleasant-spoken young man when Olin Downes interviewed him for *Musical America,* shortly before his American debut in *Pelléas*. He revealed himself to have been born in Turin of one Italian, one French parent, which accounted for the dichotomy between his two names. Like other singers before and after him, he had been a racing cyclist; had tried the law, but found it held no charms. Although ingrained in him was the French thoroughness in studying a role, he believed that the French artist sang the better for a strain of Italian blood—which at least in his case seemed to be true, although the intrinsic beauty of his voice never called forth superlatives. He ended the interview with the illuminating remark that he must hurry off to an appointed rehearsal with Caplet, and, "One knows when a rehearsal with Caplet begins, but one never knows when it will end."

At the beginning of the 1912–13 season, the tall, long-limbed young

man, with boyish and gracious manners, further explained himself to a
Herald interrogator, who thought that his brilliant red and white complexion must make the grease stick as an adjunct to his art rather unnecessary. The singer's long, low brow and strangely flat head were remarked, as well as the black hair that broke into two little curls back of
his ears, all manna to the clever, cruel caricaturists of Paris. This was the
type of new singer who takes the dramatic side of his art seriously.
Marcoux admired Massenet, he revealed, and at Covent Garden had received a telegram the past summer from the composer announcing that
Panurge (a new opera) was ready for him, and to come quickly, "as I do
not expect to be in Paris in October." Massenet's strange premonition had
been fulfilled, Marcoux recalled somberly; he had died on August 13.
Garden held a contrary opinion of the prolific composer, calling him the
"yes-man par excellence," and scornfully slashing at his hypocrisy and his
habit of writing letters "dripping with the most sickening kind of sentiment, everything underlined, not once, but two, three, or four times."
Nevertheless he had furnished vehicles for both singers, together and
apart.

Three additional French operas lay in store for Boston audiences,
which appear to have reacted affirmatively to only one: the gruesome
Habañera of Laparra, repeated from the previous season, but with a
much more appropriate heroine in Maria Gay, although she lacked
Dereyne's maddening abandon in dance. The role in which Ramon
Blanchart had strengthened his hold on the public now fell to Riddez.
Always explicit for fear he be misunderstood, the baritone wrapped and
labeled his emotions to the point of burlesque comedy. One felt sympathy
for him as a murderer, however, after hearing the singing of his victim,
the unfortunate tenor, De Potter. The best that could be said of him was
that his apparition as a ghost curdled the blood. The house took pride in
Leo Devaux's restudied staging of *Habañera*, which sharpened the contrast between the blaze and blare of the first-act fete and the somber and
dilapidated room of the murder. Zuloaga, who seems to have haunted
Parker's mind, was recalled once more in the heavy line, mass, and color.
A new third-act set showed a brown church with a rectangular tower,
crowded under a bare, sharp ridge, with graves in the foreground. The
orchestra aided in the atmospheric picturesqueness, seeming to turn
ghost itself, hunting out the spirit of the personages, and leaving burn-
ing imprints on the consciousness.

After this agonizing melodrama, Debussy seemed all the more pastel in the delicate and static *L'Enfant Prodigue*, held over from 1910–11, and in the cantata-like *Le Martyre de Saint Sébastien*, which slipped into the repertoire as a token of Caplet's *devoirs* to the master. Nothing new presented itself to audiences in the former, while the latter, unexplained by any program notes, baffled the final matinee crowd completely. One saw the vague suggestion of an altar, with two scantily dressed ladies fixed to a cross; angels with burnished halos that reflected glaring glints into the audience's eyes appeared in ranks. A woman crawling about the dim stage while the female chorus sang expressively—of what, few could guess —eventually proved to be Mme. Cerutti, miming the Saint's martyrdom. Hale questioned the comprehensibility of the Saint flopping about as if in search for a dropped coin, or extending her figure into a lifesized letter Y, and did not blame the audience for snickering. Latecomers had destroyed the effect of the prelude, and what came after seemed aimless and ineffective, culminating in a lame and impotent chorus. After intermission, *Hänsel und Gretel* assumed the proportions of a masterpiece of stagecraft. Fortunately for Bostonians' opinion of Debussy (whether or not he cared), *Pelléas et Mélisande* rang down the curtain the next evening.

13

L'AFFAIRE MAETERLINCK

In retrospect is is easy to see the relief map of Boston's third opera season dominated by twin peaks, to whose eminence all the surrounding foothills paid homage. The sense of waiting for a climax first came to notice during the interminable preparations for Debussy's *Pelléas et Mélisande*—an unprecedented forty-seven rehearsals—which took on some aspects of religious mumbo-jumbo. This tension built up again as Felix Weingartner's arrival became imminent and was detonated as he stepped to the podium to introduce Boston to its own *Tristan und Isolde*. Was it possible that in the two supreme music dramas, the puissance (as H. T. Parker would have put it) of star-crossed love held Boston in its spell for a brief season?

It seems more likely that the city, betraying purely human failings, anticipated and gloried in the personalities involved—two loving couples who paralleled the romantic duos in their respective operas. In *Pelléas* Boston looked for excitement to the playwright, Maeterlinck, and the heroine known to the world as Mme. Maeterlinck, the actress-diseuse Georgette Leblanc. In *Tristan* the spotlight played on the conductor, Weingartner, and the soprano Lucille Marcel, ostensibly Mme. Weingartner.

What would be called today the publicity value or newsworthiness of this quartet did not pass unnoticed by Manager Henry Russell. In its own right, *Pelléas* fell very low in the scale as audience bait. Always caviar to the general public, it lacked even the virtue of novelty, having been spread before Boston by Oscar Hammerstein several times in two seasons. Discussion from an artistic point of view resembled threshing over old straw, as Parker said, although neither he nor Hale could resist the temptation to do so.

When no lines formed at the box office for the première on January 10, Russell resorted to daring exploitation. As he tells it: "Apart from my dread of giving a new opera to half-empty houses, the cost of the production was so great that I feared the prospect of a heavy financial loss." Indeed, more than thirty thousand dollars had been spent on the production before the curtain went up. Even estimating a box office of five to six thousand dollars for each of five performances (too much to expect, Russell rightly feared), the opera would hardly break even.

With Georgette's approval (or so he claimed), Russell informed the newspapers that he had received a cable from Maeterlinck, saying that he would arrive in Boston in time for the première. Maeterlinck, declared Russell, had wagered a thousand dollars that he could land in New York without being recognized by reporters. "There was not a word of truth in this," Russell confessed. The poet at the time had no intention of coming to America, or even going outside the four walls of his beloved abbey home, St. Wandrille.

The Great Maeterlinck Hoax fed the public and press curiosity, with its combination of mystery, sport, and challenge, for several days. The New York *Herald* set the tone: "Will he enter New York disguised as a nobleman or in the steerage? M. Maeterlinck is confident that only the heaven-sent genius of Arsène Lupin [the character created by Maurice Leblanc, Georgette's brother] will be able to detect him."

Through the ensuing scramble to meet all incoming steamers, and even up to the last moment before the performance, Russell maintained secrecy. He dressed up a chorus man and instructed him to take a taxi to the Hotel Westminster, where the sympathetic proprietor, accustomed to the high jinks of opera folk, allowed him to register, then informed the press that a mysterious Monsieur M. had indeed arrived. The reporters' night-long vigil in the lobby went unrewarded, while at the opera house, packed to suffocation, "every man whose hair was a little longer than is usual or whose appearance was suggestive of the American conception of a poet had to undergo the disconcerting scrutiny of the curious crowd." Russell claimed to be mortified at resorting to such undignified methods, but noted that the evening's take in addition to subscriptions amounted to five thousand dollars, while the ensuing performances, lacking artificial stimulation, fell to two hundred dollars.

At the beginning of the season, André Caplet had cockily assured the arrival of Debussy, who set such great store by the conductor that he could not bear to be apart from him—"We are very closely related; always together in Paris," he boasted in a magazine interview, with a half-controlled smile. However, long before the première everybody realized that the composer was not coming.

A program booklet was circulated, containing instructions (which the critics teased as "solemnities") on how to behave at the performance: come early, be in your seats five minutes before the curtain (7:45), for there will be no seating after the opera has begun; no applause, please, or talking in the important entr'actes, which will be distinguished by the dropping of the black curtain. Applause only at the red curtain, which denotes the end of an act. Please remain seated for the orchestra postlude.

Letters to Russell from Debussy and Maeterlinck published in the booklet produced respectful attention but generated no heat. Debussy wrote in part, under the date of October 22:

"I will certainly have to renounce coming to Boston, with great regret ... from what you told me of the production and from what I have seen of the scenery [Russell showed a model to both composer and playwright and left it for exhibition at the Académie Nationale at the request of the Paris Opéra director] these temptations are difficult to resist, so certain it is that your realization will be unique. At the time of the performance of *St. Sébastien*, I saw my friend André Caplet at work ... you know his gifts as a musical director, his marvelous grasp of this art, at once so complex and delicate ..."

Maeterlinck's message bore the date of September 3:

"The designs you showed me are pure and delicious *chefs d'oeuvres*. How different from the scenery—ingenious, perhaps, but totally erroneous —of the Opéra Comique! Now ... we have attained my most ardent dreams ... the interpretation will be unique. One might say that until Boston's performance, *Pelléas et Mélisande* never existed.... The scrupulousness with which Mr. Caplet catches the most subtle and the most fugitive shades of my thought in the music has moved me more than I can express."

This tribute must have pleased both Russell and Caplet inordinately. But one wonders at Maeterlinck's sudden seeming capitulation to the charms of music. He had heretofore professed to despise it, and had not witnessed a performance of his opera to date.

Maeterlinck's gossamer play floated by itself, unaccompanied by music, at its première on May 17, 1893. Then for a London performance in 1898 by Mrs. Patrick Campbell, Gabriel Fauré wrote incidental music, which is still performed as a concert suite. Boston saw Mrs. Campbell and heard Fauré's music at the Boston theater on April 12, 1902. The story of the choice of a Mélisande for the opera became part of the legend surrounding this extraordinary work. With a loyalty that almost everyone considered misplaced, Maeterlinck advanced the claims of Leblanc, who had acted the part in the play and had already created considerable stir in Bruneau's *L'Attaque du Moulin* at the Opéra Comique, where her "unregulated intensity" frightened the manager, and in *Thaïs, La Navarraise,* and *Carmen* at La Monnaie in Brussels.

Leblanc's Carmen will probably remain unique in history. Flerens Gaevert saw her "clothed in a long robe of plaited tulle, ornamented with spangles. Her body, finely proportioned, is revealed by this indiscreet drapery, her nobly modeled shoulders and arms are bare, her hair is confined by three circles of gold in Grecian fashion. Almée? Gypsy? Daughter of the East? Princess of the harem? Byzantine Empress? or Moorish dancer? All were suggested by this fantastic, seductive costume. In a tavern, where gypsy women met soldiers, she evoked the apparition of a woman of Mantegna or Botticelli, 'degraded, vile.' " She never wearied of cheapening the original model, "but in her white diction, her blithe walk, you divine her desire of invoking something else." Gaevert's effusion undoubtedly established Georgette in the world's opinion as an exotique. She acted Lady Macbeth (translated into French by her adoring poet) in the garden and woods of St. Wandrille. She made Maeterlinck's heroines her own: Mélisande, Ariane, Joyzelle, Monna Vanna. She became the only link between him and the world.

At the time she was prone to giving song recitals of a singular nature, called *"auditions lyriques mimes,"* in which she sang in whatever posture pleased her at the moment. She even made Schubert wildly erotic, turning *"Sei mir gegrüsst"* into an affair of threshing arms, sculptural attitudes, and a cry of exasperated, fainting flesh, a Paris reviewer commented. Faithfulness to this strange creature, further described in what must have stood as the prize understatement of the decade as a "talented but not a restful person," led Maeterlinck to Debussy's flat, where the poet, seeking

the part of Mélisande for Georgette, is said to have challenged the composer with an upraised cane. Meeting the defiance of the ailing musician's
wife, he retreated. Georgette lost out in spite of this intervention. Director
Albert Carré decided that the affairs of the Opéra Comique, particularly
in the casting of Debussy's new opera, would be better served by the
presence of a young Scottish-American soprano, Mary Garden, who had
recently made a startling surprise debut in the third act of *Louise*.

Leblanc failed in another sortie against the bastions of the Opéra
Comique when, in spite of Maeterlinck's renewed partisanship, Lucienne
Bréval won the part of Monna Vanna in Février's setting of the play.
Boston was to make up to her partially for that slight also, for Russell
mounted the play especially for her, in addition to *Pelléas* with Fauré's
music.

The glamorous Georgette arrived in Boston clad in a leopard coat, a
brown beaver hat trimmed with parrots' wings, and a long veil of golden
brown chiffon. Her raiment encompassed a low-cut, short-sleeved terra
cotta blouse and a short dark blue velvet skirt, with patent leather shoes
and gray gaiters. A huge diamond, held by an invisible gold filet, glittered
like a headlight from her forehead. Her hair spilled out around all this
trimming in loose twists of rather dull yellow. "She was a tall, untidy
woman," the girl reporter summed up succinctly. Women invariably saw
through the poses. This writer added the comment that when Leblanc had
studied Carmen in Granada with a gypsy, she acquired every authentic
element, including fleas.

Georgette later made herself available to interviewers, who found her
arrayed in Grecian costume, a style somewhat invalidated by the panther
skins thrown on here and there. She at once proclaimed her credo: that
her husband's plays suffered artistically unless interpreted by someone
who understood them. The writers correctly divined this to be a reference
to herself. She loftily proposed to make a study of American womanhood,
perhaps believing that she could assist them to aspire to a higher realm
of culture and spirit. By observation and not by intuition, she insisted,
she was already beginning to apprehend our civilization. Somewhat
baffled by her efforts to plumb philosophical depths, the newspapermen
nevertheless always accorded her a good press, if space and descriptive
detail are criteria. Later in the season, she condescended to bestow upon
Boston (still rather reserved, yet secretly curious), a sample of another

art: her intimate lecture recital. For the moment, however, the opera was the thing.

Six years after the Paris première, Oscar Hammerstein broke the first American lance for *Pelléas*, producing it at the Manhattan Opera House in February, 1908, with virtually the original cast: Miss Garden; Jean Périer as Pelléas; Hector Dufranne as Golaud; and Jeanne Gerville-Réache as Geneviève. Vittorio Arimondi replaced the original Vieuille as Arkel, Mme. Sigrist, instead of Blondin, was Yniold, and Campanini conducted, whereas Messager had presided over the première. Boston saw Hammerstein's cast twice in April, 1909, with the exception of Dalmorès as Pelléas, Vieuille restored to the role of Arkel, and Emma Trentini as Yniold. When the third performance came along in April 1910, Devries sang Pelléas, Huberdeau Arkel, and De La Fuente conducted.

This type of information, which Hale delighted to shower on his readers before every new experience, refreshed Boston's memory and prepared its receptivity to the opera. Without doubt, the revolutionary *Pelléas* needed cultivating, as Mary Garden had insisted in 1908. It took four years for Paris to establish it firmly in repertoire; at first, people would whistle and cry out. At one performance three young men in the first row whistled all through a scene. But applause from the balconies after each scene drowned the hisses. The upper reaches of the theater caught the spirit of the piece first. Perhaps this was true of Paris, but Boston galleryites remained unconvinced, possibly because they remained absent.

The two high oracles of Boston's press gloried, along with the manager and a tiny coterie of admirers, in the beauties and mysteries of Maeterlinck's drama and Debussy's music. Four performances within a January fortnight, with the cast intact, offered unexampled opportunity for study, reflection, and deepening enjoyment. "This lonely and incomparable work," in Hale's words, survived even the snobs, the delirious Pelléastres. "It will probably remain unique; perplexing, perhaps, to the student and the antiquary of future generations, who will regard it as a strange manifestation of poetic individuality in a grossly material and commercial age."

The Boston realization did not entirely satisfy Parker, who found Caplet's orchestra ampler in volume, less fine in texture, than the Ruhlmann (Opéra Comique) or Campanini (Manhattan) approach. *Pelléas* thus became more tangible, more a music drama of poetic and tragic romance, and less one of dream and vision. In the new amplitude, it lost some gentleness; in the new exactness, some mistiness and remoteness were sacrificed. Although never before had Debussy's music seemed so exactly mated to the smallest minutae of the drama, the orchestra became, instead of an iridescent web enclosing and pervading, an explicit element. Caplet's version "tended to lessen glamoring vagueness and shadowed mystery," and to heighten the fate-haunted drama. In the older representations, "if we stirred in our stalls, we felt the phantoms would vanish; last evening they asked—and received—our applause."

Mlle. Leblanc's Mélisande ran in an entirely different vein from the remainder of the players, a circumstance that undoubtedly provoked a sense of uneasiness. Parker found some excuse for her posings, "plainly modeled after illuminated borders of medieval missals," and her faculty for expressive listening and the ability to suggest a personage by telepathetic stillness. But for Hale all these qualities were marred by her self-consciousness, and the studied attitudes remindful of quaint stained windows. "The actress stood in front of Mélisande. Yet fortunate moments occurred when the voice gave the right and only accent to the text, when one had a glimpse of Mélisande's soul." He preferred to wait for final judgment on later performances. When that judgment day arrived, Mlle. Leblanc's vocal and histrionic accomplishments faded into miniature scraps of tinted parchment beside the very real yet completely dreamlike Mélisande of Mary Garden, whose innocence proved a stumbling block to her husband, caused her lover to be slain, and yet was recognized by the wise old grandfather. Hale's own innocence prompted his remark on Mlle. Leblanc's performance—her chief attraction lay in the fact that she was Maurice Maeterlinck's wife.

The Golaud of these January performances elicited from Parker the opinion that the opera should be named for the wronged husband instead of the guilty lovers. Vanni Marcoux, bowing upon the American scene in the first of the operatic portraits that were to be unveiled one after another, each more compelling than the last, mounted to a lonely peak of genius in the fleeting hours between curtain and curtain.

"The half had not been told us," said Hale of the reputation that had preceded the baritone from Paris, Brussels, and London. The voice, used solely for dramatic purposes, the facial expression, the sobriety and significance of gesture, the authoritative bearing, built to a dominating individuality. In a rare outburst of superlative, Hale concluded: "This was one of the most striking performances I have seen on the opera stage during the last thirty years."

Parker compared Marcoux to Forbes-Robertson in the Maeterlinck play. His impressive physical aspect, informed with a masculine vigor and a quick intelligence, electrified the spectators, while his ability to convey character delighted the critics. He seemed to embody the weight of middle age without its bulk. His diction was clear and easily understood, colored vividly with gusty or haunting moods. This was no base spy, but a human being, torn tragically by doubts.

No other character matched his standard as Golaud at this first performance, although much could be said for the richness of Maria Gay's voice as Geneviève, and the gentle serenity and goodness of Edward Lankow, whose voice Debussy was said to have proclaimed exactly the right one for which he wrote Arkel. Debussy's opinion was apparently justified in Russell's eyes, for Lankow assumed the role of the old king in each of the five performances in 1911–12 and the two in 1912–13. He suited the part physically too, with a six-foot-plus frame and a grave, gentle mien. Bernice Fisher, the adorable Gretel and Micaela of this and the following seasons, made Le Petit Yniold altogether childlike with her tiny figure and appealing youthfulness. Her charm flickered like sunlight through the shadows of the drama, in Parker's opinion.

The one real flaw, against which all *Pelléas* audiences and critics would be forced to close their eyes and ears and sensibilities, lay in the casting of the hero himself. The best Hale could say for Jean Riddez was that he did not leap impatiently out of the frame of the picture, but Parker would not join in even this left-handed praise. This high baritone conceived Pelléas as an operatic figure, H. T. P. thought, the third side of a triangle. No glamour hung about him, no poetic suggestion, no hint of a dazed and fated spirit. He seemed capable in an operatic sense, but not as an actor in Debussy's music drama, seen either as a human tragedy or a dreamlike vision. While Boston could count (on the fingers of one hand, to be sure), stirring, glamorous, or at least provocative Mélisandes (Garden, Leblanc, and Louise Edvina, then later Lucrezia Bori and Bidu Sayao of the Metropolitan), for a fine, sensitive Pelléas it had to wait until 1934 for the Met's Edward Johnson, and again until 1945 for Martial Singher. The company's own performances always remained a trifle lopsided because of Riddez.

Another element absorbed attention in these early productions, almost to the exclusion of the music. The new and exciting principles of scenic design and lighting currently practiced in Germany and Russia were utilized in America for the first time. The ensuing season would bring their full significance and flowering with the presence of Josef Urban as chef of *mise-en-scène,* creating for proud Boston the distinction of a true and lasting scenic reform that would influence all opera in America for years. Never before in this country had the German lighting been so thoroughly and efficiently and characteristically applied as in *Pelléas.* Even *Sumurun,* a fantastic spectacle imported bodily from Berlin, would hardly prove more significant. Urban's participation in this *Pelléas* was not made clear until later, but his sets, which surprised and even shocked in 1912, became the norm for later performances at the Metropolitan, and persisted there until the revival of 1953–54, when Horace Armistead replaced them. Urban would add a new dimension to Boston's opera. Meanwhile, the decor for *Pelléas* prompted a lively buzzing.

In the first place, the squabble over the correct locale for the opera seemed to be settled once and for all. Maeterlinck had been notably unhappy with the Comique settings, although Hale twitted him slyly on his petulance, saying that a dramatist, especially when he is a mystic, is not always the best judge of stage effects. Mary Garden had pronounced the castle of Arkel to be in the cold, remote reaches of Scandinavia. But the German artists placed it in a never-never land resembling medieval Normandy.

Saliently beautiful were these sets, and artistically lighted. Many of the scenes played on a stage masked down to boxlike spaces, an innovation that did not entirely please Hale, who believed that Golaud should have been given more latitude to creep up on Pelléas and slay him, while it infuriated Mary Garden, who scolded Urban because she did not have room to turn around in. Nevertheless she coped with the cramped confines when the chips were down. The three interior scenes suggested very thick walls of old, rough stone, the rooms still and damp and dark. Sparse, heavy furniture, clumsily carved and painted in primary colors, heavy doors crossed by great colored stripes, ornamentation in bold designs painted crudely on stone or metal gave a medieval feeling. Small touches of brilliant color—the canopy of red and black and gold over Mélisande's bed and the open, illuminated missal in Arkel's gallery—relieved the heaviness. Outdoor scenes spoke of German taste: bosky forests so thick the light barely penetrated, suggesting (to Parker) Maxfield Parrish's

unreal, poetical landscapes. A vivid pictorial sense sent Pelléas and
Golaud up from a subterranean chamber into a high, narrow, shadowed
grotto, its opening a monstrous slit, through which one looked upon a
vista of blue sea touched by sunlight and overhung by an old, brown,
jutting tower. These vivid pictures, familiar to us today, caught Boston's
attention with the impact of new-minted imagination.

The lighting alone played an integral part. For several episodes, the
lights were adjusted after the curtain opened, producing the sensation of
the sudden opening of an illuminated manuscript. Lights were constantly
applied toward the coloring of the pictures. Gold sunshine fell as if by
accident on the white brow of the old king, on the green robes and young
profile of the waiting Pelléas. Golaud's lantern cast a faint flicker on the
abraded wall of the subterranean chamber. The grotto glimmered blue
until that startling moment when the moonlight's probing finger touched
it. As a spectacle alone, the production was a triumph of exquisite art.
Russell had shown himself no vain boaster, Hale concluded.

The greater shame indeed that so few Bostonians availed themselves
of this new and invigorating experience. Hale continued to fume at those
whose most telling irony was to pronounce Pelléas with a heavy and
mocking accent on the last syllable, then to laugh with an air of finality.
In this display of scorn, they only followed the example of one of their
betters, the celebrated New York Tribune critic, Henry E. Krehbiel. In
his book Chapters of Opera, he fulminated against Maeterlinck's "infantile" plays, placing Pelléas on the borderline between marionettes and
mature drama. As for the music, "unrhythmical, uncadenced, disjointed,
and ejaculatory" were his kindest expressions. To enjoy it, one must have
cultivated a craving for dissonance in harmony and found relish in com-
binations of tones that "sting and blister and pain and outrage the ear."
Otherwise, monotony was exactly the word for the orchestral color, the
mood, the dynamics, and the harmonic devices, according to Krehbiel.

The performance of the play with Fauré's music on January 30 came
as something of an anticlimax. The scenery, to be sure, provided an
illusory framework the drama had never before possessed and would
never again enjoy. But the reaches of the opera house tended to dim any
impact from the stage. Furthermore, Fauré's music, not as evocative as
Debussy's, encouraged conversation in the audience, through which its
wistful, shadowed, melancholy voice only now and then made its way
to the few attentive ears. Comparison became inevitable. Parker con-

cluded that Debussy did for the play what only the rarest actor may do, for "music begins where the spoken word leaves off in expressing sublimated emotion; it becomes at once a more poignant and allusive voice, it spins spiritual states, weaves mysterious embodiments, frees a speech of the last touches of commonness that even a poet's words cannot escape by the sheer force of long association with routine things."

The advantages lay in the perception of certain speeches unheard in the opera, speeches which made an austere, bare music of their own. Certain impersonations too evoked more meaningful images, notably Jean Duval as Arkel and René de Maupré, who made a picturesque and illusive Pelléas. Jean Durozat merely acted Golaud in an artificial manner then antiquated even in Paris. As for Georgette, she repeated the Mélisande of the opera unhampered by the vocal exigencies of Debussy's declamation. Mannered and sophisticated, she came wraithlike out of nowhere, with no tears, no tremors, but much contrivance. The audience's liveliest interest lay in the actor who impersonated Yniold, listed in the program as Sheri. Everyone knew that the charming boy, naive and piping, was Russell's younger son, Sheridan. He received floral offerings along with the adult cast.

While the scene with the servants and that with Yniold and the sheep were cut, as they were customarily in the opera, the play gained by restoration of moments Debussy did not choose to set: the chattering of the servants about the murder beside the well, and the confrontation of Mélisande by Pelléas in the tower chamber, with Yniold's innocent prattle stretching the nerves of the two silent, gazing lovers. Parker thought it a pity Debussy had not set this latter scene, as it provided marvelous opportunity for orchestral comment.

Neither Hale nor Parker had attended Russell's first play-opera experiment, when *Monna Vanna* had given Leblanc her first theatrical experience in America on January 25. Both critics, having seen Bertha Kalich in an earlier representation, preferred to cover Berlioz's *Damnation of Faust*, given by the Cecilia Society under its new conductor, Arthur Mees. Assistant critics were allowed their say about the play, and they treated the heroine with reticent respect.

Mlle. Leblanc rounded out her little stay in Boston by "lecturing" before a tiny audience in Mrs. Gardner's Fenway Court, an audience, the cynics whispered, that would have been smaller had not the Opera House sent timely aid. Being an acute and intelligent woman, she must have suspected that Boston did not take her very seriously. She was clad in long, trailing robes of mole-colored satin with cascades of lace at her throat and veils floating from either shoulder, her luxurious golden hair kept under restraint in an elaborate headdress. Tapestries framed the small stage on which she sat in a high-backed chair beside an ancient table on which rested a curious ewer, the appropriate parallel of the conventional water pitcher. She curved herself into a corner of the chair and declaimed pensively. Then she came upright in it and declaimed intently. She leaned over it and declaimed confidentially. She stood high above it and with upraised arm declaimed passionately. Occasionally she strode about, as one under nervous stress, but still declaiming.

A few songs sufficed for the little concert, remarked Parker, continuing his leisurely review. Accompanied by Walter Straram, one of the opera's assistant conductors, she intoned to music by Fauré. Her discourse concerned itself exclusively with *Pelléas et Mélisande*, which she professed to find more enchanting in its original form than as an opera. Quite frankly, she said, Debussy's music fell short of Maeterlinck's own inner meaning; it was too soft and languorous. Debussy's personages became less human, more static; of the soul, not of the body; and thus conflicted with Maeterlinck. She drew a further conclusion: that Debussy was prone to be carried away by emotion, while Maeterlinck remained always close to the source of life and instinct. Bostonians professed not to understand this profundity.

How to play Mélisande? she asked herself, answering that while Mélisande remains an *"incomprise,"* each word of Pelléas removes a veil, until, liberated, she cries her deliverance in the face of death. Boston matrons shuddered delicately at this intimation of a spiritual strip tease. She rebuked the Opéra Comique for its performance, saying that perhaps it was a racial misunderstanding, since Maeterlinck had always been appreciated better in England, Germany, and Russia than in the Latin countries. Bostonians, knowing of her discomfiture at not being chosen by the Comique, smiled slyly.

Finally, in a few courteous words, delivered in more polished and adroit diction than that in which she had "intoned," Georgette took leave of Boston audiences. Maintaining to the last that Boston's artistic atmosphere equaled that of Paris or Vienna, she sailed for Europe on February 15. She left Boston in time to miss both the first performance of *Tristan* and a recital by a recent rival for the part of Mélisande, the slim

English soprano, Maggie Teyte. Opera socialites gave her a farewell party on New Year's Eve at the Hotel Lenox; among those attending were Mesdames Converse, Fearing, Jr., Gardner, Jordan, Russell, Slater and Fiske Warren.

Astonishment and dismay filled Back Bay, where the matrons had cordially opened their salons to "Madame Maeterlinck," when the news broke in 1919 that the aging poet had married a teen-age girl on February 15. In the ensuing scramble to shift their sights, Bostonians realized with shocking clarity that Georgette and Maeterlinck had never been married at all! They were spared the embarrassment of recollecting their mistakes at the opera for by this time there was no Boston Opera Company, but over occasional tea or dinner tables the subject was quietly dropped if any tactless guest should dare to bring it up. Boston had survived the tumultuous visit of Oscar Wilde; it could brush Georgette off its shoulders like so much dust.

But the Maeterlincks continued to attract public attention. In 1920 Georgette returned to the United States and promptly "told all" to a newspaper syndicate, which made capital of the lively story. She herself had introduced the traitress to the poet's household, she cried. During preparations for a Paris performance of Maeterlinck's *Blue Bird*, Georgette had shown special interest in the eighty children in the cast, singling out for special favor the small, dark girl who played the part unromantically known as Cold-in-the-Head. This child, who was called Silver Tassel because of the ornaments on her little black cap, soon became the pet of the household, cheering the poet, who had fallen into melancholy at the death of his mother. Georgette made the mistake of leaving them alone, having naively confided her amorous history to the young woman. She, Georgette, still chafed under an indissoluble marriage with a long-vanished Spaniard. Furthermore, her subsequent life, even with Maeterlinck, had not been uneventful.

Silver Tassel, who was now called Sélysette, after one of Maeterlinck's heroines (her real name was Renée Dahon), succeeded where Georgette had not, in legalizing her position. Although the poet, with calm disregard for convention and feminine nature, invited Georgette to remain, so she wrote, she could no longer endure the presence of the man to whom she had devoted her life.

Georgette flickered fitfully in and out of the public eye until her death in 1941. She took a house in New York's Greenwich Village, and on the coldest winter day would appear in a chiffon dress and straw hat, whether from choice or penury no one knew. She continued to plunge into somewhat vague love affairs, and in spite of the traditional mattress savings bank (once thought to hold a fabulous sum of paper money), she fizzled out financially as well as artistically. In 1932 she published a volume of memoirs, entitled *Souvenirs, My Life with Maeterlinck,* which reviewed her earlier story, still one-sidedly.

In the early days of the First World War, Maeterlinck had been forced to abandon St. Wandrille, which lay too close to the battlefield. He found his perfect retreat in the south of France and built a villa, called "Les Abeilles," reflecting his twin interest in nature, expressed in *The Life of the Bee* and other books. The new home rested on a hillside between Grasse and Nice, close to Russell's villa, "La Scoperta" at La Turbie. Russell's second wife remembers many visits between the two households. One weekend the Russells' guests included not only the Maeterlincks, but Melba as well as Mary Garden, who arrived from Monte Carlo to go over the score of Montemezzi's *L'Amore dei Tre Re,* which she planned to sing in Chicago. Melba, entrenched for three weeks, insisted on moving all the furniture to suit her own tastes, which maddened Henry. But most of all he resented her singing in her bath. He loved her voice, Mrs. Russell explained, but could not bear to hear snatches of this and that, sung without purpose. On the day of Garden's visit, Melba stood for about two hours of *L'Amore* rehearsal, then appropriated the piano bench and accompanied herself in Tosti's *Mattinata.* This was too much for Maeterlinck, whose dislike for music amounted to mania. He stuck his head out of the bedroom and, to the indignation of both prima donnas, yelled "Henry, how on earth can I work with all this racket going on!"

Maeterlinck detested music on principle, rather than from knowledge and choice. Young Sheridan Russell, picking out a bit of Debussy's "Children's Corner" on the piano, confided to his stepmother that Maeterlinck had whispered, "If your father heard you playing that American ragtime, he'd be furious!"

The poet undoubtedly suffered when he was constrained to attend the gala performance of his *Blue Bird* in Albert Wolff's opera setting, which Russell arranged with the Metropolitan on December 27, 1919. To add to his misery, Russell insisted that he wear evening dress, a nuisance he had only once before endured for the sake of a friend's wedding. Fortunately the more worldly Sélysette had included a full outfit in their luggage, even remembering the decoration of the Grand Officier de l'Ordre de Léopold that King Albert had recently conferred upon him. He evinced little interest in the opera itself. Wolff, who also conducted, made no deep impression with his music.

Maeterlinck's experiences as a lecturer and Hollywood author brought even sharper disillusion. Russell had placed him confidently with J. B. Pond, a famous lecture agent, who, at the last moment, insisted that Maeterlinck deliver his message in English. What came out in Carnegie Hall on that fateful evening of January 2, 1920, was gibberish; the evening ended dismally. Pond brought suit for thirty-five thousand dollars, but Maeterlinck escaped by virtue of expert legal counsel. Russell next escorted him across the continent, where Samuel Goldwyn waited with a generous contract. With what came to be known as typical Hollywood behavior the Goldwyn studio sat passively through two plays Maeterlinck completed; then delivered the verdict: Maeterlinck was too "highbrow." After three months, the poet's party returned to the East. Goldwyn had never showed his face. It was Maeterlinck's turn to sue. He later collected forty thousand dollars.

Both Georgette and Sélysette might well have pondered the poet's words on love in a conversation with Russell at the time of the 1919 revelation. Creative artists create because they must, he began, and continued: "There is that in them—something lent them for a little while—which demands expression. Unless this is found they strangle their spirits. The love of women, or the desire for them, never implanted in a man's soul the ability to create . . . it is an aid and not a cause. The ability was there first and often finds its voice in spite of love. Believe me, the man who creates does so at the bidding of his soul, and does not owe that soul to any woman."

Or, as Philip Hale commented, apropos Maeterlinck's pressure to secure the title role in Février's *Monna Vanna* for Georgette, truly, as Corot remarked, "woman disturbs the landscape."

14

CONQUERING HELDENDIRIGENT
(Felix Weingartner)

Hardly had one pair of lovers been laid to rest when another, more substantial if not less otherworldly, rode a thunderbolt into Boston's consciousness. As Pelléas and Mélisande had monopolized January, so Tristan and Isolde filled February to the brim with passion. The Boston Opera's first real venture into the abysses of Wagnerian music drama (the perfunctory and unheeded *Lohengrin* of the first year hardly counted) afforded the most significant episode of the winter.

The performance on February 12, 1912, had everything—a heroic substitution for an ailing heroine; a new and illustrious tenor; fresh settings; and above all a world-famous conductor, who promised orchestral effulgences hitherto not experienced. Felix Weingartner, nearing fifty, had deserted both the Berlin and Vienna Royal Opera houses to become a traveling virtuoso, although retaining a post in Hamburg. He had been a guest with the New York Philharmonic for three seasons, from 1904 to 1907, and had appeared in Boston as recently as 1906 with the New York Symphony, leading a memorable performance of Berlioz's "Symphonie Fantastique." Boston knew him also as a composer, for he had played the piano part of his own Sextet in 1905. Liszt had acted as godfather to his first opera, *Sakuntala*, at Weimar, where the celebrated pianist-composer had been similarly hospitable to the young Wagner.

Hale added to a biographical account a brief note on the conductor's marriages: the first to Marie Guillerat in 1891; the second to Baroness Feodora von Dreifus in 1903. The critic openly expressed doubt about

145

the severance of the second set of bonds when the handsome conductor appeared *à deux* in Boston with his leading soprano, Lucille Marcel, who had resigned coincidentally from the Vienna Opera to accompany him on his tours, being the object of the favoritism of which he was accused. The singer did not hesitate to affix his name to hers with a hyphen the following season, so it may be presumed that all legal matters had been expedited at some time during the three years that Boston knew and admired them, and "Madame" Weingartner was accepted in Back Bay parlors as "Madame" Maeterlinck had been.

All personal prejudices foundered and were lost under the tremendous tidal wave of that first *Tristan*. Even Hale dropped his former fretful preoccupation with the "illogical" and "silly" libretto and with what he termed the ludicrous potion scene which suggested to him that a sharp attack of colic had overtaken the lovers. He had prophesied that in spite of its music of wondrous beauty and overwhelming strength, *Tristan* would be relegated to the library shelves when *Lohengrin* and *Meister-singer* were still holding the stage. Now he came perilously close to eating a few earlier words and confined his dissatisfaction with the drama to some aspects of the staging, notably the absurdity of the ship. "How was it steered?" he wondered. "Only Wagner knows, and the secret is buried with him." After meting out their just deserts to the singers, the *Herald* critic awarded the highest honor to Weingartner. Of recent virtuoso performers, Gustav Mahler had shown a fine sense of proportion and respected the singers, but was overly academic. Arturo Toscanini shared the two good qualities, but imparted too Italianate and romantic a glow to the music. Weingartner's orchestra sang a marvelous song, with the stage but not above it; with sonority but never with noise. His control seemed not tyrannical but easy. In short, the composer and interpreter were one.

The glamour of youth still lingered about the tall, spare figure. His appearance proclaimed him a scholar and a gentleman, a combination specially tailored for Boston. The fresh-colored face with the small, rather tight mouth was sheltered under a dominating forehead that surely denoted high intellect. His bearing before the audience showed the patient courtesy of a man absorbed in his work. A little stick at the end of his long right arm served to give his curiously stinging beat, while his left hand curved the phrase. Occasionally his whole body vibrated to the emotion of the music. At climaxes he seemed to gather all his strength and fling himself bodily, mentally, and emotionally upon the music.

At rehearsal, an observer commented that if anything should happen to disable the index finger of Weingartner's left hand, he would lose half his eloquence. It warned, halted, corrected flats or sharps, subdued or stimulated. The maestro issued reproof only occasionally, and in a mild tone. One could judge his severity by the language he chose: German if he was excited; French if he stopped to think; English if he paused further to remind himself that the Boston orchestra was not necessarily replete with fluent linguists. His general air of placidity showed an unwillingness to burn up his vitality ahead of time.

The results were clear at the performance. Although the orchestra had rehearsed only briefly under the new master after its preparation by Conti, the men seemed transformed. Their number had been increased to seventy, with twelve extras when required, and Pierre Henrotte (later with the Metropolitan Opera orchestra) engaged as concertmaster. A new solo cello, clarinet, and bass, and the strengthening of each choir had already produced results. More individual virtuosity also manifested itself. The conductors, especially the young ones, had learned not to overdrive. The men, being human, awaited Weingartner in moods divided between eagerness and apprehension. They need not have worried. By definition the master was one to get along with his players. This marvelous orchestra never overwhelmed the singers, but rather seemed to open, to enhance, to shade their songful speech. The real protagonist of the opera resided in the pit.

Still, enough room existed for appreciation of the singers. In Boston it had always been the procession of Isoldes that evoked prose poems: Rosa Sucher leading off in Boston's first *Tristan* April 1, 1895, then Katherina Lohse-Klafsky in 1896, both with Damrosch's German company; later the ineffable Metropolitan prima donnas Lillian Nordica, Lilli Lehmann, Milka Ternina, Gadski, and most recently Olive Fremstad. Though the De Reszke brothers enjoyed lionization along with two heroines, Nordica and Lehmann, the Tristans (aside from Jean De Reszke's) had provided ample poundage but had hardly pulled their weight artistically. Burgstaller, Kraus, and Burrian belonged in the history books but not in public affections. Then in 1912 Russell came up with a German tenor of truly heroic pretensions, a Dutchman who looked the part, sang with cantabile as well as strength, and as Hale delightedly commented, did not mistake palsy for passion.

Jacques Urlus dominated the stage from the moment of Tristan's dramatic entrance. His simple yet imposing bearing, the absence of tricks and mannerisms, but above all, the voice that kept its singing tone through the hero's strenuous utterances of joy or agony set him above any German tenor Hale had heard in *Tristan*. Russell showed justifiable pride in introducing Urlus to America. The next season, Gatti-Casazza claimed him, and the Amsterdam-born singer remained with the Metropolitan until 1917. His inauspicious New York debut as Tristan, when he lost his voice completely, was soon forgotten; one critic proclaimed him "the most valuable tenor acquisition in years." In addition to his vocal excellences, he seemed to the eye one of the most fascinating exponents of the fearless hero, Siegfried, since the beautiful, long-legged Max Alvary.

Isolde had been intended for Nordica, but the stately prima donna turned up voiceless on the day of the première. The seriousness of her defection can be imagined: no replacement for the taxing role existed in Boston, and a desperate call to Gatti in New York brought the dire news that of the Metropolitan's two Isoldes, Fremstad and Gadski, the former was due to appear on the stage of the Met that very night, while Gadski was laid up with a sprained ankle. To Russell's impassioned plea, Gatti agreed to sound out Mme. Gadski. It was then eleven thirty in the morning. Allowing a half hour for the Metropolitan general manager to reach Mme. Gadski, Russell phoned again at noon. In spite of her swollen ankle and her husband's protests, the gallant Gadski had said *"Ja, ich singe."* She would catch the one o'clock train and be in Boston at six, in plenty of time.

Russell got out his auto and rushed to Weingartner to share the good news. To his consternation, the maestro gave every indication of lashing himself into a fit. *"Mein Gott! Verdammt!"* and other choice epithets burst from his mouth, while his blue eyes blazed. Russell finally calmed him down, to learn that the fair Johanna was accustomed to sing the score with Toscanini's cuts, whereas his, Weingartner's, occurred in quite different places. The orchestra and the other singers would be thrown into hopeless confusion.

Russell had gone too far to let this setback daunt him. Quickly sending for a *Tristan* vocal score, he induced Weingartner to pencil in his particular deletions, dispatched the book with an assistant conductor to meet Mme. Gadski's train in New London, and prayed that the singer's vaunted musicianship would hold up. The messenger found the good lady already in Isolde's first-act costume, and in the two hours on the New Haven, singer and conductor feverishly rehearsed new material and cues. At the opera house, while Gadski made up, Weingartner himself took over. The curtain rang up punctually at its early hour, seven thirty. In the audience sat three hundred chagrined Nordica fans, who had accompanied the singer's husband, George W. Young, on a special train from New York. They swallowed their disappointment as Gadski triumphantly carried through, with ankle bandaged but no injury noticeable to brain or throat. In fact, both Hale and Parker found her vastly improved over previous performances. Hale noted a gain in tonal variety and aesthetic intelligence. Parker declared that while she had of old stopped at the surface of song, now Isolde as well as Gadski sang in her tones. This prima donna, who had impressed interviewers in former years with her human qualities, so "comfortable, generous, and German," became even more German in the first years of the war and lost her popularity in America. Before this, Boston heard her several times. Gatti took advantage of her warm reception as Isolde to cast her, during the spring visit of the Metropolitan, as Elisabeth in *Tannhäuser*, Santuzza in *Cavalleria Rusticana*, and Aïda, all within four days. In 1913–14, Russell invited her for one *Meistersinger*, which, though Hale described Eva as not one of her best parts, prompted Gatti to show her again in the role, along with that of Elsa in *Lohengrin*, in 1915–16.

The three other principal singers in *Tristan* offered little that was new, although Edward Lankow, in assuming the role of King Marke, brought on a favorite comment from Hale, who added him forthwith to the company of operatic bores he fondly listed now and then. It had always been the American fashion to deplore the length of Marke's monologue in the second act, and rare is the singing-actor who can keep an audience—or critics—alert through its entirety. To the roles of the lovers' companions, Louise Homer as Brangäne and Pasquale Amato as Kurvenal brought richness of tone and eloquent acting. The Italian baritone had never sung the role at the Metropolitan.

The novelties of the staging demanded a share of excited attention. New to America in 1912 was Urban's great yellow curtain on the deck of the ship conveying Isolde to Cornwall. It filled the whole stage space. When raised, it disclosed a high stern of rudely carved woodwork, heavy of joist and beam, and more suggestive of the primeval world than usual, thought Parker. Hale added to his scorn of the first-act ship several objections to the second-act investiture, the garden of Marke's castle with a tower from which Brangäne watches. The garden seemed insignificant, the castle frowned and dominated, no space showed for a path to the forest from which the king would return to surprise the lovers. Furthermore, the amorous pair had to sit on an unromantic spot resembling the steps of a public building. The third-act scenery Hale found of rare beauty. Parker described it as all sea and sky in the background; a small court bursting with a great plane tree; a high, brown, crumbling, weather-wasted castle.

Costumes seemed properly primitive, in frank reds and blues, broad leathers and metal bosses. "As Gadski knows," the critic remarked, "the day is past when Isolde voyaged in a white negligee." Urlus affected a red doublet and kept his legs armored even at night in the garden. In a later performance, he amended this fault.

Nordica slipped into her rightful place at the matinee of February 17, singing with a display of true vocal art that Hale suggested was currently ignored or flouted at Bayreuth, where what he called the "false" traditions of Cosima (Wagner's widow) and her son were respected. The rumors that Nordica had suffered a stroke proved entirely false. Such malicious winds are invariably created in any tiny vacuum a stage personality leaves in her progress; let her not appear once or twice, or seek seclusion over a short period, and immediately the word trickles through: So-and-so is dying of whatever ailment is fashionable at the time. At the turn of the century, Emma Calvé, the healthiest of mortals (she died in 1942 at the ripe old age of eighty-four), was pursued by a newspaper rumor of her imminent demise from cancer. She did little to contradict it except to keep singing; perhaps she even encouraged the ghouls by letting it be publicized that she had, in a moment of morbid fancy, designed her own tombstone.

Nordica apparently suffered from a recurrent neuritis. Her voice showed its effects, lacking brilliance in stormy passages, but her art rose to greater heights in compensation. Hale made amends for all his previous peevishness by comparing this performance favorably with her Isolde of 1901, which had not only taste, emotion, brilliance, and power that suggested a great reserve force, but also was the impersonation of a character of flesh and blood. He added that she elaborated still further at this performance.

New servitors lent interest to this *Tristan* and that of February 21. Otto Goritz, the masterly Peter in Boston's *Hänsel und Gretel*, came from the Metropolitan to sing Kurvenal. He impressed Parker with his large vocal energy and masculine devotion to his master, touched with very direct, simple, primitive feeling. Jeanne Gerville-Réache fitted rather clumsily into Brangäne's trailing robes. Completing a record that Boston justly termed glorious, the fourth performance on February 23 brought no new disclosures of Kurvenal's character as exemplified by the Metropolitan baritone Herman Weil, but introduced a cherished mezzo-soprano to Boston as Brangäne. New York had compared Margarete Matzenauer favorably to Marianne Brandt and Ernestine Schumann-Heink. She had shed a golden glow on Amneris, the role of her Metropolitan debut, on Kundry, the *Walküre* Brünnhilde, Ortrud, and Orfeo, among other roles. Her voice, so rich and sonorous, capable of such infinite gradations of color and emotional depiction, had cast a spell in New York. Boston felt its impact immediately. Next to Marcoux, Parker found her the most interesting character to grace the roster. He admired her finely cut profile and alert and expressive great dark eyes; her long black hair added a touch of lustrous color. The voice—very full, even, and resonant, a mezzo that ran deep without a trace of contralto thickness or clumsiness, and in its top revealed almost a soprano quality— nearly cloyed by its richness. In fine, "no such voice has been heard here within easy recollection."

The Hungarian-born, German-trained Matzenauer would come back next season to sing two performances of Isolde, encompassing the leap from the lower to the higher range, the lesser to the mightier role, with ease and distinction. Boston heard her Isolde before the Metropolitan. She sang it in New York (in English) only after the war moratorium on German opera. Perhaps she sang in Boston the more fervently for having married her Tristan, the Italian Edoardo Ferrari-Fontana. Indeed, she was carrying his child under the Irish princess' capacious robes. (The marriage did not last long, however.) Otherwise, Matzenauer vouchsafed only Metropolitan performances (Fidès in *Le Prophète* and Amneris in *Aïda*) to Boston.

Weingartner had hardly drawn breath in a marathon few conductors would care to attempt, nine performances within twelve days: *Tristan* on Monday, *Tosca* on Wednesday, *Faust* on Friday, *Tristan* on Saturday matinee; then a concert on Sunday, *Aïda* on Tuesday, *Tristan* on Wednesday, *Hänsel und Gretel* on Thursday matinee, and, finally, *Tristan* on Friday. He said farewell to the gala accompaniment of wreaths of various sizes presented by Russell and other admirers. The enraptured audience buzzed and applauded as Nordica blew kisses "à la Tetrazzini," Parker commented acidly.

Weingartner had wrought an astonishing transformation of Boston's operatic spirit, along with the revitalization of the orchestra. His *Tosca* had "searched out exactly the right Puccinian ambience" while his orchestra played as well as if the opera were *Tristan*. His *Faust*, but for a contretemps that marked one of the rare mechanical mishaps on the Boston stage, showed his shaping and commanding force, although it did not mark a rediscovery as had *Tosca*. He inspired all the singers in *Aïda*, after a somewhat unpromising start. The audience applauded for him at mid-entr'acte, startling all old hands, for such a demonstration had never before occurred in Boston. He "told the tale in the voice of the orchestra" at the helm for *Hänsel und Gretel*. Sooner or later, the orchestra men, unaccustomed to his level of intensity, were bound to flag. Their letdown came in the Sunday concert, when they showed themselves unable to give eloquence to Beethoven's Fifth Symphony.

Taking the beat from her illustrious partner in the pit, Lucille Marcel shared in his *réclame*, as Tosca, Marguerite, and Aïda. While not a passionate actress, she showed definite conceptions of each character. Her Tosca seemed a woman of a higher sort, Hale thought, whose deep love for Mario received a mortal wound at his apparent faithlessness, and who gloried in the murder of Scarpia—an original touch. She attempted no new stage tricks in *Faust* but adhered to old traditions. She neither wriggled, crawled, nor sobbed through Aïda's tragedy, confining the characterization to her voice, which as always displayed strong, full, rich quality. Hale remarked that it might be as well to cast two Aïdas as two Juliettes—or two Traviatas, by the same token—to span the different vocal and dramatic requirements of the first and last acts of these operas. But he felt it more important that Aïda's voice should possess sensuous beauty, like Marcel's, rather than the clarion call of the purely dramatic soprano, since the greater part of the role is emotionally lyrical. In a Beethoven song and Mozart arias, Marcel confirmed the critics' good opinion of her vocal qualities at the Sunday concert, with Urlus as an expressive partner.

Parker as usual expended twenty words to Hale's two. He saw Marcel's Floria Tosca as a subdued design, deliberately wrought, an ordered foil to the ferocities of Marcoux.

The Marcel voice as demonstrated in Boston seemed a far cry from the clamorous shrillings which were said to have made her famous. Recommended by Jean De Reszke, she stepped into an *Elektra* performance in Vienna, taking the place of the heroine at short notice. Evidently the then strange music, which Ernestine Schumann-Heink, suffering through one performance as Klytaemnestra, characterized as "a frightful bellowing from a set of mad women," did not bother the young Lucille. Weingartner complimented Boston for recognizing what Vienna had not—that the charm of Lucille's singing lay not only in her voice, but in her personality.

Born in New York under the name of Wasself, Marcel had the advantage of piano lessons from a remarkable teacher, Alexander Lambert. With this foundation and four years of voice training with Mme. Serrano, she flitted very early in her life to Berlin, thence to Paris, where she encountered the beneficial domination of Jean De Reszke. The chain of recommendations led from the famous tenor to Weingartner, and thence to Strauss and the Vienna *Elektra*.

Buxom, with large, expressive eyes, a wide mouth that pressed dimples into service as it smiled, Marcel exuded vigor and a certain earthy charm that belied her lyricism on stage. She perched in a box at every Weingartner performance (when she wasn't singing, of course) and greeted her hero with a beaming face and a waving arm and hand at his every entrance. The frankness of it all surprised the reticent New England folk of boxes and parquet.

Weingartner immediately made his voice heard. Fond of explaining himself and the technique and art of music, he issued a pamphlet on conducting and gave interviews freely, peppered with aphorisms, shrewd sayings, and pronouncements on musical styles. Strauss seemed all "noise," and indeed, like Debussy and D'Indy, displayed more style than ideas. Although he considered Bruckner rather a fad, he placed his firm faith in the diatonic scale of Bach and Beethoven—good news for Boston. Although he lived only two blocks from Karl Muck, who returned in triumph to lead the Boston Symphony for his second tenure, beginning in 1912, there is no evidence that the two men, adversaries in the Berlin situation that had resulted in Weingartner's departure, made up their differences under Boston's benign influence.

15

THEY ALSO SERVE

Backstage and below stage in an opera house an orderly chaos reigns. Preoccupied little men scurry around from dark corner to dark corner, carrying notebooks and gesticulating with pencils; bawling out incomprehensible orders to each other; hurrying with a sure step past ropes drawn vertically taut and dirty canvas flapping from high, hidden booms, over platforms painted a gangrenous green or a fake stone-gray; or merely standing and waiting. Once the curtain is up, the pattern becomes clear. That one is an electrician: his cues are all set, and all he has to do is to make sure the man on the switchboard knows them. That one is a technical wizard: every piece of scenery has been built to fit and painted to design; every bit of the puzzle will fall into place, and the medieval castle or peasant hut will take on solid reality—or lighter fantasy. This one watches the huge face of the clock: between one tick and another his raised hand flashes down; the waves of the heavy curtain slowly part, poise for an instant as if undecided, then sweep widely upward out of sight. Spaced at intervals behind the scenery, which shows heavenly blue to the front but is drab and braced at the back, stand the assistant conductors, interested only in what is visible through peep holes in the back drops.

Their duties are most often those of glorified office boys; they wait for the rare night when, baton in hand, they will be giving their colleagues signals instead. Meanwhile, one of two or more of them perch on ladders or crouch in corners behind the scenes, anxiously watching the countenance (too often, to their minds, Mephistophelean) that contorts and writhes in the tiny, piercing light on the conductor's desk, but even more tensely observing the hand and stick as it rises and falls and circles and chops. They must anticipate this hand. As it descends, they must have already sketched that descent to a singer, a trumpeter, a small group of instruments, or even a big chorus, from whom the conductor is obscured. One of these subordinates, acting as prompter, will don a coverall and climb from below the stage into a little tower whose top rises above the footlights. Translating the maestro's signals from a rear-view mirror, he reinforces the beat while shouting the first word of every singer's vocal entrance, often adding a strange pre-echo effect to the music.

Below the stage floor, in cells too murky to yield their shadows to the bare bulb no matter what its wattage, the servitude strikes a note of grimness. Push a button and the silent machinery all around suddenly breaks into a vicious hum; pull a lever and the ceiling opens, letting down a little square curiously covered with what castle carpet or grassy sward lies above. Onto this square steps a motley figure: devil or goddess has been summoned to the crust of the earth from its bowels. Given the proper pushbutton, the apparition will arrive safely at earth level.

They still talk in Boston about the time when Satan got trapped in his own realm. It was of course a performance of *Faust*, not an ordinary repeat, but a fine gala in the middle of Felix Weingartner's first week as guest conductor. Everyone showed a case of nerves to begin with. Weingartner knew that Lucille Marcel, the Marguerite of the evening (and his own true love), felt slightly ill. She had sung Tosca two nights previously, and the first excitement had worn off, leaving her not quite up to another effort. The tension persisted past the curtain and infected the entire crew. Below the stage floor sat Russian-born Alexander Smallens, in his first American job, waiting a cue to push a button. Above, an ambitious new electrician pulled too many levers at once and—poof! went a fuse below. It couldn't have occurred at a worse moment. Smallens pushed the button on cue. But no little square descended. The trap door didn't budge.

Then the fun started. As required by the story, the old Doctor Faust in his study resorted to desperate measures to recall his youth, summoning help from another world with a cry, "À *moi!*" Nothing happened. Half-fearful, he looked about him as if searching for information from his millions of books. From behind his white beard, Faust became more and more the tenor Zenatello, casting glances ever more sharply at the spot where from lower regions should come his visitor. At last, from below, a muffled voice: *"Me voici!"* But no apparition. Standing beside Smallens, dressed in the sleek green habiliments he affected as Méphistophélès, Vanni Marcoux was too expert an artist to let his cue pass; the equally experienced Zenatello chimed in from above, so that for a moment the Boston audience witnessed a unique duet between the Devil in Hell and Man on Earth.

Weingartner, by this time fuming and worrying about Lucille, did an unprecedented thing: he dropped his baton and, brushing musicians to the right and left of him, made for the underground door to backstage. From his seat in the seventeenth row, Manager Henry Russell picked up the phone that connected him with the mechanical staff and ordered the curtain down. As the music quieted, the buzz in the auditorium rose to compensate.

No explanation was offered; Weingartner reappeared and took up the stick to begin just before where he had left off. Again the moment arrived that had betrayed everybody. Méphistophélès by the libretto is required to hand Faust the fateful goblet to drink. Marcoux had given up all idea of using the trap and had made a fast sprint to the wings. The curtain rose again on his entrance. Only part of the string section joined in Weingartner's distracted beat; the harried conductor once more jumped down and flailed a path through violins and cellos, while Pierre Henrotte, the concertmaster, sprang to the podium, but too late to prevent cacophony. His moment of glory subsided; Weingartner returned, mopping his high, glistening forehead, and gave the signal to turn back all pages.

Faust began all over again. This time the Devil emerged from the alcove in Faust's library. Several jokesters urged the retention of this bit of business, considering it highly appropriate that the philosopher's learned books should yield such diabolical magic. Alexander Kahn, the company's press oracle, capitalized on the incident as a sign of the Opera House's displeasure at Marcoux's imminent departure. Russell, perhaps superstitiously, perhaps not, did not cast the popular baritone as Méphistophélès again until another season had gone by.

This contretemps, and another the same season, remained unique in the Boston Opera annals. The second incident occurred during a *Trovatore* on March 13, when the water pipe burst, incapacitating the hydraulic machinery that controlled the asbestos curtain. For fully five minutes, the audience watched in fascination as the line of demarcation between them and Maria Gay, being pitifully abused by the Count De Luna's soldiers, crept inexorably downward. Gay and the chorus men were virtually on their knees, heads lowered sideways, trying to get their message across in the ever diminishing space. Finally, not an inch remained. Moranzoni signaled his men to silence, then lifted his baton for a selection or two to while away the time. Fifty minutes went by. The audience, smelling no smoke, sat quietly. At last the performance resumed—in front of the asbestos barrier. Zenatello omitted his suave aria, "Ah sì, ben mio," but sang "Di Quella Pira" with great abandon, and the "Miserere" and "Ai nostri monti" scenes proceeded as if their proper backgrounds were present.

"Good old *Trovatore*," mused Hale, apropos this disjointed performance. Always a breeding ground for anachronisms and unlikely bits of business. He remembered that in Maretzek's company many years before, Ferrando, Di Luna's captain, wore a huge sombrero instead of an ornate helmet, and that a bygone Leonora daintily carried a lace handkerchief throughout her trials in all four acts.

No opera house is without its bat, or the cat that crosses the stage, sublimely indifferent, during Aïda's passionate importunity to her gods. A stage manager's laxity will allow student supers to go on with their twentieth-century trouser legs and shoes peeping beneath their Egyptian robes; a medieval band in *Die Meistersinger* or *Aïda* will sport rimless glasses under pancake chapeaux or towering headdresses. Too realistic an actor will, as in the case of Rodolfo Fornari, put more energy into his part than called for. When this Marcello threw his hat at Musetta in the third act of *La Bohème*, he cast off his wig as well. Opera would not be opera without these ridiculous moments.

But for the most part, Russell's fairly expert staff worked competently to assure smooth performances. Still, the life of an assistant conductor or stage director held few joys. The pay Smallens described as measly—in fact, a list of the payroll of 1911–12 later unearthed shows him to have received only $611.00 for the season, next to the lowest fee of $555.60, which was taken in by Walter Straram, a Frenchman who later gained a place in the world press as conductor and partner of Ganna Walska, the Polish-American socialite singer. Among the half-dozen assistants in Boston, salaries ran as high as $1,932.44, paid to an Italian with the unlikely name of Clandestini; or $1,653.95, paid to Charles Strony, who in the next two seasons would pick up the cream of the conducting assignments. All of the assistants scrounged for extra jobs, finding them usually as coaches for various singers. Smallens coached Edmond Clément in *Louise*, giving ten lessons at five dollars a lesson. And Arnaldo Schiavoni, who made twice Smallens' salary, charged only three dollars a lesson, to Smallens' disgust. Schiavoni would get real conducting jobs as well in the season of 1913–14, while Smallens, whose bristly, independent attitude won him none of Russell's love, was being held down to two Sunday concerts and then was cut out of an important work because his oboe soloist complained to Russell that Smallens had tried to make him change his conception of the solo part of Bizet's "L'Arlésienne" Suite. The oboist, after all, maintained that he had played the work under the original conductor, Colonne, in Paris, and upstaged Smallens decisively.

After Caplet had relented in his disdainful attitude toward the younger conductor, Smallens was summoned to Russell's presence one morning. He had just about decided to give up music, take his mother's advice, and go back to his original study of medicine. The conversation with the impresario went like this:

Russell: "I don't like your character."

Smallens: "I don't like yours, but we are not engaged in character tests here."

He prevailed; even got a raise of ten dollars a week, and gave up medicine for good. But never under Russell, indeed, not until the Boston Opera Company had been reconstituted in 1915 by Max Rabinoff, did Smallens come into his own as a conductor.

Meanwhile his chores—and his colleagues'—duplicated and multiplied. At one time, Smallens would coach the magnificent Ernestine Schumann-Heink from the wings as she sang the gypsy Azucena in German, surrounded by Italian colleagues in *Trovatore*. These instances of mixed language then occurred frequently in the opera houses of the world, and were treated philosophically. Boston registered additional instances: Clément singing Rodolfo in French, Garden doing all of Tosca but "Vissi d'arte" in French.

The most stirring example of this divergency in language revolved around a *Tristan* in 1913. Carl Burrian, the Metropolitan tenor who had sung the Boston performance on January 31, a Friday, knowing that his wife was mortally ill, returned to New York for a Siegmund in *Die Walküre* the following Thursday, then notified Boston that he was sailing for Germany because his wife had died, and he could not sing the Saturday matinee. Frantic telephone calls produced no substitute: Jacques Urlus was firmly committed to his Metropolitan debut on the crucial date; Charles Dalmorès, whom Chicago counted on for the role, was still on the high seas. A rumor reached Russell; tranquilly dwelling in New York, as the husband of Margarete Matzenauer, was the Venetian Edoardo Ferrari-Fontana, considered the most romantic tenor since the ineffable Jean De Reszke, and Italy's and South America's favorite Tristan. Russell begged the tenor to oblige. He agreed. Only then did the nagging problem arise: what language would he sing? His Wagner had been entirely in the Italian tongue. Would he try to learn the German and so keep the homogeneity of the performance? He reluctantly agreed to that too. Only a few hours remained; Ferrari-Fontana spent them closeted with Samuel Endicott, the young coach chosen for the task of Teutonizing him. Endicott recalls that the task proved impossible from the start. After about twelve pages, the towering tenor stormed up to the piano, grabbed the heavy score, and threw it across the room, shouting, *"Finito! Finito! Non posso più!"*

But he persisted until curtain time. Safely negotiating the shoals of the first and second acts, a goodly portion of which is taken up by a duet with Tristan's lady love, he foundered on the reef of the third act, which is almost entirely the tenor's. Weingartner had been fuming through the minutes and hours. Minnie Saltzmann-Stevens, the new Isolde, a charming American and one of the few genuine pupils of Jean De Reszke, who had come from Chicago to make her Boston debut, labored under uncertainty caused by having had to make a mere piano runthrough do for a real rehearsal. A small storm backstage at second act intermission resolved itself into one stubborn fact: Tristan would sing Italian or else. The order passed down. Prompters bristled at every strategic point in the wings, while in the box Smallens and Ralph Lyford squeezed together for the final scene, the former throwing Italian words to the dying Tristan, the latter German cues to Isolde. No one in the audience seemed to mind. And Ferrari-Fontana won the right to sing another Tristan, entirely in Italian, two nights later.

Several of the assistants must have thought the millennium had arrived early in the 1912–13 season, when Caplet fell ill and Strony succeeded to two *Thaïs* performances (both with Mary Garden); Lyford (who had begun as assistant chorus master and one day would found the Cincinnati Zoo Opera) received the nod for *Lucia,* and Horace Britt, later well known as a cellist, took over part of a Sunday night concert. At another concert, Anthony Dubois, who had hitherto acted mainly as a prompter, received the baton to accompany his Belgian confrère, the leonine violinist, Eugen Ysaÿe, who played the Vieuxtemps Concerto in D Minor, Lalo's "Symphonie Espagnole," and Charles Martin Loeffler's transcription of Chabrier's Scherzo. Loeffler, who had been a first violinist in the Boston Symphony until 1903 and who now held a comfortable position as a composer, rose up in the audience to acknowledge applause for his work. Ysaÿe, it was said, perpetrated a few small slips in technique, "little clouds of unevenness, no bigger than a man's hand." In the emergency atmosphere, everything was forgiven. The Boston Symphony, too, was undergoing a period of minor strain. Karl Muck, newly returned to his old post, suffered a short illness, during which Otto Urack, a new cellist, ascended to the podium for three concerts. It was quite a week among the "petits maîtres."

Generally the assistants had nothing more elevated to do than to make sure the cannon shot in *Tosca* came off to the second, one passing the beat along to another, who banged a big bass drum. It took seven men to ring the bells in the prelude to the third act of the same opera, each one grimly watching a different signaler and hoping for the best. Or Smallens would spend a half hour holding a leafy branch against the tower on a *Pelléas et Mélisande* set, while Caplet and Urban discussed the artistic possibilities of the shadow. Fortunately for Smallens' sense of accomplishment, they used the branch in performance.

Arnaldo Conti, the Boston Opera Company's first conductor, got a clever idea for *Otello* one day, and instructed Endicott to go down into the pit and warm up the organ fifteen minutes before the curtain.

"Be there; watch me," said Conti. "And when I cue you, put your foot on the three lowest pedals. You'll see."

The resultant roar approximated nicely the pounding of surf on rocks suggested by the orchestral storm at the beginning of Verdi's Shakespearean setting.

The Boston Opera House possessed what at the time was considered marvelous facilities for making steam. Several operas call for obscuring clouds. Although Wagner's *Die Walküre* was not in Russell's repertoire, other companies later availed themselves of the fine "magic fire" effects made possible by a row of pipes set just under the removable floor boards in front of the prompter's box. Electric fans would hoist streamers of red and yellow striped cloth fluttering into the air; mixed with the steam, they simulated tongues of flame most realistically.

Assistant *répétiteurs* learn the hard way; and promotion seldom is one of the rewards of their job. Its benefits lie in the value of hoarded experience, which, to win honor, they must carry on to new surroundings. The penchant for practical joking that is shared by opera personnel high and low probably runs sharpest among these harried yet bored young men. Combined with professional insight, the genius for contriving embarrassing situations burns fiercely within them. Leo Devaux, a secondary tenor who had spent one year at the Metropolitan, then joined Boston in its second season and became French *régisseur* in 1911–12, offered a tempting target. Several of the assistants thought him a fussy ignoramus. In preparing a *mise-en scène*, Devaux would interleave his piano score with transparent papers busily inscribed with notes to himself and others, a practice in good standing with other stage directors before and since. Straram and Smallens found the score for *Louise* unguarded one day. With mischievous alacrity they interchanged the sheets until what applied to Act I turned up in Act II and vice versa. The distraught Devaux couldn't clear up the confusion for hours.

Répétiteurs and *régisseurs* were privy to moods and character revelations on the part of the singers, great or lowly, who moved across the stage or sang and spoke at their bidding. Prompting from the wings one night, Smallens noted that Melba, elevated upon her balcony, became more and more annoyed as the young and handsome Lucien Muratore, below her, poured out Roméo's soul in Gounod's song. Maintaining the entranced pose of charmed girlhood, the diva muttered, as the tenor's ovation mounted, "It doesn't pay to be an opera singer, Smallens. Have you any idea what they did for me at my twenty-fifth anniversary in Covent Garden? No? Well, all I got was twenty-five shillings' worth of red roses."

The next instant she was all music, sending Juliette's farewell to the ears of her lover and to the hearts of the rapt audience. The assistants, though often harshly opinionated, showed respect where due. "This was the greatest voice, bar none," recalled Smallens. "Each tone was like a pearl in all registers."

Smallens' introduction to another side of operatic life came at a party given for the press by Alexander Kahn, the lively public relations chief, at the Lenox Hotel. The young conductor had never had a cocktail in his twenty years; the resultant glow inspired him to universal friendliness. He remembers dancing on a table; dancing with Olin Downes, one of the few critics who deigned to show up. Neither Hale nor Parker came. Downes helped him home like a real chum.

In the hierarchy of the stage, Delfino Menotti ranked uppermost for three years as general *régisseur*, retiring when Josef Urban took over the direction as well as the designing in 1912. Menotti, a quiet, cultured Italian gentleman, formerly a baritone, exerted a beneficent influence by character and ability. Oreste Sbavaglia, a capable *routinier*, presided over the chorus, which increased in efficiency each year.

Whatever the jealousies and bickering of the artistic personnel, an opera house staff, backstage or "house," generally forms a loyal and knowing group, a working team of character and color that any business man would be proud to command. Head technician or wardrobe mistress, office boy or head usher, all mesh smoothly to provide the frame for the living picture on stage.

Boston's opera house boasted a good share of these personages, from the venerable Charles F. Tukey, formally known as superintendent of the building, but more familiarly as the Irish Cerberus of the stage door, to Albert Lothian, the genie of the box office. Tukey was a quiet man, with an all-seeing eye and a tongue that held its freight for a few chosen ears; he missed nothing that went in the back entrance but kept his counsel well. Lothian, a cheerful soul, whose very dreams provided hilarious anecdotes, was ever ready with the bright word, the quick retort. He feared nobody, genuflected to no sacred cows, and even brought Mrs. Jack Gardner up short when she stretched privilege beyond limits. Much as he admired the taste of Boston's *grande dame*, he could not find it in his heart to let her slip in through the back of the house, having given her ticket to a guest, then ask the usher to place a seventh chair in her box.

"I'll have to charge you for an extra seat," he told her.

Furiously she snapped: "People drop in."

"Yes, because you 'drop in' at the stage door," he retorted.

Even at Al's funeral, two of his friends could not resist telling his widow how Al had scored over Mrs. Jack. The switchboard operator in the opera office had long suffered that lady's queenly ways: she would come in hurriedly "just to make a phone call," then would depart as precipitately.

"I didn't dare ask her for a nickel," said the girl to Mrs. Lothian. "But

Al came in one day and caught her at it. 'Mrs. Gardner,' he said, 'you surely don't want this switchboard girl to pay for your calls out of her modest salary—and that's what she's going to have to do!' I tell you, she was mad! She put down five cents and flounced out. But she kept on being nice to Al. He was the only one who stood up to her."

Al Lothian had long ago endeared himself to Eben Jordan, Jr., not only for his sterling qualities, but because his father had chaperoned Eben, Isadore Braggiotti and Herbert Dumaresq on their sally round the world as young men. Lothian Senior, a gifted musician, had conducted the orchestra at the Boston Theatre, trained many actors and musicians, and brought up his own sons to be theatrical men. One of Al's brothers chose footlights; another became manager for the Colonial Theater when Al reigned over the box office, and a third acted as personnel manager to Mrs. Patrick Campbell. All three got together at one of Mrs. Campbell's engagements. The running joke of those days was the size and grandeur of ladies' hats. One imposing dame in a proscenium box refused the usher's request to doff her bonnet.

"Do you realize who that is? That is Mrs. John Jacob Astor!" a member of her party protested loftily.

The lady's identity couldn't have mattered less to Al, who said so in several blistering words. His victory was Pyrrhic; the lady kept her hat on and left the theater.

Lothian was Jordan's inevitable choice for treasurer of the new Boston Opera's box office; a similar post was opened to him later at Jordan Hall, where he remained for thirty-five years. The trust and affection between the two men ran deep and steady. Jordan, never loquacious, nevertheless unburdened himself occasionally to this old friend. He confessed to weariness at certain gossip, which had it that Jordan had founded the opera house for the sole purpose of advancing his family socially.

"Absurd," Lothian quoted Jordan as saying. His wife, a member of an old Philadelphia Quaker family, put social advantage last in the scale of values; his daughter was totally without that kind of social ambition and could make her way by her charm and character. Lothian fumed at this misunderstanding of the motives of a fine and generous man. Why, Major Higginson, for all his prestige, and for the indirect benefit he received in the business world for his patronage of the Boston Symphony, never put as much into the orchestra as Jordan did into the opera, Lothian maintained.

Lothian's loyalty extended to Ralph Flanders, controversial manager of
the New England Conservatory, and for a time intimately connected with
the opera management, who with Jordan was responsible for Lothian's
long stay at Jordan Hall. Whatever his way with countless schemes for
increasing his own and others' capital, and whatever the difficulties his
somewhat devious mind led him into, he possessed the quality of un-
faltering friendship. He continued in positions of trust after the opera
company's dissolution, managing the Boston seasons of the Chicago and
Metropolitan companies for a time.

Al was in a strategic position to defend the morals of the opera house.
Behind his cage, he appeared to be at the mercy of subscribers and occasional ticket buyers, but grumblers seldom escaped unscathed.

"So you don't want to come to the opera because you think the tenor
is immoral? Better not listen to Wagner or Verdi either!"

Al believed that Jordan exercised the same tolerance. What if Russell
seemed as extravagant in his moral life as in his budget? You can't run
people's private lives.

The unorthodox family situation of the Russells was an open secret to
Lothian and his wife, who in later years lived in the very apartment that
Alice Nielsen had occupied. (Mrs. Lothian is still there.) Russell could
walk from his own roof to Alice's, Mrs. Lothian commented. But he always exercised the utmost care and tact, especially in keeping his two
sons away from any atmosphere of criticism.

As for Russell's conduct of the opera house, it was clouded no more,
and Lothian believed even less, than many another's by the shadow of
the "casting couch." That vulgarity, rife in the theater, infected the opera
only to a minor degree, he maintained. In New York, no one would
have complained. But every Bostonian who owned a box or subscribed to
an orchestra seat felt himself or herself the guardian of public morals
and never hesitated to speak up.

The Shuberts kept Lothian on at the Opera House for a while. Al's
father and the elder Shubert had been acquainted. Napier Lothian told
Al about the old man, who, when the sons began to be successful, tried
in vain to get recognition and money from them. In revenge, he would
take a peddler's tray and stand in various theater lobbies hawking shoe-
laces to embarrass his ungrateful progeny.

Al failed in only one undertaking in his long and useful life. He attempted to teach Maria Gay English. One day he asked Russell to paint on his door the word "Private" in nine languages.

"I have a pupil," he explained. "You're not the only teacher."

Gay had a leading part in the English version of *Martha,* and in one speech she had to say, "Goodness gracious!" Lothian volunteered to coach her. He seldom heard an actual performance, but occasionally repaired to the second balcony for an hour or two of rehearsals. When the *Martha* night arrived, he managed somehow to slip away from his post at the crucial moment.

"Goodness grass-ious!" the mezzo uttered. Lothian quit teaching on the spot.

16

PRIMA DONNAS AND PORTENTS

"The days of resurrection continue," sighed H. T. Parker, as the Boston Opera season of 1911–12 drew to a close. Emma Calvé had woven glittering bits of mosaic into the fabric; Lillian Nordica had risen up grandly as the majestic Isolde; and Emma Eames had uttered what proved to be her last syllable from the opera stage as recently as December. A vague rumor persisted, said Parker, pursuing this line of thought quite logically, that Lilli Lehmann was being considered for next season's Donna Anna. Ernst Van Dyck, now in Brussels, might still be worth hearing in declamatory song. And if Jean De Reszke had not definitely retired, Boston might reconstitute opera as opera was in the America of the nineties. This process held out appeal to those—and they were numerous in Boston—who clung to the belief that the past, operatic or otherwise, was generally superior to the present. Sometimes, he suggested, they even preferred to hear with their memories rather than with their ears; to let recollection shade their eyes from disillusion.

Eames should not have chosen Tosca as one of her farewell roles. It was simply not in her to portray a woman now frivolous, now intense, now adorably jealous. Soft gusts of emotion never swept this great lady. But, like other women of the opera stage, she remained discontented with the laurels justly hers and coveted those of others. Only a few days before the December 18 performance, she had been quoted as saying that she liked Floria Tosca because of her primitive, elemental expression of emotion.

Eames, distinguished by calmness, serenity, poise, and self-control, was the very last to portray Tosca, Philip Hale insisted.

Once before the public in this late flowering, it could be seen—at least, by masculine eyes—that her beauty endured. The feminine portion of the audience murmured a bit reproachfully—and unfairly?—at her new matronly aspect. She had not been in Boston since her Iris and Donna Anna of April 1908 with the Metropolitan. The face kept its classic profile, suggesting, when she bound her hair with silver laurel, a Roman matron of the patrician line. The voice retained its quality; the skill showed no lessening. One rejoiced in that individual, unique, crystal clearness, the fine, bell-like chime of some higher notes, silvery in cool lusters, curiously like chastity in sound to Parker. She flew in the face of the new "tradition" and sang, rather than shrieked, shouted, or "mouthed." Desdemona served her singular talents far better, and allowed her to say good-by with dignity and pathos. Even though traces of hoarseness were evident, the voice gave much to enjoy, with its rare natural beauty and the singer's mastery of her art. Thereafter she confined herself to concert singing, usually as a partner to her second husband, the dapper, distinguished baritone, Emilio De Gogorza. But she had proved to Boston that she still could provide a lesson to the majority of singers.

Between Eames' two appearances on December 18 and 22, another prima donna inserted her claims for attention. Although Luisa Tetrazzini had twinkled often in Hammerstein's galaxy, her first appearance with Russell's company was as Lucia on December 20. Her advent gave the entire house reason to join with the Donizetti chorus in its shout, "*Immenso giubilo!*" She had been ill, and the effects showed in her abstention from Lucia's highest notes, also in a gesture appealing for the audience's indulgence. But never had she shown more intelligence or warmth. The superb exhibition of vocal art embraced a pure and finely sustained legato, the ability to swell and diminish a tone, an exquisite manner of launching a phrase and ending it, truly phenomenal control of breath, and an unending flow of bravura.

It goes without saying that the audience for this *Lucia di Lammermoor* exceeded any other to date. Not since Melba's prime had such adulation been vouchsafed. An unusual number of masculine patrons could be noted, many of whom seldom went to the opera, considering it a sensuous luxury, no doubt.

No one but a lone and captious critic objected to the costuming, which would have caused a riot in the Scottish Highlands, with its mixture of tartans even among a single clan, Lowlanders to boot. Tetrazzini, who formerly wore a modified evening frock of modish cut, yielded to the budding desire for "authentic" staging to the extent of appearing in a first-act dress trimmed with tartan bands. It suggested the gowns the late Queen Victoria wore at gala evenings in Balmoral. But fitness obtained in all things, for the milksop Arturo sported silken panties of the palest and tenderest blue, matching the voice that usually comes from this character.

The prima donna's illness had given Russell the opportunity to substitute *Samson et Dalila* with Gay and Zenatello for the previously planned *Lucia*, a not entirely unhappy accident in spite of the jar to the schedule. It put an entirely French complexion on the third week, together with *Thaïs, Carmen,* and *Faust;* a little hard on Caplet, who conducted them all, but a pleasure to Russell. The manager privately expressed disdain for all prima donnas of ripe Italian figure, with their coarse, peasant habits (a board over the tub in their hotels to cook their redolent pasta sauces; no hesitance in teeth-picking or nose-blowing); but the public must be served. Russell realized that very well. "I hired Tetrazzini," he said, "but I don't have to listen to her."

The critics showed indulgence to the plump singer. As Vladimir de Pachmann remained almost the sole survivor of a vanishing race of pianists in the grand manner, so Tetrazzini seemed to perpetuate the ancient line of divas who are a law unto themselves. Even Melba had kept within the framework of an opera's story, maintaining her own dignity and that of the theater. Younger coloraturas, like Frieda Hempel and Selma Kurz, chose to follow new ways, but Tetrazzini innocently and honestly hewed to the old ones. Listeners expected her to curtsey and smile, wave her arms in embracing gestures, and kiss her hand to the audience before setting about Lucia's melancholy and mellifluous soliloquy. At a curtain call within memory, she had tossed a flower to the conductor and cried, "Thank you! Thank you!" in an ecstatically childish voice. To one observer she and the supporting flutist in the soliloquy gave the impression of two goldfish disporting themselves in a globe of clear water.

As for the famous voice, it had lost its first upper softness, but gained a diamond-like luster. The middle, rich and luscious, gave way to a queer, infantile quality in lower tones—so often a weakness in the coloratura lexicon—which she strove to hide, but which continued to be an anomaly. Her ornamentation had been perfected—the runs, trills, and dainty staccato. Best of all, she still gave each phrase its just place in the musical line. No doubt she appeared as the successor of Melba and Sembrich. Yet her real musical nature remained baffling. The question would continue to be asked: Is it all instinct?

Single performances of *Traviata* and *Barber of Seville* brought the roly-poly idol before the footlights again. The younger portion of the audience did not seem to mind that their Violetta boasted the morals of a demi-mondaine and the figure of a washerwoman. Only the high notes counted, as they always had, and the ability to project them with business-like certainty. One realistic detail horrified the oldsters. The dying Violetta, after a racking cough, inspected her handkerchief, with the care of a sanitorium patient. "Disgusting!" shuddered the dowagers.

What vocal satisfaction was wrung from the performance aside from the lady's fireworks came entirely from Zenatello's first Alfredo. Playing his father, Polese seemed to rally all the bogy-men that catch sentimental baritones if they don't watch out. He wriggled his tones, stressed the "home and mother" (in this case sister) motif for all it was worth.

The atmosphere brightened as Rosina, Figaro, and Basilio took over the stage for comic purposes. Marcoux had not been seen before in complete comedy guise; he animated the whole evening with his long, lean, black bean of a music master, interminably tall and all rolling whites of eyes. His antics knocked the last stilt from under an audience that usually sat on its dignity. That this malicious, almost sinister figure and voice could also be the brooding, bumbling Golaud seemed incredible.

The example set before her inspired Tetrazzini to livelier acting than usual. Her talents in any case lent themselves more comfortably to comedy than tragedy. In the most heartbreaking moment of *Traviata*, a spectator detected her in an open and flagrant wink at an acquaintance in the wings. The saucy minx Rosina fitted her very well, and she played up deliciously to the doddering clamors of another clever portraitist, Luigi Tavecchia, as Bartolo, as well as to the plausible, glib intrigues of Rodolfo Fornari as Figaro. In his usual high spirits, Constantino, as "love interest," provided an excellent foil to Marcoux's lean vulture of a Basilio. The same sparkling mixture never would be repeated in Boston, although Marcoux remained as the pivotal force among other changing inhabitants of Rossini's eighteenth-century Seville.

The term "prima donna" lost its exclusively feminine connotation (except for the early castrati, of course) somewhere along the course of operatic history, so the mantle now falls on the shoulders of sopranos, tenors, baritones, and basses alike. Many males in the old days—Mario, Jean-Baptiste Faure, and Luigi Lablache—were wont to receive adulation complacently, and after them Victor Maurel (for whom the term "matinee idol" was coined), the De Reszke brothers, Plançon, Caruso, Chaliapin, and in our own day Pinza, Gigli, Siepi, Björling, Corelli, and London.

Such a one was Maurice Renaud, who said his farewell to America in 1912. The Athanael of *Thaïs* and the High Priest of *Samson* had been preceded by a role peculiarly his own, the Jester in *Rigoletto*. One January showing placed him in the center of an inauspicious cluster of singers: Scotney, who seemed to try to ape Tetrazzini's childish voice without its true youthful quality; Constantino, who required long warming-up; Gay, who kept uneasy faith with the pitch; and Mardones, who wavered with the others. The hero of the evening could not himself be crowned for vocal prowess, but the strength and vividness of his communication preserved the character intact. Renaud was too acute an actor to turn Rigoletto into the awesome monstrosity Victor Maurel had made of him. Renaud above all used his imagination to live, think, move in the part he assumed, rather like the "Method" actor of today. Boston counted on seeing him as Sheriff Rance in *The Girl of the Golden West*, the role he had created in Chicago and later abandoned to Sammarco. It would have made an interesting interruption of the Galeffi-Polese-Amato spectrum. A Frenchman's interpretation of an Italian's conception of an American bad man might give good value. Even more interesting was the possibility that he might be in the cast on the one 1912 occasion when Caruso chose to regale Boston with his unique art. But Renaud bowed out.

Caruso had been promised to Russell *in extenso* as a part of the Metropolitan-Boston exchange. But one thing and another militated against his appearances. After an illness that cut him out of the Metropolitan spring tour of 1909 (when Hammerstein lent Zenatello to Gatti as a replacement), Caruso plunged into a heavy home schedule during the ensuing seasons, assuming his usual Italian roles, adding a few French heroes, and creating new ones in *Germania, Armide,* and Puccini's *Girl.* An active dislike for Boston, which culminated in his refusal to return after 1918, began in 1910, when he associated the city with the receipt of a threatening "Black Hand" letter demanding fifteen thousand dollars. A later bout of measles suffered while in the Hub may also have had something to do with it. He was severely criticized for his indifferent performance at the time. Geraldine Farrar may have influenced his prejudice. She warned him airily that Boston audiences weren't very big, but made up in coldness for their sparse numbers. It wasn't really cricket for Deeney, as her old Melrose friends called her, to put off her colleague thus; but then she had old scores to settle with Russell and never lost an opportunity. A considerable school of thought still maintained that she, as a Boston girl and freshly arrived home after European triumphs, should have been chosen as the star of the Opera House first night. After the Opera House began to operate, Farrar appeared therein only with the Metropolitan on tour, treating her delighted home-towners to three favorite Puccini heroines, Carmen, and two strangers: the Goose Girl in Humperdinck's *Königskinder* and the elevated laundress in *Madame Sans-Gêne*.

Caruso's high spirits, which led him into foolery that often disrupted stage decorum, found no sympathetic echo in Russell's breast. The egg pressed warmly into the hand of a colleague; the coatsleeves sewed up for Colline to struggle vainly against; the top hat filled with water; these childish pranks passed under the indulgent eye of Gatti-Casazza but left the Boston manager chilly. Caruso did what he could, however, to increase the jollity of Boston. Coming before the curtain for one of innumerable curtain calls after *The Girl*, he drew his outlaw's pistol and fired a blank jubilantly into the air. Even the applause couldn't absorb the shocking sound. Boston would have preferred his New York stunt: grabbing Destinn around her ample waist and turkey-trotting her into the wings.

Caruso's fee had been set in a letter from Gatti-Casazza at two thousand dollars per performance; this was in 1910–11, when the tenor did not appear. However it cannot have gone above twenty-five hundred, for this was the limit set by the tenor himself in days when he could have commanded the sky. In one season Russell paid Eames two thousand dollars each for her two appearances; and parted, albeit ruefully, with eighteen thousand dollars for Tetrazzini's half dozen, which made her fee the highest of any but Weingartner's comparable three thousand dollars for each performance. So it cannot have been entirely a financial consideration that kept Caruso out of the Boston Opera House. The box office justified almost any fee paid to the country's operatic idol. Rather it was Russell's ever recurrent opposition to the "system"—plus, of course, the tenor's own wishes in the matter. Henry made another stab at his favorite target at the beginning of the 1912–13 season. In phrases more grandiose and stuffy than usual, he set forth his credo, giving the effect of a parchment scroll, chastely illuminated:

"I do not in any wise overlook or belittle the value in any performance of a skilled and eminent artist, but I cannot but regret and also vigorously oppose any custom or tendency which has as its ultimate end the glorification of the personality of the singer at the expense of the artistic rounding out of the opera representation as a whole."

Let it be said that Russell tried. But the vital need for the golden ones—golden in the sense of their box-office magnetism as well as their aura—and at the same time the growing indifference of the public to all except Caruso and Tetrazzini, pointed an ominous finger toward the future. The shadow began to creep into a corner of the picture as early as Eames's appearance at the head of the fourth week, in 1911–12. The audience's behavior aroused disquiet on the part of observers. Here was a long-admired favorite, awarding to Boston her operatic *adieux;* surely an occasion that should be gala. Instead, the parquet and boxes, the usual Monday night subscription phalanx, received the diva with only a mild rattle of applause.

The causes were not far to seek, Parker thought. Eames fulfilled all that was expected of her, but Boston had begun to take its opera for granted, no matter what was set before it. Four performances a week, and prima donnas might come and go; the old joys and enthusiasms had thinned out into habit. Furthermore, the seatholders' butlers and maids, all too often sent along as proxies, did not possess the experience of the seatholders, limited as that might have been, in the ways of showing appreciation whether they felt it or not. Only sporadically did a display of personal enthusiasm and delight bubble up from the rather sluggish mass below gallery level. In the heights of the house, gaping space all too often betrayed the rectangular backs of seats that should have been obscured by human curves.

Jordan's three-year period of cushioning behind the scenes would soon end; his advisers busied themselves with plans and alternatives. By January the situation had become acute. Mayor John F. ("Honey Fitz") Fitzgerald, who bequeathed to his famous grandson, John Fitzgerald Kennedy, no musical talent stronger than a penchant for rendering "Sweet Adeline," knew a good civic thing when he saw it. He made an honest attempt at this crucial moment to exempt the Opera House from taxes.

Support appeared in the journals for his point of view, but the crushing weight of the opposition made itself felt immediately. A letter to the editor in the *Transcript*, over the signature of Frank Seiberlich, former chairman of the Committee on Taxation in the House of Representatives, who then became a Senator, dismissed assistance to opera as a "dangerous precedent." In an adjoining column, the editor gave this conservative viewpoint a nasty raking over, citing the narrow spirit that had defeated exemption for the Museum of Fine Arts, another deficit institution. Opened on the same night as the Opera House, the Museum had swelled its artistic reputation while mourning that it alone of important art repositories in America received no municipal support. On January 13, Representative Cummings of Boston filed a bill providing for the city's purchase of the Opera House and for a sum for its annual maintenance, at the rate of five cents on every thousand dollars of its assessed valuation. It got nowhere.

Rumors trickled southwestward, so that in mid-January a New York paper predicted that the Boston Opera House would close. Jordan and Russell were forced to indignant denials. Then Jordan put it squarely up to the public in a circular letter published on February 7, in which he revealed that he would no longer assume the annual deficits after this season. Twenty or thirty generous friends had volunteered to help just this once, but he and they would not answer for a fourth season or beyond without broader assistance. He offered the company a rebate in rental for the next three years, which would account for an annual saving of $60,000. The boxholders had been asked to raise their ante by February 15, which would result in an advance over the past of $90,000. In addition, he was now asking the public to raise $150,000, which would bring the available maintenance fund to $300,000, to be used over the three-year period. This was thought to be sufficient, as the expected income, based on previous years, would be around $600,000, while the cost of running the company would be at least $750,000. If by some miracle the full amount of the fund was not used, contributions would be returned after prorating. The boxholders knuckled under meekly, with a 90 per cent vote of confidence. They got off more cheaply, Jordan reminded them, than similar patrons in New York. Their most expensive seat cost only a little more than $10, while the least they could spend for one place was $7.50. "Middle classes" (so-called by one blunt editorial pen) could begin to register their contributions, now that the thoroughbreds were safely tucked into their boxes and stalls.

From mid-February until mid-April, the papers played a kind of game with the campaign, printing the box scores each day. A few of the old reliables sprang immediately into action. In the $5,000 class were Mrs. Robert D. Evans, a Gloucester widow; Mrs. J. Montgomery Sears; and Frank E. Peabody, of Kidder, Peabody. Larz Anderson pledged $1,000 for the first year only; the Hollander Dry Goods' $1,000 presumably was meant to be stretched over the three-year period, as was the Bayard Thayers' and the Baylies' $2,000 apiece. Alexander Cochrane headed the list of ten givers of single thousands. Alexander Steinert, the music merchant, obviously meant to give a thousand ultimately, as his first offering was $333. Less powerful but equally welcome pump primers were His Honor, Mayor Fitzgerald, with $200, and H. T. Parker, with $25. Surprisingly for Boston, which traditionally liked to hide its benefactions behind closed doors or anonymity, few chose coy initials or other disguises, the most munificent being "A Friend," to the tune of $1,000. As the days sped by, the sums dwindled, although a few names—Frothingham, Minot, Moses Williams, several Searses, Amorys, and Coolidges— were sprinkled among what tactless persons called the "little people."

Cheerleaders interpolated shouts of encouragement at intervals. A letter from Cardinal O'Connell to Jordan expressed a sense of civic duty and gratitude for his noble generosity to Boston: "Good opera is distinctly a refining influence and possesses a high educational value." Henry Russell wrote on February 24 that it pleased him deeply to see the fund being swelled by sums of from $5 to $25, a clear indication that enjoyment of the opera was not confined to the well-to-do classes.

On March 5, Mayor Fitzgerald's petition for tax rebate was heard before the Commission on Cities, with Judge Corbett appearing for His Honor. He contended that the Opera House was a losing proposition, and if not for the generosity of one philanthropic citizen in particular, it could not continue. Because of its educational work among the poor, it should be helped by the city.

He couldn't have chosen a more vulnerable position. It immediately raised the question of ticket prices for the "poor." The acknowledgment that one dollar was the very bottom price brought the peevish (and slightly irrelevant) question from Chairman Newhall: "Could the Lawrence strikers afford this?" (These misconceptions of the functions of an opera house and its relation to a public were never cleared up in

Boston, and certainly wrecked the prospects of any favorable settlement at this meeting.) Corbett weakly responded that he couldn't answer for the mill strikers (who were just about to resume work after some strenuous months of dissention and rioting), but he was sure that many poor people patronized the opera.

How about passing a bill with the added proviso that the Opera House should be used for grand opera and nothing else? asked the chairman. Corbett murmured that he didn't know the wishes of the Mayor; the chairman's response to this interjected a political note that drove still another nail into the petitioner's hopes. "Is the Mayor the whole thing?" he demanded. It seemed that under the new charter, he was.

Whereupon Senator Frank Seiberlich rose to add a new bit of ammunition to his offensive. If the public had known, he said, that this petition was coming up, the room wouldn't have held the remonstrants. It was quite clear that Judge Corbett was representing only one individual: the Mayor. As for the non-profit status of the Opera House, it was well known that the Boston Opera Company was operated on a strictly business basis: the property was promoted and financed by Hayden, Stone & Company. And he asserted that if the opera were made exempt, exemption would have to be extended also to the Salvation Army, the Tremont Temple, the Park Street Church, and the Roman Catholic parochial schools.

"To get to that one-dollar seat," he concluded scornfully, "You have to climb more than a hundred steps."

The inadequacy of the petitioner thus exposed, the cause was lost. An inevitable slump in the fund-raising set in immediately after this defeat; then announcement of the plans for next season acted as a hypodermic. At the deadline of April 1, no amount of addition could bring the total above $110,000, however. An appeal by Jordan for $50,000 and editorials backing him up met silence. Boston could not be cajoled out of another ten-spot or thousand; even taunts about Chicago's or Philadelphia's probable response to such an emergency failed to dislodge additional pledges. Boston went about its summer with an apparently clear conscience; Jordan sailed for Europe on April 30, leaving the situation up in the air. By September 9, however, the box office showed signs of liveliness: subscriptions already equaled previous years with two months to go. It was strongly hinted that the necessary $40,000 would be made up privately; furthermore, no future general and public

appeal would be tried. Only "intimate and personal" aid would be so-
licited or accepted. In this suggestion of dismissal of public participation
in its budgetry, no one seemed to read the fate line of the Boston Opera
Company. (Hadn't Russell been re-engaged for three additional years?)
Optimism breathed down Huntington Avenue and on to the *Transcript*
office, where, obviously inspired by H. T. P., although not so initialed,
a summation of the position amused those who had the wit to see themselves as Parker saw them.

Whenever any issue captures the heart and mind of Boston [the column read in part], it becomes an institution, and, as such, a thing for
Bostonians to praise and prize; and grand opera has about reached that
stage of growth in Boston. New York has its grand opera; there it is a
fad and a fashion . . . it is just now the passion of the rich, the near rich,
and the little brothers of the rich. It does for the owners of jewels and
clothes the same office that Madison Square Garden does for horses,
automobiles and circuses; it is the showplace of the spenders, the semi-
nude, and the chatterers; but by-and-by when some other expensive
method of exhibiting raw wealth and half-naked women is discovered,
New York will flout opera, and only the galleries which love music for
music's sake will patronize it.

In Boston grand opera is now indorsed by all the churches and church-
men, and attendance at the opera places no one's morals under suspicion . . . there is a close analogy between the Boston Opera House and
the Kingdom of Heaven: it has its angels; the saints sustain it; the Jordan
refreshes and fertilizes it; the Society of St. Cecilia chants its praises; it
is open to rich and poor; and the poorer you are when you stand outside
its portals the higher you go after you enter it. The opera house repeats
the story of Dives and Lazarus. When last heard from Lazarus was resting
in Abraham's bosom while the malefactor was broiling in nether places;
the exact location of the patriarchal bosom is not indicated, but as
Lazarus was in a position to peek over and enjoy the rapturous vision of
Dives grilling and squirming, the presumption is that the patriarch and
pauper were occupying front seats in the gallery while Dives was in the
pit, or as we term it, the orchestra chairs.

This gem of irony reminded Henry C. Lahee, who reprinted it in his
Grand Opera Singers of Today, of Lord Nelson, who, not wishing to see
certain signals, applied the telescope to his blind eye. Disregarding all
storm signals, however, the opera company chose rather to adopt the
motto of another great seaman: "Damn the torpedoes! Full steam ahead!"

Act IV

17

TALES OF EIGHTY NIGHTS—AND A FEW MATINEES (1912–13)

In his fourth season, Henry Russell's repertoire for the Boston Opera fell into a happy balance in favor of novel elements. Standards of performance rose to unprecedented levels, while the visual aspects of production under Joseph Urban's ministrations acquired brilliance and subtlety hitherto unknown on this continent. After the first *Contes d'Hoffmann*, revolutionary in its aspect, the critic of the *Transcript* went far out on a limb in describing the event as "more finely tempered and revealing than any in America." He added that in many respects, Boston now equaled the Paris Opéra Comique, and this *Tales* compared favorably with Mahler's celebrated production in Vienna, accolade indeed from the intransigent H. T. Parker.

Russell's highest accomplishment during the Boston Opera lustrum resembled a bright mosaic, destined to break up and scatter and lose brilliance all too soon. First into the repertoire of course must be admitted that tight inner ring of staples resting on the Verdi-Puccini axis that turn up every year in all but the most experimental or most heavily subsidized opera houses. One can rattle off these entries almost automatically—*Aïda, Barbieri di Siviglia, Bohème, Carmen, Cavalleria, Faust, Lucia, Butterfly, Pagliacci, Rigoletto, Tosca, Traviata, Trovatore*—as if they were well-visited and all-too-familiar station stops in a trainman's litany. The general excellence of this baker's dozen during most of the season lay at the core of the satisfaction everyone expressed, not the least the balconyites, who sent the barometer up and up by their very presence.

But the full measure of the span of the repertoire could not be judged by these comfortable favorites, nor even by the novelties, which indeed proved weak reeds. Louis Aubert's *La Forêt Bleue* had best been left in France, for all the trouble and expense Russell put himself to in securing its American première. To mount Bizet's one-act *Djamileh* seemed a waste of money and time, particularly of Weingartner's time, as the conductor had so little of it to spend in Boston. And why restore Flotow's *Martha* to currency? many asked themselves.

Success piled up not because of these comparative trifles but rather four masterpieces of widely varied complexion, which entered the repertoire for the first time: *Les Contes d'Hoffmann*, Offenbach's swan song, which opened the season; Mozart's *Don Giovanni*, upon which Weingartner wrought his magic; Charpentier's *Louise*, to which Russell beat the Metropolitan by eight years, although Hammerstein had introduced it first to America; and Wolf-Ferrari's *I Giojelli della Madonna*, anticipating the Met by thirteen years.

Also holding fresh appeal, either because of different casting or continuing superiority, three operas retained from the second season and four from the third completed the prepossessing array. Puccini's *Fanciulla del West* continued to exert a strong fascination for Boston audiences. *Hänsel und Gretel* remained a gem of supernatural fantasy and skillful staging, though the music seemed dull to Parker when Wagnerian and no better when light than Offenbach, Lecocq, Suppé, or Strauss. *Otello* still provided a towering experience in the lyric theater. Repeated from the third season were the three French successes, *Pelléas et Mélisande*, *Samson et Dalila*, and *Thaïs*, while the overpowering *Tristan und Isolde* once more lent much-needed Germanic substance to the otherwise all-Latin (always excepting *Hänsel*) calendar.

The roster, too, shared in the flowering, more lustrous names gleaming than ever before. The conduit from the Metropolitan seemed finally to have been unblocked: no barriers stood in the way of appearances by Frances Alda, Lucrezia Bori, Emmy Destinn, Olive Fremstad, Frieda Hempel, Marie Rappold, Lila Robeson, and Ernestine Schumann-Heink. On the masculine side, Boston had to be content with one appearance each from Enrico Caruso (in *Pagliacci*, his second and last with the company), Carl Burrian (Tristan), Umberto Macnez (the Duke in *Rigoletto*), Riccardo Martin (Pinkerton), Pasquale Amato (Rance in *The Girl*), and Willy Buers (Kurvenal in *Tristan*). John McCormack brought vocal distinction to four tenor parts. Otto Goritz and William Hinshaw divided the role of Peter in *Hänsel und Gretel* between them, one to four; Herman Weil sang Kurvenal twice; Andrés de Segurola took bass parts in *Bohème* and *Faust;* Adamo Didur played Leporello to all three Don Giovannis; and Antonio Pini-Corsi twice assumed the two buffo roles in *Bohème.* Thus the Metropolitan had fair representation in Boston, which Boston's contribution to New York—Alice Nielsen, Maria Claessens, and Edward Lankow—hardly matched. (The status of a young baritone, Anafesto Rossi, is not clear. He appears on both rosters, but sang much more often in Boston.)

Even more to Russell's credit, the foundation of the local company stood secure. Louise Edvina added a new and brilliant note to the sopranos, whose ranks already included Elizabeth Amsden, Fely Dereyne, Bernice Fisher, Lucille Marcel, Carmen Melis, Alice Nielsen, Lillian Nordica, Evelyn Scotney, and the ever scintillating Luisa Tetrazzini. Mary Garden seemed one of the family by now. The faithful Maria Gay and Jeska Swartz upheld mezzo-soprano standards. Russell still could count on Edmond Clément, Giovanni Zenatello, and Jacques Urlus, first magnitude tenor stars, and, with a bow to Chicago, Charles Dalmorès. Vanni Marcoux outshone the other baritones, for such names as Rodolfo Fornari, Giovanni Polese, and Jean Riddez conveyed competence rather than splendor. Three good basses made their department solid: Lankow, José Mardones, and Luigi Tavecchia.

The season got off on the right foot immediately on November 25 with Offenbach's *Tales.* In Urban's illusive settings, the poet's three adventures (with the doll Olympia, the courtesan Giulietta, and the singer Antonia) passed as in a dream, the only reality the prologue and epilogue in the tavern where he relates them. Not only were the settings new, but the score itself had undergone surgery and patching at the hands of the conductor, André Caplet, so that the performance differed materially from Hammerstein's earlier exhibitions, and from the Metropolitan's, which would be seen later that season. With more diligence than taste, Caplet wielded the shears and pastepot. He can hardly be blamed: this opera has suffered almost as many mutations and disputations as Mussorgsky's *Boris Godunov.* Caplet could not benefit from certain later discoveries about Offenbach's intentions. The habit of omitting either or both Prologue and Epilogue, and dropping the Muse, Hoffmann's defender, from either or both, has muddled the otherwise fairly clear line of the story. As intended, the Muse appears at the very first, declaring that she will follow Hoffmann through his fantastic affairs and claim him finally for her own. She then throws off her robe to show the trousered costume of Niklausse, Hoffmann's companion in adventure. This accounts for the part being sung by a mezzo-soprano, otherwise not explicable. Hoffmann is saved for her by his drunkenness, and has forgotten all his other loves (who are at last seen to be one woman in several identities).

Without actually realizing it, the audience should have been able to follow the threads of common identity between the parallel characters in each act. Urban had devised a color scheme that worked exactly like musical leitmotives. Affinities in color and design in the four women's costumes, the prevailing somberness of the evil figures of the four men (three of whom wore the same dull red hair), the splotch of angry bright red of the servant's figure in all three acts, tied these individuals together.

Maurice Grau had brought the opera to America first in 1882, giving it a "completely mounted" production at the Fifth Avenue Theatre on October 16. Offenbach quite naturally still labored under his previous reputation as a frothy musical comedy composer. But this remarkable music reminded the *Times* critic of Meyerbeer and Gounod combined, a compliment which Offenbach nevertheless might not have appreciated.

Hammerstein's revival in 1907 restored the original dialogue, but cut each act here and there and tinkered with the prologue. Gatti-Casazza's version did nothing to clarify the plot. Caplet succeeded in further snarling the originally logical threads, omitting songs for Niklausse and the comedy episode of Franz, Antonia's servant. For another, he transferred the chorus in praise of wine from the prologue to a bridge leading to the first act, which he "composed." Hale caviled after the third performance at Caplet's arbitrary addition of instruments and his own recitatives, which replaced the spoken dialogue.

Boston appreciated the opera for its color, its spectacle, and the singing of several of the principals. Not in recollection had a production been so well prepared or fused with such skillful synthesis and symmetry, Parker remarked. Not the least effective element was Caplet's conducting, which showed fine understanding and imagination.

In choosing the redoubtable Vanni Marcoux as the single dark-voiced protagonist, Boston became the second American company to assign all four roles embodying Hoffmann's enemy to one singer (Hammerstein had used Renaud). The Met didn't get around to this logical casting until much later. Another quadruple masculine role is that of the four servants, which more often than not are assumed by the same *comprimario* tenor.

The more varied demands on Hoffmann's three loves usually cause a prismatic split in the soprano ranks, with the minor role of Stella dealt to a lesser claimant. Russell followed the accepted schizophrenic procedure, giving Olympia to Bernice Fisher (replaced by Evelyn Scotney at the fourth performance and by the newcomer, Frieda Hempel, at the fifth); Giulietta to Elizabeth Amsden for the entire series; and Antonia to Louise Edvina until the final showing, when Lucrezia Bori stepped in. Myrna Sharlow walked through the miniscule part of Stella at each performance.

Clément, singing the part for the first time anywhere, was the ideal Hoffmann by all counts. Slim, romantic in manner as well as contour, the tenor showed grace and elegance, a masculinity yet a dreaminess that accorded well with the poet's sudden changes from introspective melancholy to flaring action. His musical speech, clean, plastic, adroitly shaded, evolved into cantilena more beautiful than any yet heard from him.

With all these gifted apparitions on stage, Marcoux still dominated in voice and action. Parker reveled in describing the four roles, all different, all subtly and imaginatively created, which left no doubt of the singer's own will at work, his disregard of such tradition as already existed in this flamboyant work. Dr. Coppelius, the scorcerer, appeared as a greasy, leering, tattered, and vagabondish peddler of magic, weird and forbidding in glance and accent. Dappertutto, another embodiment of Hoffmann's adversary, was converted from a Chevalier of the eigtheenth century to a kind of silent, baleful Marquis of Steyne, albeit in a bourgeois coat and boots, chewing bitterly upon his lust for possession and vengeance. Dr. Miracle, Antonia's Nemesis, billowed in, enveloped by great black flowing robes, a necromancer of the middle ages. His gaunt, skeleton-like hands, piercing eyes, wheedling and snarling tones bespoke an uncanny bird of prey. As for the Counsellor Lindorf in prologue and epilogue, he appeared the taciturn, middle-aged materialist. A sordid and sinister vein, sharply etched, correlated the four impersonations. At the third performance, Marcoux made definitive changes in Dr. Miracle, discarding the bald, pale head and enveloping robes, and appearing as a mask of death, with curling dark hair, in black riding dress with a cloak over his shoulders and shining boots. This rendered him less like Méphistophélès and more like Death disguised as a quack. Hale's most revealing comment on this *tour de force* came at the end of the season, when he accused Marcoux of being in reality a basso cantante and suffering vocal damage by taking baritone parts, notably this quadruple Offenbach responsibility. Jean Riddez, the four-ply menace of the final performance, returned to tradition in makeup.

Frieda Hempel had been intended for the part of the charming doll, Olympia, but the attractive blond German pleaded illness even before the Metropolitan season. She had come out victorious from a trying experience, which doubtless contributed to her indisposition. Reading with horror an account in a Berlin newspaper which accused her of having partaken in an "orgy" in order to win a decoration from Leopold, the King of Belgium, she immediately instituted libel proceedings. Her vindication was complete, but the wear and tear on a prima donna's nervous system must have been excruciating. She made her Metropolitan debut as Marguerite in *Les Huguenots* (scheduled originally for opening night) on December 27, and added the Mozart Queen of the Night, Rosina, and the very Olympia Russell had planned for her before she came to Boston. Appraisal by The Hub thus had to wait until her Rosina in *The Barber of Seville* on January 20. Bernice Fisher, who learned the role of the Doll in six weeks, won a somewhat ambiguous estimate from Parker, who said that her flights of song came as though from the throat of an automaton, which of course she was supposed to be; but the compliment could be taken two ways. Olin Downes gave her "exceeding credit" for her coloratura finish and security. Hale summed it up to his own satisfaction by the curt epithet: "Not vocally suited."

Elizabeth Amsden irritated Parker on another score: her Giulietta seemed far too cool and ordinary of voice, and too detached and dignified of manner—a matronly New England lady and not a gorgeous Venetian harlot. Perhaps it was too much to expect of the Boston-born girl, although by this time she had had considerable opera experience in Europe and had gone through a season of dramatic heroines at home: Aïda, Santuzza, Minnie, Leonora, Marguerite, and Ricke in *Germania*.

She deepened in stageworthiness as the season drew on, especially in her new role as Elvira in *Don Giovanni*.

Antonia's passionate lyric music found an exquisite exponent in a new singer, Louise Edvina, whose vivid personality, aided by big black eyes of singular brightness, brought additional brilliance to Offenbach's most sympathetic heroine. A Canadian who had married the socially impeccable Honorable Cecil Edwardes, son of a British peer, she had gradually risen in the professional world after earlier study in Paris with Jean De Reszke, and had created for Covent Garden (where Manager H. V. Higgins favored her specially) contemporary roles such as Louise and Maliella (*Jewels of the Madonna*). She changed her name from Martin to a Latin version of her husband's surname. In the first of two seasons with Boston, she groped in timid innocence through the strange world of *Pelléas et Mélisande*, and projected a Louise that was as interesting as her Tosca was commonplace. Her clear vitality of spirit was one of her most attractive qualities. Her limpid and even voice, with its pure, sensuous quality, held great charm, even though produced in the "open" French manner. She showed expertness in shading and molding and coloring. "Very modern" as an actress, she sang too well for the ancients to flout her on that score. Hale continued to like her best as Antonia, going so far as to term her "ideal."

Minor characters in *Hoffmann*, particularly the men, provided some pleasant surprises. Luigi Cilla, relegated for two seasons to Roderigo in *Otello*, Parpignol in *Bohème*, or Nick in *Girl of the Golden West*, made capital of the four servants, Andres, Cochenille, Pitichinaccio, and Franz, even without the last-named's comedy ditty. Each character blossomed as an individual, humorous and pictorially zestful. Ramon Blanchart as Crespel and Ernesto Giaconne as Spalanzani let these two ancients come through clearly and expressively in both speech and song. Giaccone patiently waded through all five Boston seasons, shouldering more small roles than any other comprimario, averaging more than a dozen operas and about forty-five appearances a season. Elvira Leveroni's Niklausse disturbed Parker; she seemed physically unsuited for masculine attire, and lacked a light youthful touch.

All three of the important "novelties" provided frames for the talent of Edvina. In *Jewels of the Madonna*, although the wildness was written into her music, she brought to it only keen intelligence and skill—not enough. "She apprehends it more than she feels it," Parker remarked. Melis, who took over for three performances, had the advantage of birthright for this sort of character—it would be impossible to imagine her as Antonia, for example. Each to her own. Melis vividly portrayed her growing passion for the bully Raffaele. It seemed a pity that her Maliella could not be joined by Marcoux's Raffaele, but Melis put up with Blanchart, while the carelessly insolent, wantonly domineering Marcoux, with his vicious and sensual face and lean, strong body, played opposite the comparatively tepid Edvina.

Both newspapermen stirred their critical spoons reluctantly in the unsavory brew of Wolf-Ferrari's squalid story, hesitating to taste the "realism" that repelled. For once, Parker showed more restraint than his rival colleague. Was it a reviewer's business to suggest that a creative artist had better have been doing something else or something more like what he had done before? Wolf-Ferrari happened to have written sublimated, introspective, mystical, and beautiful chorales in his *Vita Nuova,* also the merry and sparkling little opera bouffa, *The Secret of Suzanne,* and the adroit and sprightly operatic comedy, *The Inquisitive Women* (these last two gracing the Metropolitan's repertoire at that moment), which recalled Mozart and Rossini. Now he chose the hot, fierce, highly colored melodies of life in the slums of Naples. We should be concerned only with the exposition of his design, execution, and the results. "Sometimes," Parker concluded, "it is good to clear the critical air."

Hale proved less lenient and philosophical. His indignation reached moral heights, rather in the manner of New York's Krehbiel, who never ceased to take offense at librettos that departed too far from the plumb line. Wolf-Ferrari's frank stage directions were not carried out completely by Zenatello, fortunately for the sensibilities of the audience, but still enough boldness remained to throw Marcoux's Scarpia in the shade. There was every reason to believe the opera would be popular in Boston. If this could be said to show the composer's versatility, it also showed his arms stretched out to the public with both eyes firmly fixed on the box office. "We will think we are attending a glorified performance of the Follies of 1912!" Hale fulminated.

Parker thought that, in this opera, Boston's ballet had not yet been spurred to heights; Hale had a cool word for the chorus: they sounded like the Apollo Club singing a wild Bacchanalian ditty. If all the elements did not fuse at first try, Russell counted on this warmblooded piece to continue to draw, penciling it in for a half-dozen hearings the following year.

Of loftier musical import, the introduction of Mozart to the Boston repertoire weighed the scales in Russell's favor. After all, as Hale admonished, no opera company without *Don Giovanni* and *Figaro* could plume itself on its quality. Russell could manage only one this time—the incomparable *Don Giovanni*. It was to be expected that with two big brains at work on the production, something extra special would result. Weingartner was trusted to preserve the musico-dramatic verities, while Urban designed a set that would keep the action flowing.

It is the current ideal to keep Mozart intact as written, an ideal seldom attained because of the length of the opera, its production difficulties, and the thorniness of casting seven major roles and one only a shade less so. Somewhere along the line in the past century of American productions, one or another element has got lost, been restored, shelved once again. The poor tenor is too often deprived of one of the two arias that make his part bearable; Donna Elvira must do without her exacting "Mi tradi" or sing it in an unaccustomed place in the action; the saucy final sextet is excised or allowed to remain. Each generation takes its own liberties with what has been called the "world's greatest opera," so that it should not be surprising to find even a man of as high probity as Weingartner feeling justified in putting his personal mold on the sprawling score.

"No cuts," he insisted in a long interview in the *Transcript* two days before the première. No cuts, always excepting. This time it was the "banal anti-climax" of the "moralizing" sextet. Omitting this he considered not tampering with the work of a genius, but merely "perfecting" it. To the transposition of Donna Anna's great aria from her chamber to the cemetery (which he acknowledged to be "impudent" although permissible), he added the switch of Elvira's "Mi tradi" from a later scene to the earlier street scene. But no one seemed to consider this meddling. As for the element of tragedy in the work, "you have to keep the premonition of something essentially wrong" as announced by the first somber theme in the overture. "It is drowned out in frivolity and bravado, but suddenly it recurs in a sharp little stab of tragedy. The distinction has to be made between the two manners, just as it has to be made between the open and intimate parts of the score."

Weingartner expressed little sympathy with the current German idea of dramatizing the arias by pantomime and action. But a present-day conductor might term equally incongruous Weingartner's final touch—to add a string quartet to the "dry" recitative accompaniment, traditionally a solo harpsichord.

For the sake of any *Don Giovanni* at all, these innovations were respectfully received, although Hale demurred at one piece of stage business, which kept the Commendatore's statue off his horse and behind the scenes in the cemetery. This created a feeling of remoteness and made Leporello's terror and Giovanni's bravado less convincing. With his passion for documentation, Hale recalled that Teresa Carreño (the South American piano virtuoso, in a brief interregnum as a prima donna) had sung Zerlina in 1876, with Brignoli, an ingloriously fat figure, as Ottavio. So bulky was the tenor that a flippant critic wrote that in *Roméo et Juliette* he should have been hoisted to the balcony by a derrick. Hale mused over the Metropolitan casts of 1884 and 1898, the former with Christine Nilsson (Elvira), Emmy Fursch-Madi (Anna), Sembrich (Zerlina), Giuseppe Kaschmann (Giovanni), Italo Campanini (Ottavio); the latter with Nordica, Lilli Lehmann, Sembrich, Victor Maurel, Edouard De Reszke, and Thomas Salignac, the poor, bleating Ottavio, who "made a mess of things." Even the earlier and (to him) better cast had not given unalloyed pleasure because of long stage waits; Hale had received the impression that it was little more than "set pieces in costume." Any *Giovanni* after these would be a treat. Still, when Gustav Mahler conducted the opera with the Metropolitan in Boston on April 9, 1908, he did not consider matters much improved, and warned his compatriot-colleague, Karl Muck (then presiding over the Boston Symphony) not to attend, complaining that the singers were not first class. This seems heretical to a generation that worships in retrospect the hallowed names of Eames, Scotti, Farrar, and Bonci, but maybe Mahler was partly right, for Boston also got the routined Robert Blass instead of the exciting Chaliapin as Leporello; the lesser Rita Fornia for the greater Gadski as Elvira; and Farrar, though beloved by Boston, was taking the place of Sembrich as Zerlina. Perhaps Muck did come to the performance four years later; no evidence could be uncovered to prove or disprove his presence in Weingartner's audience.

He would have witnessed a lineup of preponderating worth, its strongest musical links the revelatory John McCormack; Alice Nielsen, also rather surprisingly showing a true Mozart style; and Vanni Marcoux in the title role. Emmy Destinn's greatness as an artist never came into question and was fully revealed in the great florid aria ("Non mi dir") in the graveyard, but early moments found her not wholly in the Mozartian vein. Elizabeth Amsden made an honest and brave attempt, but the first act aria soared beyond her capabilities. When she did not attempt too large an utterance, she gained the decorative beauty that seemed to one writer the only reason for Elvira's arias. Nielsen possessed this decorative quality to a high degree. The comely soprano had been absent for a whole season and a half, and stepped back into a warm, personal welcome.

McCormack distinctly bore away the honors. Both of his arias evidenced exquisite taste and abounded in display of the highest vocal art. Few could match him in the suavity of phrase and the adroit leading of return melodies; the light elegance of his tone and accent captivated critics and listeners, who would later disrespectfully dub him an Irish balladeer. Unhappily for his adoration of Mozart and the supremacy of his vocalization, these Boston performances remained unique in America. Gatti-Casazza preferred Leo Slezak, Carl Jörn, or even Jacques Urlus for the part of Tamino in *The Magic Flute,* the only Mozart on the Metropolitan boards during McCormack's short periods there. For another Ottavio he would have to be content with Lilli Lehmann's invitation to Salzburg in the summer of 1913. By the three companies other than Boston—the Met, Chicago, and Hammerstein's—the personable tenor was confined to Italian heroes of not much greater brain power than poor Ottavio, but with less demanding floridity and purity of style. How frustrating this proscription must have been is indicated in the biography, *I Hear You Calling Me,* by his widow, Lily. She counted his favorite operas, out of the twenty-one he could sing, as *Giovanni* and *Bohème,* and quoted him as saying: "I love *Don Giovanni* so much I stand in the wings and listen to every note. As a result, I can sing everybody's part." He wanted to stand or fall by his recording of "Il mio tesoro," the second of those two glorious arias. Indeed, at one of the Boston performances, Lily says that John achieved his "big moment" when Weingartner laid down his baton and led the applause for this heavenly flight of song.

Adamo Didur, who made his Boston debut as Leporello, showed a consistently conceived impersonation, effective in its way. Hale would have preferred an oilier rascal and more respect for the second part of the catalogue song. The comical Tavecchia showed himself a capital Masetto, and Mardones' voice suited the Commendatore's music.

All of these characters pivoted around the central figure, that of the restless, amorous Giovanni. It was, as always, Marcoux's creation of a character that held most fascination. The handsome rake, in handsome costume, was graceful, light-footed, warm in wooing, not too ironical in his treatment of the scorned Elvira, humorous with his toady Leporello, yet always his superior and master, his tones not always bearing the sensuous beauty of the music, but gaining in suppleness and suggestion of natural and spontaneous speech in music.

Comfortably set in the assurance of a viable cast and production that excelled all expectations, how was Russell to anticipate that his leading man would be the victim of one of those bizarre stage accidents that happen far less often than might be expected, what with the lethal properties of sandbags, trailing cords, slippery light banks, and other all-too-identifiable flying objects? After the event, which was variously described as a blow from the descending curtain and a misjudged fall at the onslaught of the ghostly statue, rumors began to leak out that Marcoux had been "warned," and came to the stage a prey to nervous alarms. A fortune-teller had predicted death on stage, just as once before Caruso's composure had been shattered by a dire prophecy. Furthermore, Marcoux had neglected to wear a lucky locket given him by Jordan's daughter. And the performance fell on a Friday.

Russell turned immediately to Blanchart, who had obliged him in the contretemps with Baklanoff in 1910–11. Blanchart saved the day once more, this time in a role he knew. He managed some remarkable stage business, with many humorous little strokes, and his voice did not lack for beauty of tone. However, the rich golden-brown garb of Marcoux in the first act could not be drawn over the portlier legs of his replacement. Blanchart's improvised costume consorted poorly with Urban's all-over design: Zerlina's gay touches of green, and the brilliant salmon bodice and flounces or lavish brown and green brocade of Elvira. Blanchart's achievement, however, seemed the more creditable in view of the many years he had not sung the part. Around him, the production solidified, and most of the singers appeared more at ease. The third performance gave increased pleasure, although Edith Barnes (later

to become celebrated in Chicago and New York as Edith Mason) replaced Nielsen, who had set off once again on her concert travels. By
this time Marcoux had recovered enough to send out notes of thanks
for flowers and souvenirs and hundreds of consolatory messages. He
remained in sick bay, however, until February 22, when he appeared
to great rejoicing opposite Mary Garden in *Louise*. A single Méphistophélès on February 26 ended the contribution of Russell's most vaunted
male drawing card. The final four weeks of the season limped on without him.

Tristan, one of the solid successes of the season in spite of the earlier
mishaps, attained something near perfection at its seventh representation by the company in March. To Parker it seemed the most memorable, the most complete, most revealing, most exciting *Tristan* the
company had given. For one thing, it was the first that had not suffered
a handicap of one sort or another. Olive Fremstad partnered Ferrari-
Fontana wonderfully: "the music in their two throats had melting ardors";
Gay as Brangäne and, as Kurvenal, the Metropolitan baritone Herman
Weil (his only Boston role) were secure and practiced.

Neither did singers' troubles plague the final *Tristan* when Nordica and
Urlus returned. The most radical change possible occurred with the
accession of Caplet to the podium at this performance. The Frenchman
had been itching to get his hands on Wagner and would succeed all
too thoroughly the next season. Caplet's way with the huge *Tristan*
orchestra prompted Hale to believe that his old friend Alfred Hertz of
the Metropolitan was there in the pit, riding the whirlwind and directing the storm, so boisterous were the sounds issuing therefrom. Parker
refused to hear the performance, sending a second-stringer. Had he
known that Nordica would sail that fall for a world tour, never to return,
he might have put his seal upon her last operatic notes. Hale accorded
a valedictory: she was "again in her highest state." Urlus by this time
offered a familiar Tristan; so fickle is the affection of critics that Hale
yearned for a more romantic figure, having seen something near perfection in Ferreri-Fontana.

As for the novelties, Parker's unwonted indulgence for *La Forêt Bleue*
proved vain. His plea to banish the obsession with masterpieces, a part
of the pet American fallacy that led us to try to isolate opera from other
pleasures of the theater, may have roused echoes in a thousand breasts,

but this pastiche of fairy tales, linked into an amiably meandering narrative, would please (according to Hale) only children and elderly persons who liked to see the little heroes of their youth.

The libretto, arranged with considerable skill, found its composer wanting. The first act seemed the weakest; the second reminiscent of Debussy, not only in atmosphere but in melodic line; the whole was pastel, fragmentary. The singers had spent long and wearying hours in preparation—Jeska Swartz had even used part of her precious time in Paris on it. As a result of that long and close identification, Swartz remains faithful to the memory of *The Blue Forest,* and remembers her enjoyment at playing Tom Thumb. Bernice Fisher, her perennial partner in such high jinks, was an adorable Red Riding-Hood. These two made the fortune of *La Forêt Bleue,* Parker insisted. And for once Jean Riddez distinguished himself, evolving a creation out of the Ogre, rightly extravagant but without burlesque; humorous without buffoonery. The others had less luck: Carmen Melis found the Princess' music alien to her voice, style, and understanding; Ferdinand De Potter sang harshly as Prince Charming; Elizabeth Amsden was lost as the Fairy.

Djamileh, which Hale damned as indescribably boresome, seemed a favorite of Weingartner's. His wife intended to sing it in Hamburg, so she, at least, got some satisfaction out of its lifeless music. The audience showed delight at Urban's imaginative settings, the deep reds, gold arabesques, the great circular window, and the white flowers on lattices in Haroun's chamber.

The only other feature designed to enliven was the dance by Frieda Casson, who postured Orientally in so decorous a manner that even the mayor of Boston, "that sweet, white flower of garrulous innocence, need not have averted his eyes," Parker jibed.

Every manager tries *Martha* from time to time. Its sweet melodies may have given a few old-timers a thrill of rediscovery but aroused little enthusiasm otherwise. The English translation fell on unwilling ears. It could be understood anyway only from the lips of that expert trained in operetta, Alice Nielsen (whom Russell undoubtedly meant to placate for his confirmed indifference and neglect). Only Wolf-Ferrari's delicious *The Secret of Suzanne* (also for Nielsen), gave real value in the novelty list, though decidedly fluffy and insubstantial.

Two days before the premiere of *Forêt Bleue,* Russell did attempt something different: a performance out of subscription and for the first time in Boston of *L'Arlésienne,* with music by Bizet. He imported a company of Canadian actors headed by Paul Marcel, and assigned Caplet and the opera chorus, orchestra, and ballet to the task. A failure at its première in 1872, the score had been neglected until the revival of *Carmen* at the Opéra Comique, but subsequently had become a pillar of strength at the Odéon. Bizet wrote some twenty-seven numbers for *L'Arlésienne;* the ballet music is often interpolated in the fourth act of *Carmen.* Caplet used the original score, which called for a small ensemble of twenty-six, although for a concert version this has always been greatly expanded.

Again, the whole thing seemed hardly worth the trouble. In the cavernous auditorium, the music sounded thin, though all too often the only *raison d'être* for the whole project. When the play came through at all, which was infrequently, because of the provincial character of the actors, the music seemed superfluous. *L'Arlésienne* could not be considered the most successful of Russell's experiments.

An artistic administrator shuffling operas, first-and-second-rank singers, conductors, and four sets of subscribers can be compared to a man trying to complete a jigsaw puzzle on the heaving deck of a small boat in choppy waters. Russell possessed an instinctive flair for this type of puzzle, but seldom attained his ideal of keeping casts intact because of accidents and indispositions, as well as satisfying the customers' desire for variety, and juggling the desires—and contracts—of singers for conflicting roles.

The game of musical chairs permitted the introduction of new singers. None ingratiated herself more genuinely to Boston in 1912–13 than Lucrezia Bori. She created an atmosphere of personal charm, physical attractiveness, and musical artistry that thoroughly captivated the city. Her very reticence pleased the conservative Bostonians. Endearingly she had said: "I want to come to that big opera house in my slippers, with as little noise as possible." In her spirited defense of her forebears (although she had elided her name because of the certainty of invidious attribution, she protested that the Borgias were not all wicked poisoners), Boston was quick to approve the respect for family that paralleled its own ancestor worship. Hale twitted her gently on the name, saying that "her tones do not stab; they do not poison."

The romantic story of her "discovery" had penetrated to Back Bay two years previously. In the Metropolitan's descent on Paris in the late spring

of 1910, Gatti-Casazza had introduced Puccini's version of the Manon
Lescaut story to an audience that had hitherto acknowledged only
Massenet's. Lined up for the première were Caruso, Amato, and the always controversial Lina Cavalieri. On this occasion the soprano had decided to wait out a ruptured appendix rather than scar her perfect
epidermis or alternatively she had not wanted to leave the side of her
latest companion. At any rate, as Alexander Smallens said, if she awoke
with a wrinkle, she stayed in bed. The part of Manon fell vacant perilously
close to performance date. Andrés de Segurola, who had heard a young
Spanish singer as Mimi in Milan the year before, urged Gatti to send for
her. Bori immediately became the beloved *"toute jeune fille"* of Gabriel
Fauré's description. In 1912, fortuitously for Bori, Hempel's detention in
Europe postponed her opening-night Metropolitan debut in *Les Huguenots,* and *Manon Lescaut* was substituted, bringing Bori the double honor
of a debut on opening night and singing with Enrico Caruso.

Boston claimed Bori's first Mimi in America, on November 27. *Rigoletto,* which marked her second appearance with the Met, this time in
Brooklyn, was repeated in Boston but never again in New York—only in
Atlanta. Its out-and-out coloratura role suited her less than the more lyric
parts, although she remained an affecting Violetta. Gilda was the only
role in which she pleaded guilty to allowing her ambition to run a little
ahead of her art, as one Boston paper put it. Boston would hear her much
later as Massenet's Manon, as Mélisande, and as Mignon. In her youthful
bloom, the Mimi, Antonia, and the ensuing season's Butterfly and Fiora
(*L'Amore dei Tre Re*) provided treasurable moments. Paying a compliment to her graceful figure, Hale wished far distant the day when the
exercise of lungs and diaphragm would result in an outward and un-
seemly development that would rivet the attention. He lived long enough
to assure himself that such an awkward accretion of flesh never blurred
the svelte outline of this singer's girlish figure. Parker succumbed to the
appeal of her lustrous black eyes and hair. The warm quality of her voice
peculiarly fitted it for lyrically emotional parts, such as Mimi. Her
remarkable poetic and dramatic gifts carried out her conception of the
little Paris seamstress with faultless logic to its tragic conclusion.

This performance of *Bohème,* the first of three in which Bori would
enchant Boston, held a good earnest for Russell's ambition to forego
"stars" in favor of a tightly knit ensemble. The standard reached higher
than in almost any previous production of the Puccini favorite. So, at

least, believed Olin Downes. Parker approved the exuberance of the Bohemians, which Hale on the contrary found too boisterous. Bori's "conversational" singing brought all the more relief after the stress and fury of Pulcini, Polese, and De Segurola, three of the comrades.

The tenor, Léon Lafitte, embarking on the first of two years in America, pleased Downes and Hale as Rodolfo, with his vibrant vocal quality, but later showed himself no Haroun (*Djamileh*) or Julien (*Louise*). In the summing up of the season, Hale called him an honest bourgeois, but the next season he found numerous virtues in the singer's versatile accomplishments in three languages, going so far as to term him that rare bird, "a tenor who thinks." Arthur Wilson took a little of the gloss off of this estimate by complaining in the *Globe* that Lafitte's Duke in *Rigoletto* could by no stretch of the imagination be considered a pursuer of women, or true to any other but his own wife. Perhaps this straightforwardness also militated against his complete success as the fickle Lieutenant Pinkerton, who abandoned Bori's Cio-Cio-San.

The Japanese child-bride would continue to be one of Bori's cherished roles in Italy and South America, although she never sang it again in the United States. The reigning favorite, Geraldine Farrar, had her own grasp firmly on the kimono and obi of Butterfly, as well as on the services of the live geese in Humperdinck's *Königskinder* (another role Bori sang exquisitely). Later, when Bori returned to the Met, the pattern did not hold so rigidly, but the trend seemed toward heftier Cio-Cio-Sans—Elisabeth Rethberg, Maria Müller, and Florence Easton.

How fragilely beautiful Bori made Butterfly is evident from her photographs. How imaginatively she sang is revealed by Parker, who said she seemed the youngest of many, tremulous rather than fired, to the end a bewildered and desperate child. New York could feel the poorer, deprived of this delicate yet poignant characterization. Boston remembers it still.

18

LEGEND TO THE LIFE
(*Mary Garden and Vanni Marcoux*)

"Banned in Boston!" The words send a shiver of delight through many an author who envisions his sales mounting as the proscription takes hold. Boston's opera found itself under the same threat early in its fourth season, although the Watch and Ward Society played no part. Puccini's *Tosca*, Mary Garden, and Vanni Marcoux provided the fissionable elements which combined to blow up into the most delicious scandal in the opera company's history.

Tosca had not yet been entirely accepted as a respectable member of operatic repertoire. Hale had grumbled at its brutality from the beginning. Its broken melodies, its passionate and revealing orchestra commentary (a "monstrous, masterly score," said the young Olin Downes), and above all, the sordidness of its subject matter, continued to preoccupy and disturb Boston, in spite of the dozen years since its première by the Metropolitan company. Boston liked to cherish its prejudices and to bolster them with every scrap of fresh evidence. *Tosca* was a horror, and that's all one could say.

By 1912 enough heroines and villains (the only two determining characters) had passed in review to allow for opinions to jell: Antonio Scotti with Ternina, Farrar, and Eames in the early Metropolitan performances; Dereyne or Melis, and a single superb example by Boninsegna, with Baklanoff or Blanchard in the first Boston years. *Tosca* had ceased to be a music drama and had become a vehicle. Comparative interpretations were all the rage; the leading role turned out to be the Camille of the contemporary opera stage in America, Parker remarked in January, 1912, when Emmy Destinn and Dinh Gilly stepped into the ranks a single time. It was the baritone's first Scarpia in America. Destinn, one of the glorious singers of the century, had not quite lived up to the histrionic demands of the part, with a scanty range of gestures and poses. She acted chiefly with her "clarinet" voice, while Gilly's steely tones mirrored a cruel police chief, not a rapier but a sword struck straight home on objects of vengeance and lust. To Boston, which developed an almost morbid preoccupation with Scarpia's character and actions, Gilly provided one novel bit: having pinned Tosca to the sofa in the second act, he suddenly released her as if thinking of his reputation—or so, at least, Parker interpreted this odd behavior.

To be bored with Puccini had almost become the fashion. After barely a decade, Puccini's melodrama had already sated Boston's public. It was common to look for contretemps as scraps for table talk. *Tosca*, like *Carmen*, breeds mishaps: the misplaced knife, the fallible candles, the firing squad with its blank cartridges, the final fatal leap of the lady from the battlements of Castel Sant'Angelo. Many were the legends about this hazardous feat, which usually involved a series of mattresses, at which the timorous prima donna peered anxiously before launching herself into space. Sarah Bernhardt, who had created the role in Sardou's play, sometimes declined to jump, it was said (no doubt because of her crippled condition), merely expiring from shock, or perhaps stabbing herself. A rather stout soprano in Toulouse also balked at the leap. As a compromise, she threw herself in front of the guns, but the firing squad, already having discharged its volley at Mario, apparently possessed no more ammunition, or at least no wits, for they allowed the lady to simulate death without a shot being fired. The furious subscribers yelled: "Jump! Jump! or we'll come on stage and push you!" A quick curtain barely saved the situation. To their credit, none of Boston's Toscas ever shied at the precipice.

It was a wonder, Parker cynically commented, that the leading role had not been transposed for aspiring contraltos, many of whom fell within the "singing-actor" category. Most of this new breed of performers "laid on harder and harder"—Ternina would seem colorless now. It was no surprise to see that the preliminary announcements of Eames' return in the role claimed that she had "heightened" her interpretation. She had to, if she wanted to stay in the picture. Melis was broad, highly colored, extravagant of action, vociferous. Farrar was beautiful but didn't sing well. Scotti used to be both sinister and human, full of telling strokes, yet variously shaded. In the present mode, Scarpia was played as the villain of melodrama: he browbeat the heroine in church, wrestled with her in his chamber, wrenched and writhed, and slapped on the histrionic color with a trowel. Nearly all subtlety and human suggestion had fled. Even the minor characters succumbed to the trend. Each Sacristan traveled further from the original human and humorous impersonation of Charles Gilibert. Conductors took the cue from the stage and piled up orchestral sonorities until singers must scream or shout; then the orchestra would suddenly break into *pianissimi* or suave cantilena. Only poor Cavaradossi or the hunted fugitive Angelotti were left to sing—and they usually overdid to match all the rest. Constantino alone still shone by virtue of his refining artistry and suavity of tone.

Thus stood *Tosca* in public and critical affections when Weingartner fused the opera into incandescence late in 1911–12, commanding Lucille Marcel, Zenatello, and Marcoux on the stage, and in the pit conducting as if *Tosca* were *Tristan*. This was Marcoux's first Scarpia, and he seemed "fiercest and frankest of all." His Roman police chief betrayed eroticism almost to mania, a mingling of cruelty, lust, and religious exultation. His face was indelibly marked with viciousness and fiendish callousness. He swiftly uncloaked Tosca in his salon and kissed her fiercely on the shoulder. He hunted, caught, and pinioned the helpless woman, barely releasing her for her piteous soliloquy. He snatched the consenting "*Si! Si!*" from her lips, and remained in a state of tremulous excitement until his death.

By the next year, Bostonians knew what to expect of him, so they thought. But they had reckoned without Mary Garden. "Our Mary" (as she was to become known to Chicago, although Boston never quite aspired to the intimate relationship) had tried on Tosca's wig in Paris that summer for the first time and liked it. (Vincent Sheean wrote of Garden that the wig was more important the the costume; once she got into the right hair for a character, she became that character.) Her initial American Tosca, on December 2, 1912, filled the eye, to be sure. The wig, a wondrous concoction of deep, dark red, "tempts the fiery colors of Besnard portraits," mused Parker. In church, she wore a bright green dress, overhung with a scarf of deepest blue. Her second-act gown contributed to the excitement the audience had already begun to feel, for it clung, all silvery, in Empire lines, like one of David's portraits of the court of Josephine. Mary herself thought that perhaps the contrast of this gleaming white against—or rather, under—Scarpia's black satin made just the difference that set this performance apart from previous ones.

The scene brought audible gasps and columns of newsprint the morning after. No one was willing to describe it accurately or in detail, and the inference to the reader who had not witnessed it depended on his imagination and knowledge of the opera. Apparently overcome by lust, Scarpia had made virtually a flying tackle and landed the lady on the sofa in an utterly compromising position. Garden left no doubt about the action, writing coyly in her book later that she lay on the lounge "to get away from Scarpia"—which does not seem exactly the most efficient means of evasion. Marcoux, she continued, "came forward with all his force, throwing himself on me."

"Maybe," wrote Parker, "this act as it is usually performed nowadays and as it was performed last evening yields some savage sensations, gratifies some primitive instincts in us as did the struggles of gladiators in Rome."

As could be expected, numerous Boston thumbs in that Monday subscription audience turned down. But it was probably Philip Hale who precipitated the near disaster. He wrote that such business in any play "would have been cut out by order of the Mayor!" This outright invitation to censorship could not be ignored. Mayor John F. Fitzgerald's office was never too busy to respond to a call to honor. The management was notified (whether by telephone or in writing was not made clear) that the next *Tosca* had better be tamed down or else. The "next" performance was scheduled for a popular Saturday evening, with Fely Dereyne and Ramon Blanchart in the contentious roles. But no one minded them. It was not in either's nature to "overdo," and neither did. No, the *Tosca* the Mayor was gunning for was coming up on a Wednesday, December 11. Russell immediately leaped into print.

"Somewhat chagrined," he felt himself to be. The musical comedies in town, which far exceeded propriety (remember, this art form invariably aroused Russell's contempt and loathing), passed unchallenged. This threat on the Mayor's part did not bode well. Russell's plaint was couched in unusually high-flown terms, even for him:

"The noting of such a paradox and especially the contacting of it on its present manifestation warrants speculation as to the artistic future growth of the city, and wakens a keen desire for a broader, healthier, and more tolerant view of high art, its meaning, and its purpose, and a better understanding of the artist's place and value in the cultural life of the community."

The Mayor retorted in kind: he resented Russell's insinuation that theater performances were allowed to pass unchallenged. He was constantly on watch and showd no partiality. He had not seen *Tosca*, but the protests were voluminous, by letter and telephone. He had always taken an interest in the opera and wished it to succeed (the evidence was plain in his attempts to secure tax exemption) and at the same time desired it to be of the highest artistic merit.

"Boston is known throughout the country as the home, during a good many months of the year, of hundreds of students at our schools, colleges, and universities; and parents of these students have the right to expect there shall be no performance at the Opera House which would be demoralizing. I think artists who appear at the Opera House can be effective without offending public taste!" he concluded.

Garden herself, discovered with Marcoux in a box at the Shubert, laughing merrily over the (uncensored) antics of Gaby Deslys in *The Passing Show of 1912,* plaintively passed the buck to the public with a gesture of *honi soit qui mal y pense,* asking: "Why should anyone go to see *Tosca* with evil in his heart?" She defended Marcoux against the charge that he had initiated all the debatable business (in later years, she even usurped credit for it), and pooh-poohed the Mayor's sternness, calling him "charming." She had forgotten, or perhaps chose to ignore, the previous occasion, much more serious, when the incumbent mayor had refused to allow Hammerstein's immoral *Salome* to corrupt the good burghers of Boston. At this later moment, Garden insisted with great dignity that she held too high a regard for her art to compromise. She would play the "sofa scene" as always.

A throng satisfactory to the management turned up the following Wednesday. The Mayor was conspicuously absent, but in his place sat the lawyer, Francis M. Carroll, while Leo Rogers, a secretary, represented Police Commissioner O'Meara. John H. Casey, the official censor, stood glumly in a lobby corner, completely uncommunicative.

"Would *Tosca* be tempered?" everyone wondered. According to the ensuing headlines, the balance seems to be in favor of a "Yes." One paper gave the lady credit, saying: "Mary Garden Toned Down." The *Post* proclaimed: "Tosca Tamed by Censors," and Olin Downes noted "a certain slight distinction between this and the previous performance." Still, whatever Garden's intentions, the initiative had to come from Marcoux. What did he do? *Musical America* mentioned that the sofa played a less important role. But Parker claimed that only those expert in noting details would have remarked any difference. Hale, however, said bluntly: "Marcoux bowed to the storm and kept both feet on the floor."

In the midst of all this *brouhaha,* the real merit of the *Tosca* performances all but got lost. Garden seemed, even to Hale, the great, authoritarian exponent of the heroine. And, wonder of wonders, she had never sung so well, not even in an earlier *Thaïs* with Hammerstein, nor in Debussy songs. For once, even her tireless detractors had to give her credit for voice, skill, intelligence, and imagination in Italian song, proclaimed Parker—although, being her individual self, she sang in French (except for the "Vissi d'arte," in which nobody could properly grasp the diction anyway, and no matter). Mistakenly, the critic thought, she and Marcoux lapsed into spoken dialogue here and there—an inevitable jar. But elsewhere she retained the pure, musical contours of the declamation.

New notes in the impersonation concerned her love, expressed by an absence of coquetry in the first act, and her deep solicitude for Cavaradossi. She entered Scarpia's room earlier than most Toscas and followed her lover into the torture chamber, abstracted, thinking only of him. The keenest stroke of interpretation occurred in the last act, when, believing Mario alive, she smiled radiantly. Discovering his death, she showed that everything went black for her; her spirit fell into nothingness. Since Mélisande, H. T. P. believed, no finer, no simpler delineation had been seen.

The Cavadarossi deserved his Tosca's concern. Dalmorès sang the role only this once in Boston, but left an unforgettable impression. Romantic, Byronic, virile, he sang with surprising freshness, and with due intensity —broken by the fashionable sobs, Parker said in an aside—and with a new and stirring tang of baritone quality. He was, in short, manlike and not tenor-like.

Marcoux seemed to several observers to have modified his original fierce Scarpia, which had reached a point of brutality beyond which it seemed impossible to go, but he still betrayed to Parker the acrid contrasts of hypocrisy and pietism, which caused him to pray while torturing Tosca. This monstrous personage defeated itself a little by its own broad "exercises." (One wonders here if Parker's "types" had not betrayed him by virtue of his unreadable scrawl, and if he did not mean to write "excesses." Still, the slip may have been purely Freudian.) The character of Scarpia once more laid itself open to interpretation, and in it as in Puccini's music could be found room for Marcoux's ferocities, the icy ironies of Scotti, or Renaud's subtleties of perverted cruelty and passion.

One odd little note of dissention occurred in this almost universal shudder. The *Globe* found in Marcoux's Scarpia a momentary paternal and reassuring air after Tosca had sung "Vissi d'arte," so that "one became apprehensive lest through his clemency the drama progress no further."

By November of the next year, when Garden and Marcoux staged their final Boston sparring match to Puccini's music, the story was old indeed. Hale remarked wearily that Garden's tight-fitting dress and high heels obliged her to mince, so that running from Scarpia's inflamed pursuit turned into timid avoidance of his embraces, an affair limited to the confines of the sofa rather than the free chase.

But opera buffs do not forget that when these two met together on a stage, sparks usually flew. Boston launched them as a team with the controversial *Tosca* and reveled (as far as Boston could be said to "revel") in the flame and subtleties of their partnership in *Thaïs, Louise,* and *Monna Vanna.* Unfortunately, a similar consummate experience in *Pelléas* did not come about; Garden sang only the one with Russell, with Dufranne as Golaud. Marcoux's Mélisandes were Leblanc in 1912 and Louise Edvina in 1913. When Garden led the operatic parade in Chicago, she failed at first to sign up her favorite Scarpia, being forced to play to Mario Sammarco, so bland that a critic said "even his legs are good-natured." Marcoux finally arrived for the opening of the 1913 season, and later partnered Garden in *Don Quichotte* and *Monna Vanna.*

"These are indeed Mary Garden's good days," wrote Parker early in December, 1912, after the diva had appeared as Thaïs for the first time with Marcoux. Never had she sung before with such quality of voice and vocal artistry. Her tones kept their old propulsive power and warm humanity, but now seemed full of rich songfulness and sensual beauty to boot. She had said she could sing if she would; now she had given proof of it. She glorified Massenet's music and even (and for Parker, this represented a descent into improper usage that marked great emotion) "glamored" it. Her Thaïs with Renaud the year before had seemed unnecessarily prudish. The 1912 impersonation was called by Hale incomparable, unique. To Downes, she gave off transcendent eloquence and power even when sitting motionless under a palm tree.

With Marcoux she threw every resource into singing and acting, sure of an elastic and equally skilled response; with anyone else, as in a performance with Henri Dangès the next year, she met no resistance and carried all her impulses too far. When Marcoux was restored to the cast several days later, she immediately ceased to debase her gifts by exaggeration and "chose the finer answer," as Parker said. He could not understand why, with such boundless capacities as a singer and actress, she elected to "make perverting use of them." It seems clear that the presence or absence of a favorite partner provided at least part of the answer. One critic speculated afterward on the wholesomeness—to Mary— of perhaps seeing another version of Thaïs—Cavalieri's, for example.

This would have infuriated Garden, for the beauteous Lina had provoked the one stormy rivalry of her Hammerstein years. Hammerstein, desiring to use Cavalieri's services to the full, announced her in a *Thaïs* for a Friday night. He found out his mistake the minute the *affiche* went up on the Manhattan Opera wall. Garden threatened to sail on Saturday if that upstart sang "her" role on Friday. After some face-saving bluster, Oscar gave in. Mary later wrote that *she* sang Thaïs that Friday and ever afterward.

As for Marcoux, his first Athanael in 1912–13 brought back the old skill in intonation, regard for the course and flow of melody, familiar sonority, eloquence, and diversity of color that Parker thought he had sacrificed for the rough, broken, ill-pitched tones of the multiple villain of *Tales of Hoffmann*. Hale remarked again that his natural bass-baritone voice had suffered by taking these baritone roles. Athanael suited him; his fervor did not descend to ranting; his intensity did not degenerate into melodrama. As Anatole France's anchorite, in his yellow, gleaming robes, he suggested to Parker the mosaics at Palermo, a distinctly Oriental, even Byzantine figure.

The tenor in no case mattered as much, although Dalmorès complemented the other two with his striking portrait of the voluptuary Nicias and his skill in singing, as Max Lippman, Ferdinand De Potter, and, in 1913–14, Louis Déru could not hope to do. The tired score by this time had ceased to interest anyone. Caplet veered from the delicate, subtle, and significant in his treatment to the coarse and blatant, and now and then merely the neat and unobtrusive. When he fell ill, the best anyone could say for his substitute, Strony, was that he followed with alacrity some small changes Garden made as she went along.

Of all the operas that could be definitively tagged "Garden's repertoire," Charpentier's *Louise* certainly led the list. In its third act, the slim, almost boyish lass had rocketed to fame with "Depuis le jour" that Friday the thirteenth of April, 1900. Ready after months of study by herself, she calmly appropriated the place, if not the costume (she weighed barely ninety-eight pounds and had no "figure" to speak of) of Mlle. Marthe Rioton, the creator of the role at the Paris Opéra Comique. Unknown until that moment, except to the American Sybil Sanderson, who had befriended her with a generosity most atypical of one prima donna vis-à-vis another, and who introduced her to Albert Carré, director of the Comique, Garden at once enslaved André Messager, the fiery conductor, as well as Carré (both of whom, according to her book, added the tender passion to professional admiration), and brought *tout Paris* to her slim feet. *Louise* became her undisputed possession for two hundred subsequent hearings, while poor Mlle. Rioton was given the role of Hänsel, and, as Mary remarked with the kindness that kills, "was perfectly enchanting in it."

It is strange that Boston did not react unfavorably to the moral tone of *Louise*. H. E. Krehbiel had loosed a storm of righteous indignation in New York, when Hammerstein had introduced it, writing that "coupled with the story, which glorifies the licentiousness of Paris and makes mock of virtue, the sanctity of the family tie, and the institutions upon which social stability and human welfare have ever rested and must forever rest, the music may also be set down as immoral." Instead, Russell's audience seemed to worry only about the length of the opera. For what it was worth, Boston could take what pride it chose in the fact that it was hearing *Louise* in almost its entirety for the first time in America on December 18, 1912. Even at the cost of suburbanites' convenience, it was good to see the work of Charpentier respected for once, Parker decided, although the *longueur* of its four-hour stretch struck Hale as appalling. The Monday-night audience seeing its second representation agreed with Hale. By the time of the Saturday matinee subscription, pressure had been exerted and the score pruned by twenty minutes, taken chiefly from the scene of Montmartre at dawn, with its rag and coal pickers, vendors of artichokes, bird food, and carrots, chair mender, junk man—the myriad "bit" parts that elongate the cast of this opera beyond all others. A fragment of the lovers' ecstatic duet also fell under the knife. Hale remained philosophical about these excisions, remarking that he could do with even more; however, the third act might be better sacrificed than the second, a view with which sympathizers with Charpentier's attempt to portray the "little people" of Paris undoubtedly agreed. This Montmartre scene did provide the background of Louise's story, Parker contended, yet the opera remained understandable without it. Surely it was better to nibble than to bite off whole scenes. Seidl, he maintained, used to cut a measure here and there, and nobody knew unless he had the score in his lap. *Louise* so treated would sacrifice only what is weakest, the conventional, old-fashioned operatic prancing. However, the sewing-room scene remained too closely knit in music and action to endure cutting, and as for the first and final acts, even the old Munich conductor, who received each new score with a smacking of lips and a "Now first for the cuts!" would spare them.

Campanini had instituted cuts in *Louise* similar to those now used in Boston, so that it was no shock to Garden when she stepped into the cast at the final performance in 1913, on February 22, although the deletion of any measures must have caused pain to so complete an artist.

At first Mary seemed restless on the stage in *Louise*, agile and flexible; "as loose as ashes" in Hale's words. Her eagerness gave human form to what might otherwise be a mere sociological problem. Charpentier's characters all too often aired theories not musical, prated of income and capital and free love in hifalutin' rhetoric not always translatable into plain decent English (and not understandable in French either). Not even the temporary discomfiture of her hero, who fell to the ground from his balcony when the railing broke, deflected Garden's impersonation.

The voice? Hale preferred to minimize its importance: Parker thought she elected to use it wondrously in "Depuis le jour," which in long memory had not sounded so thrilling; but elsewhere it repelled more often than it stimulated the imagination, and occasionally departed obviously from Charpentier's design. In the first act she cried "Paris! Paris!" apparently to music of her own invention.

What astonished everyone, even those who participated, was the audience's reaction. Little by little, Parker marveled, untutored Boston (as they used to call it in New York), was making progress in operatic manners and customs. At Garden's seasonal leavetaking, the throng proved worthy of the tradition of the Metropolitan or Manhattan, remaining through the unconscionable length of *Louise,* to stand and applaud until the management lowered the lights. "After nearly four seasons, we are at last 'really' operatic," Parker remarked smugly.

Garden had found an ideal father ready-made for her, as Marcoux had deepened his accomplishment in the part, new to him that season, until it was a rare theatrical portrait. He might have stepped upon the stage off the streets of Paris. His contentment with the workman's life, the joy of his own fireside, his affection for Louise, the peasant shrewdness and bonhomie, all flowed out of his singing in the first act. At the end, his broken spirit, his piteous tenderness and blind anger showed in his tones. This, announced Parker—and all the others agreed—was a complete characterization in terms of the music drama, one of the greatest in years, worthy to stand by his Golaud.

Léon Lafitte, whose single Julien met competition with Marcoux, appeared straightforward, hardly romantic, not at all Byronic. Earlier in the season, Clément had better graced the part, and Zenatello had shown himself not too Italianate to sustain illusion. The Mother gave Maria Gay one of her best roles, a strongly marked, wholly admirable performance. The minor singers, particularly Edward Lankow, Luise Van Aken, Elvira Leveroni, and Ernestine Gauthier, attracted Hale, although he later chided Gauthier, who played the impish apprentice in the sewing-room scene, for thinking herself a chief character.

Louise remained the penultimate partnership for Garden and Marcoux with the Boston company; only *Monna Vanna* would be new the next (and last) season, as will appear. Public imagination had no choice but to feed on the association of these two blazing temperaments, and to create the image of them as lovers offstage as well as on—although oddly enough, *Monna Vanna* provided the only ground for this relationship; otherwise, their relationships were those of villain-heroine (*Tosca*), savior-sinner (*Thaïs*), and father-daughter (*Louise*). The passion entertained by the gentleman in each case for the lady could not be denied, but it remained unrequited, even in the case of the renegade daughter.

Mary Garden is forever disavowing this or that colleague or "gentleman friend" as a lover in her book, but she mentions Marcoux only in connection with the *Tosca* incident and is much more absorbed by her "innovation" of making the placement of candles by the murdered

Scarpia's outflung hands seem to be a last-minute inspiration than by the baritone's personal attraction. She continues into an anecdote with the introduction: "It was while I was scandalizing the Bostonians with my candid version of Tosca . . ." with no credit to her fierce and handsome vis-à-vis. It seems possible that even the amount of "romantic" interest she permitted herself in other channels never was doled out to this personable singer. He entered her life as an ideal working partner and perhaps sounding board for her vivacity and occasional outbursts of flirtatious charm, and departed it the same way. About the time that he was acting paternally to Garden's Louise, he received the news that a divorce from his second wife had been accomplished. Garden had immediately to deny that she was marrying him on the spot. He lingered in single blessedness until the summer of 1914, when on the American Independence Day, after the close of the Boston Opera season in Paris, he married a French dancer from the Théâtre Antoine by the name of Madeleine Morlay. One account insisted that she was a rich widow, and another featured a picture of her with her hand on the head of a stuffed tiger—all grist to the portion of Boston's public that liked a gossipy tone to its opera news.

Henry Russell, almost infallible about a singer's prospects, judging by their first impact on him, mistook Mary completely. It was not generally known that she had been an early pupil of his in London, in the days when the quiet Scottish mouse had grown no protective armor. She would never make the grade in grand opera, he predicted. At twenty, her shyness, her wistful docility, her devotion to family and country showed her to be a sweet lass, nothing more. The ineffable showmanship appeared only after the piercing lights of notoriety had shone upon her, mixed with the beams of fame and achievement. She told Mrs. Russell that the moment before she had to sing "Depuis le jour" for the first time, she turned her back to the audience and whispered to herself: "Now or never!" It was "now." From the moment of her debut, the private Mary seemed to disappear; the legend blossomed. Mary Garden's legend runs in many channels, flashing many-colored glints from its shallow surfaces, glittering under arc lights, as various as its observers.

The public Mary could utter no word that was not reproduced in headlines within hours; by the same token, words she never said clung to her by attribution, adding to the legend. In turn she appeared great lady, shrew, gamine, supreme artist, girlish prattler, *femme fatale*. The "real" Mary that hid behind these phases had been born of bitterness, disillusionment, deep resentment, and humiliation. Love spelled frustration; friendship meant too much taking, too much giving.

To an associate and admirer, the pianist George Copeland, she appeared as a *grande dame*, with a flow of conversation that commanded a whole dinner table, and an unfailing courtesy to the host; never did she dine but the next morning five dozen roses appeared with her card of thanks. The slim figure that never varied an inch from year to year owed its felicities to a diet that also never varied.

"She loved to come to dinner quietly, being bored by doormen and footmen and apartment and hotel life," Copeland recalls. "It was always the same menu—even until she was seventy-six. A thin soup, grilled fish or meat, one vegetable, and two glasses of champagne with fruit. She could wear a dress that showed her back to be perfect, like a girl's. " 'I feel right this way; why should I spoil it!' she would say if you urged her to change her habits."

Boston may have been cited as her "favorite city" in her somewhat slapdash encounters with the press, but privately to Copeland she remarked that "its first attitude toward any work of art is: 'What is there about it we don't like?' " She recalled Boston's "good old opera days in Mechanics Hall, when the ideal of dress consisted of a white shirtwaist, a black skirt, and an old mackintosh, all smelling of violet perfume." She slyly noted that she was surprised, considering where the opera house was built, that anyone found out opera was being given there.

While she was dining with Copeland one night, a Metropolitan Opera official offered her a box for several performances. "I'm not at all sure, but I don't think I shall go," she replied. "The real reason is, I suppose, that I don't care for *variété*." Then, to add salt to the wound: "You see, I have thirty-four roles in three languages which I have learned completely. Sixteen were written for me." And, she didn't have to add, "I don't want to see anything less perfect."

The imperious artist, thorny in close association, recalls herself vividly to several colleagues. About the same time that Geraldine Farrar provoked from Arturo Toscanini the rebuke: "There are no stars, mademoiselle, except in heaven!" Garden was waging her own war for supremacy over a conductor, André Caplet. The tiny boxed-in setting for several of the scenes in *Pelléas et Mélisande* irritated Garden beyond restraint. She flounced in and out of them at rehearsal, muttering under her breath. Taking her own time, she made one entrance so belatedly that Caplet rapped sharply with his stick and called to her. Sauntering to the footlights, she poised above him and looked down arrogantly.

"Monsieur André Caplet," she drawled, "I will come when I am ready. You will wait." Then, a few decibels higher: "I don't know if I'll sing anyway—these sets are so————small. I can hardly turn around!"

But turn around she did; the rehearsal resumed; Caplet swallowed his pride and resentment (though swearing privately that he would never conduct for that woman again—of course he did); and the eventual performance was magical perfection.

Garden's eccentricities often led conductors and stage directors a merry chase. During the full season (1921–22) in Chicago when she reigned as "directa" (the title she chose for herself), she determined to discipline her chief conductor, Giorgio Polacco, who was going to continue his job, while she would be giving up her administrative post. She learned the news, according to Alexander Smallens, as the company was about to open in Denver, April 17. Sending Howard Potter, the company secretary, to Polacco, she informed him his services would not be needed for that night's *Thaïs*. Smallens would conduct.

That young man had never laid a baton on *Thaïs*, nor, almost more importantly, had he ever been in the pit when Mary walked the stage. At 7:45 P.M., with no rehearsal behind him, he beheld Miss Garden in the doorway.

"Good evening," she said smilingly. "Just one thing: do you hold the last note of my last aria? I haven't the faintest idea what I do in *Thaïs*."

This cannot have reassured the young conductor, who proceeded to lead the score from the printed page—and to pray. Mary made her entrance as the Alexandrian courtesan and went on rather languidly. He followed diligently as best he could, but soon she became very capricious, jumping two bars, and leaving him to unscramble.

In the wings, she said: "I'm very gay this evening; you must forgive me."

With considerable temerity, he warned her he would pursue his own course, let the songs fall where they might.

"She followed like a lamb," he said, "but I never got the assignment again. She had disciplined Polacco, but from then on he saw to it that he alone conducted *Thaïs*."

The legend gathered sparkle along the way—the tantrums, the cheerful contradictions, the aphorisms, the lofty advice to young aspirants. But it is as the great artist that Mary Garden most commends herself to memory. In Boston, her Mélisande remains imperishable. Even for those who never witnessed her impersonation, the name of Garden is linked with Debussy's heroine, her white figure a "tranquil, gentle wisp caught upon the strange, bleak winds of fate, whirled in and out of the shadows"; she brought to Boston and its critics a vision "unique upon the opera stage and in the finer theatre of the imagination and vision each may set for himself."

Certain investitures will remain inextinguishable: a Japanese kimono suggests Farrar's Cio-Cio-San; Carmen's shawl can feel at home on no shoulders but Calvé's; Falstaff's body-padding fits no frame but Victor Maurel's; the clown costume must be filled by the bulky body of Caruso. So it is Mélisande's wig that signifies Garden, the incredibly long wig that was made from the hair of beautiful blond girls all over Brittany, strand by strand. When Miss Garden returned to America in the late forties to lecture, she dwelled long and lovingly on this wig. "You must have it to be Mélisande," she repeated over and over.

It is always amusing and instructive to witness different interpretations of a role, Philip Hale believed. For one thing, it incites discussion and comparison. Although we are often told that a composer declares this or that woman an ideal heroine, the fact is that composers are as a rule easily satisfied, or even grateful, if only the public will applaud. Debussy was a certain exception to this. He, who had written in Garden's score, "You alone will remain the woman and the artist I had hardly dared hope for," continued to remember her, for when the choice of a new Mélisande came into question in 1908, he asked for someone "with an accent"—Garden's exotic French remained the ideal, especially after the sharp, all-too-clear emissions of the really French singers fell on the ear—and the selection fell on the English girl, Maggie Teyte, she of the "petit accent." Pelléas had dropped out of the Boston repertoire when Miss Teyte made her debut there in 1914, so the chance for that comparison never arose. Neither did Chicago see Miss Teyte in the role during her three seasons; it bore Miss Garden's chop mark. In fact, America waited until 1948 for Maggie Teyte's Mélisande at the New York City Center, and by then, memories had dimmed, even of Miss Teyte's former glories. Still, a few old-timers breathed grimly, "You should have seen Garden."

19

OPERA URBANIZED

Already acknowledged remarkable in its flair for occasional elaborate productions, the Boston Opera in its fourth season blazed out in new stage designs and colors that showed the way to all America. The opening opera, *Tales of Hoffmann,* brought the prophecy that a revolution in settings and lighting would one day be credited to the innovations at the Boston Opera House.

The one man responsible for the new visual appeal of the Boston Opera stage was Joseph Urban, a portly, almost Rabelaisian gentleman from Vienna, whose outward preoccupation with the delicacies of *haute cuisine* at once built up a huge girth and disguised the true demoniac energy of the creative genius. Behind the smoke screen emitted by a hundred Turkish cigarettes, Urban worked fourteen hours a day. His name had appeared little in the previous season, being cloaked under the title of the Viennese firm of Lefler, with which he worked. To Boston the new settings for *Pelléas et Mélisande, Tristan und Isolde* and *Hänsel und Gretel* had been presented as examples of Russian and German design and lighting. Urban's hand had also added touches to *Samson et Dalila, Germania, Werther,* and *Habañera,* while his files contain photographs of sets for *The Pipe of Desire,* and *The Sacrifice* of 1910–11.

At last he was recognized as a new force at the opera, when his formal engagement was announced in the spring of 1912. Not only would he act as chief designer, but he was put in charge of the stage. To round out the department, two Viennese designers, two minor *régisseurs,* and

211

three assistant stage managers were ticked off to complement him, and the former property master, Robert F. Brunton, was promoted to technical director.

This was the man whose own life could best be described as baroque. Born in Vienna in 1872, he studied and worked with Baron Karl von Hasenauer, who built the Imperial Museums of Art among other impressive Vienna structures, with Professor Heinrich Lefler, and Dr. Paul Schlenther, director of the Vienna Holfburg Theater. His earliest achievement was a prize for illustrating Poe's *Masque of the Red Death*.

At twenty-three he was summoned by the Khedive of Egypt to decorate a palace (where he acquired his taste for Turkish tobacco at the Khedive's own insistence); then he remodeled a castle for Count Esterhazy in Vienna and decorated Vienna's Town Hall and the Tsar's bridge in St. Petersburg. A tinge of theatricality occasionally spoiled his architectural efforts, but was not amiss when he began to express himself fully and magnificently on the stage itself. Before he came to America the second time, he concocted a dramatic presentation for the coronation of the English King George V in 1910.

Urban can be said to have done as much if not more than Florenz Ziegfeld in glorifying the American girl: he provided backgrounds and costumes that set off the beauty of Ziegfeld's girls to perfection. For his first assignment from the great showman in 1914, he procured hundreds of gelatine capsules containing medicine for ailing horses from a veterinarian, and strung them like beads for a shimmering curtain that turned to fairy-like fabric under colored lights. Meanwhile, he drew eyes to himself as he splashed the Boston stage with color. Hollywood of course heard of him and commandeered his services. During the Florida land boom, he was swamped with commissions for clubs and ostentatious homes by Drexels, Huttons, and other old and new rich folk. New York knew him best for the Ziegfeld Theatre on Sixth Avenue, the New School for Social Research, the Atlantic Beach Club, and the Central Park Casino. He stuck his graying head into many speakeasies, decorating their interiors as well as his own.

The Metropolitan Opera acquired his services in 1917, and he continued to brighten that stage (with some fifty scenic productions) as well as a dozen New York theaters until his death in 1933. "His able and easygoing ways . . . predestined him for the Metropolitan of the twenties," asserts Irving Kolodin in his history of that organization. Urban's re-

markable set of plans for a new opera house concocted in 1927 met with
the fate of all attempts at replacing the old yellow brick building on
Broadway and Thirty-Ninth Street until Lincoln Center materialized.
America, which he was to adopt as his own in 1917, felt the touch of
his exotic brush first at the Austrian exhibit of the St. Louis Exposition
in 1904; he never saw his last contribution, the futuristic buildings of
the Century of Progress in Chicago in 1933–34.

Urban's stage designs have become so familiar to us now, and even
so old-fashioned (his *Tristan* sets lasted four decades at the Met, until
1959), that it is difficult to imagine the furor with which America greeted
them then. First, color made its impact, employed always in relation to
lighting. Critics and viewers recoiled at first from the clear, almost harsh
primary colors, which responded so vividly to stage lights. The famous
"Urban blue," a carefully cherished secret, became widely celebrated.
Fifty men were said to guard the sacred vat in which it was mixed at his
Yonkers studio. That came later, however; his first workshop was set up
by Eben Jordan at Swampscott, where a *Transcript* writer explored the
premises one October day before the 1912 opening. "The greatest factory
of illusion in our country" boasted floor space of 150 by 75 feet, occupied
almost entirely by canvas stretched out to be painted. This was stage
technicians' first experience with scene painting from above, so to speak.
Following the sketches made to a scale of one twenty-fifth by the two
Viennese artists, Weber and Kamerzell, after Urban's original design,
painters drew outlines with charcoal fastened to a long stick. The paint,
mixed very carefully to be "light-proof," was splashed on by enormous
brushes, while gigantic palettes on wheels followed the painters around.
Because the color must not be allowed to dry until the entire canvas was
covered, speed was of the utmost necessity, and the strain on the painters
became heavy as hours and days wore on. The movement, expertness, and
speed reminded the onlooker of a polo game. What most amazed the
novice was the technique of "pointillage," by which paint was splashed
rather coarsely and without too much attention to detail. Distance and
four-colored lighting would accomplish the miracle.

In an adjoining room, the wives of the two Viennese artists presided
over a sewing bee; here leaves were attached to painted gauze and any
other necessary stitches taken. A carpenter shop manufactured what
scenery would not be hung. Everything eventually found its way to the
painters. This colorful assembly line astonished the writer, who soberly

called attention to the expense of such a factory. Nearly a year, day and night, had already been consumed before the opening, with a hundred people working for a mere eighteen-week season.

Urban called the setup "our opera republic." He guided its functions from a new studio in an annex built the previous summer (with extra money put up by Jordan) just behind and adjoining the opera house, to the design of the original opera house architect, Parkman B. Haven. In addition to the two rooms occupied respectively by the musical director (Caplet) and the artistic director (Urban), the architect made space for chorus and ballet rehearsals.

Sketches had already appeared to suggest an opera to come, the opening *Tales of Hoffmann,* showing clearly an ensemble that summoned the fantastic atmosphere of the opera. Now, little pasteboard boxes, two feet wide, their fronts scooped out and "many strange things within," revealed the curious manner in which Urban worked. He first sketched settings in his mind and on chance scraps of paper. Then he built colored objects—no flat drawings, but only models. Colored plates of furniture and important props drawn from these models went to the prop man for verification, thence to the manufacturers. His costume sketches struck an American manufacturer as astonishing, not only in their beauty of color, but in the very grouping of designs. He would draw and color in minutest detail two or more characters in relation to each other, thus revealing not only a unified color scheme, but a dramatic unity as well: "... certain harmonic effects should be accentuated on the stage; the motive in the orchestra is my cue for the stage," he wrote. The privileged could peep into the curious little manuscript Urban used for rehearsal: dozens of typed pages, synopses of the action, stage business, tricks for candlelight, electrical cues.

The dossier of an opera would contain every imaginable outline of staging and costuming. Pages of copious notes in German script, or sometimes typed; hand-drawn ground plans which showed the disposition of larger furniture, platforms, and vegetation; lighting plots, platform plots, lists of ground cloths, lists of props with lavish illustrations, often in color; graphs for drop and flat scenery; shoe plots; outlines for the wigmaker and coiffeur (M. needs a blond moquage, R. a peruque, full and red; S. a gray mustache, etc.); costume details and groupings in exquisite ink and water color drawings; often photographs of the entire effect or some detail, occasionally corrected in ink and pencil so that you knew the master had amended the scene after the first performance.

Although *Pelléas et Mélisande* and *Tristan* had already presented opportunity for judgment of the new style in decor, the first real colored pennant to be attached unmistakably to Urban's mast fluttered over Offenbach's *Les Contes d'Hoffmann*. For the first time in American theatrical history, every element of the stage—scenery, costumes, properties, and direction—came from a single hand. Even the auditorium in which the audience gathered to witness these marvels had felt the touch. A new curtain within the familiar sweep of deep red velvet showed matching deep red, but embroidered in designs of wrought silver, simple yet fanciful repeated crowns and shields. Its pure line and color gave the keenest pleasure. Even the exterior asbestos curtain had been made seemly by a covering of gray, broken by parallel stripes of the same deep red, a color scheme already anticipated by the program cover, neat but rich.

It is doubtful if Boston quite realized that a revolution had taken place in its midst, although to give the first-night audience credit, a little shiver ran almost audibly through the auditorium as each new picture was revealed on the stage. Still, the reception could be called little more than placid. Comments in intermission seldom rose to a more feverish pitch than "It is well put on." Once, to be sure, mild applause greeted a scene, but to call Urban before the footlights lay quite beyond the imagination of this elegant crowd. Only at the end, after the Antonia scene, did clapping become long and insistent, from which the new singer, Louise Edvina, could take heart even more than Urban.

Urban had discarded footlights and other "outworn" means of illumination in favor of newer devices, soft and suffused glows over the faces of the singers. The Prologue and Epilogue played in the brown darkness of the cellar tavern, spotted by the vivid blue coat that was the operatic badge of Hoffmann, the hero, and suggestive of the painting of Dutch masters. This scene occupied the whole stage. When the curtain fell on it, an inner proscenium arch remained visible, doors at either side opening to permit the entry of Spalanzoni's guests to a ballroom, a stage within a stage. This semi-circular chamber glittered gold on gray, flooded with a rich orange light. The colors of Veronese and Tintoretto—or even more aptly, Beardsley's atmosphere—enhanced the Venetian scene. Black slaves, gorgeously clad, made color rigid and statuesque; the magic and languor of flesh contrasted lushly with mysterious blue walls guarding the landing place of gondolas. Two great fountains plashed at the sides. Antonia's modest room, low-studded, isolated, pale in greens and yellows, with ox-eye windows, glinted under the wan glamour of twilight. Cold moonlight played over the dead girl at the last. Through each of these scenes stole an evil spirit in black, Hoffmann's satanic genius, and at the feet of each of the poet's dead loves, a servant crouched, a splotch of vivid contrasting red.

No one doubted Urban's artistic purpose and sincerity, but Hale frankly didn't like the boxed-in ballroom, opining that to relegate the action to a remote height dimmed its brilliance. He had previously objected to certain similarly confined scenes in *Pelléas* (notably the castle exterior in the first act, and the scene of Pelléas' murder in the castle grounds) and would again complain about *Louise*. Still, the *Hoffmann* production suggested a peculiar atmosphere of strange beauty and *diabolerie*.

An estimation in the *Transcript* after the first of the year, when *Louise* had passed in review, summed up Boston's attitude toward the innovation. "We are told to take the scenery in a new way," the account ran, "not as an actual reproduction of life, as in Belasco; not as a conventional excuse for reality, such as large colored cutouts of Christmas pageants; not in reproductions of mid-century paintings and spasmodically three dimensional, as in opera. "We should instead feel the emotion expressed in staging."

This was pretty highflown, even for Boston. One could accept the adjuration in *Pelléas et Mélisande*, where the designer was on safe ground. *Tristan* had been acceptable too, following the familiar size of Wagner's concept, although the great billowing yellow curtain in the first act seemed preposterous on any sailing vessel. Still, it was built to the general size of "grand" opera, and therefore not outside the pale. The scenes of garden and sea showed more beauty, originality, and imagination than usual, but remained essentially unstartling. *Tales of Hoffmann* went a bit farther, with a new color spectrum and those curious doors at the sides of the proscenium; still, it could be taken in stride.

Quite a fuss had been raised over *Hänsel und Gretel* this year. When last February new scenery appeared, few realized that Urban had a hand in it, although many agreed with Hale that the production brought credit to the management. Others deplored the boxed-in forest, not at all realistic, but more like a Boecklin painting; and many voiced unkind words for the great gold stairway on which angels shone, themselves shaped of molten gold, contrasting vividly with the gorgeous blue background. The second performance drew an audience largely composed of children, who were not disposed to find fault with scenery. Between then and the following December 28, the golden staircase was removed, and a border illustrative of the folk tale framed the scene charmingly but obscured the view for too many. Letters from irate subscribers flowed in. Two days later, the border remained in place, but had been tilted or juggled somehow so that the view no longer was obstructed. The management was trying to please the customers. But the cries for the missing staircase continued to mount. What amused those in the know was that Urban had not committed a desecration on some other holy of holies; he had merely made changes in his own work. "Early" Urban had already become classic, then passé.

Louise at last confirmed the suspicion that had been engendered in the previous Urban operas: that the new scenic conceptions were most vulnerable at the point of lighting. Boston's technicians had not quite measured up to the unprecedented demands; or perhaps Urban's experiments had not quite jelled. The trouble went back as far as *Tristan*, where lighting plays quite as vital a role as the orchestra or singers. The lighting in the first act, bright outside Isolde's tent, contrasts with the twilight treachery within; the second-act's pale moonlight increases to brilliance as Tristan rushes in and Isolde meets him, then fades until the whole stage is dark. Signs of dawn strengthen until Tristan receives his mortal wound in cold and hard daylight. Light is the essential element in the third act, the element that produces Tristan's suffering and delirium. The drama ends in an infinite, empty gray.

That the second act of Urban's first *Tristan* passed in a blazing glare Parker attributed to the singers asking for more light. The performance of *Hänsel* that evoked so many complaints found the electrician in a state of confusion: he sent white glares to Gertrude's face instead of red from the kitchen fire; bright sunlight patched the forest too boldly, then switched in an instant to sharp, clear moonlight.

Pelléas had suffered from nervewracking contretemps. What was said by Arthur Wilson to be the first revolving stage in America caused abrupt pauses and stage waits. It was scrapped immediately.

Urban's ideal lighting subtleties, which became so familiar, constituted a *cause célèbre*, discussed endlessly in the Boston of 1912. What to Urban seemed desirably dim, an intensity low enough to blend his colors and project them properly, struck the literal Bostonians as just plain too dark. They felt deprived if they could not watch this singer's lips or that one's beauty. So up went the lights, and out the stage door went Urban's careful plans. Subjected to unsubtle lighting, *Pelléas* sets seemed "painty" and lacking in effects of distance. They resembled an overexposed negative, with its glaring contrasts in black shadow and highlights. It was all "theatrical" instead of illusive.

Walking the line between reality and illusion, Urban's decor for *Louise* could best be described as impressionistic. Deliberately cutting off many square feet at the sides and top, he designed Louise's room irregular in shape, with certain definitely ineradicable impressions of a room in which the girl and her parents lived—this was no canvas box, but the emotional evocation of a neat, poor dwelling. The Butte at down provided an excellent example, with its row of tiny houses of mixed and "dabbled" colors, the flecks of contrast here and there combining into a total picture of glowing tints. Evidence exists that Urban used a real photograph as a model. His free employment of solid, square corners covered with pointillage conveyed masonry such as one had never seen, but that might just possibly exist somewhere. It remained unrealistic even with the realistic action in front of it.

Still another effort to make opera express the facts of life in their actual environment, Wolf-Ferrari's *The Jewels of the Madonna* gave Urban a free hand to create. He began, according to Parker, where the words left off. The first-act square by the sea seemed drenched in hot, clear sunshine. Through great arches, the sea shimmered in blazing brilliance. Color ran madly through the festival of the Madonna and the celebrant procession. By contrast, the second-act garden, where Gennaro wins Maliella's favors by giving her the jewels he had just stolen from the Madonna, was bathed in the deep soft blue of the Italian sky, Whistlerian in prospect, with its tall trees, crumbling old houses, tranquil sea glinting in the moonlight. Though offering less opportunity for design, Urban's set for the third-act bare room served the composer's purpose, suggesting a subterranean evil but not amplifying it. It lay to the designer's credit that the extreme accent on realism asked by the plot and the music did not pull him into mere vulgarity.

In *Don Giovanni*, another new production for Boston, Urban came squarely up against the ideas of the conductor. Fortunately he had worked

often and well with Weingartner in Vienna, so that their thoughts chimed
on this opera as on many others. They would restore *Giovanni* to two acts
from the prevalent five; would not change scenery visibly, but use every
resource of the modern stage—except, of course, the revolving platform,
which by now was out of favor—to avoid long waits between the many
scenes. The stage, as well as the orchestra, would be reduced in size, so
that the production would be of chamber proportions, a consummation
devoutly desired by Hale. The new curtains would serve to deaden sounds
on the stage behind, while scenes were being played in front of them.
The chief changes brought about were the placement of the Inn to which
Donna Elvira comes opposite the Don's house, so that action moved
swiftly from one to the other; the transfer of Donna Anna's aria of lament
to the beginning of the cemetery scene, so that it became a chant over
her father's grave, thus eliminating the scene in her room; and the ending,
where instead of an unillusive descent to hell, the statue seized Giovanni
by the hand, the whole banquet room was enveloped in flames, and after
a quick change of scene, the Don was seen lying dead at the feet of the
statue, once more in the cemetery. Though not yet a definitive stroke of
the imagination, the solution was judged workable and plausible. Urban
once more used the framed stage, with a portal at side front, which might
by now be accepted as standing for "Urban *fecit*," Hale commented. The
lighting, *mirabile dictu,* was thrice admirable, he thought, although perhaps too bright in the opening scene.

A set of singular originality distinguished Bizet's *Djamileh,* seen once
fleetingly in February. Then in March, Urban designed sets for Aubert's
La Forêt Bleue—a brown village and a great ranked forest (not blue,
however), a castle that seemed to rise out of nothingness, vistas of skies,
sun, and moon. To read in his notebooks that the props consisted of rocks
from *Carmen* and *Girl of the Golden West,* grass mats from stock, dead
leaves from *The Girl,* ivy, flowers, and dry wood from stock, is slightly
disillusioning. However, a stuffed wolf and litter and a large tumbler for
the Ogre to drink blood from were freshly requisitioned. At that, the
production cost was reckoned in six figures. No one was inclined to take
any other part of this opera very seriously, except the cast, which had
slaved over it.

Distinctly Urban characteristics were the false proscenium openings to
alter the shape of the stage; the use of a single large object right in the
middle, against all academic principles (the statue in *Don Giovanni,* the

tree in the third act of *Tristan,* a bridge in *Faust*); and the graduated thicknesses of gauze transparencies in *Pelléas.*

New Urban touches distinguished a half-dozen repertoire operas, which benefited thereby in varying degrees. For *Bohème,* it was a matter of details of staging; a new vivacity and bustle, truly Latin in its exuberance, among the four Bohemians; the charm of a suggestion of winter sunlight that threw the shadow of bare boughs on the snow in the third act; the still, dark figure of Colline centered at the final moment with Rodolfo prostrate on the dead form of Mimi behind him. In *Butterfly,* the new setting did not mirror Japan faithfully, knowing ones said; furthermore the electricians betrayed Urban again in turning the lovers' faces a ghastly green as the moonlight faltered. Yet the fall of dusk on the mountain gave a moment of beauty. In a subsequent performance, the technicians still had not gained control of their tools; a critic slyly blamed the tenor's violence, however, for frightening the sky into extraordinary chromatic effects.

Some operas seemed already beyond revivification. The hopelessly commonplace *Thaïs* yielded only in the picturesque illusion of a new row of houses in the street scene and the curtaining of Thaïs' chamber, which added mystery, luxury, and remoteness. *Samson et Dalila* offered more opportunity. In a single performance, Urban's influence could be plainly spotted. The walls and portico of Dagon's Temple now showed rugged and stern; Dalila's maidens were recostumed in cool and shimmering white, while the vivid striping of the Jews' dresses seemed almost Bakstian.

Urban never did succeed in completely taming his technical crew in Boston. Probably the overbalance of rehearsal time accorded to one or two operas each season reacted unfavorably on his department, as on others. Furthermore, he never got Hale to capitulate to the boxed-in stage for certain operas. Nevertheless, this wizard of color and materials and light transformed the Boston stage and made it the first to adopt the new ways that later became bywords. The plump Viennese remains in memory the single most important figure in Boston's finest season. His magic was not only for the eye; it awakened the imagination and sent the spirit soaring.

20

IMPRESARIO IN THE LIMELIGHT

At the pinnacle of the fourth season, in the midst of Weingartner's visit, when the effect of Vanni Marcoux's absence had been slightly blunted by the gallant intercession of Ramon Blanchart—indeed, on the very day that the third and last performance of *Don Giovanni* drew the accustomed Saturday matinee audience to the Opera House—the lid blew off.

A new magazine made its debut in Boston. Premonitory rumblings had heralded the advent of *Music Magazine and Musical Stage Review*, subtitled *The National Music Weekly*—an advance circular had titillated the public and undoubtedly outraged the opera management. Now newsvendors stood in front of the house on the Huntington Street side, urging patrons to "Get your *Music Magazine* here . . . read all about the opera! Ten cents!"

Those curious subscribers who handed over their dimes received, and later tried hard to conceal, a twenty-page sheet about eleven by fourteen, bearing on the cover an unidentified photograph of Henry Russell, who looked more than usually diabolical. In the bottom margin ran the line: "Commencing in this number 'The Dr. Cook of Grand Opera.'" (The allusion pointed to Dr. Fred A. Cook, the surgeon, whose claims to discovery of the North Pole in 1909 had been proved false after the revelations of the true discoverer, Robert Edwin Peary.) Surreptitious peeks at its first page revealed a photograph of André Caplet, and though its caption had been set in rather small type, a good many were able to make it out: "His elevation to the post of chief conductor at the Boston Opera

221

House is hardly explained by his artistic attainments!" That was enough to elicit gasps and covert glances from neighbor to neighbor. "Everyone" guessed what was meant. The article itself covered more than two pages. Adding a turn to the screw, an anonymous reviewer cut the Boston Opera performances to ribbons, bearing down heavily on Urban and on the weakness of the conducting staff, while a similarly unrevealed correspondent dipped his pen in treacle to describe the doings at the Metropolitan and Chicago operas. The clue to the magazine's intent could be spotted in the absence of the editor's name. A space had been left in the masthead, where the sheet's personnel might be expected to be listed. (It was filled in the second issue by a [perhaps] symbolical line drawing of a satyr playing panpipes.) But the identity of the pen behind the poison came to light quickly. It was not hard to discover that the editor was Philip Kahn, whose brother Alexander had been hired as press representative for the opera company in 1911 and dismissed, according to Russell, a year or so later. None but the consequential columns of the magazine remained anonymous; the otherwise innocuous reports all bore presumably bona-fide by-lines.

Whether or not opera officials had attempted to prevent the publication, as the editor alleged in his opening paragraphs, on February 15 the newsstands became denuded of copies in the twinkling of an eye. The first issue, and the three that followed, rapidly achieved the status of rarities. Only a few copies exist today outside of libraries.

Exercising the human right to believe the worst, some horrified readers must have felt, at the least, an uneasy doubt, and must have asked themselves questions. Could it be true that Russell had so grievously mismanaged the business affairs of the opera, that Jordan was guilty at best of errors of judgment and at worst of insincerity of purpose, that singers received their pay in cash instead of by check, with the clear implication of a "kickback"? And so on and so on, as the reader penetrated further into a thicket of barbed innuendo and direct thrust. The tone of righteous indignation adopted by the pamphleteers extended also to Russell's private life. Caplet's engagement was examined "on its merits"; the impresario's exercise of a lordly *droit de seigneur* over certain attractive prima donnas was more than hinted at.

"Many are the tales whispered about," the account ran, "and many are the instances that will be cited—from the one involving the young beginner who was forced to appeal to the Board of Directors, to that which forced a famous prima donna to reject an offered contract because of [alleged] insulting importunities."

No names were named here, but if one turned to page eleven, a clue appeared in the final lines of a story headed "A Great American Soprano": "This sterling artist was lost to Boston audiences because she differed with Director Russell as to the course an ambitious girl should adopt in order to achieve artistic success." In the middle of the column was a charming picture of Mme. Marguerite Namara-Toye. The claims advanced for her by this staff writer mounted to laudation that should have embarrassed any singer lesser than Sembrich: "Discriminating critics of both continents proclaim her as the greatest living Mozart singer, and one who is gifted with the most beautiful voice heard since the time of Patti." She was at the moment embarking on a concert tour, having also distinguished herself in operetta. Boston would hear her that year at the Copley Plaza.

Still beautiful and fascinating today, Mme. Namara gives her own account of these doings. She has dropped her married names—among them Toye and Bolton (Guy)—in favor of the *nom du théâtre* given her by a benefactress who introduced to her Russell when she was still Marguerite Banks, fresh from Europe and complete with mother-chaperone. Namara maintains firmly, with a delicious smile and flutter of her astonishing eyes, that she gained time on the dreadful day Henry bearded her in his sixth-floor office by flinging an inkwell at him where he stood by the window (whether the inkwell was full or empty is not stated). Whereupon the beleaguered girl ran down five flights of steps in the empty building—empty, that is, except for Fred Toye, a company secretary, who championed her cause and whom she later married. The name of Banks appeared on the first season's roster, but it goes without saying that she did not sing. Her appeal to the "Board of Directors" (presumably Jordan himself) had no effect. Russell's second wife avers that it was a disagreement over which role Mme. Namara would play on stage rather than in private which brought about the clash. A decade or so later the volatile Namara visited the Russells on the Riviera and ostensibly buried the hatchet, even though Henry continued to harbor an unforgiving sentiment.

The prima donna who allegedly upheld her honor with hauteur and a refusal to sign remained a mystery to the public. A number of other *fameuses* never appeared with Russell, but whether by their choice or his is not clear in all cases.

The main article went on (with our brackets): "A coward by nature, Henry Russell is daring in his deeds. He never walks alone at night, he never sleeps alone in his apartments [note the plural], he fears his own shadow, and still he braves public opinion and risks disclosures . . .

"While it is fairly questionable whether or not the Boston Opera House added to Boston's renown as an art center, it is undeniable that it has caused more scandalous gossip than any other art institution, even with a ten-fold longer existence [not necessarily—the mere fact of the institution being in Boston had a great deal to do with it] . . . the consistent reports that 'something is rotten in Denmark' have already won for Boston a rather undesirable publicity" [including this].

"Russell must not hide behind the beautiful words of a friendly press," a writer scolded in the second issue. "He must not assume the part of a martyr. He must come out into the open and show some evidence of having made good. Failing that, he ought to resign."

Russell did neither; he sued for criminal libel.

Jordan's reaction had been to call an executive meeting of the board at the behest of Russell and present to the public an expression of complete confidence in his general manager. Otto Kahn came specially from New York to lend his support.

The *affaire scandaleuse* ended almost before the ink had dried on the magazine's fourth—and final—issue. One month from its debut, the editor was found guilty of the charges and, according to Russell's account, sentenced to jail.

"Only wealthy fools or the simon pure can afford to sue," Morris Ernst remarked in his book on libel and slander entitled *Hold Your Tongue.* Russell obviously was neither, yet he won his suit. The defense seemed thrown into confusion by the district attorney's demand that a bill of particulars be shown. The trial was adjourned for a day, opening on March 14—fortunately not a matinee day. A decidedly operatic air pervaded the courtroom. Rows of singers, subpoenaed as witnesses for the defense, sat uneasily and chattered nervously. A disappointed throng milled about outside the door, while the tedious impaneling of the jury droned on, then heads came up as the indictment was read.

The defendant had criticized the plaintiff for alleged mismanagement of the company, and wanted to know why a deficit existed when more than five hundred thousand dollars had been subscribed, and why singers were paid in cash instead of by check, and if the manager's private secretary collected agent's commissions in the name of the company. The defendant charged that the plaintiff had failed previously in England as an impresario, and had had a race-track man playing "angel" for his "disastrous" journey across the United States. Also he had become rich within three years; his manner of living had changed. "Nothing but the trains *de luxe* for him and his, for it is the Boston Opera Company that foots the bills even when Mrs. Russell and the little Russells travel in Europe," the magazine had stated, going on to (allegedly) quote the "so-called" business manager, William Macdonald, as saying that "Caplet's hotel bills while in Europe would cause a millionaire to turn green with envy." The editor added: "And Caplet is but an adopted member of the Russell family."

The defense hurriedly filed its bill of particulars, including days and dates of certain "acts." Such as was not "scandalous," reported the *Globe* cautiously, was allowed by the judge to remain, and the defense was permitted to give evidence. But evidently the defense believed that its case was irreparably weakened without the censorable material. Whereupon Judge Brown held that the magazine article itself, offered in evidence by the government, was *prima facie* libelous and ordered a verdict by the jury of "guilty." The opera stars, listed as Swartz, Zenatello, Gay, and Scotney (Nielsen had been summonsed but was in Chicago), breathed a sigh of relief. Nina Russell had been served with a subpoena, in spite of Henry's protest at the cruelty of the action, for Nina lay ill in the Fenway Hospital, the victim of melancholia caused by the ruthless tearing at the already frail fabric of her life.

Laying about him in all directions, Philip Kahn had jibed at the newspapers for their policy of concealment and complacency, quoting the *Saturday Evening Post* as saying that "there is undoubtedly a certain subserviency to department stores—the largest advertisers; but usually all the department store wants is suppression of shoplifting items." Linking this up with Boston's Jordan and his flourishing emporium added one more jab below the belt. And music critics cannot have been pleased to read that they gave the impression of writing "under orders" and that "some of them are under personal obligation to Director Russell."

The papers retaliated with their classic defense: silence. When one of their own family, no matter how remote the cousinship, steps out of line, the others close ranks and present a formidable cold shoulder to the offender. The trial received matter-of-fact coverage; otherwise, no blaze for the scandal-minded could be kindled with the aid of one's morning or evening newspaper.

Russell's public exoneration lay in the verdict, as well as in the previously published statement by the board. It was never thought necessary to explain the "race-track" angel, in reality Lord Grimthorpe, who had indeed put up the money for Russell's unsuccessful season in London, but who apparently had lent nothing but his presence to one American tour.

The dignified rebuttal by the board of the charges of extravagance on the part of the management (notably Russell) seemed to satisfy everybody, although there was not much opportunity then (nor is there now, in view of the paucity of reliable material) to form an independent judgment. The board's public statement follows in part:

"The executive committee also compared expenses with other companies, both in the aggregate and in detail. The figures afford convincing testimony of the economy, prudence, and care with which the affairs of the Boston Opera Company have been managed. It has reached a high standard in less than three years and justifies the claim to support and approval of the opera-loving public. The committee takes pleasure in publicly expressing unqualified confidence in Mr. Russell's absolute integrity, and appreciation of the skill, efficiency, and faithfulness with which he has conducted the affairs of the institution."

Signatures included nine of the seventeen members of the committee: Messrs. Jordan, Converse, Blanchard (secretary), Otto Kahn, Fearing, Herbert Sears, Baylies, Burnham, and Flanders (no longer business manager but still a member of the board).

And that was that. While the water was hot, the management threw in the plans for next season, more or less successfully diverting attention. Hale's grave comment on the situation of the two characters most chivied in the fracas fell like balm on their wounded spirits. Russell and Urban, he said, had faced before the footlights two sorts of opposition and detraction: from those who abide by tradition and convention and are uneasy and irritable at any departure or innovation; and those who disdain to understand the purpose or result of any new method and are content to deride it. It was a wonder, he added, that Urban had been able to accomplish what he did, in view of the hampering attitudes and derision he had met. In addition he had to learn a new language.

His professional torment assuaged for the moment, Russell could divert one stream of thought to his personal life, which was in a far more chaotic state than the newspapers or the public or his defamers suspected. Unfortunately for the precarious balance of his already vulnerable status, Henry found his emotions seriously engaged for the third time in his life. It had happened literally at first sight. The little scene involved Jeska Swartz, who, near the beginning of the season, returned from her study in France for the forthcoming novelty, *La Forêt Bleue*. Pausing at the stage door one afternoon to greet Russell, she was caught with the manager in a pushing horde of youngsters pouring out of the house from a special matinee. Russell, quick-witted and quick-tongued, smiled ironically at her, their eyes on a level barely a foot above the heads of the children, and remarked, "All mine—if gossip is to be believed."

"They vastly overrate you," retorted the mezzo-soprano.

Henry laughed appreciatively, then his face sobered and whitened. Jeska followed his gaze. The children had cleared the vestibule and just entering it was a girl, very young, with a soft oval face and enormous shining dark eyes. She asked, "Is this the way into the theater?"

Henry muttered assent, and stood aside to let her pass. Then he turned to Jeska, still spellbound, and demanded, "Did you see that? What do you think?"

"She's the prettiest girl I ever saw," said Jeska dutifully.

"No—but—" Henry's voice dropped to a whisper, "when Nina was that age, she looked exactly like that!"

From that moment, Henry began his life all over again. Jeska, having witnessed the beginning, was able to follow the threads as few others in the company could. Henry summoned all his deviousness. The last person to learn of the new state of affairs was, of course, Alice Nielsen. An open break that left scars on the two sensitive women, although they never actually met face to face, did not occur until late in 1913, after a strange and trying summer in Europe. Donna Shinn was then twenty-one.

"Who in the world is Miss Shinn?" Henry asked with some asperity after a bombardment of telegrams from Thomas Nunan, music critic of the San Francisco *Examiner*, suggesting that he hire her. Nordica had spoken too of the young western singer she had heard a half-dozen years before, when the San Carlo troupe played in San Francisco. Donna missed meeting Henry by five minutes on that occasion. At the urging of Nordica, Nunan, and other San Francisco friends, Donna's father, an attorney prominent in state politics and reclamation projects, took Donna to Boston for an audition with Henry. But the elusive manager was out of town, and the little party turned homeward without meeting him. The second pilgrimage to the East brought about the accidental encounter at the stage door.

Donna had appeared with the Lambardi company on the coast and believed in her own capabilities and destiny, although her unworldiness prevented the sharpening of aggressive weapons to achieve her aims. Neither she nor her equally naive mother suspected any oddity in the fact that Russell never allowed her to sing in public. Even at her audition, he had cut her short after a few bars of the *Lucia* Mad Scene. At the insistence of Caplet, Straram, and Jordan, who sat in the audience, he allowed her to proceed with "Charmant oiseau" from David's *The Pearl of Brazil*, but closed the audition with celerity and drew her aside on the stage. Taking both her hands, he said, "Little girl, I am going to do everything for you!"

Incredulous at her own good fortune and bedazzled by its prospects, the young girl floated through the ensuing months in a rainbow cloud. She may have wondered why, when Straram wanted her for Antonia in *Tales of Hoffmann* and Garden put in a bid for her to sing in Chicago, Henry refused, giving as an excuse that she needed maturing for the big roles. He kept her steadily at rehearsal. Nielsen did not rejoin the company until February for two performances as Zerlina, then went away for another month. When she returned, two new roles, Martha and Suzanna, together with a short illness, assured her undivided concentration. Donna, blissfully ignorant of Nielsen's private role, made a friend in an unexpected quarter. Nina Varese took the girl under her wing, even chaperoning her on the European voyage Henry arranged immediately after the season's close in 1913. Donna's mother went back to California.

Henry had contrived an ingenious if costly way to give his new singer experience: he built an opera company around her. Ostensibly to try out several singers he had tentatively engaged for Boston, he hired the theater in a little North Italy town near Como (by an ironic coincidence called Varese, Nina's stage name) and gathered a catch-as-catch-can troupe. Donna remembers that Marguerite D'Alvarez, the brilliant, dark-eyed beauty who had sung with Hammerstein in New York and London, was the Amneris in a performance of *Aïda* in which she provided the only hit in a comedy of misses. Russell used up two tenors before a third was allowed to stay on the stage and sing. The first two met with "Partì! Partì per ferrovia!" (freely translated as "Get out of town" with the suggestion that the railroad was handy) as soon as they opened their mouths on "Celeste Aïda." Even the third singer, whom Donna remembers as being Slezak, didn't please the entire audience, and those who dissented continued to shout and shake fists at the satisfied customers. During most of the performance, the audience displayed healthier vocalism than the singers.

On the following night, the timorous Donna appeared before the inimical crowd as Suzanne, in Wolf-Ferrari's little opera. To her amazement, not a sound came from the listeners—not even a catcall. But neither was there a sign of applause. When the curtain went down on the same stony silence, Donna retired to her dressing room heartbroken. Caplet, who had coached her, tried to put it off on the Italians' dislike of Wolf-Ferrari, but Henry callously remarked that she was lucky they didn't throw things. The next day she saw scrawls on the walls of the house that warned: "We don't want children singing in this theater." Henry, driven by emotion that overpowered good sense, carried this experiment a trifle too far for comfort. If, as seems probable, the venture was embraced in the Boston budget, it proved an expensive audition indeed.

Nina's complacence, even connivance, in acknowledging and protecting Donna became firm policy when she realized that Henry was serious about the girl. Through many harrowing scenes in the months to come, she remained a steadfast friend. Donna thought of her tenderly, almost as a mother. After the inevitable showdown with Nielsen, Nina took Donna once again to Europe, for the Paris season of the company. Now Henry wanted a divorce. Nina of course consented, although it came too late for her own happiness. After Caplet died in 1925, Nina moved to the Riviera, to be near Donna and Henry, who stood by to console her. Henry, it seems, always cherished for his first wife some emotion—respect? reverence for a memory?—possibly identified with his adoration for his mother. Gradually Nina picked up the skeins of life, beginning to take an interest once again in the career she had abandoned to marry Henry. In the twenties, she appeared in several plays in New York, among them Zoë Akin's *Papa* and *Peter Ibbetson* with John Barrymore. She outlived Henry by four years, dying in 1941.

With Donna, for the first time in his life, Henry became almost domesticated. Nina had sensed that this might be so. Henry was always "softer" with the younger woman, she believed. He and Donna lived a great deal of the year in the villa at La Turbie, or in an apartment in Monte Carlo, where Sheridan, Henry's younger son, came to join them. Sheri had gone to Paris to school for a year after the Boston Opera closed, then studied cello and played a great deal until he became deaf in one ear. His uncle, Sir Landon Ronald, occasionally held out a helping hand, but could not really forgive Sheridan for not attending his school. Never subjected to as much of the *sturm und drang* of his parents' existence, Sheri grew up a happier lad than his older brother, Tosti.

Tosti's full name, Henry Tosti Russell, was bestowed in honor of his father and Paolo Tosti, the buoyant songwriter and teacher. After his father's death, he chose to be called Henry, evincing a pride in his heritage that never deserted him. Toughened early to disappointment, he developed a doubting, questioning mind, saved from complete cynicism only by a fundamentally loyal and affectionate heart. D'Annunzio played a leading role in his early disillusionment. The poet came to lunch one day, one of the rare occasions when Tosti's mother and father were together, he remembers. Henry primed his son on table topics. At a certain moment, receiving a kick on the shin, Tosti inquired brightly about the poet's prowess as a glass blower. D'Annunzio, flattered by the boy's interest, promised to send him some examples of the fragile art. But he broke his promise.

"I discovered from his insincerity that all men are equal," Tosti recalls. "There is so such thing as a great man. From then on, I always checked everything and questioned everybody. This made me a good journalist." He won a gold plaque for a remarkable scoop: the United Press publication of Edward VIII's abdication before it was announced in the House of Commons.

Puccini, perhaps not a great man, but certainly a kind one, helped to redress the balance slightly in favor of a belief in humanity. Crossing the English Channel one day in typically dirty weather, Henry and Puccini, both superb sailors, braved the spray and talked music. Puccini expressed a desire to greet Henry's son, whereupon Tosti was summoned, green and shaking, from the cabin. Clinging to the companionway railing in agony and trembling, he staggered to his father across the dancing deck. Puccini grabbed the boy by the elbows and lifted him high, then kissed him on both cheeks.

"I liked him so much, I felt ungrateful, not to respond more heartily," said Tosti. "But at least I didn't throw up on him. He liked people, one of his great charms. I resent those who called him common and vulgar."

With something of Henry's energy and versatility, Tosti set about keeping himself busy in Boston. Sheridan genuinely liked practicing the cello, but Tosti turned Philistine when a violin was placed in his hands. He resorted to the time-honored dodge of concealing a book—an exploit of Buffalo Bill's—in his Ševčík exercises, and playing over and over the only two lines of music he had memorized. His British tutor, knowing little about music, seldom noticed the horrid sounds that came from an injudicious mixture of Czech and Wild West cultures. The boy conceived for Timothée Adamowski, the Boston Symphony concertmaster who consented to teach him, a loathing that was warmly reciprocated. Finally Henry gave up and allowed his son to go to business college on Boylston Street. Typing had it all over piano or violin playing, Tosti thought. Still he didn't relinquish music altogether. He formed an orchestra of sixteen or seventeen children, as well as a chorus of fifteen, and aspired to the life of a conductor. Bluffing it out—he couldn't read music two bars' worth—he gave concerts in the opera house foyer, playing *Carmen* selections and accompanying the indulgent Alice Nielsen in *Faust* arias. "A piece of damned impudence," he labeled it when he was older and less daring.

More successful was the model stage Tosti built with the help of Robert Brunton, the property chief, and Walter Hearn, the baggage master. Brunton showed the boy how to build the superstructure from which to hang curtains and scenery. Hearn, with his enormous fat body that "moved stomach on stomach," perspired in rivers as he went about the dirty work backstage. He was devoted to the family, and Henry and Nina trusted him with supervision of Sheridan and Tosti. Both boys liked and respected him for his straight look and uncompromising honesty.

When the miniature stage was complete, with three racks of lamps— orange, green, red, blue, and white, enough even for the sunset in *Thaïs* —Tosti gave select performances to the accompaniment of records. Nielsen dressed the three-inch puppets that served for actors.

Tosti got his electrical equipment by the expedient of barter. The tough-looking individual who provided the tiny lamps and wiring discovered his customer's connection with the opera house and demanded, "Got any free tickets?"

"Sure," replied Tosti. "You got a smoking?"

The term translated to mean evening clothes, the ruffian allowed as how he owned a tuxedo and suggested that the orchestra was the location for him. Tosti plucked two five dollar seats almost every Saturday night for him.

A good many hours were spent cheerfully by the children in the disposal of "paper" to fill the house. The amount of their activity formed a good barometer of the success of any opera. All too often, Business Manager Macdonald would turn over a hundred seats in the balcony for the boys to distribute. Tosti, being old enough to stay up at night, heard almost every performance, absorbing by osmosis the gamut of opera and learning to love it.

Other links existed between the company and the Russells. Maria Paporello, the ballet mistress from 1911 onward, married Giuseppe Maschiaghi, Henry's valet, and opened a dancing school in Boston. She wrongfully accused Tosti of stealing fifty dollars, whereupon her husband, loyal to the Russells to a point of fanaticism, beat her severely. He had nearly given his life for the boys. On a miserable cold night in London he had carried Tosti and Sheri out of a blazing building, breaking his leg as he jumped; then despite his pain had summoned the fire engine. The boys loved to hear him tell the story and begged Giuseppe to show them the knot on his leg which was a souvenir of the broken bone. He cooked for Henry too, specializing in a tasty risotto.

Henry's private secretary, Randolfo Barrocchi, showed an unfriendly aspect to the boys. Tosti believed he hated Henry, although he imitated him in dress, down to impeccable spats. The boys cared little for him; his habit of drenching his nearly bald head with perfume and bestowing exaggerated care on a luxuriant mustache was enough to put them off. He too married a ballet dancer, which complicated everybody's life. Tosti believed him a master of intrigue and distrusted him accordingly, although Nina was said to like him. He remained a figure of mystery, the center of numerous storms and disturbances, as long as the company existed.

Tosti, with his desperate yearning for a home, never found one until he made it for himself. He was always being sent away somewhere to school. The worst time was in Frankfurt-am-Main, where he and Ben, Nielsen's son, endured the rugged discipline of a German school. The masters thought nothing of pulling a boy by the ear until that organ tore away from the head. Ben, a little older and tougher than Tosti, came unscathed through the horrors. It always grieved Tosti that his father treated Ben with far more kindness than himself.

Donna, so close to Tosti in age, became an ally, although she unwittingly made trouble for him. Possibly as a reaction against his father's meticulous habits of dress, Tosti affected as much sloppiness as he could get away with. Donna remarked in a teasing though kindly manner about a particularly rakish hat Tosti sported. Henry at once chimed in, like a Henry James father choosing words dipped in sarcasm and disdain that found their target in the boy's sensitive skin.

A similar trifle set off a reaction that delivered the *coup de grâce* to this strained father-son relationship. When Tosti, seeking the affection that had always escaped him, married at a ridiculously early age, Henry came, reluctantly, to visit one day in Paris. He immediately began to rag Tosti on his taste in suitings and ties. This was more than Tosti's loyal French wife could bear.

"Why don't you then buy him some new ones!" she exploded.

Henry never saw his elder son again. Tosti went to Portugal to live soon after. Henry existed very well without the youth of the human species; he despised "brats." It was in some part their propensity for procreation that inspired his dislike for Louise Homer and Ernestine Schumann-Heink. By some possible extension of this prejudice, Henry showed no patience for feminine weaknesses. He did not suffer prima donnas' husbands lightly anyway, but professed to be doubly irritated by one particular specimen who presented himself regularly to the impresario with the excuse: "My wife cannot sing tonight; we have the curse."

Paradoxically, or so it might have seemed to those detractors who accused him of out-Juaning Don Juan, Henry is said to have shown little need of the casual gratification of sex impulses that appears to be usual for a man of his métier. It is possible to believe that his "casting couch" was less occupied than gossip would have it. Henry loved to take it out in talk, however, quoting Oscar Wilde on every occasion when Boston was sure to be shocked. Donna thought he liked to model himself on Lord Darlington of *Lady Windermere's Fan*. He showed himself the complete Puritan where Donna was concerned; she was allowed no rouge, no lipstick, no decolleté dresses. With the masculine possessiveness that neatly dovetails with other characteristics of so self-centered a man, Henry kept Donna as much of a child as possible during the seven years of their marriage. Fortunately for her independence of character, she discovered a talent for writing, which she later put to good use as a press agent, a short story writer, and a playwright.

Although it ended in divorce, the marriage of Henry and Donna could be called successful on its own terms. Its termination was by agreement, another instance of the solicitude all Henry's women showed for his welfare. Donna actually gave Henry up to another wife for his own good. Donna's father had died in 1919, the year of her marriage. Her mother, visiting the Russells in France in 1925, became ill, and Donna was forced to accompany her home. After six months, she granted Henry a Paris divorce. With his third marriage. Donna may well have pondered the turn of the wheel that brought her back to Nina's situation.

Act V

21

THE SWAN BEGINS ITS SONG
(1913–14)

The handwriting on the wall was plain. In retrospect, it is possible to read, for "Mene, mene," *Meistersinger* and *Monna Vanna,* and to decipher the riddle of the baffling fifth season of the Boston Opera Company. Although *Monna Vanna* provoked curiosity and provided the annual "incident" without which an opera company could hardly be said to be normal, *Die Meistersinger* exerted the strongest influence on Russell's schedule. Wagner's great lyric comedy drew the blood and juice out of the Boston corpus, leaving it too anemic to nourish the remainder of the repertoire. The blame for this could of course be laid directly at Russell's door, but Caplet's growing ambition undoubtedly exerted equally strong leverage.

If *Meistersinger* had proved worth waiting and sacrificing for, the absence of other fresh material might not have debilitated public interest and company morale to such an extent. But its success fell short of sensation. Did Caplet's enthusiasm atone for merely pitchforking other operas onto the stage? Philip Hale asked his readers at the end of the season. The answer had already sounded in the perceptible waning of public interest.

Russell seems to have had his mind elsewhere. Hastily he followed Gatti-Casazza's lead and mounted Montemezzi's *L'Amore dei Tre Re* after its resounding success at the Metropolitan in January, and thus almost casually produced the one new artistic triumph of the year. He had first call on the services of the tenor who created the part of Avito at

237

the Milan première the previous April, the handsome Ferrari-Fontana, who had rescued *Tristan*. Russell signed him for several roles this year, but unaccountably overlooked the Montemezzi—or allowed Gatti to beat him to it without challenge.

After it was all over, H. T. Parker found a few things to say that must have planted barbs in the already sensitive façade of the opera board, if not in the toughened hide of its debonair director. Perhaps it would be fairest, the critic began, to call this a period of transition, beset by chance adversities. At the head of his list of misfortunes was Clément's absence, then the domestic bereavement of Gay and Zenatello (Gay's two young daughters had died within one month), successive illnesses, then the Christmas blight, and the mistakes in policy, leading off with the sacrifice on the altar of *Meistersinger*. The lack of a "chief" conductor loomed most significantly. Russell had always been remiss in this department, frequently expressing his distaste for "prima donna" conductors and entrusting too much to *routiniers*, too little to the talent of a Weingartner. Caplet's domination seems almost sinister in the light of the neglect of Weingartner, who got all his operas except *Otello* second-hand this year. Perhaps his other obligations kept him away until the last month in Boston, but Russell should have planned accordingly and left a plum or two for his most eminent leader. Caplet's shadow fell too heavily on the young Frenchmen Strony and Tournon to allow their profiles to emerge, while Moranzoni, who carried the burden of fifteen Italian operas, seemed an old familiar story, competent as he was. Boston, if it had realized its lack, could have looked toward New York and sighed for a Toscanini, a Polacco, and a Hertz. At least the latter's thunders might have shaken the lethargy out of the orchestra and boxes.

But Boston was not quite aware of what was going on in its handsome five-year-old opera house. A restlessness and a new querulousness poisoned the atmosphere. The boxholders, without a genuine love of opera as a foundation, were sated: attending had become a boring obligation rather than a lively pleasure. The only bright hope seemed to lie with what Parker "without offense" termed the "middle classes." The balconies had waxed as the lower levels waned; still the new growth put down roots only gingerly. Management and directors seemed not to possess the green thumb with which to cultivate this garden and bring two auditors springing up where one used to be.

What did the public want anyway? Parker thought they were fed up with Puccini, with *Aïda* and *Traviata* and *Lucia*—even with Tetrazzini. Not so much new as different pieces might satisfy their craving. And as for singers, too many had been retained (no names mentioned) in the face of public dislike, while the budget would not allow for the eminences everyone desired. "An unsolvable problem," he concluded.

The only remedy proposed was to shorten the season to twelve weeks, thus reducing subscription prices and hedging against boredom. After all, as Hale reminded them, Boston could not boast the large floating population of New York, where hordes go prepared and anxious to spend money. Furthermore he pointed out a detrimental feature of the opera house—no standing room. But, he reasoned, this had all been true in the past; had been discussed thoroughly before. What was wrong now? One could always fall back on the excuse that many Bostonians felt poor at the moment. Railroad stocks were depressed; dividends fell low. Even more portentous, the sixteenth amendment to the Constitution had taken effect on February 25, 1913. Incomes, "from whatever source derived," would henceforth be subject to Federal tax. No longer would a man with a million dollars be considered a millionaire pure and simple.

None of these circumstances by itself should have inflicted mortal injury on Boston's newest cultural body. Perhaps the nagging Boston conscience had functioned all along to the detriment of the opera—the conscience which forbade any enjoyment unless a worthy charity stood open-handed in the background. If Boston didn't invent the "charity ball," currently scheduled almost nightly on every metropolitan social calendar in America, Bostonians were early birds in the field of philanthropical fund. The conscience had long since been squared for the city's Symphony. But opera *per se* still smacked of naughtiness, and the local peccadillos only intensified the generality.

The season opened brilliantly, as usual. The extent of the dominance of the *Meistersinger* project, however, may be judged by Russell's selection of an opening opera. Instead of newly mounting a work, as in the preceding two seasons, he chose the box-office sensation of 1912–13, *Jewels of the Madonna*. Possibly cynical about first-night audiences, who by tradition would rather stare at themselves than at the stage, Russell competed for their attention only by offering several singers new in their parts, and by including more spirited and wanton action in the Camorrists' den (although admittedly Wolf-Ferrari's specific directions could not be carried out).

As if in unconscious response, the ladies gathered in boxes and orchestra reflected the garish colors of the stage to an unprecedented degree. Never before had such a blaze of green, orange, geranium, ruby, and gold shone under the opera chandeliers, while diamond ornaments glittered in hair, at the throat, on wrists and fingers. The few notes of black bespoke mourning. One dashing lady (an Ames) stood out as an exception. Beneath the hem of her black velvet gown, startlingly short, trim ankles and feet directed the eye to the latest fad, slippers and hose in the same color, a pulsating crimson.

If *Jewels* did not quite strike fire, the onus can be laid on the two leading personnages, Maliella and Rafaele. Louise Edvina had not warmed up to her task from the previous season; she still thought the part rather than felt it. And the dapper Mario Ancona, that tried-and-true baritone of at least twenty years' experience, had learned along the way how to sing and escaped twenty faults of the new generation, but, as Parker deplored, showed little character in his first appearance with the company. Ferrari-Fontana suited the robust masculinity of Gennaro, but unfortunately for the drama, turned directly to the audience in his hour of ruin. The attractive Marguerite D'Alvarez, who had deeply impressed Donna Shinn the summer before, made her Boston debut, and though the part of the mother Carmela offered little for display, her deep, rich, warm voice, a true alto, promised delights to come.

"Opera always begins well in Boston," Parker remarked, whether ominously or optimistically is impossible to tell. The more sanguine view was borne out by the first three weeks, which brought *Monna Vanna,* the debuts of the tenors Lucien Muratore, Giovanni Martinelli, and Vincenzo Tanlongo, the baritone Henri Dangès, and the bass Pavel Ludikar, all investments with potential gilt edges; a Garden-Marcoux *Tosca,* two Matzenauer and Ferrari-Fontana *Tristans,* Bori's only *Butterfly,* Garden's *Thaïs,* and D'Alvarez's Amneris and Dalila.

At least a handful of the Boston opera public felt ready and primed for *Monna Vanna,* having witnessed Maeterlinck's drama with Georgette Leblanc two seasons previously. The story of the Florentine commander Prinzivalle who offers to lift a siege of Pisa if Monna Vanna, the wife of the Pisan commander Guido, will come to his tent at night, held no surprises; but the tension evoked by the daring of the lady, avowedly bare under her long cloak as ordered, should have retained the power to rasp Boston nerves. Mary Garden thoroughly destroyed this illusion, however, by the frankness of her costume, contradicting all precedents, and confirming actor-manager Wilson Barrett's accusation that she had a mania for showing the smoothness and whiteness of her skin. Her conception of Vanna insulted the dramatist and the intelligence of her audience, Hale fumed. She revealed bare arms, shoulders, and "demesnes that there adjacent lie," in a diaphanous affair of rosy red that assaulted the eye, that might have served neatly at a students' ball in Paris, but that hardly sugested an enveloping mantle. "Sometimes," Hale mused, "it seems as if Miss Garden were possessed by the demon of perversity, wishing to be original at any cost." It was a wonder that she contented herself with kissing Prinzivalle on the brow in the scene where he, discovering that Monna Vanna was a childhood friend, spares her and offers to lift the siege anyway. Judging from Miss Garden's demeanor, the music should have been that of Thaïs before her conversion.

Henri Février's opera paid the price for this latest whim of the uncontrollable diva, an extortion it could hardly afford. Aside from the drama, whose verities thus disappeared, Russell's latest novelty featured the superb acting of Vanni Marcoux, some stunning designs by Urban, and unusually evocative stage direction by Leo Devaux—all these not seriously disturbed by the music. In the light of its laborious contrivance and inconspicuous workmanship, Hale wished that Février had borrowed more freely from other composers. The Prelude to Act III, called "The Anguish of Guido," should be retitled "The Anguish of the Hearers," he wrote savagely.

Marcoux should have been left to himself to express Guido's distress, for the singer elevated the part, making it worthy of being included in that litany of great operatic portraits that Hale was fond of reciting (on this occasion reaching back to include Emil Fischer's Hans Sachs, presumably in honor of the current *Meistersinger*). Furthermore, the baritone's voice had never responded so willingly to his intention.

Many feminine hearts stirred at the sight and sound of Lucien Muratore, the new tenor from the Paris Opéra. Of commanding presence and splendid physique, his manly bearing compensated for a face less subtle than his art. Although two sets of hearers would forever squabble about his ability to restrain and refine his full and noble voice, its sensuousness and stirring quality remained a passionate partner to his sense of stage. His dramatic flair had been developed in his early years, for Muratore belonged to that extremely rare category, actor turned opera singer.

He had played leading roles opposite Mme. Réjane at the Odéon before the Opéra Comique captured him in 1902. Three years later he moved to the Opéra. Many composers chose him to create roles in new operas— indeed, he had been the first Prinzivalle in *Monna Vanna* in 1909. So practiced an artist had he become that one admiring critic claimed that he could "assume with success any role short of a decapitated midget." Although this Boston debut probably marked his first partnership with Garden, they met again in Chicago, where the tenor sang, with one interruption for war service, until 1922.

Muratore's preparation for *Monna Vanna* had included elaborate research into costuming, a procedure he always followed. He claimed it was more a case of love for his work than moral honesty that prompted him to such close attention to detail; at any rate, the results gave that touch of authenticity that impresses even though it is not immediately perceptible. He had found a genuine Renaissance dalmatic (a state robe, really an outer vestment worn by church officials) for Prinzivalle, although his armor could not be genuine, for it would weigh more than fifty pounds. He looked forward to creating the hero in Zandonai's *Francesca da Rimini*, which Russell planned after its première in Turin in February 1914; then he would wear genuine armor, if only for a few minutes. A Greek scholar had taught him to use a real antique bow for Fauré's *Pénélope*, given the previous March in Monte Carlo. So it went. For example, he conceived his Faust (the role of his Boston debut) from Dürer's "Maximilian of Austria," his Herod from the Memling painting.

"It is unworthy to rent a costume," he insisted. "When the costume is right, I feel I *am* Roméo"—a parallel to Mary Garden and her dependence on wigs.

For those who liked a bit of gossip, Muratore held further interest. He had just married the lady whose beauty was best described by the French as *troublant*. Her name was Lina Cavalieri and trouble was her shadow. In her brief seasons with the Metropolitan and Hammerstein, she had proved more divisive than magnetic. Boston had seen her *Tosca*—the visual aspect outweighed the vocal, being, as Andrés de Segurola described it, a delectable combination of "white Caucasian ermine, glowing white satin, and luscious flesh, topped by the deep green of emeralds of tiara, necklaces and brooch."

Her private exploits outran even Mary Garden's in providing front-page fodder. When an involvement in a divorce suit was said to come close to Metropolitan interests, that opera house found an excuse to close its roster to her. Hammerstein welcomed her. But in addition to inciting Mary Garden to riot by claiming a *Thaïs* performance, Lina is supposed to have stirred up rivalry between French and Italian forces, and even to have contributed to Campanini's departure from Hammerstein's purlieus. Nevertheless, the conductor engaged her for at least one season in Chicago. In June, 1910, she married Robert Winthrop Chanler of the Astor dynasty. By September the marriage ended, amid mountains of newsprint, but a substantial lump of the Chanler fortune remained in the lady's slim, white—and greedy—fingers. Whatever her motives in previous marriages or entangling alliances, she seems to have married Muratore for love. At least, she displayed one of the strongest emotions that are said to be handmaidens to the tendor passion: jealousy.

Muratore had formerly been married to Marguerite Bériza, an intelligent, graceful soprano from the Paris Opéra Comique, with a dark, passionate face, heavily shadowed eyes, and full mouth, who by chance had been engaged by Russell and had already appeared in *Faust, Tales of Hoffmann,* and *Bohème.* Her best singing would be accomplished in *Louise* later in March, for although she made every role individual, her voice tended to shrillness in upper reaches. She had a small theater of her own in Paris by this time.

When Mary Garden fell ill for the first time in her career (according to her she never missed a performance, but the records prove her wrong), a performance of *Manon* had to be shelved on February 21. Bériza, who sang under a weekly contract, had been asked to step in, but gossip had it that Cavalieri refused to let Muratore sing Des Grieux, thus forfeiting his thousand-dollar fee.

Bériza was quoted as saying: "That woman broke up my home! If she ever speaks to me, I'll scratch her eyes out." Apparently she retained no resentment toward Muratore. For when on February 27, Russell approached her with a proposition she had every right to refuse, she jumped at it. Would she sing Monna Vanna the next afternoon? Would she indeed! It meant polishing up the role she had observed only in the Boston rehearsals and going on cold the next afternoon, but she counted on that full-length mantle to warm her up, not to mention the proximity to her former and presumably still cherished husband.

Cavalieri's reaction was predictable. After she had ended a domestic

Mad Scene on a note high above the staff, she recollected that the thousand dollars would be welcome. She herself had been ill, she claimed with pathos, and not able to earn money. So she would let Muratore out, but on a leash. According to one account, she told him: "I will be there, and if you give that woman one unnecessary kiss, one caress that looks real, I shall go down and break up the opera." According to Russell, she knew nothing about the substitution and turned ghastly pale and seemed to echo the words of the equally unknowing tenor, "*C'est affreux!*" when his former spouse greeted him with "*Je viens comme vous l'avez voulu.*"

Lina brooded in a proscenium box, her great midnight eyes ablaze, her mouth set in sullen curves. Bériza, demure on stage, had not hesitated in the wings to share her glee with her friends. Summoning up her talent as an actress, she did her best to make Muratore uncomfortable, knowing that each affecting gesture meant a bad half hour for Lucien afterward. Her revenge was fully gratifying, for in addition to the personal (though momentary) triumph over Cavalieri, she must have given one in the eye to Garden. Several critics sprang gratefully to her banner, Arthur Wilson claiming that Maeterlinck's character lived on the stage for the first time, while Olin Downes praised her second act (the vital one) as far superior to Garden's. It was pleasant, Wilson wrote, to see that she had taken note of the dramatic lines and explicit directions for costuming. Here was no suggestion of an adventuress who found her errand merely a stimulating diversion; nor was she amiably curious about what her captor would do. Rather, she appeared a woman of adamant will, resolved on sacrifice. When she agreed that she wore nothing but her cloak, you believed her, the garment from chin to toe giving a more perfect illusion of nudity beneath than the boldness, scantiness, and brazen impudence of Garden's garbled version. As for Muratore, many professed to believe that he sang with unwonted ardor, indeed, as one inspired.

The story of *Monna Vanna* seemed made to order. After Vanna and Prinzivalle discover their childhood friendship, Prinzivalle lifts the siege, and for this is considered a traitor by his own men. He and Vanna escape to Pisa, but Guido, refusing to believe in his wife's innocence, throws Prinzivalle in jail, thus alienating Vanna, who turns her affections to Prinzivalle and helps him escape. They live happily ever after.

No situation could have been better suited to arouse the green demon in Cavalieri. What must she have thought of the following dialogue!

P. "You know me not again? Do I recall nothing to you?"

V. "Is this the boy I knew? But stay, perchance there is something—for still you seem to smile as you smiled when a boy . . ."

P. (taking her hand) "I cover it with kisses. Yet you show no reluctance—bear me no despite for this cruel ordeal!"

Then Vanna sang: "But we speak of myself as though life took no account of others. Too much we forget all that another suffers, while we beguile the hour with a smile at the past."

Cavalieri could hardly restrain herself. But the curtain fell at last; the triangle dissolved.

Meistersinger finally got onto the stage on January 23. Was it worth all the trouble? Parker thought so; Hale disagreed, but the latter's chronic irritability at the complete Wagnerian *corpus* had to be discounted. For the affirmative, Parker concluded that never in this country, not even at the Metropolitan, had all concerned realized so complete a job. Wilson leaned to the negative, believing at the end that the encroachment on the rest of the repertoire had not been warranted. More than one observer bemoaned the absence of Weingartner (and his wife's Eva) until the final pair of six performances. Parker, however, stood up for Caplet, proclaiming the orchestra as at one with him. The number of rehearsals should have ensured this unanimity at least. Wholly to the local credit, in addition to the sharply drilled instrumentalists, was the chorus, which had been equally well trained. No one could complain of the ensemble work in the mighty masterpiece.

Urban's contribution came under dispute, Parker calling his sets a part of life, not a frame for it, and finding them rich in suggestions of Nuremberg; Hale, though seeing many picturesque qualities, wished for more open and spacious effects. In the second act, he complained, there was nothing to hide the lovers from Beckmesser, not even darkness.

Of the seven principals, four came from the Metropolitan: Carl Jörn as Walther; Johanna Gadski as Eva; Robert Leonhardt as Beckmesser; and Carl Braun as Pogner. The Bostonians were Pavel Ludikar as Sachs; Jacques Jou-Jerville as David; and Lydia Rienskaya as Magdalena. Even in the rather frequent shuffling of casts, Metropolitan replacements were called on for Walther (Urlus), Beckmesser (Goritz), Pogner (Griswold and Witherspoon), and Eva (Hempel). Later Léon Lafitte took over Walther four times, Taddeuz Wronski got two chances at Pogner, and Lucille Marcel-Weingartner sang Eva twice. William Hinshaw, who had just left the Met, came up for Hans Sachs twice. Leonhardt's admirable Beckmesser (the program with unconscious aptness spelled the pedant "Heckmesser") avoided the sin several of his predecessors had committed in acting like low comedians; in fact, this town clerk and judge of music showed overweening conservatism. How he would have raved against M. Claude Debussy!

In all this pageantry, Ludikar stood out for the gentle gravity and quiet humor of his Sachs, well planned and totally lacking in unctiousness. It was the seventh of ten roles in which the Czech bass-baritone displayed conspicuous intelligence, versatility, and schooling.

Hale further expressed his dissatisfaction with the other characters and ideas: Jörn was not the romantic Franconian knight, but a "walking gentlemen," continually rehearsing a song so that when performance time comes, the effect is largely discounted; Gadski's Eva was rather sophisticated, with a querulous, pettish, pouting note. Braun's Pogner, while nobly sonorous, might well figure in that gallery of operatic bores Hale had so often listed (this time he added the Flying Dutchman and the Harper in *Mignon*). He finally boiled over after the third performance, allowing some of his indignation to find vent. *Meistersinger*, he began, would be described by a press agent today as satire with a "love interest." A pity that it was not of a reasonable length: "Would that it had been put in a duck press and the best of it extracted!" Its heavy-laden humor became painfully elaborated in the street row. This is all very well for Bayreuth, where the visitor has nothing else to do but to go to bed early the night before, rise, take a cold bath and do a few gymnastic exercises, walk, then rest till opera time. At intermissions he fills himself with ham and beer, thus enduring the next act.

"They order these things well at Bayreuth; but the gaseous waters during waits in America are not so beneficial," Hale concluded.

L'Amore dei Tre Re turned out to be the nine-days' wonder of the season, the three performances occurring within that span: February 9, 14 (matinee), and 18. Montemezzi's gain was Zandonai's loss: the latter's *Francesca da Rimini* was hastily abandoned in favor of *L'Amore* (and Cavalieri lost the chance to display an intricate costume). Russell imported Bori, Ferrari-Fontana, and Amato for three of the leading roles and supplied Ludikar from the Boston nucleus as Archibaldo. All three New York singers had become well routined in this new opera, for four Metropolitan performances preceded Boston's first. The opera made a deep impression on Boston's cognoscenti, while it could not have failed to hold the more general public by its highly charged drama, its flow of impassioned melody, and its colorful settings. Hale paid Monte-mezzi the highest tribute in his lexicon, saying that it was impossible to separate the music from the poem. The music seemed to him singu-larly original, following neither Wagner nor Debussy nor the later Verdi, and free from any taint of Puccini-ism. Sem Benelli's tragedy may be taken as literal: the love of the old King Archibaldo for his son; that son Manfredo's adoration of a wife who scorns him; Prince Avito's requited love for that same woman. Or deeper symbolism may be found by those who care to search. The three kings love Italy, personified by Fiora, who hates her conquerors, father and son, and loves and dies for a prince of her own people, Avito. The scene where the blind Archibaldo finds and strangles the woman who has betrayed his son, then staggers off with the lifeless corpse slung over his shoulder, is one of the most gripping in opera.

Boston had the unique opportunity of comparing two Fioras: the charming, natural heroine of childlike simplicity, perfection of voice and vocal art that Bori set so winningly on stage; and the original of Luisa Villani, who conceived the character as more mature and passionate. Hale deemed Villani's Fiora one of the chief impersonations of the sea-son. Her Desdemona, too, impressed the critic as conveying unusual emotional depth. The California soprano, who would be heard widely with various traveling companies, had appeared to advantage in a Boston *Trovatore* in 1910–11 and would sing at the Metropolitan in 1915–16, but unfortunately for New York, *L'Amore* did not grace the repertoire that season.

Ferrari-Fontana, as was to be expected, advanced Avito's cause with great authority, and added to a native fervor the bonus of rare vocal quality and remarkable dramatic intelligence. Amato's sensuous tones never pealed more resoundingly (in fact, Hale accused him that season of over-boisterousness, asking: "Did the shouting of Ruffo spur him on to rivalry?"). When Ancona succeeded him as Manfredo, things quieted down, but Amato's juicy voice was missed. Ludikar made an impressive Archibaldo, but in Boston's eyes no one could surpass Marcoux, who took the final performance. Roberto Moranzoni came into his own, if anyone had ever doubted his quality, with these performances. The importance of the continuous orchestra web (recalling in technique if not in idiom the later Verdi, *Pelléas et Mélisande,* and Wagner's music dramas) put a fourth king in the pit.

If *Meistersinger* had not been allowed to accept too many transfusions from the rest of the repertoire, the season would have been rewardingly balanced in favor of substantial musical treats, as the previous one had been. The four new productions and repeats of a dozen works that climbed close to or actually attained masterwork status—*Giovanni, Tristan, Otello, Hoffmann, Manon, Louise, Gioconda,* the sure-fire *Jewels, Secret of Suzanne,* and re-Italianized *Martha,* the sumptuous *Samson et Dalila* and the fading *Thaïs* (for Garden) overbalanced the fourteen old standbys.

But Boston betrayed its basic unsophistication by wearying of the old sweet songs, while at the same time lacking the true opera buff's willingness to revisit the work an infinite number of times for the sake of different singers—or of comparing the growth or decline of the same singer in a role. This pastime offered fewer joys than before, it seemed, even to the handful of initiates; after Muratore, most of the newcomers either fizzled after the first blazing burst of press-rocketry or tarried so briefly that their personalities had no time to settle comfortably into Boston's memory. One exception was Marguerite D'Alvarez, who returned Boston's appreciation for her glorious contralto voice and skill by some warm compliments in her autobiography, *All the Bright Dreams.*

The Boston Opera House was the most artistically managed of all American opera houses, she maintained (Hammerstein's, Chicago's, and San Francisco's formed her basis for comparison); everything was done to achieve perfection. She had starred in Russell's catastrophic summer venture in Varese, where he had told her "he admired my performance but I must diet—my proportions were too Latin for anything but character parts in America, and impossible for a Carmen." (Russell's astuteness was later borne out when her single performance of the gypsy was branded dull and logy, totally unsuited to her, by Hale, the only exception to a catalogue of praise for her other roles.) The singer credits Hale with tremendous assistance in her career, ruefully calling his criticisms "analytical to the point of surgery, but always brilliantly constructive."

The singers met socially at the Jordans, which made it all much easier, D'Alvarez thought. She particularly enjoyed working with the two chief conductors, and cast a sidelight on one of them: "André Caplet was one of the most interesting of the many conductors; he was simple and intriguing, intelligence spurted from his eyes, and it was thrilling to sing under him. We rehearsed alone together and the next day my perfume was detected by the nostrils of his jealous mistress—how strong were the perfumes then!—and he begged me not to wear it any more at rehearsals."

Moranzoni she found charming and human. "His calm was extraordinary for an Italian, and whenever he made a correction it was done with humor and tact."

Maggie Teyte did not count her early Boston experiences worth mentioning in her somewhat tame version of an autobiography, *Star on the Door,* but Boston found her enchanting as Mimi and Zerlina, though not spontaneous as Butterfly, when she darted in from Chicago, where she was in the midst of her third season. The tiny, exquisitely formed Miss Tate (who changed her name so that the French tongue might find it compatible) appeared wrenlike to some observers ("a little dear, just as cute and sweet as she can be"), but behaved more like a hummingbird. She flitted brilliantly from place to place, never staying very long, revealing an independence of character and toughness of mind that paralleled her elder compatriot singer, Mary Garden, but never equalling Garden in the grand prima donna *beau geste* or the wilful bestowal of supreme talent on unworthy interpretations in search for "something different." When she made headlines, it was usually in behalf of righteousness: once she threatened to horsewhip an arrogant stage manager; another time she arranged for the Philadelphia claque leader to be trapped in her apartment in the act of demanding five hundred dollars to ensure that she not be hissed.

Teyte followed Garden as Mélisande at the Opéra Comique at the instigation of Jean De Reszke, with whom she was studying; but she never quite supplanted her rival, although she had reason to consider herself a proud successor. The two never met on the stage except in Massenet's *Cendrillon* with the Chicago company. Absurdly young as

Mélisande (nineteen), she was only twenty-three when she entered American opera annals as Cherubino in Mozart's *Le Nozze di Figaro* with the Chicago troupe in Philadelphia on November 4, 1911.

Teyte and Marguerite Bériza made their Boston debuts as the girls in *Bohème*, presenting a fresh, youthful pair of grisettes. Teyte's voice bore upward and undistorted the long curve of Puccini's melody and caught the characteristic suspense that underlies it, while phrasing and coloring to Mimi's moods, Parker wrote. Bériza, according to Hale, showed rare taste in dress, made Musetta vivacious, acted with artistic intelligence and no vulgar romping. Teyte's Mimi would continue to move Boston listeners in two later seasons when another impresario intrepidly picked up the pieces of Russell's broken empire and briefly seemed to have mended the vessel.

Teyte's first Rodolfo was the versatile Léon Lafitte, who sang ten roles fairly well, but distinguished himself signally in none. Her second poet showed a different stripe, a brawny, bellows-lunged Italian, who was destined for an illustrious career at the Metropolitan for more than three decades and was even considered as Caruso's successor by many. Giovanni Martinelli cannot have been flushed with happiness over his initial reception either in New York or Boston, however. Critics spoke well of the strong, clear, resonant voice, but regretted that he forced it to the point of abuse, his frank and pleasant face swelling visibly with the effort. His actions suggested that he had been rushed onto the stage before being thoroughly taught or mastering the repertoire.

Martinelli lived to see such criticisms modified as he himself learned to modulate the voice and restrain the passion. He retired in 1945 to become the grand old man, honored and sought by all. *Tosca, Aïda,* and *Bohème* were his Boston operas (one less by a *Butterfly* than at his concurrent Metropolitan engagement). Although Puccini had selected him for the European première of *Fanciulla del West*, he never sang it at the Met until its revival in 1929, after Caruso's death.

Late in the season, Boston managed to work itself up to a state that might be described as mildly agog over a new singer, who had been hailed in London as the "new Patti." Felice Lyne's one performance as Gilda had produced hysterical headlines on both sides of the ocean. The wily Hammerstein's fine hand lighted the fuse to prove he was still the blazing old fireworks master; in Lyne he had a dud, as events turned out.

Russell predicted the course of the new American star, for although he hired her to sing a single Gilda in March, it was simple, cynical obeisance to the public, with no real conviction of her value. When the London sensation broke, Henry cabled his agent in Milan to demand why he hadn't heard her before. The answer: "You did, and told her to go to musical comedy"—ticket to limbo in Henry's book. He visited her in her London dressing room. She shook her finger at him, saying, "You see, Mr. Russell, you were wrong about me!"

"I wasn't wrong, my dear," Henry replied smugly. "You are a rocket. If you will take my advice and go into operetta, you may have a lasting success."

He watched sardonically as the Boston public allowed her the biggest personal success of the season; then doubtless prided himself on predicting her fall. Although she was considered worthy of several performances in the Paris season of the Boston company and of partnering Baklanoff in a couple of *Rigolettos* in the aftermath (as the Boston post-Russell seasons came to be called), the Missouri-born singer soon departed for oblivion.

Trailing a cloud of lawsuits, an old friend paused in his stormy passage between continents to sing a half-dozen performances before he went to jail. Florencio Constantino had been at the heart of the first Boston years, together with Alice Nielsen and the conductor, Arnaldo Conti, who had trouped with Russell in the San Carlo company. He was never too tired to sing four times a week; not once did he disappoint an audience or refuse to sing. Russell, who had held him on an extensible leash until he broke away in 1912 to form his own troupe in Argentina, where he was very popular, said admiringly that Constantino never offered excuses, something that could be claimed for no other tenor.

Never in the same bracket as Caruso or Bonci, and by now outclassed by Zenatello, Constantino's durable lungs still had in them the power for a Radames, a Rodolfo, a Faust, two Almavivas, and an Enzo within little more than a month's span. But his legal entanglements made better headlines. In January, he won a hundred-thousand-dollar breach-of-promise suit misguidedly hurled at him by one Marcelle Hontabot, a French cabaret singer, only to face a demand for fifty thousand dollars from Joseph Gravina, a bass who had appeared in Boston once in 1912–13 (when Constantino was absent), and who presumably had not caught up with him until now. Gravina's grievance stemmed from a rash gesture by the tenor, who, as Almaviva, in a mock duel with old Dr. Bartolo, had pinked the bass in the eye in a New Orleans *Barber of Seville*.

On level ground when it came to fellow singers, Constantino stepped out of his league when he tangled with managers. Not at all satisfied with his season or the terms thereof, he asked balm to the tune of $14,300 from Russell in May (outcome not stated, but practically a foregone conclusion), then almost immediately found himself in the toils of that inveterate old litigant, Oscar Hammerstein. Constantino had been fending off Oscar for several years; now retribution arrived. Like a true Samson, he claimed a woman had betrayed him. In a voice "like a Seraph's note," he explained to an interviewer that this Dalila, a private citizen immune to a tenor's charms, had put the finger on him. Pathetically he described his incarceration:

"I go to stone house in lower end of city near river. I smell river breeze. Cold and damp. Gives me creeps. See cage, think of dog. Reminds of prison scene in opera. But real, I real actor. No audience. I indignant. Perspire freely. No singing. No whistling. Man hands me broom. Met others with brooms. No one knew me [the crowning indignity]. Allowed to go home. Caught ten-thousand-dollar cold." (Whether this amount went for doctor's bills or toward the thirty thousand dollars awarded to Hammerstein for Constantino's breach of contract in going to Boston five years previously is not clear.)

With all his faults—irresponsibility well ahead in the list—there was something endearing about Constantino's frank "tenorality." He belonged to the old school that came on stage to sing to the audience rather than to his fellow artists; at his first entrance, he would cast an appealing, propitiatory glance at the top gallery before uttering a word. His great dismay at discovering that Faust also played on the legitimate stage paralleled Tamagno's horror at the revelation that *Otello* had first been a play and that Salvini had beat him to the character.

The highest note of nostalgia, which linked past to present, chimed appropriately late in the season. Nellie Melba, ever divine, her quarrel with Russell ever smoldering under the pearly surface, consented to honor Boston with a final Mimi and Juliette. The date with Roméo found his heroine ailing, and Nielsen obliged, though suffering from a virus herself. On the morning of the March 7 matinee *Bohème*, the famous throat remained closed. Russell persuaded Melba to go to the theater, promising to keep an understudy in readiness. At curtain time minus fifteen, Melba could get out only a hoarse whisper. But she agreed to get into her costume, while the substitute clambered hastily into *hers*, and to explain her defection in front of the curtain, so that the audience would believe her truly ill. This strategy received its reward in sympathy for the ailing prima donna as well as for the lucky understudy, Myrna Sharlow, a promising young American who had sung dozens of small roles during two seasons and as recently as January 31 had been promoted to a Saturday-night essay at Mimi. Sharlow's success in this lucky break carried on the tradition. Extra rewards (Micaela and Suzanna) fell to her before the season's end; she was taken to Paris for a small role, went on to Chicago, and later appeared one season at the Met.

Melba meanwhile nursed her throat while Russell pondered restitution. The Monday-night audience should be treated to a combination of the best features (for Melba) of the two operas she had missed. Perhaps it had been planned all along, but the "star night" smacked of a gesture of atonement and was received as such. Carefully charting her course among the girlish roulades demanded of her, the aging soprano still evoked tumults of applause. Russell surrounded her with his best casts; Muratore and Marcoux in *Roméo*, and a new and well-graced baritone Henri Dangès, in both operas, with Bériza as Musetta and a new young tenor, Vincenzo Tanlongo, agreeably voiced as Rodolfo. This was March 16; only two weeks remained before the Saturday night potpourri that closed the season.

Anticipating the sixth season, Russell spread a rich carpet, promising many things to all people. He had heeded the critical grumbles and guaranteed that Weingartner would return, possibly to do *Walküre*, his own *Cain and Abel* (on the verge of its première in Darmstadt), and an opera of Gluck's. Other novelties might be *Boris Godunov*, the displaced *Francesca da Rimini*, Messager's *Béatrice*, *The Marriage of Figaro*, and *Madame Sans Gêne* (the Giordano opera was also scheduled for Geraldine Farrar at the Metropolitan, but it was a sad and safe bet that another would sing it in Boston). Furthermore, Russell counted on the presence of the best singers, among them Bori, Destinn, Edvina, Garden, Gay, Matzenauer, Nielsen, Marcel, Clément, Marcoux, Ferrari-Fontana, Martinelli, Muratore, Tanlongo, Teyte and Lyne, with the addition of Maria Barrientos, a Spanish coloratura who would go to the Met in 1915-16, and Rosina Storchio, who had created Butterfly. The season would open after the first of the year, on January 4, with an *Otello* re-staged by Urban. Boston had been borrowing the Met's scenery all this time. The new production would be christened in Paris, as would several of the novel operas.

Blithely waving from the top deck of the S. S. *Olympic*, Russell left this rosy prospect and sailed away on March 28 to France. Many of his company would board the *Lapland* the next day to join him in the City of Light for their greatest adventure, arranged by Russell and the director of London's Covent Garden as a joint undertaking.

Everything had been done to make the send-off auspicious. The *Lapland*, largest vessel ever to enter Boston harbor (18,694 tons), had been specially routed there from New York, but few of the two hundred passengers already aboard in first class objected. If this courteous gesture had only been paralleled by efficiency! The *Lapland* docked several hours late, while a milling crowd of five thousand shivered on the windy dock. They had gathered from all corners at 10 A.M. or thereabouts, marching through one street after another, to such cheering crowds as stayed away from church for the purpose. General William Oakes was in charge of the parade; former Mayor Fitzgerald (he had been succeeded by Curley) headed the committee of the combined City Club and Massachusetts Real Estate Exchange, with the approval of the Chamber of Commerce. Other civic and several Italian groups joined in, determined to show their bias in favor of culture.

As the lines converged on the narrow pier, potential passengers could hardly be disentangled from celebrants. "Opera Stars Hurt in Crash!" *The New York Times* proclaimed next day, detailing the casualties as feminine faintings, an injury "about the stomach" to Manager Macdonald, who had to be carried to his stateroom, and the loss of Mme. Lafitte's handbag and tickets, among other depredations. In the uncontrollable struggle, the formal program had to be abandoned; speeches went unuttered, and musical notes died aborning. Myrna Sharlow did manage to sing "Dixie," after the *Lapland* arrived; it was the only tune known to both the singer and the ship's band. The American and French anthems also broke through the confusion. Visitors tried to buy refreshments on board, but there were none to be had. At last, the *Lapland* pulled away from the pier at 2:45 P.M. bearing a bruised and ruffled operatic complement, and leaving behind a disheveled but cheering citizenry. Mayor Curley, already sagacious in office, never showed up.

22

"PARIS TOUT EN FÊTE . . . OH, PARIS! PARIS!" *

Every American impresario, especially if he originates in Europe, sooner or later is seized by the desire to go back to show off his new accomplishments. To this desire is joined the dream of wealthy backers of opera, for whom the idea of a national opera syndicate holds perennial appeal anyway, while an international cartel is doubly enticing. Perhaps it was not so much due to Gatti-Casazza's ambition as to Otto Kahn's that a Metropolitan company was shipped eastward in 1910; Gatti had, after all, too recently arrived from Italy and was just beginning to find his footing in New York. But Henry Russell succumbed to the itch in his fifth season in Boston. The New York financier, Kahn, always Russell's champion, once more hovered in the background, but was not allowed or more likely did not want to play solo angel. A distinguished committee to handle administration was assembled by Russell and Harry Higgins of Covent Garden, including Baron Frédéric d'Erlanger (the millionaire composer), the Marquess of Ripon (representing the Royal Opera of Covent Garden), Eben D. Jordan (Boston Opera), Gatti-Casazza, Kahn and Clarence Mackay (Metropolitan), and Lord Grimthorpe, Russell's one-time patron. Sir Ernest Cassell, the London banker, had subscribed fifteen thousand dollars, and Lord Rothschild was also mentioned. The group, tagged "Anglo-American" from the first, signed a five-year lease on the new Champs-Élysées Theatre, and proposed to create a permanent organization to "show" Paris, according to Russell. It was said to be capitalized at three hundred thousand dollars, although Russell had admitted

* From *Louise,* by Gustave Charpentier.

255

to Kahn in February that he and Higgins thought seventy-five thousand dollars more than enough. Not only the Italian repertoire would be explored in the original language, but Wagner's operas, in their entirety, would be given *in German* for what was said to be the first time in the French capital. To further ensure audience interest, Russell resorted to a technique perfected in America: the women's committee. After they had been convinced of the success and prestige of the season, the Princess Murat, the Duchess d'Aosta, Princess de Polignac, and Mrs. Edgar Stern graciously allowed their names to be used.

Among welcoming hands across the sea, conspicuously limp were those of local opera managements and their press satellites, although they attended certain performances in force, notably the openings. Kahn and Gatti had experienced the insular jealousy of the Parisian establishment five summers ago and had survived, but not without skirmishes and scars. Paris opera purveyors needed no legitimate grievance apart from the basic threat of competition to turn jaundiced eyes on the invaders. The Metropolitan's alleged shabby treatment of a French contralto, Marie Delna, had served neatly as a trumped-up excuse for hostility on the part of certain critics and a section of the public that included several well-known composers. One or two of these critics had been won over by the simple expedient of hands under the table, the old-world equivalent of the new-world *lagniappe;* an increasing audience had taken the lure of Caruso, Toscanini, Amato, and the unexpectedly delightful *Manon Lescaut* with Bori. A current complaint concerned the disappointment of André Messager, Paris composer and conductor, at the failure of a deal with Russell. Messager counted on heading the French wing in Boston next season and producing his own *Béatrice*. When he stipulated that a young soprano at the Opéra, said to be one Andrée Vally, be engaged simultaneously, Russell refused in an unaccountable access of virtue. (Russell's search for a new French conductor posed the question, soon academic, of what he intended to do with Caplet.)

Always outwardly cool, Russell bade fond farewell to the last of his black hairs before the season even started, it was reported in the *Globe*, which faithfully followed the pilgrims' progress abroad. The distracted manager wrote Kahn that the situation was chaotic: Higgins and the local impresario had failed to get advance publicity, boxholders, and subscriptions; no prospectus had been prepared and the opening week's repertoire had not been decided as late as April; but above all he, Russell, had experienced the utmost difficulty in retaining artistic control against Higgins' inroads. The latter had vetoed *Otello* with Ferrari-Fontana as an opener and insisted on *L'Amore dei Tre Re* (with Edvina, of course, and what Henry called an "inferior" baritone, Giordano Paltrinieri, who later served many years as a Metropolitan *comprimario*). Henry commented vindictively that *Amore* had fizzled out, so that a third performance was canceled. The committee would not verify Weingartner's contract; the conductor finally settled for two hundred dollars a performance. Russell's final and rather smug judgment: his own performances—including *Otello* —had been successful both financially and esthetically.

In the meantime Russell had to intervene in the smallest problems. Sadly questioning its necessity, impressed on him by the portly Frenchman who owned a monopoly, he interviewed fifty *ouvreuses*, the women ushers who make life bearable or miserable for the customers. These women generally paid about twenty dollars for the privilege of working first-class theaters, confident of profit in tips. Russell was sorely tempted to fight the system, but soon yielded gracefully, conducting a brisk inspection of the fifty damsels and even deigning to select their badge of office —a dainty white apron and a white rose in the hair.

Backstage, Henry gave a curtain lecture to the chorus, which, like the Metropolitan's aggregate before it, provided the liveliest material for Parisian gossip and curiosity. The comely American girls viewed the wicked city somewhat timorously at first, settling in quiet pensions in the Alma *arrondissement*, and venturing out only in pairs, like French *gendarmes*. They soon found themselves "less molested than on Huntington Avenue," and discarded the hatpins with which they had armed themselves, beginning to enjoy the masculine attention paid them on the streets. A number learned enough French to move into apartments on the Left Bank (of course not alone, but in duets, quartets, or even octets) and to patronize the shops ("Oh, you Galeries Lafayette!" exclaimed one, who had begun to feel queer in her conservative Boston clothes).

Russell was luckier than Gatti-Casazza in his theater, for where the Metropolitan manager had been forced to cope with the superannuated Châtelet, which reminded the technicians of a dilapidated old barn, the Boston troupe moved into surroundings up-to-date as well as beautiful. Gabriel Astruc, who had acted as local agent for the Met's appearances, had subsequently been prime mover in the construction of the Champs-Élysées, which had opened on March 31, 1913, with Berlioz' *Benvenuto*

Cellini. Less than a year later, it stood abandoned. Its resuscitation at the hands of the Anglo-American troupe had gone a long way toward winning the Parisians' good will; they were never ones to view a dark theater complacently.

Boston's technical crew was spared the makeshifts that the Met had been forced into, and Urban's scenic investiture seems to have fitted nicely in the new house after some minor adjustments. True to promise, Russell produced a completely new staging for *Otello,* while *Masked Ball* and *Parsifal,* never having been included in Boston's repertoire, must have been hastily assembled after arrival.

A canny rearrangement of the audience chamber to place the boxes in front of the cheaper seats, while allowing for more of the latter, augured well. Astruc's loss was partly attributed to the disadvantageous situation of the *haute monde.* Russell's reward was to see all the boxes taken, chiefly by the American set. Prices slightly undercut Astruc's, the boxes commanding $10 and $6, the orchestra $5.50, the balcony $2.25, the gallery $1.75, with a student rate of 40¢.

Messager showed no hesistancy in juggling his calendar to oppose Russell, but the Opéra could not shift one important date: plans of royalty are not disarranged as lightly as opera schedules. A state visit by King George V and Queen Mary of England had been indelibly inked in for April 21, including a gala at the Opéra on April 22, which could under no circumstances be shifted to the next night in order to conflict with Russell's public dress rehearsal. Grateful for this small favor, Russell affected indifference to Their Majesties' presence so near and yet so far from the Champs-Élysées, letting it be known in Boston that it was just as well not to arouse further the already erupting jealousy of the Opéra. (He reacted similarly to a visit from the King and Queen of Denmark a little later.) He was not even advertising the season heavily in the French press, for the same reason as well as the added fear of provoking the ancient accusation of "Yankee bluff."

As curtain time drew near, one unexpected hitch threatened to stay the whole opening performance. The French could not be held responsible this time; it was the petty tyranny of the Ricordi publishing empire. Tito Ricordi, who had already made trouble by refusing Russell's company permission to perform *Tosca* and *Butterfly,* but had condescended to be photographed directing Louise Edvina and Vanni Marcoux in a bit of business for *L'Amore dei Tre Re,* suddenly discovered at rehearsal that he did not approve of the soprano's tempi. Edvina stood on her rights as an interpreter; Russell, who could not afford to antagonize the favorite of Harry Higgins any more than the head of Ricordi's, hastily arbitrated. The solution was not made public, but the dress rehearsal took place as scheduled. Russell sighed with relief to jump that obstacle, for the only two other sopranos familiar with the role of Fiora—Bori and Villani— were at the moment in America.

In the glitter of jewels and reputations, the audiences of April 23 and 25 compared favorably: the Tweedledee of the dress rehearsal matching the Tweedledum of the opening. A sprinkling of nobility, rarefied society, and the upper echelon of artistry graced both, with the weight of the professional world more heavily cast at dress rehearsal. High diplomacy nodded from the boxes at the opening in the persons of various members of President Poincaré's suite, American Ambassador and Mrs. Herrick, British Ambassador and Lady Bertie, and Italian Ambassador and Signora Tittoni. In one audience, halos of light spread around Principessa di Stigliano Colonna, Comtesse de Gallifet, and Lady Lowther, while in the other the Princess Murat, Grand Duke Paul, Princess de Lynar, Marquise de Lastèyre, and Marquise de Jancourt added radiance.

Dress rehearsal brought out the artistic élite of Paris. In intermissions, a buzz of excitement identified composers Claude Debussy, Gabriel Pierné, and Montemezzi himself; Mme. Réjane and Maurice Bernhardt of the theater; the great Jean De Reszke and his wife; and Emma Eames with her husband, Emilio de Gogorza. (The stately American soprano later came out with a dignified paean for Russell, his courage, and his ability, wishing him luck in his formidable undertaking. For as Dumas *fils* once said to her: "*Nous autres français, nous n'aimons pas la musique. Ce que nous aimons, c'est la musique militaire et la chansonnette.*" In spite of this delinquence in taste, however, the French ought to take notice, because the first to profit from Russell's international ventures would be French musicians and artists, whose fame would be spread far and wide.)

Bostonians in the audience, led by Jordan and his wife and daughter, spotted Zina Brozia, currently appearing in Massenet's *Hérodiade* and *Radda* (a drama after Gorki) at the Gaité Lyrique.

Gatti had tempted his first-night audience with Caruso, Destinn, Homer, Amato, and Toscanini, set like jewels in the gilded trappings of *Aïda*. Russell counted on the new sensations of Montemezzi's music drama, which indeed aroused more than perfunctory admiration for its intrinsic worth and for the gifted performers. Particular warmth greeted Vanni Marcoux, whose qualities as a magnificent lyric interpreter were already well known, and who strengthened his hold on Paris with his expressive, violent Archibaldo. (Learning that he was to be married in July, the market women from Les Halles, who had fervently patronized the Gaité Lyrique in the old days, sent him drifts of flowers.)

Edvina, already well liked for her Louise at the Comique, played Fiora with an "interior flame, and with pretty attitudes knowingly voluptuous," said the *Arsenal* critic, who added that she sang with perfect grace in a voice that had taken on notable amplitude. Her second-act costume caused gasps, even in sophisticated Paris, for under a flowing orange mantle, her gown exceeded in exposure even the point to which Kitty Gordon (of the famous back) had descended. The *Globe* back home hinted that Edvina's Fiora would add to her Boston reputation. Newcomers Ferrari-Fontana and the Italian baritone Francesco Cigada, gave pleasure as well. One odd note appeared in *Le Monde Musical,* which, while deeming the interpretations of the first order, found the architecture of the décors strictly American (whatever that might mean), although the lighting and the *mise en scène* were perfect. Altogether, the Anglo-American debut was a success in spite of Russell's private thoughts.

Messager waited until now to show overt enmity. Russell had announced a first *Otello* for April 30, whereupon the Opéra decided that that very same night was the only possible time for a dress rehearsal of the latest novelty, Alfred Bachelet's *Scémo*—not world shaking, to be sure, but a dress rehearsal imposed sacred obligations on the Opéra public. Russell countered by postponing *Otello* to May 5; the Opera in turn put off *Scémo,* whereupon Russell went ahead anyway. Later, when *Parsifal* came up for the third time at the Champs-Élysées, the Opéra hastily and childishly threw the French version into exact opposition.

A new quarrel arose with the Opéra Comique, which in the first place announced *Don Giovanni,* provoking Russell into abandoning the Mozart work, then objected to Russell's proposed use of *Bohème* in the Comique itself, rather ungraciously, considering that the affair was designed as a benefit for the Comique's own pension fund. Russell offered to withdraw the Puccini work, which was a favorite at the Comique, but the ever powerful Ricordi firm intervened through its Paris representative, M. Gentien, and reestablished an *entente cordiale.* "Opera War Averted," read the headline of May 24.

Henry bowed diplomatically in public about this time, complimenting Albert Carré, the old chief of the Comique, as the greatest *metteur en scène* that the French school had produced, and pronouncing himself happy at some equally laudatory remarks from M. Carré, printed in an interview of all the Paris theatre managers by Pierre Veber. Furthermore, M. Gheusi, presently at the Comique, had recently shown unmistakably friendly feelings. And still more, he (Russell) had met the incoming director of the Opéra, M. Rouché, who clearly did not regard Henry as an interloper.

The interpretation of Puccini's *Manon* by the"Anglo-Americans" was, according to Arthur Pougin in *Le Ménestrel*, incontestably remarkable on all points, and conferred the highest honor on Russell's troupe. Maria Kousnezoff, the petite Russian soprano, *"artiste adorable"* who had already won friends both at the Opéra and the Comique, and Giulio Crimi, young Italian tenor, carried the honors. Both would be heard later in Chicago, and Crimi sang from 1918–22 at the Metropolitan.

The postponed *Otello* brought Melba's return after ten years, a nerve-wracking ordeal for the prima donna. She confessed her nervousness to the press, a delicate shudder accompanying a bell-like peal of laughter. Volunteering that Russell was indeed a splendid director, and that the company contained superb talent, she dimmed the effect of her praise somewhat by adding: "It is supported by unlimited capital; what more could be asked?" But she did not hesitate to declare that she was trying to get the company to come to Australia.

Great travel plans floated on every breeze these days. The first flush of success had encouraged the cartel-minded to promise artists a contract in every port. Why, they could sing at the Champs-Élysées, the Opéra, the Opéra Comique, then in Covent Garden, at the Metropolitan, in Chicago, Philadelphia, Boston, and perhaps even Australia. The web was confidently spun. No cloud appeared on the clear blue of the world cyclorama. Even that trouble in Mexico (Vera Cruz had been occupied by American Marines on the very day of Russell's dress rehearsal, and headlines broke out in a rash of war scares) had not disturbed the Paris social season, which was just beginning to get under way.

Melba needn't have worried. The critics were more than polite to her. Nevertheless, she endured a bad hour or two, for the audience, whether Parisians or Americans, tittered audibly throughout the first two acts. Donna Russell tells the story: "Then when she sank down on the prie-dieu and sang the 'Ave Maria,' the entire audience hushed. I'll never forget her voice in that aria. It was divine—I can still hear it ... the greatest voice of all time. No one has ever matched that quality. When she had finished, the audience rose in one body to applaud her.

"Henry always said that Melba's cold personality was a testimony to the greatness of her voice. Tetrazzini had to throw kisses and act like a clown to win her public ... Melba won by the sheer perfection of her technique and the unearthly quality of her voice.... Strange as it may seem, men were mad about her. Most of her pearls, which were as famous as Queen Alexandra's, came from the Duke of Orléans. When she was our guest in Monte Carlo, she read me a letter from the Duke, and wept as she read. He was devoted to her long after middle age."

A similar sentimental mood, only slightly tinged with an occasional comment on the diva's tendency to leave all acting to impulse, persisted through two more Desdemonas and a Mimi during the Boston season in Paris, the latter at a benefit given at the Opéra Comique for its pension fund, and with John McCormack making his bow to Paris as Rodolfo.

Before Wagner stormed to the Champs-Élysées, one more Italian masterpiece was unveiled, eliciting from the Paris *Herald* the dazed inquiry: "Have the golden days of Italian opera returned?" It would seem so, from the packed houses—Princesses, Grand Dukes, Marquises, and Earls multiplied in dizzying, almost geometric fashion, while the ranks of society, art, and music swelled to include *tout Paris*. And what had they gathered to see? "Not the latest production of musico-choreographic neurasthenia, not a Russian ballet danced by overdressed women and underdressed men. No. An Italian opera, an old Italian opera, the most traditional Italian of Italian operas, Verdi's *Masked Ball;* four acts of conspiracy, love, sorcery, and murder dressed in melody, not melody hidden in an orchestral maze, but melody naked and unashamed, supported by an orchestra based on a big guitar reinforced by a street band."

Emmy Destinn, who had shared in the happy clamor after the Metropolitan's *Aida* four years before, headed the international cast, which included the "rich and powerful" tenor, Martinelli, the experienced Ancona, and little Maggie Teyte. The soprano who had succeeded Garden as Mélisande continued to enchant the French capital with her voice and piquant figure in Wolf-Ferrari's *Secret of Suzanne,* and by her exploits on the Chantilly golf course, where she played with Francis Ouimet, the American open champion (and incidentally with her husband, Dr.

Eugène Plumon). Ouimet, Chick Evans, and other patrons of the links, who had been among the *Lapland's* passengers, returned the compliment by filling a box for the opera.

About this time came the flattering news that Queen Mary had summoned three of Russell's sopranos to participate in a London gala: Melba, Destinn, and Edvina. Destinn sang later in *Pagliacci* in Paris, with Ferrari-Fontana (substituting for Martinelli) and Ancona, in the double bill with *Secret of Suzanne*. The French, through fond of *badinage*, found Wolf-Ferrari's frothy "trifle" too long. They admired Marcoux's Count Gil, however; this favorite could do no wrong. The double bill would be repeated, introducing to Paris the charming young Italian, Claudia Muzio, who would go on to greater heights in America, and an *Otello* was mounted to show off the talents of the two Weingartners. Then only one Italian revelation remained to breast the German tide, which foamed in on May 20. This was a mid-June pair of *Barber of Sevilles*, which brought the controversial Felice Lyne before the French public. The affair "lacked the sacred fire," the *Gaulois* critic complained, although McCormack undoubtedly possessed the most beautiful voice of the new world (while remaining an *"acteur froid"*), Amato was remarkable, and Marcoux always *très grand artiste*. But the Rosina collaborated a bit too heartily with Meyerbeer, singing his "Pardon" waltz (more formally known as the Shadow Song from *Dinorah*) in the lesson scene. Tavecchia as Bartolo seemed to the *Ménestrel* man the only true Italian exponent.

Like all European capitals, Paris had settled in the groove of hearing its own language on the opera stage, and, left to its own devices, would probably still react chauvinistically to the idea of importing a whole exotic troupe for the purpose of hearing lyric drama in German, though occasional hybrid performances have always slipped into even the best-regulated opera houses. In later years it was possible in the Paris Opéra to hear Tristan ask. "Bin ich in Kornwall?" and Kurvenal reply: "Non, maître, voici Karéol!" But before the Boston season, the nearest to an all-German performance in what was said to be forty years had been the single act of *Tristan* (the second) that the Metropolitan had included in a gala in 1910, with Fremstad as Isolde, Burrian as Tristan, Louise Homer as Brangäne, and Allen Hinckley as Marke. Russell's ten performances of three Wagner music dramas in twenty-six days thus staked a claim on the history books.

With the advent of the "German" season, Russell's troupe achieved a goal he had never reached in Boston: a phalanx of superior conductors. First on the podium came Albert Coates, the zestful and expansive Russian-born, who had assisted Nikisch at Leipzig and about the time of the Bostonians' Paris visit had been called by Sir Thomas Beecham to Covent Garden. From 1920 on, Coates often visited America. Artur Nikisch himself, a true romantic figure of the generation, came to take over the third *Tristan* and swept the public to emotional experiences of a high order. Felix Weingartner arrived to lead *Meistersinger* and *Parsifal*, bringing with him that schoolmasterish didacticism that so amused the French, although many, including the critic of *La Presse*, looked to him to "readjust" the misinterpretations that Wagner had fallen into in France. Knowing his Parisians, Weingartner sent to all the papers a short note which exhorted the public to be on time for *Parsifal*, so that they might properly appreciate the very special character of the work. (The threat of closed doors materialized, leaving many intransigent Frenchmen outside during the *longeurs* of the Prelude.) Several papers took this curtain lecture in good part; others gave it the "ho-hum" treatment.

Egon Pollak, the Czech leader currently at Frankfort, had been invited to conduct Wagner at Covent Garden this same year and would appear in Chicago in 1915. In Paris he assumed command of the two final *Parsifals*, and led the act of *Tristan* at the climactic gala on June 19. The indefatigable Pierre Monteux, whose orchestra occupied the Champs-Élysées pit, was scheduled to appear on the podium, but apparently became too preoccupied with the Russian ballet (which intermittently flashed across the Opéra stage, bearing the celebrated Vaslav Nijinsky in clouds of color and excitement), although a Belgian magazine reported his presence at the helm for one *Tristan*.

The Italian forces had already been immensely strengthened by the presence of Ettore Panizza, who was exclusively responsible for *Manon Lescaut,* two performances of *The Masked Ball,* and the double bill. This Argentine-born Italian had spent six seasons at Covent Garden, would go to La Scala in 1916 and assist Toscanini as principal, beginning in 1921, then make his American debut with the Chicago Opera. Much later, he succeeded Tullio Serafin at the Metropolitan in 1934, remaining until 1942.

Perhaps it was too much to expect of the captious critics that they swallow with a smile this large foreign body. One or two of them choked on the League of Nations in the *Tristan* cast: an Isolde and a Kurvenal from Dresden (Eva van der Osten, the first Octavian in *Der Rosen-kavalier,* and August Kiess), a King Marke from Frankfort (Johannes Fonss), a Tristan from Copenhagen (Peter Cornelius), a Brangäne from Sweden (Julia Claussen), and a conductor from England (Coates). "One cannot improvise with Wagner or Mozart as one can with Verdi and Puccini," the *Liberté* reviewer remarked tartly, ignoring the fact that all these performers bore the stamp of experienced Wagnerians, regardless of nationality. Another critic thought the representation homogeneous but without fire; still another would not even allow cohesiveness.

The only leading *Tristan* singer who appeared later on the American scene was Claussen, the statuesque mezzo-soprano, who had indeed already sung at the Chicago Opera and would spend many happy seasons at the Metropolitan after the war. Only one genuine top-rank "Bostonian" participated in the German *sängfest,* and even she (Marcel-Weingartner) might be considered rather on the international side. From Boston, Elvira Leveroni, Taddeuz Wronski, Louis Deru, and Lorenzo Fusco were listed as performing lesser roles; others undoubtedly filled roles too minor to be listed. Several who came directly from America bore the preferential brand of the Metropolitan: Matzenauer, Leonhardt, Urlus, Amato. All others were European, assembled chiefly through Higgins, but partaking of continental, chiefly Teutonic, blood and background.

Even Paris critics could not accomplish the impossible; and it did seem impossible to find any fault whatever with *Meistersinger.* One writer even strung out his adjectives like matched pearls: "admirable, unforgettable, living, light, gay, poetic, and zestful." Another vowed that he had never heard a representation so just, so exactly appropriate to its national character. The restitution of a masterpiece honored the efforts of the interpreters, among them Mme. Weingartner, Johannes Sembach (the Walther, who was immediately engaged for the Metropolitan, stayed until the war, and returned afterward) and Paul Bender (the Sachs, who did not reach New York until 1922). A courteous reception also awaited a real veteran, Anton Van Rooy, who in two performances recalled memories of his Metropolitan Sachs to those Americans who went back as far as 1899. But above all, the credit belonged to Weingartner. (What might the Boston season have been if he had taken the reins from Caplet! many remarked.) He was allowed to bask in an aura of warm approbation exactly one week, until *Parsifal* opened—or rather, closed—the Champs-Élysées doors at the unheard-of hour of 7:30 P.M. A deep hush fell over the capacity audience, gathered despite the disagreeable necessity of having to venture out in evening clothes in broad daylight. When Weingartner was about to raise his baton, a stirring suddenly ran through the house, and cries of *"Fermez les portes!"* were hurled from scores of places in the upper galleries. The Paris *Herald,* reporting the unprecedented incident, remarked that "indignant Wagnerites brook no exception to the rule that no one be admitted during the Prelude." Parisians, who ordinarily took their *Parsifal* in smaller doses and with a grain of indulgence, experienced the Bayreuthian rule for the first time. Five hours later, they staggered out onto the boulevard, many still exalted or professing that high state, many simply exhausted.

The fact that Wagner's *"Bühnenweihfestspiel"* (Stage Consecration Festival Play), in Gallic proportions and translation, had been all the rage at the Opéra since January aroused pugnaciousness in several quarters: how could it be done any better, even in German, and uncut? Notwithstanding approval of most of the singers, which ranged from polite in the case of Matzenauer's Kundry (but *évidemment* she could not be compared to an artist of the quality of Lucienne Bréval) and Sembach (intelligent, correct, appreciably clean diction), to unstinted praise for Carel van Hulst ("an Amfortas indeed superior to any we have"), part of the Paris press turned away from Weingartner, even though the audience continued to grow. Gaston Carraud in *Liberté* led the pack of dissenters. Weingartner may have professed to receive a benison from the Master himself, but had never lifted the baton at Bayreuth except by chance for the very last act of *Parsifal* in an emergency at the end of the 1882 season [The conductor wrote, however, a history of the festival town in 1896]. Though Richter *et al* may have shown individual temperaments, they all partook of the same spirit, a pious flame cherished by modest and profound artists. "I can assure you," M. Carraud swore solemnly and passionately, "that in Weingartner's interpretation exists nothing, nothing, nothing of that spirit."

M. Carraud took one final and devastating jab at Felix *infelice: "Mais M. Weingartner, vous l'avez appris aussi, est le chef d'orchestre qui conduit 'Parsifal' le plus vite* in the world. [His English.] *Saluons ce record."*

Egon Pollak met no such invective when he took over the last two performances. By then, the critics had evidently written themselves out. The public meanwhile continued to fill the Champs-Élysées, to the satisfaction of Russell's *amour propre.*

Disasters are not made to order for opera benefits, but it seemed almost as if history were repeating itself when on May 29 the Canadian Pacific S. S. *Empress of Ireland* was run down by the collier *Storstad* in the St. Lawrence River on her way from Quebec to Liverpool, and sank with an estimated 1,191 aboard. Four years previously, Gatti had thrown the resources of his company into a benefit for the survivors of the foundered submarine *Pluviôse*, raising two hundred thousand francs and giving a massively distinguished audience the *Tristan* act that heralded Russell's German sortie. Now the Anglo-Americans propelled themselves with equal vigor into the cause, enlisting society matrons to replace the *ouvreuses* as program sellers. Russell chose a double bill for June 17: *Masked Ball* with *Secret of Suzanne* as a curtain-raiser. The Verdi work introduced a new soprano, Rosa Raisa, "a revelation," who would rise to full eminence in Chicago. Pasquale Amato, who had sung Amfortas in German a few days before, reverted to his native Italian as Renato. Both Raisa and the baritone distinguished the *Pagliacci* of the company's farewell on June 19, the gala that showed Matzenauer and Ferrari-Fontana as husband-and-wife Tristan and Isolde, with Amato and Eleanora de Cisneros as the servitors. An act of *Barber of Seville* completed the glorified vaudeville. President Poincairé bought a box, which he failed to occupy, but not another seat was vacant.

To everyone's astonishment, the May heat, which had devitalized the chestnut trees and pedestrians alike, broke into cold sullenness with a drop from 28.8 to 5.3 (Centrigrade of course). Paris shivered, then rallied for a gay June season. The icy winds failed to shake a series of lavish balls, or to carry away the lines that formed at the Bernhardt Theatre to see the Divine Sarah in repertoire. Customers didn't budge from the Châtelet, where Loie Fuller danced such fantasies as Debussy's "Nuages" and Stravinsky's "Firebird" with the Orchestra Colonne; nor from the Opéra, where Stravinsky also colored the Russian Ballet, and where on opera nights one might hear Maurice Renaud in *Le Vieil Aigle* of Raoul Gunsbourg, or Muratore in *Monna Vanna*, or Marcel Journet in *Walküre;* nor from the Opéra Comique, where Marguerita Sylva was singing *Carmen*, Marie Delna still reigned in *La Lépreuse*, and *Pelléas et Mélisande* enjoyed several repetitions. Nor for that matter did chattering teeth prevent hundreds of requests for tickets for the final Boston performances at the window of the white building on the Avenue Montaigne.

Although furs and boots replaced organdies and parasols, *la belle société* scarcely faltered on its appointed rounds. The opera company became a cynosure for generous hostesses. In her magnificent mansion on the Rue Faubourg St. Honoré, Mrs. Edgar Stern arranged many evenings, one of which was graced by the dancing of Dorothy Jordan. Paris, even in a wintry springtime, seemed exceedingly good.

That it was a fateful springtime affected few of the American wayfarers. Most of the opera company sailed for home on the *Cincinnati* conscious only of a job well done. On June 21, the Paris *Herald* patted itself on the back for reassuring businessmen, including Jesse Isidor Straus, and dispelling the gloom American newspapers insisted on spreading. Why, they had even forgotten the Mexican incident!

Jordan returned to Boston, confident, as was Russell, that the opera would spend another season in the Champs-Élysées. It was even rumored, though later and sadder advice contradicted the optimism, that the undertaking just concluded would break into the black. The Paris Opéra finally confessed that Russell's competition had cost it more than six hundred thousand dollars.

The opera world betrayed vastly more concern at the shocking news that Cleofonte Campanini had let Mary Garden go. In her place would reign her ancient enemy, Marguerite Carré, who had driven her from the Comique in jealousy and then queened it over the house her husband directed. Now it seemed that positions would be reversed: Garden would go back to the Comique. But the war prevented the switch.

As for Russell, he felt justified in sunning himself for a while on the Riviera, in a villa at Cap Martin offered by that same Mme. Stern who had so often shown hospitality in Paris. Messager had brought Henry to this Lady Bountiful. Though surrounded by the usual Italian entourage indispensable to an opera manager even *en vacance,* Henry managed to enjoy himself deeply, motoring, swimming, and sailing, with Donna as companion. Blissfully shutting his eyes to any possible discord, he traveled up to Paris in July, only three weeks before the irrevocable August 4, to receive a decoration from the German Kaiser for the Wagner performances, bestowed at a formal banquet in the German Embassy, where Baron von Schoen had frequently entertained the Teutonic singers and conductors. Henry believed this to be the final gala in the embassy.

The Kaiser's attentions could not have been more ironically timed. Henry soon found himself on the wrong side of the fence. He was pointed out as the friend of Baron von Schoen, as the purveyor of German opera only weeks before the war—as, in short, a spy. Wherever he walked, menacing frowns would accompany him. He hired a bodyguard and appealed to the wife of the British Ambassador, who was staying on the Riviera with her niece. Lord Bertie's influence, together with the intervention of Lord Grimthorpe, at last forced on Henry's enemies the perils of interference with a British subject.

By this time, Henry's Italian coterie, now aliens, had hastily bundled themselves across the border, leaving him and Donna alone in the huge villa. They moved into Monte Carlo, where the Casino had closed, and Henry continued quite calmly to plan for the Boston season even after war broke out. The blow fell in September. A cable from Jordan announced the closing of his house, as well as Chicago's, giving as reason (according to Henry) the serious financial conditions in America. Henry considered this most unfair, as America was taking no part in the war, but could not find it in his heart to blame Jordan, who had borne so heavy a financial burden. He wrote: "Otto Kahn shared my views on the subject, and with his usual sense of justice decided to keep open the Metropolitan."

It was not in Henry's nature to give up easily. He managed to get passage to America and in December was shuttling back and forth from New York to Boston, seeing Kahn at one end and Jordan at the other, in the endeavor to get control of the Boston Opera House. Philadelphia and Chicago appeared in the picture as well, but Henry's ambitions ranged even higher. He wrote Kahn: "It is, as you know, my eventual hope to merit the directorship of the Metropolitan some day. I say this without any disloyalty to my friend Gatti, who I believe regards me as his legitimate successor. 'Il saper a[s?]perttare' [Know how to wait]—an axiom I know how to value."

Kahn had written him rather ominously that the Century Theater (designed as a Metropolitan adjunct) was losing money at an alarming rate, which meant that he was losing it. "It is a pretty expensive privilege nowadays to rank as a protector of the arts," he concluded dryly. But he came to Henry's rescue in personal matters, advancing several thousand dollars for his living expenses.

Henry sailed sadly back to Europe in February, 1915. Impoverished, he and Donna took refuge in the palace of Prince Dominico Orsini in Rome, where at least great names in politics and society kept them chilly company. By March, 1916, Henry was haring over the map of

Europe pulling strings to free Vaslav Nijinsky and his wife and daughter —as well as the impresario Serge Diaghilev—from their incarceration as prisoners of war in Vienna at the behest of Kahn, who wanted the illustrious dancer for a spring season at the Met. After harrowing adventures, Nijinsky arrived in New York, but Henry was absent. He would have nothing to do with the ballet; offered the job as manager by Diaghilev, he refused almost contemptuously. His one-time secretary, Randolfo Barrocchi, got the post. Only opera would satisfy Henry. He pursued several ideas, notably a project shared with Jean De Reszke—an effort to inaugurate an international opera training center at the Champs-Élysées—but here he was balked by many circumstances. Not the least was the theater's ownership, now transferred to the Polish siren, Ganna Walska. A dinner party was arranged so that Henry could meet Ganna. Donna Russell tells the story:

"But we've already met, Mr. Russell," said Ganna. "In my home in New York."

Henry squirmed, but continued bravely, "I'm so anxious to hear you sing."

"Oh, you've heard me! You thought I was terrible. You allowed me to sing only three bars before you stopped me."

Henry didn't get the theater.

After his ill-starred trip with Maeterlinck in 1919, Henry embarked on the tour of Australia with Melba that was once again to change his personal life. He and Donna took under their wing the stage-struck daughter of Lord Dufferin and Ava, the Lady Patricia Blackwood. Henry was soon writing to Kahn for assistance in Pat's ambition. And, after his second wife and he were divorced "in a very friendly manner," he invited the financier to his and Pat's wedding on June 4, 1926. Another and rather startling element of the friendship between the two men showed here. "I may be married in the clothes you gave me!" Henry added. "Don't forget your promise to reduce your valet's wardrobe in my favor." It was Henry's great fortune to resemble Kahn from the neck down; he professed to wish fervently for more likeness from the neck up. Kahn showed his indulgence and liking for both Henry and Pat until the end.

23

AFTERMATH

The opera house stood dark and silent, stripped as bare as though gutted with fire. Jordan had at last given up. Russell, already returned to Europe, was stunned by the news that on May 11, 1915, the Boston Opera Company filed voluntary bankruptcy proceedings in the United States District Court, stating its liabilities to be $215,570, its assets $78,900. No creditors were secured except for taxes and duties on certain imported scenery still in bond. (What this last can have been still remains a mystery. Probably the new settings used in the Paris season were only just coming home.)

Jordan himself appeared as the chief creditor, the principal item being $30,780 advanced in open account. Of the $30,000 already paid in by subscribers, $28,306 was assigned to the former benefactor. No mention is made of an attempted refund, which may have left the public a trifle restive. Among other creditors were auditors, legal counsel, the Metropolitan Opera for $1,088 in rentals and artists' services, the *Musical Courier* for $400 worth of advertising, and a half-dozen or so artists' and administrative contracts. Randolfo Barrocchi put in for $2,040, William R. Macdonald for $2,125, and Rudolph Vavpetich (who had begun on a lowly rung in the management but would go on to higher places in New York's concert business) for $1,132. Russell himself claimed $6,019 in addition to disbursements for the European trip in the amount of $13,677. But these represented merely the top tenth of the iceberg. Concealed somewhere in Russell's effects in Europe were

271

dozens of artists' contracts, believed to mount up to more than $170,000. These of course were declared terminated.

Later evidence revealed that the amount listed as owed to the Metropolitan missed the truth by almost one tenth. It was, in fact, $9,066.79 by November 1915. Correspondence that grew more and more strained in tone shuttled between William Macdonald and Robert Jordan on the Boston side and John Brown, the Met's comptroller, with an occasional assist from Otto Kahn. Russell had been a trifle negligent about paying his bills, it seemed; the account with the Met for rental of scenery, props, and costumes, and for artists' contracts, fell into arrears as early as 1911. Periodic settlements reduced it somewhat, but at the time of the bankruptcy Boston still owed more than $8,000 (to which certain shipping charges were added) for services that included rentals for the productions of *Meistersinger, L'Amore dei Tre Re, Don Giovanni, Otello,* and *Rigoletto,* as well as technical department loans and a share of a fee for Jeanne Maubourg, a French mezzo-soprano.

Furthermore, Brown had had a devil of a time coaxing sets and props back into the fold, away from Boston's grasp. Still not returned by 1914 were the entire trappings for *Otello,* one newel post from the set of *Roméo et Juliette,* props for *Germania,* a stove for *Werther,* and a *Tristan* ground cloth (the large cloth that covers the stage and its splinters and dirt).

Friendly relations seemed likely to be sundered when a Boston lawyer wired that the correspondence between Jordan and Kahn had been mislaid in the hullabaloo over vacating the house; when he finally found it, matters were not mended by his suggestion that the Boston debt had been offset by a counterdebt incumbent upon the Met. This was too much even for Kahn, who had, out of friendship for Jordan and Russell, not pressed the obligation too hard. The financier wrote that the Met's claim was for "goods" actually delivered; that the Met had never been remiss in its payments for Boston artists; that he had wanted to be "neighborly," and never thought for a moment that Jordan and his colleagues "would permit us to be penalized." He concluded that the debt was also a debt of honor.

Jordan, stung by one more evidence of his opera management's slipshod way of doing business, replied that he would pay the sum out of his own pocket—as indeed he did. The check for $9,066.79 duly arrived.

In these sad days of disillusionment, when the beautiful and still new opera house seemed doomed to a shabby existence at the fitful mercy of road shows (ironically Massachusetts Institute of Technology experts pronounced it acoustically unfit for anything less than grand opera), a glimmer of good cheer suddenly appeared. The news got around that another courageous impresario was willing to restore grand opera to its rightful throne in the fall of 1915.

The eleven express wagons that had been working around the clock to remove boxes of scenery, costumes, electrical fixtures, and props reversed their direction and brought the complete paraphernalia back again. The familiar faces of Joseph Urban, Robert F. Brunton (technical director), and other staff members appeared once more in the workshops and on stage. "Under New Management," the opera house began to come to life.

Max Rabinoff was the man who so greatly dared. As Hammerstein's associate, he had appeared as early as 1908, and quickly became American representative for his countrywoman, Anna Pavlowa, who began her tours in 1909, appearing at the Metropolitan for two seasons with Mikhail Mordkin and with Russell's company in 1910–11 and 1913–14. Rabinoff had also managed opera in Montreal. Feeling himself to be an intimate in Boston opera circles, he plunged into the new undertaking with the immense gusto that has never failed in a long and variegated career.

His first step was to buy up the Boston scenic investiture for forty-seven operas, many of them Urban's new designs, others the older but still serviceable and beautiful settings by the Italian Stroppa. The bankruptcy receiver had been pleased to let them go for a sum so modest that one hesitates to believe it possible. Rumor placed the price at ten thousand dollars; Rabinoff failed to deny it.

His successful tours with Pavlowa led him to the threshold of a startling new idea. He would combine the two theatrical elements and "introduce a new art to America"—really two art forms "of a novel character." These were to be known as "mimo-choreographic" and "mimo-dramatic" grand operas. For the uninitiated, Rabinoff had his representative Howard Potter prepare an elegant prospectus, not only for Boston but also for the several cities he planned to visit on tour with the "Boston Grand Opera Company" in conjunction with the "Pavlowa Imperial Ballet Russe." Pointing out that until Pavlowa's advent, America had known choreographic art only as perfunctory divertissements miscalled ballets, the exposition continued with definitions of the new art forms.

"These works are neither exclusively grand operas (as we know them) nor yet exclusively Russian ballets (as Mlle. Pavlowa has introduced them). They are a combination of each, put together in a symetrical [sic] whole ... While there is a general similarity in the 'mimo-dramatic' and 'mimo-choreographic' grand operas, the line of differentiation between them is sharply drawn ... The mimo-dramatic grand opera story is sustained by means of pantomine, which requires the highest efficiency from those artists entrusted with this branch of the interpretation. Mimo-choreographic grand operas are constructed with a view to disclosing marked opportunities for consistent and illustrative dancing which shall form an integral part of each opera."

It all boiled down, in Boston's opinion, to the fact that some operas contain better ballets than others. To justify the equal terms for prima donna and prima ballerina (who was said to be a partner in finance as well as performance), such works as Auber's *La Muette de Portici* (mimo-dramatic) and Rachmaninoff's *Aleko* (mimo-choreographic) would be revived, while a new work, *The Enchanted Garden* to music by Josef Holbrooke, would be conducted by the composer himself. (The latter two never materialized, at least in Boston).

As for the operas *per se*, the natural choices were *Gioconda, Aïda, Faust,* and *Carmen*, while all others were chosen for their comparative brevity, in order that Pavlowa might claim the second part of the bill. The only exception seems to have been *Otello*, for Rabinoff scarcely wanted to waste Urban's new settings and the presence of Villani, Zenatello, and Baklanoff in his company. Pavlowa had additional solo innings on two Saturday nights, with all-dance programs.

Seven weeks were originally announced for Boston; these were cut down to five, and eventually the fifth was halved. Before the November 15 opening, the company appeared in Chicago, St. Louis, Detroit, Toronto, and New York (at Hammerstein's old Manhattan Opera House). After Boston, they visited Washington.

If for no other accomplishment than introducing *L'Amore dei Tre Re* to the several cities that had never heard it, Rabinoff deserves an individual place in American opera annals. He opened with the Montemezzi work in Boston, restoring Villani to her original role and giving Zenatello and Baklanoff the opportunity to add vital characters to their galleries. The presence in the pit of Roberto Moranzoni seemed still another link to the but lately departed troupe, possibly an earnest that all might yet be continuous and well. But under the necessity to include the lovely dancer in each bill, Rabinoff added a scene from Gluck's *Orfeo*, which dragged the evening out too lengthily for Boston.

At the end of a fortnight, Philip Hale was able to answer the question he had put to himself on opening night: "Is it possible that opera in Boston is out of fashion?" The disheartening conclusion: "Yes."

No one could dispute the quality of the performance, he argued. The leading singers, most of them already Boston favorites, brought international reputations; lesser parts were well sustained; the orchestra and chorus were first class; the scenery and costumes would do credit to Paris, Vienna, or Berlin. Furthermore, the incomparable Pavlowa bestowed her grace and beauty freely. Yet the attendance as a rule proved pathetically small. Who could blame Rabinoff if with all his zeal and high artistic purpose, he felt obliged to abandon the enterprise? Boston evidently either wished no opera at all or would remain content with a short season of the Metropolitan at its own convenience. So Boston would rank on the musical map with Atlanta, he concluded cuttingly.

Many new delights were added to familiar experiences before Rabinoff did indeed break off the season on December 15, 1915. The "authentic" Butterfly of the Japanese soprano, Tamaki Miura, seemed fresher, more graceful in its joy and pathos than any other. Hale commented that those sopranos who boasted of their studies of Japanese as preparation for Cio-Cio-San should be reminded of Emma Abbott, who in her early days of barnstorming was said to visit a madhouse in order to play Lucia. Such striving for realism hardly seemed necessary. A native Butterfly was, of course, another matter.

Maggie Teyte's first Boston Nedda impressed Hale as the best since Mme. Basta-Tavary had appeared with an otherwise wretched company with a ludicrously inadequate orchestra some years ago. Olive Fremstad's first Tosca in the Hub showed superiority to any since that of Milka Ternina, at least in acting. The second act was ennobled by the beautiful artist, not in the manner of a nymph pursued by a satyr as painted by Jordaens or Rubens. For once the sofa was merely a decorative article of furniture and not a playground.

Luca Botta's Rodolfo, in a performance of *Bohème* that brought out the largest and most brilliant audience so far, surely was no starving poet, but a well-nourished gentleman who had taken excellent care of his voice. This proved pleasing, smooth, pure, free, expressive, and skillfully employed. The third act, with Teyte's pathetic and charming Mimi, probed deeply into the meaning of text and situation. Elvira Amazar, a newcomer, showed a pretty little body and the voice and vivacity of a soubrette. Her rich admirer Alcindoro should have been a Russian Grand Duke, or at least a rich Brazilian on holiday. Boston missed by some fluke the distinction of claiming Amelita Galli-Curci's American debut. The coloratura was announced by Rabinoff but did not appear. Her subsequent debut was with the Chicago company as Gilda on November 18, 1916.

The rejuvenescence of Auber's old score, *La Muette de Portici* (known also as *Masaniello*) could be credited as a gesture to operatic history, as it had influenced lyric drama very strongly and for many years was enormously popular. Boston had first seen it in 1828. Felice Lyne appeared as the Princess Elvira, with Pavlowa dancing the mute heroine. The five acts dragged on interminably, it seemed, with long intermissions adding to the weight of the evening. The first planned performance had been put off till the second week because of the illness of a tenor, George Michailoff, whose bearing was still apologetic on November 23. The work received only one repetition.

Of the erstwhile sensation, Miss Lyne, Hale said that it would be well to forget the "roaring and the wreaths" of London. Judged without these appurtenances, the coloratura seemed colorless. She also sang a Gilda and her first Marguerite in Boston, in a *Faust* that achieved more importance for Baklanoff's first Boston Méphistophélès. It was good, everyone thought, to have the Russian back again. He had been missed. Hale described his impersonation as dramatically ingenious and effective, if occasionally too dramatic at the expense of the music.

Other virtual "old-timers" for whom Boston reserved the warm handclap of genuine welcome included Maria Gay and Giovanni Zenatello (the tenor singing even better than before), the mezzo Elvira Leveroni, and the sterling José Mardones. In the conductor's battalion, two familiar names also appeared: Alexander Smallens and Ralph Lyford. Newcomers to the conductors' staff included a round-faced, round-bodied Russian who accompanied Chaliapin to Paris for the basso's celebrated season of Russian opera. His name, Emil Kuper, would later be spelled Cooper as he joined the Chicago Civic Opera and still later the Metropolitan.

Though audiences swelled for the initial showings of certain popular

favorites (*Faust, Aïda,* and *Bohème*), Rabinoff was never able to grasp
the loose ends of Boston's frayed confidence and reweave them into a
supporting fabric for opera. Several of the old boxholders returned to
their vantage posts: the colorful Slaters, Mrs. Gardner (conspicuous in
a headdress more bizarre than usual), the Longyears, the Larz Andersons, and Mrs. George Fearing were noted by the *Globe,* but the Jordans
contented themselves with orchestra seats.

The end did not come suddenly. Rabinoff gambled on another season,
opening on New Year's Day, 1917, but Boston kept him afloat only one
week, placing itself virtually in the category of a tour city. He chose
Giordano's *Andrea Chénier* to launch the undertaking, a performance
that Hale said deserved a crowded house, but then the company deserved
a better opera. Villani, Zenatello, Baklanoff, and Moranzoni divided
the honors between them. One additional novelty, Mascagni's melo-
dramatic *Iris,* which Conried had reluctantly mounted for Emma Eames
in 1907–08 and Gatti had revived for Bori in 1914–15, pleased Boston
no more than before, although the petite Miura could always charm an
audience. Hale found the libretto repulsive, the music dull and futile.
Mascagni shot his bolt in the opening hymn, he maintained. And in the
last act, both librettist and composer joined Iris in the sewer where she
had flung herself. *L'Amore dei Tre Re* wore well, however, and the usual
sprinkling of favorites served to introduce popular singers.

Well, what excuses could one offer this time? Hale pondered. Last
year Rabinoff had been told he came too early. So he came late. But
Boston had spent all its money at the Allied Bazaar. Many were tired
of their charitable work, multiplied since the war. It was too soon after
Christmas. It was New Year's Week. The weather remained unfavorable.
The evangelist William (!) Sunday proved a strong counterattraction to
a conscience-ridden community.

Rabinoff, deemed a brave man on all counts, nevertheless conceded
his defeat at the hands of Boston's inertia. Perhaps if he could have
mounted *Götterdämmerung,* Back Bay would have turned out in full
force, attracted by a funeral of such spectacular proportions. No lesser
mourning was due from the opera house for its builder and benefactor.
Jordan would never see it again, either from his box or an orchestra seat.
He had collapsed on the golf course and died at his summer home, "The
Rocks" in West Manchester, on August 1.

The spirit had gone out of him in 1914, and he had parted with the opera's physical property in February, 1916. The purchasers, J. Sumner Draper, Mark Temple Dowling, and J. Murry Howe, traded, in what was called probably the largest deal in actual exchanges ever registered, the Niles Building, a fireproof mercantile structure containing 15,200 square feet on City Hall Avenue, next to City Hall itself—a new property, already largely rented. With the Opera House went the adjoining eight-story warehouse on St. Stephens Street, as well as the Park Riding School and the Regent Garage.

Two years later, Messrs. Draper and Howe sold the house to the Shuberts, who already owned the theater that bore their name, as well as the Majestic (formerly Jordan's property), the Wilbur, and the Plymouth. The price was reputed to be a million dollars. Under their absentee ownership, E. C. Smith carried on as local manager, filling contracts with the Chicago Opera, which in the ensuing decades paid nine visits of a fortnight each. Campanini's and Mary Garden's rather specialized repertoire held novelty if not invariable magnetism for Boston operagoers. In the first season, 1917–18, *Isabeau* (Mascagni), *Thaïs* and *Jewels of the Madonna* seemed attractive; later works to which Boston never quite became accustomed were *Aphrodite* by Camille Erlanger (*not* the Baron who had assisted Russell's Paris adventure), Puccini's *Triptych*, Rimsky-Korsakoff's *Snegourotchka*, Massenet's *Jongleur*, *Sapho*, and *Hérodiade*, Alfano's *Resurrection*, Giordano's *Jest*, Honegger's *Judith*, and Cadman's *Witch of Salem*. Filling in the 143 performances of the nine seasons were more conventional works.

The Metropolitan slipped in a season after Rabinoff's first, endeavoring to fill the vacuum with twenty-five performances, several of them its own new material. Thus Boston heard its first *Rosenkavalier*, probably its first *Boris Godunov*, and its first and undoubtedly last *Der Widerspenstigen Zähmung* by Hermann Goetz (which quite simply translates into *The Taming of the Shrew*). Bostonians who remained loyal to the ideal of their own opera may have felt comforted at hearing once again a few of the singers who had been lent by the Metropolitan to Russell: Rothier, De Segurola, Alda, Martinelli, Amato, Leonhardt, Homer, Scotti, Goritz, Rappold, and Gadski among them, while Barrientos, who had been announced by Russell, and Sembach, who had distinguished himself in the Paris Wagner performances, finally appeared in Boston. Gatti brought the first *Parsifal* since Conried's pirated performances of 1904–05, and otherwise allotted enough appearances of Caruso and Farrar to satisfy the star-hungry, the latter portraying a new heroine as well as the old favorites: the saucy laundress in Giordano's *Mme. Sans-Gêne.*

"You see," the Boston Opera Company's detractors exclaimed, "we don't need an opera company of our own! We can get all we want without the fuss and bother!"

The Metropolitan tried again in 1917–18, competing with the Chicago troupe, giving nine performances, with Caruso in *Le Prophète,* and introducing Claudia Muzio and the Swedish Marie Sundelius, who came to live in Boston. Leoni's *L'Oracolo,* a grim story of Chinatown, which offered Scotti a fine acting part, was new to Boston. The Met yielded to Chicago's superior attractions after this and repaired the break only after fifteen seasons had flowed past. Since that return in 1933–34, the New York visitors have missed only one wartime spring in their very first touring city.

Boston jogged along comfortably for a few decades, occasionally reading in the papers that another brash attempt to storm their operatic bastions was brewing; complacently wearing "I-told-you-so" expressions when these ill-advised invasions invariably collapsed either of their own inadequacy or their indifferent reception—often both. The tourists meanwhile kept coming—good, bad, and merely mediocre. One troupe bore the San Carlo name, with the redoubtable Fortune Gallo at its head; Boston's memories hardly stirred to recall Russell's early company. German companies arrived; Aborn continued to offer a mixture of light opera and operetta in English; during the WPA days, a company was hastily assembled, its chief claim to fame being that it provided the background for the debut of Eleanor Steber, a Renoir-like beauty from West Virginia, who was studying at the New England Conservatory. She went on to more glorious realms, winning the Metropolitan Auditions of the Air in 1940.

With the new movement toward opera in a language the natives could understand and the rapidly opening doors of schools and colleges to the lyric art form, the Hub was persuaded to accept, and even help to nourish, several younger groups. But the golden frame of true "grand" opera remained empty. The house on Huntington Avenue lost its pride bit by bit. When in 1940 the whisper of its doom circulated, one cynical writer stated frankly that he didn't care. "What good is an opera house with only ten days or so of opera?" he argued. For a few weeks, the letters columns of the dailies were peppered with protest. William R. Hall, who played in the original opera orchestra from 1909 to 1914, suggested an appeal to a foundation. Others with long memories bemoaned the desecration of planning a supermarket where Jordan's house—it was still called that—had played host to culture for so long. Northeastern University, which was beginning to spring up sturdily a little further out on Huntington Avenue, was said to have its eye on the opera house corner in the forties, but this rumor went underground for a time.

Bereft of its proper tenants, except for brief moments, the building took on a more and more forlorn aspect, its terracotta crumbling under age and occasional lightning bolts, its halls growing dingier, its seats noisier, its carpet thinner, its backstage quarters seeming to contract as newer equipment and methods became known—although not invariably used by visitors. Nothing becomes obsolete so fast as stage machinery.

Mystery still surrounds the various reports that the building was or was not safe. After one inspection, a police cordon was thrown around the building. This was the last straw for the Shuberts, who gave up after almost forty years, and let the building go to a construction company, which in turn sold it to Northeastern University on September 25, 1957. On November 6, two years before the building's golden anniversary, the fatal order of demolition was signed. The question of the true condition of the building never was settled and soon became academic. Spokesmen for one faction vouch for the soundness of the foundation. The thirteen-foot-thick concrete slab below the stage sat as firmly as before. Structural weaknesses above ground were cited. Might they have been repaired? We shall never know.

One grim winter day in 1958, the long, slender arm of the crane poised at the farthest point of its arc, suddenly reversed its direction and whipped the limp line into a taut fury, sending the big steel ball to strike the first blow against the great brick wall. Soon one could see ghastly daylight through the gaping hole of the stage.

What Cyrus Durgin, contemporary music critic of the *Globe*, called "Operapathy" took firm hold of Boston's citizens. Only a few sprang to the defense of the opera house, and their futile cry consisted of "Why don't *they* do something about it?"—never "I." Boston's opera house died in dust; Boston's operatic past succumbed with hardly a whimper.

The first spark of revival of interest in a potential resident company was kindled by the protean Boris Goldovsky with his New England Opera Company, which among other achievements gave the formidable Berlioz work, *Les Troyens,* its American première in the opera house. Mr. Goldovsky, who had as his chief goal the training of young singers, and who has put his stamp on many of the current generation of talented opera singers, eventually concentrated on his touring company and on purely educational pursuits.

The future poses several questions. Boston's most faithful visitor, the Metropolitan Opera, has been obviously unhappy with the former movie palace that bears the name Metropolitan but no other relationship. In the spring of 1965 the company is moving for its annual spring week into the new Prudential Insurance Auditorium, part of the complex that is rising on Huntington Avenue on the site of old Mechanics Hall. The Boston Opera Association, with Talcott M. Banks as president, sponsor of these yearly galas, perforce has adopted a wait-and-see attitude, a nice Bostonian blend of reserve and sanguinity, about the new auditorium.

Meanwhile, a new and energetic resident company called the Boston Opera is making its own record while aspiring to succeed to the old opera's glory and to become truly "grand." Its director, Sarah Caldwell, has already shown the daring and imagination of the genuine impresario, mixing among the better-known staples of repertoire such controversial fare as Alban Berg's *Lulu* and Luigi Nono's *L'Intolleranza,* and such restorations as *I Puritani,* the original *Boris Godunov,* and *Les Contes d'Hoffmann.* Miss Caldwell displays an ability to galvanize a large section of Boston's public. Her first success arrived coincidentally with the razing of the old house; the tendency to call her Boston's phoenix is irresistible. She has presented a number of important singers, including Joan Sutherland and Boris Christoff, in her casts, and has herself conducted a number of operas.

At the moment of transition, history is still being written. The need for a physical plant is paramount; under a new roof the new Boston Opera may continue to blossom.

THE BOSTON OPERA COMPANY
1909–1914

CASTS

*Including tour appearances in the
United States and Paris (in order
of singing)*

Key to abbreviations:
  (c) conductor
  (d) American debut
  (T) tour only
  (?) could not be
      verified

1909–10

November 8

La Gioconda (Ponchielli)
  Conti (c)
Barnaba: Baklanoff (d)
La Gioconda: Nordica
La Cieca: Meitschik (d)
Zuane: Pulcini
Isepo: Stroesco
Enzo: Constantino
Laura: Homer
Alvise: Nivette (d)

November 10

Aida (Verdi)
  Conti (c)
Ramfis: Mardones (d)

Radamès: Leliva (d)?
Amneris: Claessens
Aida: Boninsegna
King: Archambault (d)?
Messenger: Giaccone
Priestess: Freeman (d)
Amonasro: Baklanoff

November 11

La Bohème (Puccini) (for
  Lakmé)
  Conti (c)
Marcello: Boulogne (d)
Rodolfo: Constantino
Colline: Mardones
Schaunard: Pulcini
Benoit: Tavecchia

Mimì: Nielsen
Parpignol: Stroesco
Alcindoro: Mogan
Musetta: Lewicka (d)?
Customs Officer: Dunstan

November 12

Lakmé (Delibes) (for **La
  Bohème**)
  Conti (c)
Nilikantha: Nivette
Lakmé: Lipkowska (d)
Hagi: Stroesco
Mallika: Freeman
Rose: Pierce (d)
Frédéric: Fornari (d)
Ellen: Parnell (d)

282

Gérald: Bourrillon (d)
Mrs. Benson: Leveroni (d)

November 13 (mat.)
La Bohème
Same as Nov. 11 except:
Luzzatti (c–for Conti) (d)

November 13
(first "debut" evening)
Aida
Same as Nov. 10 except:
Ramfis: Perini
Radamès: Hansen (d)
Amneris: Leveroni
Aida: Parnell
Amonasro: Boulogne

November 14
Concert
     Goodrich (c)
Boninsegna, Boulogne,
   Mardones, Henrotte
   (violin), Conti-
Berenguer (harp),
Lyford (organ)

November 15
Lakmé
Same as Nov. 12

November 17
Pagliacci (Leoncavallo)
     Conti (c)
Tonio: Boulogne
Canio: Leliva
Beppe: Balestrini
Nedda: Pierce (for
   Bronskaja)
Silvio: Picco

Cavalleria Rusticana
     (Mascagni)
     Conti (c)
Turiddu: Constantino
Santuzza: Noria
Lucia: Rogers
Alfio: Fornari
Lola: Freeman

November 18
La Gioconda
Same as Nov. 8 except:
La Cieca: Leveroni
Laura: Claessens

November 19
Aida
Same as Nov. 10 except:
Radamès: Hansen (Leliva
   replaced him in Acts III
   and IV)
King: White

November 20 (mat.)
Cavalleria Rusticana
Same as Nov. 17 except:
     Luzzatti (c)
Turiddu: Leliva
Santuzza: Boninsegna

Pagliacci
Same as Nov. 17 except:
Canio: Hansen scheduled;
   Leliva substituted
Nedda: Lewicka

November 20
Lakmé
Same as Nov. 12 except:
Nilikantha: Archambault
Lakmé: Davenport (d)

November 21
Concert
     Goodrich (c)
Bronskaja, Roberts, Bour-
   rillon, D'Alessandro (d),
   Fornari, Lyford (organ)

November 22
Rigoletto (Verdi)
     Conti (c)
Duke: Constantino
Borsa: Giaccone
Countess Ceprano: Pierce
Rigoletto: Baklanoff
Marullo: Pulcini
Ceprano: Dunstan
Monterone: Perini
Sparafucile: Nivette
Gilda: Alda
Giovanna: Rogers
Page: Swartz (d)
Maddalena: Leveroni

November 24
La Bohème
Same as Nov. 11

November 25
Pagliacci
Same as Nov. 17 except:
Canio: Goiri
Nedda: Lewicka

Cavalleria Rusticana
Same as Nov. 17 except:
Turiddu: Leliva
Santuzza: Boninsegna
Lola: Roberts

November 26
Don Pasquale (Donizetti)
     Conti (c)
Don Pasquale: Pini-Corsi
Dr. Malatesta: Fornari
Ernesto: Bourrillon
Norina: Nielsen
Notary: Mogan

Cavalleria Rusticana
Same as Nov. 17 except:
Santuzza: Boninsegna

November 27 (mat.)
Lakmé
Same as Nov. 12

November 27
La Bohème
Same as Nov. 11 except:
     Luzzatti (c)
Rodolfo: D'Alessandro
Mimì: Savage (d)
Musetta: Di Pesa (d)

November 28
Concert
     Goodrich (c)
Nielsen, Baklanoff, Idzow-
   ski (d), Rogers, Stroesco,
   Picco, Perini

November 29
Aida
Same as Nov. 10 except:
Radamès: Constantino
Amneris: Olitzka

December 1
La Traviata (Verdi)
     Conti (c)

Violetta: Lipkowska
Flora: Rogers
Marquis D'Obigny: Dunstan
Gastone: Giaccone
Alfredo: Bourrillon
Baron Douphol: Pulcini
Annina: Leveroni
Giuseppe: Stroesco
Germont: Boulogne
Dr. Grenvil: Perini

December 2

Rigoletto
Same as Nov. 22 except:
Gilda: Lipkowska

December 3

Faust (Gounod)
  Goodrich (c)
Faust: Bourrillon
Méphistophélès: Nivette
Valentin: Boulogne
Wagner: Vanni
Siébel: Freeman
Marguerite: Noria
Marthe: Rogers

December 4 (mat.)

La Traviata
Same as Dec. 1 except:
Alfredo: Leliva

December 4

Cavalleria Rusticana
Same as Nov. 17 except:
  Luzzatti (c)
Turiddu: Oggero (d)
Santuzza: Kirmes (d)
Lola: Roberts

Pagliacci
Same as Nov. 17 except:
  Luzzatti (c)
Tonio: Picco
Canio: Hansen
Nedda: Schroeder (d)
Silvio: Pulcini

December 5

Concert
  Goodrich (c)
Boninsegna, Olitzka,
  Bourrillon

December 6

La Traviata
Same as Dec. 1 except:
Alfredo: Constantino

December 8

Madama Butterfly
  (Puccini)
  Conti (c)
B. F. Pinkerton: Leliva
Goro: Giaccone
Suzuki: Freeman
Sharpless: Fornari
Cio-Cio-San: Nielsen
Yakuside: Mogan
Imperial Commissioner:
  Rizzi
Bonze: Archambault
Yamadori: Pulcini
Kate Pinkerton: Swartz

December 9

Cavalleria Rusticana (for
  Don Pasquale)
Same as Nov. 17 except:
  Luzzatti (c—for
    Conti)
Santuzza: Boninsegna
Lola: Roberts

Ballet of Night
Loie Fuller and her Muses

December 10

Rigoletto
Same as Nov. 22 except:
Ceprano: White
Gilda: Lipkowska

December 11 (mat.)

Aida (for *Madama
  Butterfly*)
Same as Nov. 10 except:
Radamès: Cartica

December 11

Rigoletto
Same as Nov. 22 except:
  Luzzatti (c)
Duke: D'Alessandro
Rigoletto: Boulogne
Ceprano: White
Sparafucile: Archambault
Gilda: Davenport

December 12

Concert
  Goodrich (c)
Bronskaja, Constantino,
  Mardones
Henrotte (violin)

December 13

Lakmé (for *Madama
  Butterfly*)
Same as Nov. 12

December 15

Faust
Same as Dec. 3 except:
Faust: Constantino
Marguerite: Nielsen

December 16

La Traviata
Same as Dec. 1 except:
Violetta: Bronskaja
  (for Nielsen)
Marquis D'Obigny: Vanni
Alfredo: Constantino
Annina: Rourke
Germont: Fornari
  (for Formichi)

December 17

Il Trovatore (Verdi)
  Luzzatti (c)
Ferrando: Perini
Leonora: Boninsegna
Inez: Pierce
Di Luna: Boulogne (for
  Formichi)
Manrico: Cartica
Azucena: Fabbri
Ruiz: Giaccone

December 18 (mat.)

Faust
Same as Dec. 3 except:
Siébel: Roberts
Marguerite: Alda

December 18

Madama Butterfly
Same as Dec. 8 except:
B. F. Pinkerton: Kolumbin
Suzuki: Leveroni
Cio-Cio-San: Lewicka
Imperial Commissioner:
  Perini

December 20
Il Trovatore (for *Madama Butterfly*)
Same as Dec. 17

December 22
Carmen (Bizet)
Conti (c)
Morales: Pulcini
Micaela: Lipkowska
Don José: Constantino
Zuniga: Archambault
Carmen: Gay
Frasquita: Lewicka
Mercédès: Freeman
Escamillo: Baklanoff
Dancairo: Stroesco
Remendado: Giaccone

December 23
Aida
Same as Nov. 10 except:
Radamès: Cartica
Aida: Hoffman (d) (?)
Amonasro: Formichi
  (d) (?)

December 24
La Gioconda
Same as Nov. 8 except:
La Gioconda: Boninsegna
La Cieca: Fabbri
Isepo: Vanni
Laura: Claessens

December 25 (mat.)
Carmen
Same as Dec. 22 except:
Micaela: Bronskaja
Don José: Bourrillon
Escamillo: Boulogne

December 27
Carmen
Same as Dec. 22 except:
Micaela: Bronskaja
Don José: Bourrillon
Escamillo: Boulogne

December 29
Lakmé
Same as Nov. 12 except:
  Goodrich (c)
Nilikantha: Baklanoff

Ellen: Kirmes
Gérald: Idzowski (for Bourrillon)

December 30
La Bohème
Same as Nov. 11 except:
Marcello: Formichi
Mimì: Alda
Musetta: Bronskaja
Customs Officer: Balestrini

December 31
Carmen
Same as Dec. 22

January 1 (mat.)
Il Trovatore
Same as Dec. 17 except:
Di Luna: Formichi

Note: Company went on national tour. See tour casts at end of season.

February 7
Carmen
Same as Dec. 22

February 9
Don Pasquale
Same as Nov. 26 except:
Don Pasquale: Tavecchia
Notary: Stroesco

Il Maestro di Capella (Paer)
Conti (c)
Benetto: Balestrini
Barnaba: Pini-Corsi
Gertrude: Lewicka

February 11
Lucia di Lammermoor (Donizetti)
Conti (c)
Normanno: Vanni
Enrico: Fornari
Raimondo: Perini
Lucia: Lipkowska
Alisa: Pierce
Edgardo: Constantino
Arturo: Giaccone

February 12 (mat.)
Madama Butterfly
Same as Dec. 8 except:
B. F. Pinkerton: Hansen
Suzuki: Leveroni
Imperial Commissioner: Picco
Kate Pinkerton: Kirmes

February 12
Il Trovatore
Same as Dec. 17 except:
Leonora: Hoffman
Azucena: Olitzka

February 14
La Bohème
Same as Nov. 11 except:
Musetta: Bronskaja
Customs Officer: White

February 16
Faust
Same as Dec. 3 except:
Valentin: Blanchart
Marguerite: Dereyne
Marthe: Leveroni

February 18
Mefistofele (Boito)
Conti (c)
Mefistofele: Mardones
Faust: Constantino
Wagner: Stroesco
Margherita: Alda
Martha: Leveroni
Elena: Boninsegna
Pantalis: Claessens
Nereo: Vanni

February 19 (mat.)
Don Pasquale
Same as Nov. 26 except:
Don Pasquale: Tavecchia
Notary: Stroesco

Dance of the Hours
  (from *La Gioconda*)

February 19
Carmen
Same as Dec. 22 except:
Micaela: Bronskaja
Don José: Kolumbin (for Bourrillon)

Zuniga: Gantvoort
Carmen: Dereyne

February 20
Concert
Goodrich (c)
Boninsegna, Bronskaja,
Savage, Roberts,
Idzowski, Blanchart,
Nivette, Gantvoort,
White, Chorus

February 21
Mefistofele
Same as Feb. 18 except:
Margherita: Nielsen

February 23
Les Huguenots
(Meyerbeer)
Conti (c)
De Nevers: Blanchart
Tavannes: Giaccone
Raoul: Constantino
De Cossé: Vanni
Marcel: Nivette
Meru: Perini
De Retz: Pulcini
Urbain: Dereyne
Marguerite: Bronskaja
Ladies of Honor: Kirmes,
Leveroni
Valentine: Boninsegna
St. Bris: Boulogne
Bois-Rosé: Oggero
Maurevert: Archambault
Couvrefeu: Pulcini
Thoré: White

February 25
La Gioconda
Same as Nov. 8 except:
La Gioconda: Boninsegna
La Cieca: Fabbri
Laura: Claessens

February 26 (mat.)
Mefistofele
Same as Feb. 18 except:
Margherita: Nielsen

February 26
Lucia di Lammermoor
Same as Feb. 11 except:

Lucia: Bronskaja (for
Lipkowska)
Edgardo: Cartica
Arturo: Oggero

February 28
Madama Butterfly
Same as Dec. 8 except:
B. F. Pinkerton: Hansen
Suzuki: Leveroni
Imperial Commissioner:
Picco

March 2
Mefistofele
Same as Feb. 18 except:
Margherita: Nielsen (for
Alda)

March 4
Lakmé
Same as Nov. 12 except:
Goodrich (c)
Mallika: Roberts

March 5 (mat.)
Les Huguenots
Same as Feb. 23 except:
Marcel: Mardones
Valentine: Parnell (for
Boninsegna)
Couvrefeu: Fanos

March 5
Faust
Same as Dec. 3 except:
Valentin: Baklanoff
Siébel: Swartz
Marguerite: Nielsen
Marthe: Leveroni

March 6
Concert (including
Wagner excerpts)
Goodrich (c)
Nielsen, Bronskaja,
Roberts, Hansen,
Stroesco, Baklanoff,
Nivette, Henrotte
(violin)

March 7
Tosca (Puccini)
Conti (c)
Angelotti: Perini

Sacristan: Tavecchia
Cavaradossi: Constantino
Tosca: Boninsegna
Scarpia: Baklanoff
Spoletta: Giaccone
Sciarrone: Pulcini
Shepherd: Leveroni
Jailer: (?)

March 9
Lucia di Lammermoor
Same as Feb. 11 except:
Luzzatti (c)

March 11
Don Pasquale
Same as Nov. 26 except:
Don Pasquale: Tavecchia

The Miserly Knight
(Rachmaninoff)
Act I (in Russian) First
time in Boston
Baron: Baklanoff

March 12 (mat.)
Tosca
Same as March 7 except:
Cavaradossi: Jadlowker
Tosca: Dereyne
Scarpia: Blanchart
Jailer: Orchard

March 12
Rigoletto
Same as Nov. 22 except:
Luzzatti (c)
Ceprano: White
Gilda: Bronskaja
Giovanna: Kirmes
Page: Martuccia
Maddalena: Swartz

March 14
Lucia di Lammermoor
Same as Feb. 11 except:
Luzzatti (c)

March 16
Il Barbiere di Siviglia
(Rossini)
Conti (c)
Fiorello: Pulcini
Almaviva: Constantino
Figaro: Fornari
Rosina: Lipkowska

Dr. Bartolo: Tavecchia
Basilio: Mardones
Berta: Kirmes
Sergeant: Giaccone

March 18

Tosca
Same as March 7 except:
Tosca: Dereyne
Jailer: Stroesco

March 19 (mat.)

La Traviata
Same as Dec. 1 except:
Violetta: Nielsen
Flora: Pierce
Marquis D'Obigny: Vanni
Germont: Blanchart

March 19

Lohengrin (Wagner)
(in Italian)
Goodrich (c)
Herald: Pulcini

King Henry: Mardones
Telramund: Blanchart
Elsa: Dereyne
Lohengrin: Hansen
Ortrud: Claessens

March 21

Rigoletto
Same as Nov. 22 except:
Luzzatti (c)
Ceprano: White
Gilda: Nielsen
Giovanna: Kirmes

March 22

The Miserly Knight
Same as March 11

Pagliacci
Same as Nov. 17 except:
Tonio: Baklanoff
Canio: Constantino
Nedda: Dereyne
Silvio: Fornari

March 23 (mat.)

La Bohème
Same as Nov. 11 except:
Goodrich (c)
Rodolfo: Jadlowker
Mimì: Lipkowska
Musetta: Bronskaja
Customs Officer: White

March 23

Tosca
Same as March 7 except:
Sacristan: Mogan
Cavaradossi: Bourrillon
Tosca: Dereyne
Scarpia: Blanchart

March 24

Mefistofele
Same as Feb. 18 except:
Margherita: Nielsen
Elena: Dereyne

TOUR 1910

PITTSBURGH

January 3

Aida (Verdi)
Conti (c)
Ramfis: Mardones
Radamès: Constantino
Amneris: Gay
Aida: Boninsegna
King: Archambault
Messenger: Giaccone
Priestess: Freeman
Amonasro: Baklanoff

January 4

Lakmé (Delibes)
Goodrich (c)
Nilikantha: Nivette
Lakmé: Lipkowska
Hagi: Stroesco
Mallika: Freeman
Rose: Pierce
Frédéric: Fornari

Ellen: Kirmes
Gérald: Bourrillon
Mrs. Benson: Leveroni

Followed by dance diver-
tissement by Thamara de
Swirska to Grieg's "Peer
Gynt" Suite and other
short pieces

January 5 (mat.)

Lohengrin (Wagner)
(In Italian)
Conti (c)
First time by company
Herald: Archambault
King Henry: White
Telramund: Baklanoff
Elsa: Sara Anderson (for
Nordica)
Lohengrin: Hansen
Ortrud: Olitzka

January 5

Carmen (Bizet)
Conti (c)
Morales: Pulcini
Micaela: Bronskaja
Don José: Constantino
Zuniga: Archambault
Carmen: Gay
Frasquita: Lewicka
Mercédès: Freeman
Escamillo: Boulogne
Dancairo: Stroesco
Remendado: Giaccone

January 6

La Bohème (Puccini)
Luzzatti (c)
Marcello: Formichi
Rodolfo: Constantino
Colline: Mardones
Schaunard: Pulcini
Benoit: Tavecchia

Mimì: Nielsen
Parpignol: Stroesco
Alcindoro: Mogan
Musetta: Bronskaja
Customs Officer: Huddy

January 7
Lakmé
Same as Jan. 4 except:
Gérald: Kolumbin

January 8 (mat.)
Madama Butterfly
(Puccini)
Conti (c)
B. F. Pinkerton: Leliva
Goro: Giaccone
Suzuki: Freeman
Sharpless: Fornari
Cio-Cio-San: Nielsen
Yakuside: Tavecchia
Imperial Commissioner:
Rizzi
Bonze: Archambault
Yamadori: Pulcini
Kate Pinkerton: Kirmes

January 8
Rigoletto (Verdi)
Luzzatti (c)
Duke: Constantino
Borsa: Giaccone
Countess Ceprano: Pierce
Rigoletto: Baklanoff
Marullo: Pulcini
Ceprano: White
Monterone: Perini
Sparafucile: Nivette
Gilda: Alda
Giovanna: Kirmes
Page: Swartz
Maddalena: Leveroni

CHICAGO

January 10
Aida
Same as Jan. 3

January 11
Lakmé
Same as Jan. 4 except:
Gérald: Kolumbin

January 12 (mat.)
Carmen
Same (?) as Jan. 5 except:
Don José: Leliva (for
Bourrillon)

January 12
La Bohème
Same (?) as Jan. 6

January 13
Rigoletto
Same (?) as January 8

January 14
Madama Butterfly
Same (?) as January 8

January 15 (mat.)
Faust (Gounod)
Goodrich (c)
Faust: Kolumbin (for
Bourrillon)
Méphistophélès: Nivette
Valentin: Boulogne
Wagner: Vanni
Siébel: Freeman
Marguerite: Sylva
Marthe: Leveroni

January 15
Les Huguenots
(Meyerbeer)
First time by company
Conti (c)
De Nevers: Formichi
Tavannes: Giaccone
Raoul: Constantino
De Cossé: Vanni
Marcel: Mardones
Meru: Perini
De Retz: Pulcini
Urbain: Freeman
Marguerite: Bronskaja
Ladies of Honor: Kirmes,
Leveroni
Valentine: Boninsegna
St. Bris: Boulogne
Bois-Rosé: ?
Maurevert: Archambault
Couvrefeu: Pulcini
Thoré: White

January 17
Carmen
Same as Jan. 5 except:
Micaela: Nielsen
Escamillo: Baklanoff

January 18
Lucia di Lammermoor
(Donizetti)
Luzzatti (c)
Normanno: Vanni
Enrico: Fornari
Raimondo: Perini
Lucia: Lipkowska
Alisa: Pierce
Edgardo: Constantino
Arturo: Giaccone

January 19 (mat.)
La Bohème
Same as Jan. 6 except:
Marcello: Boulogne
Alcindoro: Tavecchia
Customs Officer: White

January 19
Il Trovatore (Verdi)
Luzzatti (c)
Ferrando: Perini
Leonora: Boninsegna
Inez: Pierce
Di Luna: Formichi
Manrico: Cartica
Azucena: Olitzka
Ruiz: Giaccone

January 20
La Traviata (Verdi)
Conti (c)
Violetta: Lipkowska
Flora: Freeman
Marquis D'Obigny: Vanni
Gastone: Giaccone
Alfredo: Constantino
Baron Duphol: Pulcini
Annina: Pierce
Germont: Formichi
Dr. Grenvil: Perini

January 21
Lohengrin
Same (?) as Jan. 5 except:
Elsa: Osborn-Hannah (T)

January 22 (mat.)
Madama Butterfly
Same (?) as Jan. 8

January 22
Lakmé (Acts I, II)
Same as Jan. 4

Pagliacci (Leoncavallo)
Conti (c)
Tonio: Boulogne
Canio: Leliva (?)
Beppe: Balestrini (?)
Nedda: Sylva
Silvio: Picco

January 23
Concert
Goodrich (c)
Formichi, Hoffman, Hansen, Olitzka, Nielsen, Cartica, Bronskaja, Pierce, Giaccone, Perini.

ST. LOUIS

January 24
Aida
Same (?) as Jan. 3

January 25
Lakmé
Same as Jan. 4

January 26 (mat.)
Lohengrin
Same (?) as Jan. 5

January 26
La Bohème
Same (?) as Jan. 6

January 27
Carmen
Same (?) as Jan. 5

January 28
Rigoletto
Same (?) as Jan. 8

January 29 (mat.)
Madama Butterfly
Same (?) as Jan. 8

January 29
Pagliacci
Same (?) as Jan. 22
(With dance divertissement? or "Lakmé"?)

INDIANAPOLIS

January 31
Lakmé
Same as Jan. 4

Followed by Thamara De Swirsky in dance divertissement

CINCINNATI

February 1
Carmen
Same as Jan. 5 except:
Micaela: Nielsen
Escamillo: Baklanoff

February 2
Lakmé
Same as Jan. 4

Followed by Thamara De Swirsky in dance divertissement

February 3 (mat.)
Lohengrin
Same as Jan. 5 except:
Herald: Orchard
Elsa: Osborn-Hannah

February 3
La Bohème
Same as Jan. 6 except:
Marcello: Boulogne
Customs Officer: White

SPRINGFIELD

February 5 (mat.)
La Bohème
Same as Jan. 6 except:
Marcello: Fornari
Alcindoro: Tavecchia
Customs Officer: White

February 5
Cavalleria Rusticana
(Mascagni)
Luzzatti (c)
Turiddu: Kolumbin
Santuzza: Boninsegna
Lucia: Leveroni
Alfio: Picco
Lola: Freeman

Pagliacci
Same as Jan. 22 except:
Luzzatti (c)
Canio: Cartica
Beppe: Giaccone
Nedda: Bronskaja
Silvio: Pulcini

PROVIDENCE

March 28
La Bohème
Same as Jan. 6 except:
Goodrich (c)
Marcello: Boulogne
Customs Officer: White

March 29
Carmen
Same as Jan. 5 except:
Goodrich (c)
Don José: Bourrillon
Zuniga: White
Carmen: Dereyne
Frasquita: Savage
Mercédès: Roberts

March 30 (mat.)
Madama Butterfly
Same as Jan. 8 except:
B. F. Pinkerton: Hansen
Suzuki: Leveroni

March 30
Rigoletto
Same as Jan. 8 except:
Rigoletto: Blanchart
Gilda: Bronskaja
Giovanna: Swartz

NEW HAVEN

April 1
La Bohème
Same as Jan. 6 except:
Marcello: Boulogne
Alcindoro: Tavecchia
Customs Officer: White

April 2 (mat.)
Carmen
Same as Jan. 5 except:
Goodrich (c)
Don José: Bourrillon
Carmen: Dereyne
Frasquita: Savage
Mercédès: Roberts

April 2
La Traviata
Same as Jan. 20 except:
Luzzatti (c)
Violetta: Nielsen
Flora: Pierce
Annina: Leveroni
Germont: Blanchart

1910–11

November 7
Mefistofele (Boito)
Conti (c)
Mefistofele: Sibiriakoff (d)
Faust: Lassalle (d–for
Constantino)
Wagner: Stroesco
Margherita: Alda
Marta: Claessens
Elena: Melis (d)
Pantalis: Claessens
Nereo: Giaccone

November 9
Rigoletto (Verdi)
Goodrich (c)
Duke: Constantino
Borsa: Giaccone
Countess Ceprano: Roberts
Rigoletto: Baklanoff
Marullo: Pulcini
Ceprano: Huddy
Monterone: Perini
Sparafucile: Mardones
Gilda: Lipkowska
Giovanna: G. Fisher
Page: Swartz
Maddalena: Claessens

November 11
Otello (Verdi)
Conti (c)
Montano: Pulcini
Cassio: Devaux
Iago: Amato
Roderigo: Stroesco
Otello: Slezak
Desdemona: Alda
Emilia: Claessens
Herald: Letol
Lodovico: Mardones

November 12 (mat.)
Tosca (Puccini)
Moranzoni (c–d)
Angelotti: Perini
Sacristan: Tavecchia
Cavaradossi: Jadlowker
Tosca: Melis
Scarpia: Baklanoff
Spoletta: Giaccone
Sciarrone: Pulcini
Shepherd: Rogers
Jailer: Huddy

November 12
Lucia di Lammermoor
(Donizetti)
Moranzoni (c)
Normanno: Stroesco
Enrico: Fornari
Raimondo: Perini
Lucia: Lipkowska
Alisa: Savage
Edgardo: Constantino
Arturo: Giaccone

November 14
Faust (Gounod)
Caplet (c–d)
Faust: Jadlowker
Méphistophélès:
Sibiriakoff (sang in
Russian)
Valentin: Baklanoff
Wagner: Huddy
Siébel: Swartz
Marguerite: Nielsen
Marthe: Mattfeld

November 16
L'Enfant Prodigue
(Debussy)
Caplet (c)

Lia: Nielsen
Siméon: Blanchart
Azaël: Lassalle

Pagliacci (Leoncavallo)
Moranzoni (c)
Tonio: Galeffi
Canio: Constantino
Beppe: Giaccone
Nedda: Dereyne
Silvio: Fornari

November 18
La Bohème (Puccini)
Goodrich (c)
Marcello: Fornari
Rodolfo: Constantino
Colline: Mardones
Schaunard: Pulcini
Benoit: Tavecchia
Mimì: Nielsen
Parpignol: Stroesco
Alcindoro: Mogan
Musetta: Dereyne
Customs Officer: Huddy

November 19 (mat.)
Il Barbiere di Siviglia
(Rossini)
Conti (c)
Fiorello: Pulcini
Almaviva: Constantino
Figaro: Fornari
Rosina: Lipkowska
Dr. Bartolo: Tavecchia
Basilio: Sibiriakoff
Berta: Roberts
Sergeant: Giaccone

November 19
Aida (Verdi)
Moranzoni (c)

Ramfis: Mardones
Radamès: Areson
Amneris: Czaplinska
Aida: Melis
King: White
Messenger: Giaccone
Priestess: Savage
Amonasro: Baklanoff

November 21
Tosca
Same as Nov. 12 except:
Cavaradossi: Constantino
Scarpia: Renaud
Shepherd: G. Fisher

November 23
Otello
Same as Nov. 11 except:
Cassio: Giaccone
Iago: Baklanoff
Emilia: Maubourg

November 25
La Gioconda
(Ponchielli)
Conti (c)
Barnaba: Galeffi
La Gioconda: Nordica
La Cieca: Bonheur
Zuane: Pulcini
Isepo: Stroesco
Enzo: Constantino
Laura: Claessens
Alvise: Perini (for
Mardones)

November 26 (mat.)
Il Trovatore (Verdi)
Conti (c)
Ferrando: Perini
Leonora: Villani
Inez: G. Fisher
Di Luna: Galeffi
Manrico: Slezak
Azucena: Claessens
Ruiz: Giaccone

November 26
Faust
Same as Nov. 14 except:
Faust: Lassalle
Wagner: Letol
Marguerite: Alda

November 28
Il Barbiere di Siviglia
Same as Nov. 19

November 30
Madama Butterfly
Conti (c)
B. F. Pinkerton: Jadlowker
Goro: Giaccone
Suzuki: Fornia
Sharpless: Blanchart
Cio-Cio-San: Nielsen
Cousin: Savage
Mother: Rogers
Yakuside: Mogan
Aunt: G. Fisher
Imperial Commissioner:
Montella
Notary: Stroesco
Bonze: Perini
Yamadori: Pulcini
Kate Pinkerton: Swartz

December 2
L'Enfant Prodigue
Same as Nov. 16

The Miserly Knight
(Rachmaninoff)
Conti (c)
Baron: Baklanoff

Cavalleria Rusticana
(Mascagni)
Moranzoni (c)
Turiddu: McCormack
Santuzza: Melis
Lucia: Roberts
Alfio: Fornari
Lola: Czaplinska

December 3 (mat.)
Faust
Same as Nov. 14 except:
Wagner: Letol
Marguerite: Nordica

December 3
La Bohème
Same as Nov. 18 except:
Rodolfo: McCormack
Musetta: Camporelli

December 5
L'Enfant Prodigue
Same as Nov. 16

The Miserly Knight
Same as Dec. 2

Cavalleria Rusticana
Same as Dec. 2

December 7
Mefistofele
Same as Nov. 7 except:
Faust: Constantino

December 9
Il Barbiere di Siviglia
Same as Nov. 19

December 10 (mat.)
La Bohème
Same as Nov. 18 except:
Mimì: Lipkowska

December 10
Il Trovatore
Same as Nov. 26 except:
Moranzoni (c)
Leonora: Rappold
Manrico: Areson
(Collapsed on stage in
Act III; Giaccone, who
was singing Ruiz, re-
placed him.)

December 12
Madama Butterfly
Same as Nov. 30 except:
B. F. Pinkerton: Martin
Suzuki: Swartz
Cio-Cio-San: Melis
Kate Pinkerton: G. Fisher

December 14
La Habanera (Laparra)
American premiere
Caplet (c)
Girl: Savage
Compères: Devaux,
Fornari, Gantvoort,
Stroesco
Pilar: Dereyne
Ramon: Blanchart
Pedro: Lassalle
Father: Mardones

Blind Men: Fornari,
   Stroesco, White
Man from Madrid:
   Gantvoort
Servant: Tavecchia
Middle-aged Man: Letol
Young Man: Huddy
Woman: G. Fisher

Cavalleria Rusticana
Same as Dec. 2 except:
Turiddu: Martin
Alfio: Montella

December 15
La Bohème
Same as Nov. 18 except:
Marcello: Sammarco
Rodolfo: McCormack
Mimì: Melba

December 17 (mat.)
Otello
Same as Nov. 11 except:
Cassio: Giaccone
Iago: Sammarco
Otello: Zenatello
Desdemona: Melis
Herald: Huddy

December 17
Rigoletto
Same as Nov. 9 except:
Countess Ceprano: Savage
Rigoletto: Galeffi
Maddalena: Leveroni

December 19
Carmen (Bizet)
   Caplet (c)
Morales: Pulcini
Micaela: Nielsen
Don José: Zenatello
Zuniga: Gantvoort
Carmen: Gay
Frasquita: B. Fisher
Mercédès: Roberts
Escamillo: Rothier
Dancairo: Devaux
Remendado: Giaccone

December 22
Pagliacci
Same as Nov. 16 except:
Nedda: Melis

Ballet Divertissement
   Stier (c)
Dancers:
Anna Pavlova
Mikail Mordkin
Bronislawa Pajitzkaia
Sergei Morosev
Mikail Moisseiev

December 23
La Habanera
Same as Dec. 14

The Legend of Azyiade
(Original ballet by
   Mordkin)
   Stier (c)
Pavlova
Mordkin
Pajitzkaia
Barboe

December 24 (mat.)
Mefistofele
Same as Nov. 7 except:
   Moranzoni (c)
Mefistofele: Mardones
Faust   Constantino
Margherita: Nielsen
Martha   Leveroni
Elena: Dereyne
Nereo: Stroesco

December 24
Otello
Same as Nov. 11 except:
Cassio: Giaccone
Iago: Blanchart
Otello: Zenatello
Desdemona: Savage (for
   Melis)
Herald: Huddy
Lodovico: Perini

December 26
Il Trovatore (for *Otello*)
Same as Nov. 26 except:
   Moranzoni (c)
Leonora: Korolowicz
Manrico: Zenatello
Azucena: Gay

December 28
Aida
Same as Nov. 19 except:
Conti (c)

Radamès: Zenatello
Amneris: Gay
Amonasro: Galeffi

December 30
Carmen
Same as Dec. 19 except:
Morales: Letol
Escamillo: Gilly

December 31 (mat.)
L'Enfant Prodigue
Same as Nov. 16

Giselle (Adam/Gautier)
   (Ballet)
   Stier (c)
Giselle: Pavlova
Albert: Mordkin
Prince: West
Wilfried: Morosev
Hans: Barboe
Bathilde: Pajitzkaia
Berthe: Brown
Myrtha: Schmolz

December 31
Pagliacci
Same as Nov. 16

The Legend of Azyiade
Same as Dec. 23

January 2
Otello
Same as Nov. 11 except:
Iago: Polese
Otello: Zenatello
Herald: Huddy

January 4
Lucia di Lammermoor
Same as Nov. 12 except:
Enrico: Polese

January 6
Cavalleria Rusticana
Same as Dec. 2 except:
Turiddu: Lassalle (for
   Constantino)
Santuzza: Gay
Alfio: Polese

The Pipe of Desire
(Converse)
  Goodrich (c)
1st Undine: Swartz
1st Gnome: Fornari
Iolan: Martin
1st Salamander: Stroesco
1st Sylph: B. Fisher
Old One: Blanchart
Naoia: Dereyne

January 7 (mat.)
Madama Butterfly
Same as Nov. 30 except:
B. F. Pinkerton: Zenatello
Suzuki: Swartz
Sharpless: Polese
Cio-Cio-San: Destinn
Kate Pinkerton: G. Fisher

January 7
La Traviata (Verdi)
  Moranzoni (c)
Violetta: Nielsen
Flora: G. Fisher
Marquis D'Obigny: Huddy
Gastone: Giaccone
Alfredo: Constantino
Baron Douphol: Pulcini
Annina: Leveroni
Germont: Galeffi
Dr. Grenvil: Perini

January 9
Aida
Same as Nov. 19 except:
  Conti (c)
Radamès: Zenatello
Amneris: Gay
Aida: Destinn
Amonasro: Polese (for
  Galeffi)

January 10
Giselle
  Stier (c)
Same as Dec. 31
Followed by other ballets

January 11
Cavalleria Rusticana
Same as Dec. 2 except:
Turiddu: Lassalle
Santuzza: Gay

Lucia: Roberts
Alfio: Polese

The Pipe of Desire
Same as Jan. 6

January 13
Rigoletto
Same as Nov. 9 except:
Countess Ceprano: Savage
Maddalena: Leveroni

January 14 (mat.)
Carmen
Same as Dec. 19 except:
Morales: Letol
Micaela: Dereyne
Escamillo: Baklanoff

January 14
Tosca
Same as Nov. 12 except:
Cavaradossi: Constantino
Tosca: Dereyne
Scarpia: Polese
Shepherd: G. Fisher

January 16
La Traviata
Same as Jan. 7 except:
Violetta: Lipkowska
Alfredo: Jadlowker
Annina: B. Fisher
Germont: Amato

January 17
La Fanciulla del West
(Puccini)
  Conti (c)
Handsome: Pulcini
Harry: Stroesco
Joe: Giaccone
Nick: Cilla
Happy: Montella
Sid: Perini
Sonora: Blanchart
Trin: Devaux
Larkens: Fornari
Wallace: Mardones
Rance: Galeffi
Ashby: Gantvoort
Minnie: Melis
Johnson: Constantino

Billy: Tavecchia
Castro: Sandrini
Express Rider: Ghedini
Wowkle: Leveroni

January 18
Il Barbiere di Siviglia
Same as Nov. 19 except:
  Moranzoni (c)
Figaro: Polese
Basilio: Mardones

January 20
Aida
Same as Nov. 19 except:
Radamès: Zenatello
Amneris: Gay
Amonasro: Amato

January 21 (mat.)
La Fanciulla del West
Same as Jan. 17

January 21
Pagliacci
Same as Nov. 16 except:
Tonio: Baklanoff
Canio: Gerardi

Cavalleria Rusticana
Same as Dec. 2 except:
Turiddu: Sciaretti
Santuzza: Gay
Alfio: Polese

January 23
The Pipe of Desire
Same as Jan. 6

Pagliacci
Same as Nov. 16 except:
Tonio: Scotti
Canio: Zenatello

January 25
Carmen
Same as Dec. 19 except:
Morales: Letol
Escamillo: Baklanoff

January 27
La Fanciulla del West
Same as Jan. 17

January 28 (mat.)
Aida
Same as Nov. 19 except:
Radamès: Zenatello
Amneris: Gay

January 28
Madama Butterfly
Same as Nov. 30 except:
Suzuki: Leveroni
Sharpless: Polese
Imperial Commissioner:
Huddy

January 30
Rigoletto
Same as Nov. 9 except:
Goodrich (c)
Countess Ceprano: Savage
Gilda: Rabinoff
Maddalena: Leveroni

February 1
La Fanciulla del West
Same as Jan. 17

February 3
Faust
Same as Nov. 14 except:
Faust: Dalmorès
Méphistophélès: Rothier
Wagner: Letol
Marguerite: Garden

February 4 (mat.)
Hänsel und Gretel
(Humperdinck)
Goodrich (c)
Gretel: Alten
Hänsel: Mattfeld
Gertrude: Wickham
Peter: Goritz
Sandman: Swartz
Dew Fairy: B. Fisher
Witch: Claessens

The Miserly Knight
Same as Dec. 2

February 4
Carmen
Same as Dec. 19 except:
Morales: Letol
Escamillo: Mardones

February 5
Concert
Goodrich, Caplet,
Conti (c)
Nielsen, Bonheur,
Constantino, Mardones

February 6
La Fanciulla del West
Same as Jan. 17

February 8
L'Enfant Prodigue
Same as Nov. 16 except:
Siméon: Letol (for
Blanchart)

Hänsel und Gretel
Same as Feb. 4

February 10
Il Trovatore
Same as Nov. 26 except:
Moranzoni (c)
Leonora: Rappold
Di Luna: Amato

February 11 (mat.)
La Gioconda
Same as Nov. 25 except:
La Cieca: Leveroni
Enzo: Martin
Alvise: Mardones

February 11
Lucia di Lammermoor
Same as Nov. 12 except:
Enrico: Polese
Alisa: G. Fisher

February 13
La Gioconda
Same as Nov. 25 except:
Barnaba: Baklanoff
La Cieca: Leveroni
Alvise: Mardones

February 15
Manon (Massenet)
Caplet (c)
Guillot: Devaux
De Brétigny: Letol
Poussette: Savage
Javotte: Swartz

Rosette: Roberts
Innkeeper: Tavecchia
Lescaut: Fornari
Manon: Alda
Des Grieux: Clément
Servant: De Lieven
Count des Grieux:
Mardones

February 17
Tosca
Same as Nov. 12 except:
Cavaradossi: Gaudenzi
Shepherd: G. Fisher
Jailer: Stroesco

February 18 (mat.)
L'Enfant Prodigue
Same as Nov. 16

Hänsel und Gretel
Same as Feb. 4

February 18
La Fanciulla del West
Same as Jan. 17 except:
Rance: Polese

February 20
Manon
Same as Feb. 15 except:
Manon: Lipkowska

February 22
Manon Lescaut (Puccini)
Conti (c)
Edmondo: Cilla
Des Grieux: Bassi
Lescaut: Fornari
Innkeeper: Huddy
Geronte: Tavecchia
Manon: Melis
Singer: Swartz
Dancing Master: Giaccone
Sergeant: Pulcini
Lamplighter: Stroesco
Captain: Gantvoort

February 24
La Fanciulla del West
Same as Jan. 17 except:
Minnie: White (for
Destinn)

February 25 (mat.)

Lakmé (Delibes)
Caplet (c)
Nilakantha: Rothier
Lakmé: Lipkowska
Hagi: Stroesco
Mallika: Roberts
Rose: Swartz
Frédéric: Fornari
Ellen: B. Fisher
Gérald: Clément
Mrs. Benson: Leveroni

February 25

La Bohème
Same as Nov. 18 except:
Marcello: Polese

February 27

Manon Lescaut
Same as Feb. 22 except:
Des Grieux: Constantino

February 28

French Concert
Caplet (c)

March 1

Lakmé
Same as Feb. 25 except:
Nilakantha: Baklanoff
Gérald: Smirnoff

March 3

The Sacrifice (Converse)
World Premiere
Goodrich (c)
Chonita: Nielsen
Tomasa: Claessens
Marianna: G. Fisher
Pablo: Stroesco
Burton: Blanchart
Bernal: Constantino
Corporal Tom Flynn:
Mogan
1st Soldier: Huddy
Little Jack: White
2nd Soldier: Letol
Magdalena: B. Fisher

Gypsy Girl: Roberts
Padre Gabriel: Gantvoort

March 4 (mat.)

La Fanciulla del West
Same as Jan. 17 except:
Rance: Polese
Minnie: White
Johnson: Bassi

March 4

Aida
Same as Nov. 19 except:
Radamès: Constantino
Amneris: Claessens

March 6

Lakmé
Same as Feb. 25 except:
Nilakantha: Baklanoff

March 8

The Sacrifice
Same as Mar. 3 except:
Corporal Tom Flynn:
White
Little Jack: Gantvoort

March 9

Giselle
Same as Dec. 31

March 10

Manon Lescaut
Same as Feb. 22 except:
Des Grieux: Constantino

March 11 (mat.)

Carmen
Same as Dec. 19 except:
Morales: Letol
Micaela: B. Fisher (for
Dereyne)
Don José: Clément
Carmen: Silva
Escamillo: Mardones

March 11

La Traviata
Same as Jan. 7 except:

Violetta: Lipkowska
Annina: B. Fisher
Germont: Polese

March 13

The Sacrifice
Same as Mar. 3 except:
Corporal Tom Flynn:
White
Little Jack: Gantvoort

March 15

Tosca
Same as Nov. 12 except:
Conti (c)
Cavaradossi: Constantino
Scarpia: Polese (for
Amato)
Shepherd: G. Fisher

March 17

Don Pasquale (Donizetti)
Conti (c)
Don Pasquale: Tavecchia
Dr. Malatesta: Fornari
Ernesto: Sciaretti
Norina: Nielsen
Notary: Stroesco

Followed by Pavlova and
Mordkin

March 18 (mat.)

The Sacrifice
Same as Mar. 3 except:
Corporal Tom Flynn:
White
Little Jack: Gantvoort

Followed by Pavlova and
Mordkin

March 18

L'Enfant Prodigue
Same as Nov. 16 except:
Lia: Savage

Followed by Pavlova and
Mordkin

March 19

Concert
Goodrich, Caplet,
Conti (c)

Melis, Constantino,
Mardones, chorus

March 21
Don Pasquale
Same as Mar. 17

Followed by Pavlova and
Mordkin

March 22
La Bohème
Same as Nov. 18 except:

Marcello: Polese
Alcindoro: Tavecchia

March 24
Madama Butterfly
Same as Nov. 30 except:
Suzuki: Swartz
Sharpless: Polese
Cio-Cio-San: Destinn
Mother: Martuccia
Imperial Commissioner:
Huddy
Kate Pinkerton: G. Fisher

March 25 (mat.)
Manon
Same as Feb. 15 except:
Lescaut: Gilly
Manon: Garden

March 25
La Fanciulla del West
Same as Jan. 17

TOUR 1910–11

SPRINGFIELD

January 19
Carmen
Caplet (c)
Morales: Letol
Micaela: Nielsen
Don José: Zenatello
Zuniga: Gantvoort
Carmen: Gay
Frasquita: B. Fisher
Mercédès: Roberts
Escamillo: Mardones
Dancairo: Devaux
Remendado: Giaccone

February 22
Aida
Moranzoni (c)
Ramfis: Mardones
Radamès: Constantino
Amneris: Leveroni
Aida: Melis
King: White
Messenger: Giaccone
Priestess: Savage
Amonasro: Polese

March 28
Concert
Melis, Constantino,
Mardones

PORTLAND, ME.

March 17
La Bohème
Goodrich (c)
Marcello: Polese
Rodolfo: Constantino
Colline: Mardones
Schaunard: Pulcini
Benoit: Tavecchia
Mimì: Nielsen
Parpignol: Cilla
Alcindoro: Mogan
Musetta: Dereyne
Customs Officer: Huddy

1911–12

November 27
Samson et Dalila
(Saint-Saëns)
Caplet (c)
Samson: Zenatello
Abimelech: Mardones
High Priest: Gilly
Philistines: Giaccone,
Barreau
Messenger: Saldaigne
Old Hebrew: Lankow
Dalila: Gay

November 29
Tosca (Puccini)
Moranzoni (c)

Angelotti: Silli
Sacristan: Tavecchia
Cavaradossi: Constantino
Tosca: Melis
Scarpia: Scotti
Spoletta: Giaccone
Sciarrone: Pulcini
Shepherd: De Courcy
Jailer: Olshansky

December 1
Aida (Verdi)
Conti (c)
Ramfis: Lankow
Radamès: Zenatello
Amneris: Gay
Aida: Destinn

King: Silli
Messenger: Giaccone
Priestess: De Courcy
Amonasro: Polese

December 2 (mat.)
Carmen (Bizet)
Caplet (c)
Morales: Kaplick
Micaela: B. Fisher
Don José: Clément
Zuniga: Barreau
Carmen: Gay
Lillas Pastia: Jullien
Frasquita: Scotney
Mercédès: De Courcy
Escamillo: Mardones

Dancairo: Leo
Remendado: Giaccone

December 3

Concert
Conti, Caplet,
Goodrich (c)
Martini, Mardones, Britt
(cello), Gunn (piano);
also *Samson et Dalila,*
Act I (same as Nov. 27
except Samson: De
Potter; High Priest:
Riddez; Delila:
Claessens)

December 4

Madama Butterfly
(Puccini)
Moranzoni (c)
B. F. Pinkerton: Jadlowker
Goro: Giaccone
Suzuki: Swartz
Sharpless: Polese
Cio-Cio-San: Destinn
Cousin: Santi
Mother: Scotney
Yakuside: Olshansky
Aunt: Morella
Imperial Commissioner:
Montella
Notary: Diaz
Bonze: Silli
Yamadori: Pulcini
Kate Pinkerton: De Courcy

December 6

Thaïs (Massenet)
Caplet (c)
Palémon: Lankow
Athanael: Riddez
Servant: Barreau
Nicias: Clément
Crobyle: B. Fisher
Myrtale: Swartz
Thaïs: Brozia
La Charmeuse: Scotney
Albine: Claessens

December 8

La Bohème (Puccini)
Goodrich (c)
Marcello: Polese
Rodolfo: Constantino
Colline: Mardones

Schaunard: Pulcini
Benoit: Tavecchia
Mimì: Ferrabini
Parpignol: Cilla
Musetta: Camporelli
Alcindoro: Tavecchia
Customs Officer:
Olshansky

December 9 (mat.)

Samson et Dalila
Same as Nov. 27 except:
High Priest: Riddez

December 10

Concert
Goodrich, Conti (c)
B. Fisher, Amsden (d),
Swartz, Claessens, De
Potter, Gaudenzi,
Romito, Polese,
Mardones, Lankow,
Barreau, chorus.

December 11

Carmen
Same as Dec. 2 except:
Morales: Letol
Escamillo: Riddez

December 13

Faust (Gounod)
Caplet (c)
Faust: Clément
Méphistophélès: Rothier
Valentin: Riddez
Wagner: Barreau
Siébel: D'Oligé
Marguerite: Brozia
Marthe: Leveroni

December 15

Samson et Dalila (for
Lucia di Lammermoor)
Same as Nov. 27 except:
High Priest: Riddez

December 16 (mat.)

Thaïs
Same as Dec. 6

December 17

Concert
Caplet, Goodrich (c)
Scotney, B. Fisher, Swartz,

De Courcy, Morella,
Ramella, Giaccone,
Polese, Silli, Lankow

December 18

Tosca
Same as Nov. 29 except:
Tosca: Eames
Scarpia: Polese

December 20

Lucia di Lammermoor
(Donizetti)
Moranzoni (c)
Normanno: Diaz
Enrico: Polese
Raimondo: Silli
Lucia: Tetrazzini
Alisa: Morella
Edgardo: Constantino
Arturo: Giaccone

December 22

Otello (Verdi)
Conti (c)
Montano: Pulcini
Cassio: Diaz
Iago: Polese
Roderigo: Cilla
Otello: Zenatello
Desdemona: Eames
Emilia: Claessens
Herald: Olshansky
Lodovico: Mardones

December 23 (mat.)

Mignon (Thomas)
Goodrich (c)
Lothario: Rothier
Philine: Tetrazzini
Laerte: Leo
Giarno: Barreau
Mignon: Dereyne
Wilhelm Meister: Clément
Frédéric: Swartz
Antonio: Letol

December 26

Pagliacci (Leoncavallo)
Moranzoni (c)
Tonio: Polese
Canio: Zenatello
Beppe: Giaccone
Nedda: Melis
Silvio: Barreau

Coppélia (Delibes)
Goodrich (c)
Swanilda: Galli
Frantz: Paporello
Doll: Parker
Coppélius: Bottazzini
Burgomaster: Pulcini

December 27
Carmen
Same as Dec. 2 except:
Morales: Letol
Don José: Zenatello
Frasquita: Martini

December 29
Aida
Same as Dec. 1 except:
Ramfis: Mardones
Aida: Melis

December 30 (mat.)
Cavalleria Rusticana
(Mascagni)
Moranzoni (c)
Turiddu: Gaudenzi
Santuzza: Gay
Lucia: De Courcy
Alfio: Polese
Lola: Leveroni

Coppélia
Same as Dec. 26

December 30
Lucia di Lammermoor
Same as Dec. 20 except:
Conti (c)
Enrico: Fornari
Lucia: Scotney

December 31
Concert
Goodrich, Conti,
Moranzoni (c)
Scotney, Amsden,
Leveroni, De Courcy
Ramella, Gaudenzi,
Fornari, Silli

January 1
Otello
Same as Dec. 22 except:
Desdemona: Melis

January 3
La Bohème
Same as Dec. 8 except:
Mimì: Brozia
Musetta: Dereyne

January 5
Pagliacci
Same as Dec. 26 except:
Tonio: Scotti

Coppélia
Same as Dec. 26

January 6 (mat.)
Tosca
Same as Nov. 29 except:
Cavaradossi: Zenatello
Tosca: Destinn
Scarpia: Gilly

January 6
Madama Butterfly
Same as Dec. 4 except:
B. F. Pinkerton: Gaudenzi
Sharpless: Blanchart
Cio-Cio-San: Melis
Mother: Dolfini

January 7
Concert
Goodrich, Moranzoni
(c)
Scotney, Barnes,
Gaudenzi, Giaccone,
Polese, Barreau,
Mardones, Lankow,
Huddy

January 8
Faust
Same as Dec. 13 except:
Strony (c)
Faust: Zenatello
Valentin: Blanchart (for
Barreau)
Wagner: Olshansky

January 10
Pelléas et Mélisande
(Debussy)
Caplet (c)
Golaud: Marcoux
Mélisande: Leblanc

Geneviève: Gay
Arkel: Lankow
Pelléas: Riddez
Yniold: B. Fisher
Doctor: Mardones

January 12
Lucia di Lammermoor
Same as Dec. 20 except:
Alisa: D'Oligé

January 13 (mat.)
Pelléas et Mélisande
Same as Jan. 10

January 13
Rigoletto (Verdi)
Conti (c)
Duke: Constantino
Borsa: Giaccone
Countess Ceprano:
Morella
Rigoletto: Polese
Marullo: Pulcini
Ceprano: Huddy
Monterone: Silli
Sparafucile: Mardones
Gilda: Scotney
Giovanna: De Courcy
Page: Swartz
Maddalena: Leveroni

January 14
Concert
Goodrich, Moranzoni,
Strony (c)
Melis, Claessens, Martini,
De Courcy, De Potter,
Giaccone, Mardones,
Barreau, Leo

January 15
Rigoletto
Same as Jan. 13 except:
Gilda: De Tréville
Page: D'Oligé
Maddalena: Gay

January 17
La Fanciulla del West
(Puccini)
Moranzoni (c)
Handsome: Pulcini
Harry: Diaz
Joe: Giaccone

Billy: Tavecchia
Nick: Cilla
Sid: Silli
Happy: Montella
Sonora: Blanchart
Trin: Devaux
Larkens: Fornari
Wallace: Mardones
Rance: Polese
Ashby: Lankow
Minnie: Melis
Johnson: Zenatello
Castro: Olshansky
Express Rider: Ghidini
Wowkle: Leveroni

January 19
Pelléas et Mélisande
Same as Jan. 10

January 20 (mat.)
La Traviata (Verdi)
  Conti (c)
Violetta: Tetrazzini
Flora: De Courcy
Marquis D'Obigny:
  Huddy
Gastone: Giaccone
Alfredo: Zenatello
Baron Duphol: Pulcini
Annina: Santi
Germont: Polese
Dr. Grenvil: Silli

January 20
Aida
Same as Dec. 1 except:
  Moranzoni (c)
Ramfis: Mardones
Radamès: Constantino
Amneris: Claessens
Aida: Amsden
Amonasro: Blanchart

January 21
Concert
  Caplet, Goodrich (c)
  D'Oligé, Camporelli,
  Constantino, Fornari

January 22
Pelléas et Mélisande
Same as Jan. 10 except:
Shepherd: Barreau (role

not listed in earlier
programs)

January 24
Rigoletto
Same as Jan. 13 except:
Rigoletto: Renaud
Page: D'Oligé
Maddalena: Gay

January 25
Monna Vanna
  (Drama by Maeterlinck)
Monna Vanna: Leblanc
Prinzivalle: René Maupré
Guido Colonna: Jean
  Durozat
Marco Colonna: Jean
  Duval
Trovulzio: Leo
Borso: De Potter
Verdio: Simon Lyon

January 26
Faust
Same as Dec. 13 except:
Faust: Zenatello
Méphistophélès: Marcoux

January 27 (mat.)
Hänsel und Gretel
  (Humperdinck)
  Goodrich (c)
Gretel: B. Fisher
Hänsel: Swartz
Gertrude: Claessens
Peter: Goritz
Sandman: De Courcy
Dew Fairy: D'Oligé
Witch: Claessens

Coppélia
Same as Dec. 26

January 27
Cavalleria Rusticana
Same as Dec. 30 except:
Turiddu: Ramella
Santuzza: Amsden
Alfio: Fornari

Pagliacci
Same as Dec. 26 except:
Canio: Gaudenzi
Nedda: Barnes

January 28
Concert
  Goodrich, Caplet,
  Moranzoni (c)
Scotney, Melis, Claessens,
  Gaudenzi, Giaccone,
  Polese, Lankow

January 29
Il Barbiere di Siviglia
  (Rossini)
  Conti (c)
Fiorello: Pulcini
Almaviva: Constantino
Figaro: Fornari
Rosina: Tetrazzini
Dr. Bartolo: Tavecchia
Basilio: Marcoux
Berta: Leveroni
Sergeant: Giaccone

January 30
Pelléas et Mélisande
  (Drama by Maeterlinck)
Incidental Music by
  Gabriel Fauré
  Caplet (c)
Golaud: Jean Durozat
Mélisande: Leblanc
Geneviève: D'Oligé
Arkel: Jean Duval
Pelléas: René de Maupré
Yniold: Sheri (Sheridan
  Russell)
Doctor: Leo

January 31
Madama Butterfly
Same as Dec. 4 except:
B. F. Pinkerton: Zenatello
Suzuki: Gay
Cio-Cio-San: Melis
Mother: Dolfini

February 2
Manon (Massenet)
  Caplet (c)
Guillot: Leo
De Brétigny: Barreau
Poussette: B. Fisher
Javotte: D'Oligé
Rosette: De Courcy
Innkeeper: Letol

Lescaut: Riddez
Manon: Brozia
Des Grieux: Clément
Servant: De Lieven
Count Des Grieux:
  Mardones

February 3 (mat.)
La Fanciulla del West
Same as Jan. 17 except:
Trin: Leo
Minnie: Amsden

February 3
Tosca
Same as Nov. 29 except:
Cavaradossi: Gaudenzi
Scarpia: Riddez

February 4
Concert: Song program
Melis, Scotney, D'Oligé,
  Diaz, Montella,
  Olshansky, Mardones,
  Lankow. Conti-
  Berenguer (harp),
  Stickney (cello).
Accompanists: Strony,
  Waller

February 5
Manon
Same as Feb. 2

February 7
Aida
Same as Dec. 1 except:
Ramfis: Mardones
Aida: Melis
Amonasro: Scotti

February 9
Mignon
Same as Dec. 23

February 10 (mat.)
Faust
Same as Dec. 13 except:
Faust: Zenatello
Méphistophélès:
  Marcoux
Siébel: Swartz
Marguerite: Amsden

February 10
La Bohème
Same as Dec. 8 except:
Marcello: Fornari
Mimì: D'Oligé

February 12
Tristan und Isolde
  (Wagner)
  Weingartner (c)
Sailor's Voice: Diaz
Isolde: Gadski (for
  Nordica)
Brangäne: Homer
Kurvenal: Amato
Tristan: Urlus (d)
Melot: Pulcini
King Marke: Lankow
Shepherd: Diaz
Steersman: Kaplick

February 14
Tosca
Same as Nov. 29 except:
  Weingartner (c)
Cavaradossi: Zenatello
Tosca: Marcel
Scarpia: Marcoux

February 16
Faust
Same as Dec. 13 except:
  Weingartner (c)
Faust: Zenatello
Méphistophélès:
  Marcoux
Marguerite: Marcel
Marthe: De Courcy (for
  Leveroni)

February 17 (mat.)
Tristan und Isolde
Same as Feb. 12 except:
Isolde: Nordica
Brangäne: Gerville-
  Réache
Kurvenal: Goritz
Melot: Kaplick
Steersman: Silli

February 17
La Traviata
Same as Jan. 20 except:
Violetta: Scotney

Alfredo: Gaudenzi
Germont: Blanchart

February 18
German Concert
  Weingartner (c)
Lieder: Marcel, Urlus
Symphony No. 5
  (Beethoven)

February 20
Aida
Same as Dec. 1 except:
  Weingartner (c)
Ramfis: Mardones
Aida: Marcel

February 21
Tristan und Isolde
Same as Feb. 12 except:
Isolde: Nordica
Brangäne: Gerville-
  Réache
Kurvenal: Goritz
Melot: Kaplick
Steersman: Silli

February 22
Hänsel und Gretel
Same as Jan. 27 except:
  Weingartner (c)
Gertrude: Wickham (for
  Claessens)
Peter: Hinshaw
Witch: Mattfeld (for
  Claessens)

Coppélia
Same as Dec. 26

February 23
Tristan und Isolde
Same as Feb. 12 except:
Isolde: Nordica
Brangäne: Matzenauer
Kurvenal: Weil
Melot: Kaplick
Steersman: Silli

February 24 (mat.)
Carmen
Same as Dec. 2 except:
Morales: Letol
Carmen: Calvé

Frasquita: Martini
Escamillo: Rothier

February 24
Samson et Dalila
Same as Nov. 27 except:
Samson: De Potter
High Priest: Riddez

February 25
Concert
Melis, Scotney, Swartz,
Seydel, Ramella, Polese,
Kaplick, Lankow, White.
Accompanists: Strony,
Waller

February 26
Faust
Same as Dec. 13 except:
Marguerite: Garden

February 28
Samson et Dalila
Same as Nov. 27 except:
High Priest: Riddez
Dalila: Gerville-Réache

March 1
Werther (Massenet)
Caplet (c)
Le Bailli: Rothier
Johann: Letol
Schmidt: Leo (for
Giaccone)
Sophie: D'Oligé
Werther: Clément
Charlotte: Gay
Bruhlmann: Regnier
Kätchen: De Courcy

March 2 (mat.)
Aida
Same as Dec. 1 except:
Ramfis: Mardones
Aida: Melis
Amonasro: Scotti

March 2
Carmen
Same as Dec. 2 except:
Morales: Letol
Micaela: D'Oligé
Carmen: Calvé

Frasquita: Martini
Escamillo: Riddez

March 3
Concert: Song recital
Amsden, B. Fisher, De
Courcy, Romito,
Gaudenzi, Olshansky,
Barreau, Mardones

March 4
Werther
Same as Mar. 1 except:
Schmidt: Giaccone

March 5
La Fanciulla del West
Same as Jan. 17 except:
Trin: Leo
Johnson: Caruso

March 6
L'Enfant Prodigue
(Debussy)
Caplet (c)
Lia: Gay
Siméon: Riddez
Azael: De Potter

Pagliacci
Same as Dec. 26 except:
Tonio: Scotti
Nedda: Dereyne

March 8
Thaïs
Same as Dec. 6 except:
Athanael: Renaud
Nicias: De Potter (for
Clément)
Thaïs: Garden

March 9 (mat.)
Germania (Franchetti)
Conti (c)
Jane: B. Fisher
Crisogono: Blanchart
Jebbel: D'Oligé
Carlo Worms: Amato
Ricke: Melis
Loewe: Zenatello
Palm: Silli
Koerner: Cilla
Weber: Diaz
Luetzow: Pulcini

Chief of Police: Tavecchia
Hedwig: De Courcy
Peters: Kaplick
Stapps: Mardones
Queen: Amsden
Poliziotto: Letol
Lene Armuth: Leveroni

March 9
Faust
Same as Dec. 13 except:
Strony (c)
Faust: Jadlowker
Valentin: Barreau
Wagner: Olshansky
Siébel: De Courcy (for
Swartz)
Marguerite: Dereyne

March 11
Hänsel und Gretel
Same as Jan. 27

L'Enfant Prodigue
Same as March 6

March 13 (mat.)
Carmen
Same as Dec. 2 except:
Morales: Letol
Carmen: Calvé
Frasquita: Martini
Escamillo: Riddez

March 13
Il Trovatore (Verdi)
Moranzoni (c)
Ferrando: Silli
Leonora: Amsden
Inez: Morella
Di Luna: Polese
Manrico: Zenatello
Azucena: Gay
Ruiz: Giaccone

March 15
Germania
Same as Mar. 9 except:
Carlo Worms: Polese

March 16 (mat.)
Thaïs
Same as Dec. 6 except:
Athanael: Renaud
Thaïs: Garden

March 16

Thaïs
Same as Dec. 6 except:
Nicias: De Potter
Thaïs: Melis

March 18

La Bohème
Same as Dec. 8 except:
Rodolfo: Clément
Mimì: Zeppilli
Musetta: Dereyne

March 20

Germania
Same as Mar. 9 except:
Carlo Worms: Polese

March 22

La Habanera (Laparra)
Caplet (c)
Girl: B. Fisher
Compères: Giaccone, Cilla,
Barreau, Silli
Pilar: Gay
Ramon: Riddez
Pedro: De Potter
Father: Mardones
Blind Men: Barreau,
Giaccone, Silli
Man from Madrid:
Kaplick
Servant: Olshansky
Middle-aged Man: Letol
Young Man: Saldaigne
Women: Swartz, De
Courcy
Fiancée: Martini
Girl: D'Oligé
Little Boy: D'Oligé
Fiancé from Aragon: Cilla
Andalousians: Montella,
Diaz
Peasant: Jullien

Coppélia
Same as Dec. 26

March 23 (mat.)

Samson et Dalila
Same as Nov. 27 except:
High Priest: Renaud
Dalila: Gerville-Réache

March 23

Rigoletto
Same as Jan. 13 except:
Duke: Ramella
Ceprano: Cacici
Sparafucile: Silli
Page: D'Oligé
Maddalena: Swartz

March 24

Messa da Requiem
(Verdi)
Conti (c)
Amsden, Gay, Ramella,
Mardones

March 25

La Habanera
Same as Mar. 22

Coppélia
Same as Dec. 26

March 26

GALA PERFORMANCE FOR
THE CITY CLUB

Faust (Act II)
Same as Dec. 13 except:
Marguerite: Dereyne
Marthe: De Courcy

La Bohème (Act III)
Same as Dec. 8 except:
Moranzoni (c)
Rodolfo: Zenatello
Mimì: Melis
Musetta: Dereyne

Coppélia (Act I)
Goodrich (c)

Carmen: "Habanera"
Caplet (c)
Carmen: Gay

Aida (Act II)
Same as Dec. 1 except:
Ramfis: Mardones
Aida: Melis

March 27

Carmen
Same as Dec. 2 except:
Morales: Letol
Don José: Dalmorès
Carmen: Garden
Escamillo: Dufranne

March 29

La Fanciulla del West
Same as Jan. 17 except:
Billy: Bourgeois
Trin: Leo
Larkens: Kaplick
Wallace: Olshansky
Rance: Amato
Minnie: Destinn

March 30 (mat.)

*Le Martyre de Saint
Sebastien* (Debussy)
Caplet (c)
Scotney, Fisher, Swartz,
D'Oligé, Martini,
Leveroni, De Courcy
Symbolic Dance
performed by Mme.
Cerutti

Hänsel und Gretel
Same as Jan. 27

March 30

Pelléas et Mélisande
Same as Jan. 10 except:
Golaud: Dufranne
Mélisande: Garden
Doctor: Barreau

TOUR 1911–12

NEW HAVEN

January 18

Aida
Moranzoni (c)
Ramfis: Mardones
Radamès: Zenatello
Amneris: Gay
Aida: Melis
King: Silli
Messenger: Giaccone
Priestess: De Courcy
Amonasro: Polese

February 1

Rigoletto
Conti (c)
Duke: Constantino
Borsa: Giaccone
Countess Ceprano: Morella
Rigoletto: Polese
Marullo: Pulcini

Ceprano: Huddy
Monterone: Silli
Sparafucile: ?
Gilda: Tetrazzini
Giovanna: De Courcy
Page: Santi
Maddalena: Leveroni

March 19

Madama Butterfly
Moranzoni (c)
B. F. Pinkerton:
Zenatello
Goro: Giaccone
Suzuki: Gay
Sharpless: Blanchart
Cio-Cio-San: Nielsen
Yakuside: Olshansky
Imperial Commissioner:
Mantella
Bonze: Silli
Yamadori: Pulcini

Kate Pinkerton: De
Courcy

SPRINGFIELD

January 23
Madama Butterfly
Same as New Haven,
March 19

March 7

Faust
Caplet (c)
Faust: Clément
Méphistophélès: Rothier
Valentin: Olshansky
Wagner: Barreau
Siébel: D'Oligé
Marguerite: Dereyne
Marthe: Leveroni

1912–13

November 25
Les Contes D'Hoffmann
(Offenbach)
Caplet (c)
Lindorf: Marcoux
Andrès: Cilla
Luther: Sillich
Hermann: Chasseriaux
Nathanael: Diaz
Hoffmann: Clément
Niklausse: Leveroni
Spalanzani: Giaccone
Cochenille: Cilla
Coppélius: Marcoux
Olympia: B. Fisher
Giulietta: Amsden
Schlemil: Everett
Pitichinaccio: Cilla
Dappertutto: Marcoux
Antonia: Edvina
Crespel: Blanchart
Frantz: Cilla
Dr. Miracle: Marcoux
Voice: De Courcy
Stella: Sharlow

November 27
La Bohème (Puccini)
Moranzoni (c)
Marcello: Polese
Rodolfo: Laffitte (d)
Colline: De Segurola
Schaunard: Pulcini
Benoit: Pini-Corsi
Mimì: Bori
Parpignol: Giaccone
Alcindoro: Pini-Corsi
Musetta: Dereyne
Customs Officer:
Olshansky

November 29
Madama Butterfly
(Puccini)
Moranzoni (c)
B. F. Pinkerton: Martin
Goro: Giaccone
Suzuki: Leveroni
Sharpless: Polese
Cio-Cio-San: Destinn
Cousin: Sharlow

Mother: Wilson
Yakuside: Olshansky
Aunt: Heyman
Imperial Commissioner:
Chasseriaux
Notary: Everett
Bonze: Sillich
Yamadori: Pulcini
Kate Pinkerton: Von Aken

November 30 (mat.)
Les Contes D'Hoffmann
Same as Nov. 25

November 30
Il Trovatore (Verdi)
Moranzoni (c)
Ferrando: Sampieri
Leonora: Rennyson
Inez: Morella
Di Luna: Blanchart
Manrico: Laffitte
Azucena: Claessens
Ruiz: Giaccone

December 1
Russian Concert
Caplet (c)
Claessens, Barnes,
Von Aken, Marcoux

December 2
Tosca (Puccini)
Moranzoni (c)
Angelotti: Sillich
Sacristan: Cervi
Cavaradossi: Dalmorès
Tosca: Garden
Scarpia: Marcoux
Spoletta: Giaccone
Sciarrone: Pulcini
Shepherd: De Courcy
Jailer: Olshansky

December 4
Les Contes D'Hoffmann
Same as Nov. 25

December 6
La Bohème
Same as Nov. 27 except:
Marcello: Rossi
Rodolfo: Clément
Parpignol: Boccalino

December 7 (mat.)
Thaïs (Massenet)
Caplet (c)
Palémon: Lankow
Athanael: Marcoux
Servant: Chasseriaux
Nicias: Dalmorès
Crobyle: B. Fisher
Myrtale: De Courcy
Thaïs: Garden
La Charmeuse: Scotney
Albine: Wilsch

December 7
Tosca
Same as Dec. 2 except:
Sacristan: Everett
Cavaradossi: Sacchetti
Tosca: Dereyne
Scarpia: Blanchart

December 8
Concert: Rameau and
Debussy
Caplet (c)

Garden, De Courcy, Diaz,
Lippman, Sampieri

December 9
La Bohème
Same as Nov. 27 except:
Marcello: Rossi
Rodolfo: Clément
Colline: Mardones
Benoit: Tavecchia
Parpignol: Boccalino
Alcindoro: Tavecchia

December 11
Tosca
Same as Dec. 2 except:
Sacristan: Tavecchia
Cavaradossi: Sacchetti (for
Gaudenzi)

December 13
Thaïs
Same as Dec. 7 except:
Strony (c—for Caplet)
Palémon: Sampieri
Nicias: Lippman (for De
Potter)
Myrtale: Swartz

December 14 (mat.)
Madama Butterfly
Same as Nov. 29 except:
B. F. Pinkerton:
McCormack
Suzuki: Swartz
Cio-Cio-San: Dereyne

December 14
Lucia di Lammermoor
(Donizetti)
Lyford (c)
Normanno: Diaz
Enrico: Fornari
Raimondo: Sampieri
Lucia: Scotney
Alisa: Heyman
Edgardo: Sacchetti
Arturo: Giaccone

December 15
French Concert
Britt, Dubois (c) for
Caplet
Ysaÿe (violin)

December 16
Thaïs
Same as Dec. 7 except:
Strony (c—for Caplet)
Nicias: De Potter
Crobyle: Manley

December 18
Louise (Charpentier)
Caplet (c)
Julien: Clément
Louise: Edvina
Mother: Gay
Father: Marcoux
Ragpicker: Sharlow
Coal-woman: Phillips
Nightwalker: Lippman
Paper-folder: Morella
Scavenger: Sillich
Milk-woman: De Courcy
Ragpicker: Lankow
Policemen: Saldaigne,
Olshansky
Urchin: Von Aken
Sweeper: Leveroni
Painter: Chasseriaux
Sculptor: Bourquin
Singer: Everett
Student: Cilla
Young Poet: Giaccone
Philosophers: Pulcini,
Ouluchanoff
Chair-mender: De Courcy
Blanche: Von Aken
Marguerite: Wilson
Suzanne: Manley
Gertrude: Leveroni
Irma: Barnes
Camille: Deyrise
Apprentice: Gauthier
Elise: Sharlow
Madeleine: Wilson
Old-clothes Man:
Saldaigne
Forewoman: De Courcy
King of the Fools:
Lippman
Dancer: Galli

December 20
Les Contes D'Hoffmann
Same as Nov. 25 except:
Olympia: Scotney (for
Fisher)

December 21 (mat.)
Lucia di Lammermoor
Same as Dec. 14 except:
    Moranzoni (c)
Enrico: Rossi
Raimondo: Mardones
Lucia: Tetrazzini
Edgardo: Gaudenzi

December 21
La Traviata (Verdi)
    Moranzoni (c)
Violetta: Scotney
Flora: De Courcy
Marquis D'Obigny:
    Sampieri
Gastone: Giaccone
Alfredo: Ramella
Baron Douphol: Pulcini
Annina: Heyman
Giuseppe: Ghidini
Germont: Blanchart
Dr. Grenvil: Sillich

December 22
Russian Concert
    Caplet (c)
Claessens, Barnes,
    Gauthier, Marcoux

December 23
Louise
Same as Dec. 18

December 25
La Traviata
Same as Dec. 21 except:
Violetta: Tetrazzini
Alfredo: Gaudenzi
Annina: Phillips
Germont: Rossi

December 27
Aida (Verdi)
    Moranzoni (c)
Ramfis: Mardones
Radamès: Zenatello
Amneris: Gay
Aida: Melis
King: Gravina
Messenger: Giaccone
Priestess: De Courcy
Amonasro: Rossi

December 28 (mat.)
Hänsel und Gretel
    (Humperdinck)
    Strony (c)
Gretel: B. Fisher
Hänsel: Swartz
Gertrude: Claessens
Peter: Hinshaw
Sandman: De Courcy
Dew Fairy: Sharlow
Witch: Claessens

Coppélia (Delibes)
    Strony (c)
Swanilda: Galli
Frantz: Cronan
Doll: Downey
Burgomaster: Pulcini

December 28
La Bohème
Same as Nov. 27 except:
Marcello: Fornari
Rodolfo: McCormack
Colline: Mardones
Benoit: Tavecchia
Mimì: Donner
Parpignol: Boccalino
Alcindoro: Tavecchia

December 29
Messa da Requiem
    (Verdi)
    Caplet (c)
Amsden, Gay, McCormack,
    Mardones

December 30
Hänsel und Gretel
Same as Dec. 28 except:
    Caplet (c)
Peter: Goritz

Cavalleria Rusticana
    (Mascagni)
    Moranzoni (c)
Turiddu: Sacchetti
Santuzza: Gay
Lucia: De Courcy
Alfio: Rossi
Lola: Leveroni

January 1
Aida
Same as Dec. 27 except:
Aida: Rappold
King: Sampieri
Amonasro: Polese

January 3
Lucia di Lammermoor
Same as Dec. 14 except:
    Moranzoni (c)
Enrico: Polese
Raimondo: Mardones
Lucia: Tetrazzini

January 4 (mat.)
Louise
Same as Dec. 18 except:
Julien: Zenatello
Sweeper: Heyman
Camille: B. Fisher

January 4
Cavalleria Rusticana
Same as Dec. 30 except:
Turiddu: Romito
Santuzza: Amsden
Lucia: Heyman
Alfio: Polese

Pagliacci (Leoncavallo)
    Moranzoni (c)
Tonio: Blanchart
Canio: Gaudenzi
Beppe: Giaccone
Nedda: Barnes
Silvio: Everett

January 5 (mat.)
French Concert
    Caplet (c)
Barnes, Gauthier,
    Clément, Diaz, Sampieri,
    Britt (cello).
Accompanists: Strony,
    Straram

January 6
La Traviata
Same as Dec. 21 except:
Violetta: Tetrazzini
Alfredo: Zenatello

Annina: Phillips
Germont: Polese

January 8
Pelléas et Mélisande
(Debussy)
Caplet (c)
Golaud: Marcoux
Mélisande: Edvina
Geneviève: Gay
Arkel: Lankow
Pelléas: Riddez
Yniold: B. Fisher
Doctor: Mardones

January 10
Louise
Same as Dec. 18 except:
Julien: Zenatello
Ragpicker: Sampieri
Camille: B. Fisher

January 11 (mat.)
La Bohème
Same as Nov. 27 except:
Colline: Mardones
Benoit: Sillich
Mimì: Melis
Parpignol: Boccalino
Alcindoro: Sillich

January 11
Carmen (Bizet)
Strony (c)
Morales: Chasseriaux
Micaela: Donner
Don José: De Potter
Zuniga: Sampieri
Carmen: Gay
Lillas Pastia: Bourquin
Frasquita: Sharlow
Mercédès: De Courcy
Escamillo: Riddez
Dancairo: Devaux
Remendado: Giaccone

January 12 (mat.)
Concert
Caplet (c)
Tetrazzini

January 13
Pelléas et Mélisande
Same as Jan. 8.

January 15
Carmen
Same as Jan. 11 except:
Don José: Zenatello
Escamillo: Mardones

January 17
I Gioielli della Madonna
(Wolf-Ferrari)
Sacred-object vendors:
Saldaigne, Fabbri,
Pasquali
Macaroni-vendor:
Olshansky
Flower-girl: Manley
Water-vendor: Sharlow
Blind man: Sampieri
Ice-cream man:
Boccalino
Fruit-vendor: Ghidini
Morra players: D'Adami,
Serpellon
Totonno: Diaz
Buffoon: Cammarano
Monks: Olshansky,
Ouluchanoff
Peasant Girl: Heyman
Biaso: Giaccone
Balloon man: Zaini
Young men: Chasseriaux,
Ganelli
Girls: Manley, Musceleanu
Young Girl: Sharlow
Father: Sampieri
Nurse: Leveroni
Gennaro: Zenatello
Maliella: Edvina
Carmela: Gay
Rocco: Pulcini
Ciccillo: Cilla
Raffaele: Marcoux
Stella: Alciatore
Concetta: Sharlow
Serena: De Courcy
Grazia: Galli

January 18 (mat.)
Hänsel und Gretel
Same as Dec. 28 except:
Caplet (c)

Cavalleria Rusticana
Same as Dec. 30 except:
Turiddu: Gaudenzi

Santuzza: Melis
Lucia: Heyman
Lola: Casavant

January 18
Aida
Same as Dec. 27 except:
Radamès: Zeni
Amneris: Leveroni
Aida: Amsden
King: Sampieri
Amonasro: Polese

January 19 (mat.)
Concert
Caplet (c)
B. Fisher, Gauthier, Diaz,
Sampieri. Accompanists:
Straram, Strony

January 20
Il Barbiere di Siviglia
(Rossini)
Moranzoni (c)
Fiorello: Pulcini
Almaviva: McCormack
Figaro: Fornari
Rosina: Hempel
Dr. Bartolo: Tavecchia
Basilio: Marcoux
Berta: Leveroni
Sergeant: Giaccone

January 22
I Gioielli della Madonna
Same as Jan. 17

January 24
Carmen
Same as Jan. 11 except:
Micaela: B. Fisher
Don José: Laffitte
Escamillo: Mardones

January 25 (mat.)
I Gioielli della Madonna
Same as Jan. 17 except:
Second Monk: Sillich

January 25
Rigoletto (Verdi)
Moranzoni (c)
Duke: Ramella
Borsa: Giaccone

Countess Ceprano:
  Sharlow
Rigoletto: Fornari
Marullo: Pulcini
Ceprano: Serpellon
Monterone: Sampieri
Sparafucile: Mardones
Gilda: Scotney
Giovanna: De Courcy
Page: Phillips
Maddalena: Leveroni

January 26
Concert
  Moranzoni (c)
Dereyne, Stojowski (piano)

January 27
Tosca
Same as Dec. 2 except:
Angelotti: Sampieri
Sacristan: Tavecchia
Cavaradossi: Gaudenzi
Tosca: Edvina

January 29
Otello (Verdi)
  Conti (c)
Montano: Pulcini
Cassio: Diaz
Iago: Scotti
Roderigo: Cilla
Otello: Slezak (for
  Zenatello)
Desdemona: Alda
Emilia: Claessens
Herald: Olshansky
Lodovico: Sampieri

January 31
Tristan und Isolde
  (Wagner)
  Weingartner (c)
Sailor's Voice: Everett
Isolde: Fremstad
Brangäne: Gay
Kurvenal: Weil
Tristan: Burrian
Melot: Saldaigne
King Marke: Lankow
Shepherd: Lippman
Steersman: Diaz

February 1 (mat.)
Il Trovatore
Same as Nov. 30 except:

Leonora: Rappold
Inez: Heyman
Di Luna: Polese
Manrico: Zenatello
Azucena: Schumann-Heink

February 1
Il Barbiere di Siviglia
Same as Jan. 20 except:
Almaviva: Ramella
Rosina: Donner
Basilio: Mardones

February 3
Otello
Same as Jan. 29 except:
  Weingartner (c)
Otello: Zenatello
Desdemona: Marcel
Lodovico: Mardones

February 4
(Special for City Club)
Aida
Same as Dec. 27 except:
King: Sampieri
Amonasro: Polese

February 5
Il Trovatore
Same as Nov. 30 except:
  Weingartner (c)
Leonora: Amsden
Inez: Heyman
Di Luna: Polese
Manrico: Zenatello
Azucena: Schumann-Heink

February 7
Don Giovanni
  (Mozart)
  Weingartner (c)
Leporello: Didur
Donna Anna: Destinn
Don Giovanni: Marcoux
Il Commendatore:
  Mardones
Don Ottavio: McCormack
Donna Elvira: Amsden
Zerlina: Nielsen
Masetto: Tavecchia

February 8 (mat.)
Tristan und Isolde
Same as Jan. 31 except:

Isolde: Saltzman-Stevens
Kurvenal: Goritz
Tristan: Ferrari-Fontana
  (for Burrian)

February 8
Tosca
Same as Dec. 2 except:
  Weingartner (c)
Angelotti: Sampieri
Sacristan: Tavecchia
Cavaradossi: Gaudenzi
Tosca: Marcel
Scarpia: Polese (for
  Marcoux)

February 9
Concert
  Weingartner (c)
Marcel

February 10
Tristan und Isolde
Same as Jan. 31 except:
Tristan: Ferrari-Fontana
February 12 (mat.)

Hänsel und Gretel
Same as Dec. 28 except:
  Caplet (c)
Gertrude: Robeson
Witch: Schumann-Heink

Coppélia
Same as Dec. 28

February 12
Don Giovanni
Same as Feb. 7 except:
Don Giovanni: Blanchart
  (for Marcoux)

February 14
Cavalleria Rusticana
Same as Dec. 30 except:
Lucia: Heyman
Alfio: Fornari
Lola: Swartz

Pagliacci
Same as Jan. 4 except:
Tonio: Polese
Canio: Zenatello
Nedda: Melis
Silvio: Fornari

February 15 (mat.)
Don Giovanni
Same as Feb. 7 except:
Don Giovanni: Blanchart
Zerlina: Barnes

February 15
Otello
Same as Jan. 29 except:
Weingartner (c)
Iago: Polese
Otello: Zenatello
Desdemona: Marcel
Emilia: Maubourg

February 16
Concert
Weingartner (c)
Marcel

February 17
I Gioielli della Madonna
Same as Jan. 17 except:
Raffaele: Polese

February 19
Carmen
Same as Jan. 11 except:
Caplet (c)
Morales: Everett
Micaela: B. Fisher
Don José: Zenatello
Carmen: Garden
Escamillo: Mardones

February 21
La Fanciulla del West
(Puccini)
Handsome: Pulcini
Harry: Diaz
Joe: Giaccone
Billy: Tavecchia
Nick: Cilla
Sid: Sillich
Happy: Tommasi
Sonora: Blanchart
Trin: Devaux
Larkens: Ouluchanoff
Wallace: Mardones
Rance: Polese
Ashby: Sampieri
Minnie: Melis
Johnson: Zenatello
Castro: Olshansky

Express Rider: Ghidini
Wowkle: Leveroni

February 22 (mat.)
Aida
Same as Dec. 27 except:
Weingartner (c)
Aida: Marcel
King: Sampieri
Amonasro: Polese

February 22
Louise
Same as Dec. 18 except:
Julien: Laffitte
Louise: Garden
Ragpicker: Sampieri
Camille: B. Fisher
Madeleine: Heyman

February 23 (mat.)
Concert
Caplet, Dubois,
Tournon (c)
Melis (for Cavalieri),
Laffitte (for Muratore),
Van Barentsen (piano)

February 24
Djamileh (Bizet)
(American premiere)
Weingartner (c)
Djamileh: Marcel
Haroun: Laffitte
Splendiano: Giaccone
Slave-Merchant:
Bourquin

Pagliacci
Same as Jan. 4 except:
Tonio: Polese
Canio: Zenatello
Nedda: Melis
Silvio: Pulcini

February 26
Faust (Gounod)
Weingartner (c)
Faust: Zenatello
Méphistophélès: Marcoux
Wagner: Olshansky
Valentin: Rossi
Siébel: Swartz
Marguerite: Marcel
Marthe: Leveroni

February 28
La Traviata
Same as Dec. 21 except:
Violetta: Hempel
Alfredo: Sacchetti
Annina: Phillips

March 1 (mat.)
I Gioielli della Madonna
Same as Jan. 17 except:
Maliella: Melis
Rocco: Everett
Raffaele: Blanchart (for
Rossi)

March 1
Rigoletto
Same as Jan. 25 except:
Duke: Sacchetti
Rigoletto: Blanchart

March 2
Concert
Caplet (c)
Scotney, Kocian (violin),
Lyford (organ)

March 3
La Fanciulla del West
Same as Feb. 21 except:
Larkens: Fornari
Rance: Amato

March 5
Rigoletto
Same as Jan. 25 except:
Duke: Macnez
Rigoletto: Blanchart
Gilda: Bori

March 6
L'Arlésienne (Daudet)
Incidental Music by Bizet
Caplet (c)
(French Theater Company
from Montreal with
chorus)
Federi: P. Paul Marcel
Patron Marc: George
Dumestre
Balthazar: Claude Benedict
Francet Mamai: A. Melvil
Mitifio: C. Leurs
L'Equipage: M. Hervé

Un Valet: E. Bourquin
Rose Mamai: Marguerite
Zegarra
Renaude: C. Paul Marcel
Vivette: Lucie Marsoll
L'Innocent: L. Morelli

March 7

I Gioielli della Madonna
Same as Jan. 17 except:
Flower-girl: Phillips
Maliella: Melis
Raffaele: Blanchart

March 8 (mat.)

La Forêt Bleue (Aubert)
(American premiere)
Caplet (c)
Fairy: Amsden
Harvester: Cilla
Servant: Leveroni
Red Riding-Hood:
B. Fisher
Young Girl: Morella
Tom Thumb: Swartz
Mother of Red Riding-
Hood: Heyman
Father of Tom Thumb:
Sampieri
Mother of Tom Thumb:
De Courcy
Baker: Morella
Little Jean: Gauthier
Jacquet: Manley
Woman: Heyman
Man: Pulcini
Princess: Melis
Prince Charming:
De Potter
Ogre: Riddez
Drinkers: Cilla, Bourquin
Blanche: Sharlow
Elvire: Mullane
Pierre: Olshansky
Louis: Ouluchanoff
Frederi: Everett

March 8

Lucia di Lammermoor
Same as Dec. 14 except:
Raimondo: Mardones

March 10

Aida
Same as Dec. 27 except:

King: Sampieri
Priestess: Sharlow

March 12

Samson et Dalila
(Saint-Saëns)
Caplet (c)
Samson: Zenatello
Abimelech: Mardones
High Priest: Riddez
Philistines: Giaccone,
Chasseriaux
Messenger: Saldaigne
Old Hebrew: Lankow
Dalila: Gay

March 14

La Forêt Bleue
Same as Mar. 8 except:
Jacquet: Phillips
Page: Tryan

March 15 (mat.)

Faust
Same as Feb. 26 except:
Strony (c)
Méphistophélès:
De Segurola
Valentin: Riddez
Marguerite: Nielsen

March 15

Madama Butterfly
Same as Nov. 29 except:
B. F. Pinkerton:
Sacchetti
Sharpless: Blanchart
Cio-Cio-San: Melis
Mother: De Courcy

March 16

Concert
Caplet (c)
Amsden, Ganz (piano),
Henrotte (violin)

March 17

La Forêt Bleue
Same as Mar. 8 except:
Jacquet: Phillips
Page: Tryan

Il Segreto di Susanna
(Wolf-Ferrari)
Caplet (c)

Count Gil: Scotti
Countess Gil: Nielsen
Sante: Tavecchia

March 18

Il Segreto di Susanna
Same as Mar. 17 except:
Count Gil: Fornari

Pagliacci
Same as Jan. 4 except:
Tonio: Rossi
Canio: Caruso
Nedda: Melis

March 19

La Fanciulla del West
Same as Feb. 21 except:
Larkens: Fornari
Rance: Rossi
Minnie: Amsden

March 20

Hänsel und Gretel
Same as Dec. 28 except:
Caplet (c)

Il Segreto di Susanna
Same as Mar. 17 except:
Count Gil: Fornari

March 22 (mat.)

La Fanciulla del West
Same as Feb. 21 except:
Rance: Rossi

March 22

Faust (for Martha)
Same as Feb. 26 except:
Strony (c)
Faust: De Potter
Méphistophélès: Mardones
Valentin: Riddez
Marguerite: Amsden

March 24

Martha (Flotow)
Moranzoni (c)
Nancy: Gay
Harriet: Nielsen
Sir Tristram: Fornari
Plunkett: Lankow
Lionel: Lippman
Sheriff: Olshanksy

March 26
Tristan und Isolde
Same as Jan. 31 except:
   Caplet (c)
Isolde: Nordica
Kurvenal: Buers
Tristan: Urlus

March 28
Les Contes D'Hoffmann
Same as Nov. 25 except:
Lindorf: Riddez

Coppélius: Riddez
Olympia: Hempel
Dappertutto: Riddez
Antonia: Bori
Dr. Miracle: Riddez

March 29 (mat.)
Martha
Same as March 24

Il Segreto di Susanna
Same as March 17 except:
Count Gil: Fornari

March 29
I Gioielli della Madonna
Same as Jan. 17 except:
Maliella: Melis
Raffaele: Blanchart

March 30 (mat.)
Concert
Nielsen, Dwyer, Renaud
  (piano).
Accompanists: Waller,
  Strony

TOUR 1912–13

NEW HAVEN

January 28 (mat.)
La Bohème
  Moranzoni (c)
Marcello: Polese
Rodolfo: McCormack
Colline: Anafesto Rossi
Schaunard: Pulcini
Benoit: Sillich
Mimì: Bori
Parpignol: Boccalino
Alcindoro: Sillich

Musetta: Dereyne
Customs Officer:
  Olshansky

January 28
Carmen
  Strony (c)
Morales: Chasseriaux
Micaela: Barnes
Don José: Zenatello
Zuniga: Sampieri
Carmen: Gerville-Réache
  (for Gay)

Frasquita: Sharlow
Mercédès: De Courcy
Escamillo: A. Rossi
Dancairo: Devaux
Remendado: Giaccone

SYRACUSE, N. Y.

May

Three-day festival with orchestra, Caplet conduct-
ing

1913–14

November 24
I Gioielli della Madonna
  (Wolf-Ferrari)
  Moranzoni (c)
Sacred-object vendors:
  Cavadore, Fabbri,
  Pasquali
Macaroni-vendors:
  Canavera, Gasperoni,
  Alessandria
Flower-girl: Mandell
Water-vendor: Rieger
Blind Man: Sampieri
Ice-cream man: Boccalino
Fruit-vendor: Ghidini
Morra-players: Dolfini,
  Serpellon
Totonno: Jou-Jerville

Buffoon: Cecchetti
Monks: Tortorici,
  Neumarker
Peasant girl: Heyman
Biaso: Giaccone
Balloon man: Zaini
Young Men: Everett,
  Fusco
Girls: Mandell, Phillips
Young Girl: Missini
Father: Sampieri
Nurse: Leveroni
Gennaro: Ferrari-Fontana
Maliella: Edvina
Carmela: D'Alvarez
Rocco: Pulcini
Ciccillo: Pini-Corsi
Raffaele: Ancona
Stella: Heliane

Concetta: Sharlow
Serena: Leveroni
Grazia: Galli

November 26
Faust (Gounod)
  Tournon (c)
Faust: Muratore (d)
Méphistophélès: Ludikar
  (d)
Valentin: Ancona
Wagner: Everett
Marguerite: Edvina
Siébel: Swartz
Marthe: Leveroni

November 28
Tosca (Puccini)
  Moranzoni (c)

Angelotti: Sampieri
Sacristan: Tavecchia
Cavaradossi: Martinelli
Tosca: Garden
Scarpia: Marcoux
Spoletta: Giaccone
Sciarrone: Pulcini
Shepherd: Gauthier
Jailer: Tortorici

November 29 (mat.)
Tristan und Isolde
(Wagner)
    Caplet (c)
Sailor's Voice: Deru
Isolde: Matzenauer
Brangäne: Niessen-Stone
Kurvenal: Weil
Tristan: Ferrari-Fontana
Melot: Everett
King Marke: Ludikar
Shepherd: Jou-Jerville
Steersman: Grand

November 29
Lucia di Lammermoor
(Donizetti)
    Lyford (c)
Normanno: Fusco
Enrico: Fornari
Raimondo: Sampieri
Lucia: Scotney
Alisa: Heyman
Edgardo: Tanlongo (d)
Arturo: Giaccone

November 30
Concert
    Arnaldo, Schiavoni,
    Britt (c)
Amsden, Swartz, Marcoux,
Tanlongo. Accompanist:
Rimini

December 1
Tristan und Isolde
Same as Nov. 29 except:
Kurvenal: Amato

December 3
I Gioielli della Madonna
Same as Nov. 24

December 5
Monna Vanna (Février)
    (American premiere)
    Caplet (c)
Guido: Marcoux
Torello: Grand
Borso: Deru
Marco: Ludikar
Monna Vanna: Garden
Prinzivalle: Muratore
Vedio: Swartz
Trivulzio: Wronski

December 6 (mat.)
Faust
Same as Nov. 26 except:
Faust: Laffitte
Marguerite: Amsden (for
    Edvina)

December 6
La Traviata (Verdi)
    Schiavoni (c)
Violetta: Parnell
Flora: Mandell
Marquis D'Obigny:
    Sampieri
Gastone: Giaccone
Alfredo: Tanlongo
Baron Douphol: Pulcini
Annina: Phillips
Giuseppe: Ghidini
Germont: Neumarker
Dr. Grenvil: Sillich

December 7
Concert
    Schiavoni, Britt (c)
Scotney, D'Alvarez,
    Leveroni, Tanlongo,
    Ancona. Accompanist:
    Rimini

December 8
Madama Butterfly
    (Puccini)
    Moranzoni (c)
B. F. Pinkerton: Laffitte
Goro: Giaccone
Suzuki: Swartz
Sharpless: Ancona
Cio-Cio-San: Bori
Cousin: Missini
Mother: Mandell
Yakuside: Tortorici

Aunt: Rieger
Imperial Commissioner:
    Neumarker
Notary: Everett
Bonze: Sillich
Yamadori: Pulcini
Kate Pinkerton: Heliane

December 10
Monna Vanna
Same as Dec. 5

December 12
Aida (Verdi)
    Moranzoni (c)
Ramfis: Ludikar
Radamès: Constantino
Amneris: D'Alvarez
Aida: Amsden
King: Sampieri
Messenger: Fusco
Priestess: Sharlow
Amonasro: Ancona

December 13 (mat.)
Thaïs (Massenet)
    Strony (c)
Palémon: Wronski
Athanael: Dangès (d)
Servant: Grand
Nicias: Deru
Crobyle: Heliane
Myrtale: Swartz
Thaïs: Garden
La Charmeuse: Scotney
Albine: Rienskaia

December 13
Il Barbiere di Siviglia
    (Rossini)
    Schiavoni (c)
Fiorello: Pulcini
Almaviva: Ramella
Figaro: Fornari
Rosina: Sanborn
Dr. Bartolo: Tavecchia
Basilio: Mardones
Berta: Leveroni
Sergeant: Giaccone

December 14
Concert
    Britt, Tournon (c)
Garden, Sapin, Jou-Jerville,
Grand

December 15
Samson et Dalila
(Saint-Saëns)
Caplet (c)
Samson: Ferrari-Fontana
Abimilech: Mardones
High Priest: Dangès
Philistines: Giaccone,
    Grand
Messenger: Deru
Old Hebrew: Ludikar
Dalila: D'Alvarez

December 17
Thaïs
Same as Dec. 13 except:
Athanael: Marcoux

December 19
La Traviata
Same as Dec. 6 except:
Moranzoni (c)
Violetta: Tetrazzini
Flora: Heyman
Germont: Ancona

December 20 (mat.)
Pagliacci (Leoncavallo)
Moranzoni (c)
Tonio: Ancona
Canio: Ferrari-Fontana
Beppe: Giaccone
Nedda: Nielsen
Silvio: Everett

Ballet
Pavlova and company

December 20
Cavalleria Rusticana
(Mascagni)
Moranzoni (c)
Turiddu: Laffitte
Santuzza: Amsden
Lucia: Heyman
Alfio: Fornari
Lola: Rienskaia

Ballet
Pavlova and company

December 21
Concert
Hirst, Strony (c)

Nielsen, Heyman,
    Tanlongo, Mardones,
    Fornari, Giaccone
    (*Lucia* Sextet).
Accompanist: Rimini

December 22
Tosca
Same as Nov. 28
Cavaradossi: Laffitte
Tosca: Edvina

December 24
Lucia di Lammermoor
Same as Nov. 29 except:
Moranzoni (c)
Raimondo: Mardones
Lucia: Tetrazzini

December 26
Samson et Dalila
Same as Dec. 15

December 27 (mat.)
Hänsel und Gretel
(Humperdinck)
Lyford (c)
Gretel: Riegelman
Hänsel: Swartz
Gertrude: Robeson
Peter: Ludikar
Sandman: Gauthier
Dew Fairy: Choiseul
Witch: Robeson

Coppélia (Delibes)
Swanilda: Galli
Frantz: Boz
Doll: Caldwell
Coppélius: Cecchetti
Burgomaster: Pulcini

December 27
Il Trovatore (Verdi)
Schiavoni (c)
Ferrando: Wronski
Leonora: Frease-Green
    (d)
Inez: Heyman
Di Luna: Blanchart
Manrico: Oppezzo (d)
Azucena: D'Alvarez
Ruiz: Giaccone

December 28
Concert
Schiavoni, Britt (c)
Scotney, Androva,
    Leveroni, Oppezzo,
    Mardones

December 29
Rigoletto (Verdi)
Moranzoni (c)
Duke: Giorgini (d)
Borsa: Giaccone
Countess Ceprano: Heliane
Rigoletto: Ancona
Marullo: Pulcini
Ceprano: Serpellon
Monterone: Sampieri
Sparafucile: Mardones
Gilda: Tetrazzini
Giovanna: Heyman
Page: Phillips
Maddalena: Leveroni

December 31
Les Contes D'Hoffmann
(Offenbach)
Caplet (c—for
    Strony)
Lindorf: Dangès
Andrès: Pini-Corsi
Luther: Sillich
Hermann: Grand
Nathanael: Jou-Jerville
Hoffmann: Laffitte
Niklausse: Leveroni
Spalanzani: Giaccone
Cochenille: Pini-Corsi
Coppélius: Dangès
Olympia: Scotney
Giulietta: Amsden
Pitichinaccio: Pini-Corsi
Dappertutto: Dangès
Antonia: Edvina
Crespel: Wronski
Frantz: Pini-Corsi
Dr. Miracle: Dangès
Voice: Sapin
Stella: Sharlow

January 2
Madama Butterfly
Same as Dec. 8 except:
B. F. Pinkerton: Tanlongo
Goro: Pini-Corsi
Suzuki: Leveroni

Sharpless: Blanchart
Cio-Cio-San: Edvina
Notary: Fusco

January 3 (mat.)
La Bohème (Puccini)
Moranzoni (c)
Marcello: Ancona
Rodolfo: Laffitte
Colline: Mardones
Schaunard: Pulcini
Benoit: Tavecchia
Mimì: Teyte
Parpignol: Fusco
Alcindoro: Tavecchia
Musetta: Beriza (d)
Sergeant: Tortorici

January 3
Aida
Same as Dec. 12 except:
Ramfis: Wronski
Radamès: Oppezzo
Aida: Androva
Amonasro: Blanchart

January 4
Concert
Schiavoni, Tournon
(c)
Sharlow, Rienskaia,
Ramella, Amato, Grand
(*Rigoletto* Quartet).
William F. Dodge
(violin). Accompanist:
Rimini

January 5
La Bohème
Same as Jan. 3 except:
Rodolfo: Martinelli

January 7
Samson et Dalila
Same as Dec. 15

January 9
I Gioielli della Madonna
Same as Nov. 24 except:
Raffaele: Marcoux

January 10 (mat.)
Lucia di Lammermoor
Same as Nov. 29 except:
Moranzoni (c)

Raimondo: Mardones
Lucia: Tetrazzini

January 10
Faust
Same as Nov. 26 except:
Dubois (c)
Faust: Laffitte
Méphistophélès: Wronski
Valentin: Grand
Marguerite: Beriza

January 11
Concert
Schiavoni, Strony,
Dubois (c)
Tetrazzini, Blanchart,
Wronski; Edna Gunnar
Peterson (piano).
Accompanist: Rimini

January 12
Les Contes D'Hoffmann
Same as Dec. 31 except:
Strony (c)
Lindorf: Marcoux
Coppélius: Marcoux
Dappertutto: Marcoux
Dr. Miracle: Marcoux

January 14
Louise (Charpentier)
Caplet (c)
Julien: Dalmorès
Louise: Edvina
Mother: D'Alvarez
Father: Marcoux
Ragpicker: Sharlow
Coal-woman: Phillips
Night-walker: Jou-Jerville
Paper-folder: Mandell
Scavenger: Sampieri
Milk-woman: Deck
Ragpicker: Wronski
Policemen: Tortorici,
Neumarker
Urchin: Lasilva
Sweeper: Leveroni
Painter: Fusco
Sculptor: Grand
Singer: Everett
Student: Regnier

Young Poet: Giaccone
Philosophers: Pulcini,
Sillich
Chair-mender: Heyman
Blanche: Lasilva
Marguerite: Phillips
Suzanne: Heliane
Gertrude: Leveroni
Irma: Sharlow
Camille: Choiseul
Apprentice: Gauthier
Elise: Rieger
Madeleine: Heyman
Old-clothes man: Deru
Forewoman: Deck
King of the Fools:
Jou-Jerville
Dancer: Galli

January 15
I Gioielli della Madonna
Same as Nov. 24 except:
Totonno: Fusco
Second Young Man:
Ganelli
Maliella: Amsden
Rafaello: Blanchart

January 16
La Bohème
Same as Jan. 3 except:
Marcello: Dangès
Rodolfo: Constantino
Mimì: Bori

January 17 (mat.)
Samson et Dalila
Same as Dec. 15

January 17
Rigoletto
Same as Dec. 29 except:
Schiavoni (c)
Duke: Tanlongo
Rigoletto: Blanchart
Sparafucile: Sillich
Gilda: Sanborn (for
Scotney)

January 18
Concert
Schiavoni, Britt, Hirst
(c)

Bori, Swartz, Tanlongo,
Ludikar. Accompanist:
Rimini

January 19
Aida
Same as Dec. 12 except:
Ramfis: Mardones
Radamès: Martinelli
Aida: White
Amonasro: Amato

January 21
Tosca
Same as Nov. 28 except:
Cavaradossi: Laffitte
Tosca: Edvina
Scarpia: Scotti

January 23
*Die Meistersinger von
Nürnberg* (Wagner)
Caplet (c)
Walther: Jörn
Eva: Gadski
Magdalena: Rienskaia
David: Jou-Jerville
Pogner: Braun
Beckmesser: Leonhardt
Vogelgesang: Giaccone
Nachtigall: Everett
Kothner: Blanchart
Ortel: Grand
Zorn: Deru
Moser: Devaux
Hans Sachs: Ludikar
Eisslinger: Fusco
Foltz: Sampieri
Schwarz: White
Night Watchman: Sillich

January 24 (mat.)
Louise
Same as Jan. 14 except:
Julien: Laffitte
Urchin: Rieger
Blanche: Deck
Forewoman: Rienskaia

January 24
Les Contes D'Hoffmann
Same as Dec. 31 except:
Strony (c)
Hoffmann: Deru
Antonia: Beriza

January 25
Concert
Strony, Schiavoni
(c)
Amsden, D'Alvarez,
Sharlow, Heyman,
Oppezzo, Ramella,
Devaux, Giaccone.
Accompanist: Rimini

January 26
Faust
Same as Nov. 26 except:
Faust: Constantino
Valentin: Dangès

January 28
Die Meistersinger
Same as Jan. 23 except:
Walther: Urlus
Eva: Hempel
Pogner: Griswold

January 30
Louise
Same as Jan. 14 except:
Julien: Laffitte
Father: Ludikar
Urchin: Rieger
Blanche: Deck
Forewoman: Rienskaia

January 31 (mat.)
Il Barbiere di Siviglia
Same as Dec. 13 except:
Moranzoni (c)
Almaviva: Constantino
Figaro: Amato
Rosina: Hempel

January 31
La Bohème
Same as Jan. 3 except:
Schiavoni (c)
Marcello: Fornari
Rodolfo: Tanlongo
Mimì: Sharlow
Musetta: Heliane

February 1
Concert
Strony, Lyford (c)
Beriza, Missini,
Constantino, Mardones;

Ellen Keller (violin).
Accompanist: Rimini

February 2
Cavalleria Rusticana
Same as Dec. 20 except:
Turiddu: Ferrari-Fontana
Santuzza: White
Lola: Leveroni

Pagliacci
Same as Dec. 20

February 4
Il Barbiere di Siviglia
Same as Dec. 13 except:
Moranzoni (c)
Almaviva: Constantino
Figaro: Ancona
Rosina: Nielsen
Basilio: Marcoux

February 6
La Gioconda (Ponchielli)
Moranzoni (c)
Barnaba: Ancona
La Gioconda: Destinn
La Cieca: Leveroni
Zuane: Pulcini
Isepo: Fusco
Enzo: Constantino
Laura: D'Alvarez
Alvise: Mardones

February 7 (mat.)
Die Meistersinger
Same as Jan. 23 except:
Walther: Laffitte
Eva: Hempel
Hans Sachs: Hinshaw

February 7
Lucia di Lammermoor
Same as Nov. 29

February 8
Concert
Strony, Dubois (c)
Ysaÿe (violin)

February 9
L'Amore dei tre re
(Montemezzi)
Moranzoni (c)

Archibaldo: Ludikar
Flaminio: Giaccone
Avito: Ferrari-Fontana
Fiora: Bori
Manfredo: Amato
Maid: Heliane
Young Girl: Sharlow
Youth: Fusco
Old Woman: Leveroni

February 11

Carmen (Bizet)
Caplet (c)
Morales: Everett
Micaela: Nielsen
Don José: Muratore
Zuniga: Grand
Carmen: D'Alvarez
Lillas Pastia: Regnier
Frasquita: Sharlow
Mercédès: Swartz
Escamillo: Mardones
Dancairo: Devaux
Remendado: Giaccone

February 12

Il Segreto di Susanna
(Wolf-Ferrari)
Moranzoni (c)
Count Gil: Scotti
Countess Gil: Nielsen
Sante: Tavecchia

Pagliacci
Same as Dec. 20

February 14 (mat.)

L'Amore dei tre re
Same as Feb. 9 except:
Manfredo: Ancona

February 14

Martha (Flotow)
Lyford (c)
Nancy: Sapin
Harriet: Scotney
Sir Tristram: Everett
Plunkett: White
Lionel: Ramella
Sheriff: Wronski

February 15

Concert
Strony, Lyford (c)
Nielsen, Sapin, Ramella,

Fornari, Wronski.
Accompanist: Rimini

February 16

Die Meistersinger
Same as Jan. 23 except:
Walther: Laffitte
Eva: Amsden
Pogner: Witherspoon

February 18

L'Amore dei tre re
Same as Feb. 9 except:
Archibaldo: Marcoux
Fiora: Villani
Manfredo: Ancona

February 20

Don Giovanni (Mozart)
Caplet (c)
Leporello: Ludikar
Donna Anna: Destinn
Don Giovanni: Marcoux
Il Commendatore:
Mardones
Don Ottavio: Tanlongo
Donna Elvira: Amsden
Zerlina: Teyte
Masetto: Tavecchia

February 21 (mat.)

Madama Butterfly (for
Manon)
Same as Dec. 8 except:
Goro: Pini-Corsi
Sharpless: Blanchart
Cio-Cio-San: Teyte
Notary: Fusco
Kate Pinkerton: Reeside

February 21

Tosca
Same as Nov. 28 except:
Cavaradossi: Tanlongo
Tosca: Amsden
Scarpia: Dangès

February 22

Concert
Strony, Schiavoni,
Smallens (c)
Teyte, Beriza, Tanlongo,
Dangès; Henrotte
(violin). Accompanist:
Rimini

February 23

Monna Vanna
Same as Dec. 5

February 25

Il Trovatore
Same as Dec. 27 except:
Moranzoni (c)
Ferrando: Sampieri
Leonora: Amsden
Inez: Mandell
Di Luna: Ancona
Manrico: Zenatello
Azucena: Gay

February 27

Otello (Verdi)
Weingartner (c)
Montano: Pulcini
Cassio: Pini-Corsi
Iago: Scotti
Roderigo: Fusco
Otello: Zenatello
Desdemona: Marcel
Emilia: Leveroni
Lodovico: Mardones
Herald: Tortorici

February 28 (mat.)

Monna Vanna
Same as Dec. 5 except:
Monna Vanna: Beriza (for
Garden)

February 28

La Traviata
Same as Dec. 6 except:
Violetta: Scotney
Alfredo: Ramella
Germont: Blanchart

March 1

Concert
Hirst (c)
Scotney, Gay, Grand,
Mardones; Britt (cello).
Accompanists: Rimini
(piano); Waller
(organ)

March 2

Otello (for *Don Giovanni*)
Same as Feb. 27 except:
Iago: Ancona

March 4
Roméo et Juliette
(Gounod)
Strony (c)
Tybalt: Deru
Paris: Everett
Capulet: Grand
Juliette: Nielsen
Mercutio: Dangès
Roméo: Muratore
Gertrude: Rienskaia
Gregorio: Sampieri
Benvolio: Fusco
Friar Laurence: Marcoux
Stephano: Swartz
Duke of Verona: Wronski

March 6
Die Meistersinger
Same as Jan. 23 except:
Weingartner (c)
Walther: Laffitte
Eva: Marcel
Pogner: Wronski

March 7 (mat.)
La Bohème
Same as Jan. 3 except:
Marcello: Dangès
Mimì: Sharlow (for
Melba)

March 7
I Gioielli della Madonna
Same as Nov. 24 except:
Gennaro: Zenatello
Maliella: Stanley
Carmela: Gay
Raffaele: Blanchart

March 8
Concert
Weingartner (c)
Marcel; Schelling (piano)

March 9
Die Meistersinger
Same as Jan. 23 except:
Weingartner (c)
Walther: Laffitte
Eva: Marcel
Pogner: Wronski
Beckmesser: Goritz

March 11 (mat.)
Otello
Same as Feb. 27 except:
Iago: Ancona
Desdemona: Villani (for
Marcel)

March 11
Don Giovanni
Same as Feb. 20 except:
Weingartner (c)
Il Commendatore:
Sampieri
Zerlina: Nielsen

March 13
Carmen
Same as Feb. 11 except:
Weingartner (c)
Micaela: Sharlow
Carmen: Gay
Lillas Pastia: Agnini
Escamillo: Dangès
Frasquita: Heliane

March 14 (mat.)
Aida
Same as Dec. 12 except:
Weingartner (c)
Ramfis: Mardones
Radamès: Zenatello
Amneris: Gay
Aida: Marcel

March 14
Madama Butterfly
Same as Dec. 8 except:
B. F. Pinkerton: Tanlongo
Goro: Pini-Corsi
Suzuki: Leveroni
Sharpless: Blanchart
Cio-Cio-San: Nielsen
Notary: Fusco
Kate Pinkerton: Reeside

March 15
Concert
Weingartner (c)
Melba, Marcel

March 16
Roméo et Juliette (Acts
II, III)

Same as Mar. 4 except:
Juliette: Melba

La Bohème (Acts III, IV)
Same as Jan. 3 except:
Strony (c)
Marcello: Dangès
Rodolfo: Tanlongo
Mimì: Melba

March 18
Manon (Massenet)
Tournon (c)
Guillot: Giaccone
De Brétigny: Grand
Poussette: Choiseul
Javotte: Rieger
Rosette: Gauthier
Innkeeper: Tavecchia
Lescaut: Dangès
Manon: Dufau
Des Grieux: Muratore
Servant: Gauthier
Count des Grieux: Wronski

March 20
Rigoletto
Same as Dec. 29 except:
Duke: Laffitte
Rigoletto: Amato
Gilda: Lyne (d)
Giovanna: Mandell
Maddalena: Gay

March 21 (mat.)
Tosca
Same as Nov. 28 except:
Weingartner (c)
Cavaradossi: Zenatello
Tosca: Amsden (for
Marcel)

Coppélia (Act I)
Same as Dec. 27 except:
Swanilda: Galli

March 21
Samson et Dalila
Same as Dec. 15 except:
Tournon (c)
Samson: Laffitte
Dalila: Gay

March 22

Concert
Weingartner (c)
Marcel; Kubelik (violin)

March 23

Louise
Same as Jan. 14 except:
Julien: Laffitte
Louise: Beriza
Mother: Gay
Urchin: Rieger
Chair-mender: Sapin
Blanche: Deck
Forewoman: Rienskaia

March 25

Aida
Same as Dec. 12 except:
Weingartner (c)

Ramfis: Wronski
Radamès: Zenatello
Amneris: Gay
Aida: Marcel

March 27

Faust
Same as Nov. 26 except:
Weingartner (c)
Méphistophélès: Marcoux
Valentin: Dangès
Marguerite: Marcel (Acts
I, II); Beritza (Acts III,
IV)

March 28 (mat.)

I Gioielli della Madonna
Same as Nov. 24 except:
Gennaro: Zenatello
Maliella: Amsden
Carmela: Gay

March 28

Il Segreto di Susanna
Same as Feb. 12 except:
Rimini (c)
Count Gil: Fornari
Countess Gil: Sharlow

Lucia di Lammermoor
(Mad Scene)
Lyford (c)
Lucia: Scotney

Faust (Act II)
Same as Nov. 26 except:
Faust: Jou-Jerville
Marguerite: Beriza

La Gioconda (The Dance
of the Hours)
Schiavoni (c)

TOUR 1913–14

NEW HAVEN

February 24

Les Contes D'Hoffmann
(Offenbach)
Strony (c)
Lindorf: Marcoux
Hoffmann: Laffitte
Niklausse: Leveroni
Coppélius: Marcoux
Olympia: Scotney
Giulietta: Amsden
Dappertutto: Marcoux
Antonia: Bori
Dr. Miracle: Marcoux
Stella: Sharlow

March 24 (mat.)

Hänsel und Gretel
(Humperdinck)

March 24

Tosca (Puccini)
Cavaradossi: Zenatello
Tosca: Marcel
Scarpia: Marcoux

PARIS

April 23
(Dress Rehearsal)

L'Amore dei tre re
(Montemezzi)
Moranzoni (c)
Archibaldo: Marcoux
Flaminio: Paltrinieri
Avito: Ferrari-Fontana
Fiora: Edvina
Manfredo: Cigada
Servant: Sharlow
Youth: Fusco
Old Woman: Leveroni

April 25

L'Amore dei tre re
(Opening)
Same as April 23

April 28

L'Amore dei tre re
Same as April 23

May 2

Manon Lescaut (Puccini)
Panizza (c)
Edmondo: Fusco
Des Grieux: Crimi
Lescaut: Cigada
Manon: Kousnezoff
Geronte: Tavecchia
Musician: Leveroni
Dancing-master:
Paltrinieri

May 5

Otello (Verdi)
Moranzoni (c)
Montano: Pulcini
Cassio: Tanlongo
Iago: Marcoux
Roderigo: Fusco
Otello: Ferrari-Fontana
Desdemona: Melba
Emilia: Leveroni
Lodovico: Wronski
Herald: Pulcini

May 7
Manon Lescaut
Same as May 2

May 9
Otello
Same as May 5

May 12
Manon Lescaut
Same as May 2

May 15
Otello
Same as May 5

May 16
Un Ballo in Maschera
(Verdi)
Panizza (c)
Sam: Wronski
Tom: Grand
Oscar: Teyte
Riccardo: Martinelli
Renato: Ancona
Judge: Fusco
Ulrica: De Cisneros
Silvano: Pulcini
Amelia: Destinn

May 19
Un Ballo in Maschera
Same as May 16

May 20
Tristan und Isolde
(Wagner)
Coates (c)
Sailor's Voice: Fusco
Isolde: Van der Osten
Brangäne: Claussen
Kurvenal: Kiess
Tristan: Cornelius
Melot: Deru
King Marke: Fönss
Shepherd: Fusco
Steersman: Grand

May 23
Pagliacci (Leoncavallo)
Panizza (c)
Tonio: Ancona
Canio: Ferrari-Fontana
(for Martinelli)

Beppe: Fusco
Nedda: Destinn
Sylvio: (?)

Il Segreto di Susanna
(Wolf-Farrari)
(First time in Paris)
Panizza (c)
Count Gil: Marcoux
Countess Gil: Teyte
Sante: Tavecchia

May 25
Tristan und Isolde
Same as May 20

May 27
*Die Meistersinger von
Nürnberg* (Wagner)
Weingartner (c)
Walther: Sembach
Eva: Marcel
Magdalena: Bender-
Schaefer
David: Albert
Pogner: Fönss
Beckmesser: Leonhardt
Sachs: Bender
Kothner: Kiess

May 29
Il Segreto di Susanna
Same as May 23

Pagliacci
Same as May 23 except:
Nedda: Muzio

May 30
Die Meistersinger
Same as May 27 except:
Sachs: Van Rooy
Pogner: Fenton
David: Schwarz

June 3
Parsifal (Wagner)
Weingartner (c)
Gurnemanz: Fenton
Kundry: Matzenauer
Amfortas: Van Hulst
Parsifal: Sembach
Titurel: Wronski
Klingsor: Kiess
Voice: Bender-Schaefer

June 5
Die Meistersinger
Same as May 27 except:
David: Schwarz
Sachs: Van Rooy

June 6
Parsifal
Same as June 3 except:
Gurnemanz: Fönss

June 8
Otello
Same as May 5 except:
Desdemona: Marcel

June 9 (mat.)
(At Opéra Comique,
benefit for Pension Fund)

La Bohème (Puccini)
Panizza (c)
Marcello: Ancona
Rodolfo: McCormack
Colline: De Segurola
Schaunard: Pulcini
Benoit: Tavecchia
Mimì: Melba
Parpignol: Paltrinieri
Musetta: Beriza

June 11
Tristan und Isolde
Nikisch (c)
Same as May 20 except:
Isolde: Matzenauer
Tristan: Urlus

June 12
Parsifal
Same as June 3 except:
Pollak (c)

June 13
Il Barbiere di Siviglia
(Rossini)
Moranzoni (c)
Almaviva: McCormack
Figaro: Amato
Rosina: Lyne
Dr. Bartolo: Tavecchia
Basilio: Marcoux
Berta: Bérat

June 15
Parsifal
Same as June 3 except:
 Pollak (c)
Gurnemanz: Bender
Amfortas: Amato

June 16
Il Barbiere di Siviglia
Same as June 13 except:
Berta: Leveroni

June 17
(Benefit for survivors of
 Empress of Ireland)

Il Segreto di Susanna
Same as May 23

Un Ballo in Maschera
Same as May 16 except:
 Moranzoni (c)
Oscar: Lyne
Renato: Amato
Amelia: Raisa

June 19
Tristan und Isolde (Act I)
Same as May 20 except:
 Pollak (c)
Isolde: Matzenauer
Brangäne: De Cisneros

Kurvenal: Amato
Tristan: Ferrari-Fontana

Il Barbiere di Siviglia
 (Act III)
Same as June 13 except:
Almaviva: Tanlongo
Berta: Cunningham

Pagliacci
Same as May 23 except:
 Moranzoni (c)
Tonio: Amato
Nedda: Raisa

BOSTON GRAND OPERA COMPANY
Max Rabinoff, General Manager
(Casts verified as far as possible)

1915–16

November 15
L'Amore dei tre re
 (Montemezzi)
 Moranzoni (c)
Archibaldo: Mardones
Avito: Zenatello
Fiora: Villani
Manfredo: Baklanoff

Orfeo ed Euridice (Gluck)
 Act II
 Schmid (c)
Orfeo: Gay
Euridice: Saroya
Happy Spirit: Pavlova
 (dancer)

November 16
Carmen (Bizet)
Micaela: Scheider
Don José: Martin
Carmen: Gay
Escamillo: Baklanoff

Ballet: The Fair Maid of
 Perth (Bizet)

November 17
Madama Butterfly
 (Puccini)
B. F. Pinkerton: Martin
Suzuki: Leveroni
Sharpless: Chalmers
Cio-Cio-San: Miuri

Nutcracker Suite:
 Snowflakes
 (Tchaikovsky)

November 18
Tosca (Puccini) (for
 La Muette de Portici)
Cavaradossi: Zenatello
Tosca: Villani
Scarpia: Baklanoff

Egyptian Ballet

November 19
Carmen
Same as Nov. 16 except:
Escamillo: Mardones

November 20 (mat.)
Pagliacci (Leoncavallo)
 Smallens (c)
Tonio: Baklanoff
Canio: Zenatello
Nedda: Teyte

Ballet: Coppélia (Delibes)

November 20
Madama Butterfly (?)

November 22
Pagliacci

November 23
La Muette de Portici
 (Auber)
 Jacchia (c)
Elvira: Lyne
Fenella: Pavlova (dancer)
Masaniello: Zenatello
Alfonso: Michailoff
Pietro: Chalmers
Maid of Honor: Clément
Selva: Ananian

November 24 (mat.)
Madama Butterfly

November 24
Tosca
Presumably same as Nov.
18 except:
Tosca: Fremstad

November 25
L'Amore dei tre re

November 26
La Bohème (Puccini)
Rodolfo: Botta
Mimì: Teyte
Musetta: Amazar

Ballet: Chopiniana

November 27 (mat.)
Madama Butterfly

November 27
Ballet
Pavlova and company

November 29
Otello (Verdi)
Moranzoni (c)
Iago: Baklanoff
Otello: Zenatello
Desdemona: Villani

November 30
La Bohème

December 1
Faust (Gounod)
Moranzoni (c)
Faust: Zenatello
Méphistophélès: Baklanoff

Valentin: Chalmers
Marguerite: Lyne
Marthe: Leveroni

December 2
Cavalleria Rusticana
(Mascagni)
Turiddu: Martin
Santuzza: Villani
Alfio: Chalmers

Ballet: Raimonda
(Glazunov)

December 3
La Muette de Portici

December 4 (mat.)
Rigoletto (Verdi)
Duke: Botta
Rigoletto: Baklanoff
Gilda: Lyne

December 4
Ballet
Pavlova and company

December 6
Rigoletto

December 7
Otello

December 8 (mat.)
Ballet
Pavlova and company

December 8
Madama Butterfly

December 9
Faust

December 10
Aida (Verdi)
Ramfis: Mardones
Radamès: Zenatello
Aida: Ewell (for Rappold)
Amonasro: Baklanoff

December 11 (mat.)
Hänsel und Gretel
(Humperdinck)
Lyford (c)
Gretel: Teyte
Hänsel: Carson

Ballet: Fairy Doll

December 11
Pagliacci
Presumably same as Nov.
20 except:
Canio: Gaudenzi

December 13
Aida

December 14
Carmen
Presumably same as Nov.
16 except:
Escamillo: Mardones

December 15 (mat.)
Madama Butterfly

December 15
Gala
Aida (Act II)
Rigoletto (Act III)
Pagliacci (Act I)
Ballet Divertissement

1916–17

January 1
Andrea Chénier
(Giordano)
Moranzoni (c)
Gérard: Baklanoff
Maddalena: Villani
Chénier: Zenatello

Countess (or Bersi?):
Peralta

January 2
Madama Butterfly
(Puccini)
Guerrieri (c)

B. F. Pinkerton: Gaudenzi
(for Martin)
Sharpless: Marr
Cio-Cio-San: Miura

January 3
L'Amore dei tre re
(Montemezzi)

Archibaldo: Mardones
Avito: Zenatello
Fiora: Villani
Manfredo: Baklanoff

January 4

Faust (Gounod)
Faust: Martin
Valentin: Chalmers
Siébel: Swartz
Marguerite: Teyte
Marthe: Winietskaja

January 5

Iris (Mascagni)
    Moranzoni (c)
Iris: Miura
Il Cieco: Lazzari
Osaka: Kittay
Kyoto: Chalmers

January 6 (mat.)

La Bohème (Puccini)
Rodolfo: Gaudenzi
Marcello: Chalmers

Colline: Lazzari
Mimì: Teyte
Musetta: Riegelman

January 6

Aida (Verdi)
    Moranzoni (c)
Ramfis: Mardones
Radamès: Martin
Amneris: Gay
Aida: Villani
Amonasro: Baklanoff

REPERTOIRE, 1909–14

Including tours, Paris season (1914) and Rabinoff seasons (1915–16, 1916–17)

OPERA	09–10	10–11	11–12	12–13	13–14	PARIS	TOTAL	15–16	16–17
Aida	6 (T 3)	6 (T 1)	6 (T 1)	6	5		34	2	1
Amore dei Tre Re, L'					3	3	6	2	1
Andrea Chenier									1
Arlésienne, L'				1			1		
Ballo in Maschera, Un						3 (1*)	3		
Barbiere di Siviglia, Il		6 (T 1)	4			2	13		
Bohème, La	7 (T 8)	6 (T 1)	4	5 (T 1)	5	1	38		
Carmen	6 (T 7)	6 (T 1)	7 (T 1)	4*	2*		34	2	
Cavalleria Rusticana	6* (T 1*)	4* 2#	2*	4*	2		21	3	
Contes d'Hoffmann, Les				5	3 (T 1)		9	1*	
Djamileh				1*			1		
Don Giovanni	4*				2		5		
Don Pasquale		2*		3			6		
Enfant Prodigue, L'		5* 2#	2*				9		
Fanciulla del West, La		9	4	3			17		
Faust	5 (T 1)	4	7 (T 1)	3 (1*)	5		26	2	1
Forêt Bleue, La				3			3		
Germania			3				3		
Gioconda, La	4	3			1		8		
Gioielli della Madonna, I				7	6		13		
Habañera, La		2*	2*				4		
Hänsel und Gretel		3*	4*	5*	1* (T 1)		14		
Huguenots, Les	2 (T 1)						3		
Iris									1
Lakmé	7 (T 7)	3					17		
Lohengrin	1 (T 3)						4		
Louise				5	4		9		
Lucia di Lammermoor	4 (T 1)	3	3	4	4		19		
Madama Butterfly	4 (T 5)	5	3 (T 2)	3	4		26	6	1
Maestro di Capella	1*						1		

Manon		3		2		1	6	
Manon Lescaut		3				1	6	
Martha			2 (1*)				3	3
Martyr de St. Sébastien, Le	5		1*				1	
Mefistofele		3				6	8	
Meistersinger, Die			2			6	9	
Mignon	2*			2			2	2
Miserly Knight, The	2# 1*						5	2
Momma Vanna						4	4+	2
Muette de Portici, La								3*
Otello	5* (T 3*)	5	2	3	3	4	17	2
Pagliacci, I	5*	5*		4*	3	3*	27	3*
Parsifal		3*		2		4	4	
Pelléas et Mélisande	3*		5	2			7+	
Pipe of Desire, The	3*						3	
Rigoletto	6 (T 4)	4	4 (T 1)	3	3		20	
Roméo et Juliette	4 (1*)			3		1	1	
Sacrifice, The	4 (1*)					4	4	
Samson et Dalila		6		1		5	12	
Segreto di Susanna, Il				4*		1* 1**	9	3*
Thaïs				3		2	10	
Tosca	4	5	5	5 (T 1)			25	2
Traviata, La	5 (T 2)	3	5	5	4	3	19	
Tristan und Isolde			2	4		2	13	
Trovatore, Il	4 (T 1)	4	1	4	2	3	15	
Werther				2	3	2	2	

323

* Double bill   # Triple bill   ** Gala   + Also given as play (1912–13)   T tour

BOXHOLDERS, 1909–10

FIRST TIER

1. Mrs. H. N. Slater
2. Mrs. J. A. Garland
3. Charles F. Wright
4. Francis Gardner Curtis,
   Horatio G. Curtis, Louis Curtis
5. Mrs. John L. Gardner,
   Mrs. F. Gordon Dexter
6. Theodore N. Vail
7. William M. Wood
8. Mr. and Mrs. L. Carteret Fenno
9. Eugene V. R. Thayer
10. Miss Mary S. Ames,
    F. L. Ames
11. George A. Gardner
12. Galen L. Stone
13. Mrs. Stanley McCormick
14. Oliver Ames
15. Charles S. Bird
16. Robert G. Shaw,
    Henry S. Hunnewell
17. Edward D. Brandegee
18. Mrs. W. H. Schofield
19. Mrs. B. P. Cheney, Sr.,
    Miss Elizabeth Cheney
20. Mrs. Andrew Wheelwright,
    Mrs. J. C. Gray,
    Mrs. William Amery
21. Eben Sumner Draper
22. Nathan L. Amster
23. Mrs. Charles R. Hayden
24. S. Reed Anthony
25. Frank E. Peabody

SECOND TIER

26. John M. Longyear
27. Edwin S. Webster, Andrew Adee,
    E. W. Converse, R. M. Saltonstall,
    Margaret C. Allen
28. Larz Anderson
29. F. S. Converse, Philip Wrenn,
    George T. Rice, Theodore Burgess
30. Eleonora M. Sears,
    Alexander Cochrane,
    Katherine Abbott
31. William O. Blake
32. Lester Leland
33. Mrs. J. J. Storrow,
    Mrs. John E. Thayer,
    Mrs. Samuel Cabot,
    Miss Katherine Bullard
34. George R. Fearing
35. Bayard Thayer
36. Bryce J. Allan
37. Eben D. Jordan
38. Herbert M. Sears
39. Nathaniel Thayer
40. Henry D. Burnham
41. Charles Hayden
42. Dr. W. H. Baltzell
43. Francis Peabody, Jr.
44. Chester W. Lassell
45. Walter C. Baylies
46. William L. Parker,
    Elizabeth F. Parker
47. Thomas W. Lawson
48. Charles G. Weld
49. Frederick Ayer, Charles F. Ayer
50. Miss Fanny R. Mason
51. Robert S. Bradley,
    William B. Walker
52. Arthur E. Davis
53. Mrs. R. D. Evans
54. Horatio A. Lamb,
    Winthrop Sargent,
    William C. Endicott, John Lawrence

NOTE: A few changes occurred from year to year, and names were added when the series were divided, but 90 per cent of the boxholders remained faithful, most of them in the same location, throughout the five years.

INDEX

Artists on the Boston Opera Company roster are listed here, even if they are not mentioned in the text. The following capsule information appears after the artist's name: type of voice (*bar* for baritone, *bs* for bass, *c* for contralto, *m-s* for mezzo-soprano, *s* for soprano, *t* for tenor), and season or seasons in which they appeared (shown by hyphenated figures, sic: 09–10). T means that the artist appeared on the 1909–1910 tour only; P, that the artist appeared in Paris in 1914. Any subsequent numbers refer to text pages where their names appear.

The names of operas are in italics; the names of roles in opera entries are general references, not attributed to a specific singer. The singers' appearances in roles are listed under their own entries.